14,75

PHILOSOPHICAL PERSPECTIVES

Publication Number 667
AMERICAN LECTURE SERIES®

A Monograph in
The BANNERSTONE DIVISION *of*
AMERICAN LECTURES IN PHILOSOPHY

Edited by

MARVIN FARBER
State University of New York
Buffalo, New York

PHILOSOPHICAL PERSPECTIVES

By

WILFRID SELLARS

CHARLES C THOMAS • PUBLISHER
Springfield • Illinois • U.S.A.

Published and Distributed Throughout the World by
CHARLES C THOMAS • PUBLISHER
BANNERSTONE HOUSE
301-327 East Lawrence Avenue, Springfield, Illinois, U.S.A.

NATCHEZ PLANTATION HOUSE
735 North Atlantic Boulevard, Fort Lauderdale, Florida, U.S.A.

With THOMAS BOOKS *careful attention is given to all details of manufacturing and design. It is the Publisher's desire to present books that are satisfactory as to their physical qualities and artistic possibilities and appropriate for their particular use.* THOMAS BOOKS *will be true to those laws of quality that assure a good name and good will.*

Printed in the United States of America
S-4

ACKNOWLEDGMENTS

"The Soul as Craftsman: an Interpretation of Plato on the Good" was presented as a Bicentennial Lecture in Classics and Philosophy at Brown University in February, 1952. It has not been previously published.

"Vlastos and 'Third Man'" is reprinted from the *Philosophical Review*, volume 64, 1955, by kind permission of the editors. "Vlastos and 'Third Man': A Rejoinder" (1955) has not been previously published.

"Aristotle's Metaphysics: An Interpretation" is a revised version of a paper from which an excerpt was presented as the opening paper in a symposium on Substance and Form in Aristotle at the 1957 meeting of the American Philosophical Association (Eastern Division). It has not been previously published.

"Substance and Form in Aristotle" is the excerpt referred to in the preceding paragraph. It was published in the *Journal of Philosophy*, volume 54, 1957, and is reprinted by kind permission of the editors.

"Raw Materials, Subjects and Substrata" was presented at a conference on "The Concept of Matter," held at the University of Notre Dame from September 5 to September 9, 1961. It was printed in the proceedings of the conference (*The Concept of Matter*, the University of Notre Dame Press, 1962) and is reprinted by kind permission of the publisher.

"Meditations Leibnitziennes" is a revised version of a paper for which an excerpt was presented at a symposium on Continental Rationalism at the May, 1958 meeting of the American Philosophical Association (Eastern Division). It was published in the *American Philosophical Quarterly*, volume 2, 1965, and is reprinted by kind permission of the editor.

"Physical Realism" was contributed to a symposium on the philosophy of Roy Wood Sellars in *Philosophy and Phenomenological*

Research, volume 15, 1954, and is reprinted by kind permission of the editor.

"The Intentional Realism of Everett Hall" was presented in a series of lectures in honor of Everett Hall, held under the auspices of the Philosophy Department of the University of North Carolina.

"Abstract Entities" is reprinted from the *Review of Metaphysics*, volume 16, 1963, by kind permission of the editor.

"Classes As Abstract Entities and the Russell Paradox" is reprinted from the *Review of Metaphysics*, volume 17, 1963, by kind permission of the editor.

"The Paradox of Analysis: A Neo-Fregean Approach." *Analysis*, Supplement Volume, 1964. Reprinted by kind permission of the editor.

"Notes on Intentionality" was the opening paper in a symposium on Intentionality at the 1964 meeting of the American Philosophical Association (Eastern Division). It was printed in the *Journal of Philosophy*, volume 61, 1964, and is reprinted by kind permission of the editors.

"Theoretical Explanation," in *Philosophy of Science*, The Delaware Seminar, John Wiley, 1963. By kind permission of the publisher.

"Scientific Realism or Irenic Instrumentalism: A Critique of Nagel and Feyerabend on Theoretical Explanation," in *Proceedings of the Boston Colloquium on Philosophy of Science*, 1965. By kind permission of the publisher.

"The Identity Approach to the Mind-Body-Problem" was presented at the Boston Colloquium in the Philosophy of Science in February, 1963. It was published in *Review of Metaphysics*, April 18, 1965, and is reprinted by kind permission of the editor.

"Science and Ethics" is a revised and expanded version of a lecture given at the Phoebe Griffin Noyes Library Association, Old Lyme, Connecticut, on January 26, 1960. It has not been previously published.

W. S.

CONTENTS

PHILOSOPHICAL PERSPECTIVES

PART ONE

I

THE SOUL AS CRAFTSMAN

My AIM in this essay is to show that if the metaphysics of the later dialogues are explored with the conceptual structure of craftsmanship as frame of reference, major themes fall into place and make sense. Heretofore, these themes have proved endlessly puzzling when viewed in more piecemeal fashion, as Plato's attempt to resolve, in their ancestral form, the issues and perplexities of philosophy today. In the history of philosophy, as in philosophy itself, we must continually shift between analysis and synopsis, embracing the extremes of both. To stay at or near the middle is to be safe but uninspired. To give Kant's dictum one more twist: analysis without synopsis is blind, synopsis without analysis is empty. This essay is decidedly in the synoptic mood— perhaps outrageously so. It is, however, my experience that the finer-grained analysis of these dialogues both illuminates and confirms the large scale picture I shall draw.

My starting point is the *Timaeus*, though my ultimate aim is to sketch an interpretation of the Idea of the Good which will generate the conviction that Plato, in his later dialogues, made greater payments on the promissory notes of Book VI of the *Republic* than is generally acknowledged.

It will be remembered that in *Republic* II, Socrates points out that if someone were attempting to understand a text written in small letters difficult to read, and learned that the same text was available in larger letters, it would be sensible for him to turn his attention to the latter. In the *Republic*, the soul writ large is seen as the City and a study is made of the latter to see if its virtues and vices throw light on virtue and vice as they appear in the individual soul. In the *Timaeus*, we find the craftsman writ large as the Divine Craftsman who shapes and animates the world or cosmos in which we live. It is often said that this Craftsman who makes the world is a fiction employed by Plato to analyze the continuing metaphysical structure of a world which was never made. I am convinced that in a sense this is true. I am also convinced that it is disasterously false, if the *craftsmanship* of the Craftsman is relegated to the fiction, and is not recognized to be a central feature of the metaphysical structure which the fiction was designed to illuminate.

The *Timaeus*, in those respects which concern us, is the story of the making of a unique rational animal, which has the physical world for its body, by a craftsman who contemplates an eternal pattern. The body of this World Animal is made from an ultimate raw material consisting of "likenesses" of certain elemental physical forms, which "likenesses" spontaneously appear in the "Receptacle," that is, for our purposes, Space. This ultimate raw material becomes "worked-up" or intermediate raw material through being shaped by the craftsman into geometrically tidy particles.

Although the World Animal has both body and soul, the Pattern after which it is made plays an explicit role as pattern only in connection with the making of the world's body. This should arouse a feeling of surprise, for knowing Plato's conception of the respective places of soul and body in the hierarchy of things, we might well have expected the primary feature of the Pattern of the World Animal to be a pattern of the world's soul. And it is worth noting in this connection that its predecessor in the dialogues, The Alive Itself of the *Phaedo*, was the Form of soul and soul only. In that dialogue souls are not only items the presence of which in a body made it alive, they are themselves alive. They are, indeed, the *primary* living things, living bodies being alive in a derivative sense only, by virtue of having a living thing proper, a true animal, within. From this point of view the true World Animal would *be* the World Soul.

The *Timaeus* does, indeed, tell us that the World Soul was made, and if this making were to be taken seriously, there would have to be a corresponding Pattern. As a matter of fact, a long and complicated story is told of the making of this Soul. But, curiously enough, no reference is made in this story to a contemplation by the Divine Craftsman of a pattern in accordance with which it is made. This, I hope to make clear, is no accident.

Consider, to begin with, the materials from which the world's soul is said to be made. They are surely such as to make it clear that the making *must* be a metaphorical making, whereas the making of the world's body *need* not be. There *could* be such a thing as making the body of the world out of particles of earth, air, fire, and water. There could *not* be such a thing as making a soul out of the Being, Sameness, and Difference which pertain to Forms, and the Being, Sameness, and Difference which pertain to physical becoming.

By the time he wrote the *Timaeus*, Plato has surely come to the conclusion that souls are realities which are as unique and irreducible as the Forms, as Space, and as physical becoming. The list of "ingredients" of which Souls are "made" mobilizes the classical themes that like knows like, and that like acts on like, to account for the ability of soul to know the eternal patterns and to govern physical becoming.[1]

If the world soul is unmade, must not its maker be a fiction? Other considerations point in the same direction. Plato emphasizes both in the *Sophist* and in the *Timaeus* itself (30B) that where there is intelligence, there must be soul. Thus, the Divine Artisan, having intelligence, must be (or have) a soul. The dialogue implies, therefore, that there is at least one unmade soul at the cosmic level. And, if other things are equal, it would be a reasonable move, in the light of all that has been said, to identify the Divine Craftsman with the World Soul. If the World Soul is unmade, it needs no Craftsman to make it—and as for making the world's body, the theme of souls making their own bodies is already to be found in the *Phaedo*, where, although it is put in the mouth of Cebes, it clearly accords with the force of the argument.

---

[1]It is perhaps worth noting, in this connection, that although souls are presented in the *Phaedo* as instances of the Alive Itself, and, therefore, in terms of their role as animators of bodies, this presentation is shaped by the requirements of the concluding argument for immortality, hinging, as it does, on the contrareity of "living" and "dead." Actually, the *Phaedo* views the soul as animator as subordinate to the soul as contemplator of the Forms. This would have generated no tension if Plato had conceived of contemplation as a "motion," for, as did others, he found the essence of the living to be the capacity for spontaneous motion (i.e., the capacity to move without being moved from without). The Alive Itself could have been the Spontaneously-in-motion Itself. It is clear, however, that at the time of the *Phaedo*, the kinship of the soul with the Forms was taken to imply that in its core being the soul does not move. Aristotle builds this theme into his doctrine of the Agent Intellect by construing contemplation as activity rather than motion. Plato's course in the later dialogues was to construe soul as that which is spontaneously in motion, which is not to say that he would have rejected Aristotle's distinction (indeed, he adumbrates it!), though he would have put it to different use.

So far I have said little, if anything, which is new. However, the above considerations provide a framework within which more controversial and speculative claims can be made. The first thing to note is that to say that soul is not made, is *not* to imply that there is no Idea or Form of soul. It only implies, strictly speaking, that there is no *pattern* of soul. For patterns are to make things by. The same is true of physical becoming—in its character as the *ultimate* raw material of the world's body. This, too, is not *made*. It comes to be spontaneously, without design; though it is raw material for design. There are, therefore, no *patterns*, though there are *Forms*, of the elemental powers.

The same is, as already indicated, true of soul—with this difference: Physical becoming, considered in abstraction from all shaping and craftsmanship, is Heracleitean in character. It is a ceaseless coming into being (coming to become) and ceasing to be (ceasing to become). Souls, though *unmade*, have a genuine identity through change. They are, indeed, everlasting in the strong sense that they are without beginning or end. And the World Soul, itself a moving likeness of eternity, makes possible the moving image of eternity which is Time.

The next thing to note is that although soul is not made from a more basic raw material, souls are *themselves* raw material for craftsmanship. Souls are not made *simpliciter*, but souls are made to be good (or bad). There is, we have seen, a Form but not a Pattern of soul. On the other hand, there *is* a Pattern of the good soul, which is, indeed, as we shall see, the *key* Pattern in the Realm of Forms as providing patterns to be realized in the temporal order. Soul is confronted by two basic types of raw material, physical becoming and *soul itself*, and by the Patterns in accordance with which these raw materials are to be shaped. That the soul (its powers and propensities) *is* raw material to itself is an essential element in the Platonic conception of an art or craft of living, a familiar and central theme in the ethical dialogues.

II

To introduce the next group of considerations which I want (in craftsmanlike manner, I hope) to weave into my argument, let me return to Plato's description of the Pattern which the Divine Craftsman contemplates and seeks to realize in the world of changeable things. He refers to it as "The Animal Itself" and characterizes it as a "whole" which has all other living things as "parts." His description, as we shall see, makes essential use of a hidden ambiguity of the terms "whole" and "part." Some might say that Plato is guilty of a logical howler, but Plato puts the ambiguity to such important use that it is difficult, if not impossible, to avoid the conclusion that, as in the case of so many other "logical mistakes" or "fallacies" of which he has been accused, he was in full control of the situation. The relevant passage reads, in Cornford's translation, as follows:

> Let us. . . say that the world is like, above all things, to that Living Creature of which all other living creatures, severally and in their families, are parts. For that embraces and contains within itself all the intelligible living creatures, just as this world contains ourselves and all other creatures that have been formed as things visible. For the god, wishing to make this world most nearly like that intelligible thing which is best and in every way complete, fashioned it as a single visible living creature, containing within itself all living things whose nature is of the same order. (30C-D)

The ambiguity to which I referred above reflects the fact that Plato's terminology for the relation of genus to species refers to a genus as a "whole" and its species as "parts." From this point of view, the Form

> The Animal Itself

is a "whole" which has as its intermediate "parts" such intermediate kinds as

> The Land Animal Itself
> The Sea Animal Itself
> The Air Animal Itself

and as its ultimate "parts" such *infima species* as

> The Lion Itself
> The Tiger Itself
> The Vulture Itself.

Now it is clear to us that a Form which had "parts" in this sense (part$_1$) would not be *realizable* except *through* its "parts." Thus, if we take as our example of a genus or "whole" the Plane Figure Itself and its "parts" or species

> The Circle Itself

DIAGRAM I

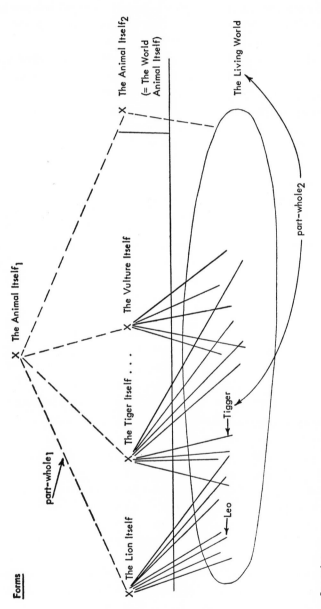

The Square Itself, etc.

it is clear that the genus or "whole" can be realized only through its species or "parts." Crudely put, nothing can be a plane figure without being a circle or a square or . . ..

It is equally clear that for Plato, The Animal Itself is realized in the temporal order as a "whole" in a different, and more familiar sense (part$_2$) (i.e., as a living thing which includes all other living thing as "parts" in the sense in which each of us, to use an illuminating anachronism, includes cells of various kinds as parts). Thus the phrase "The Animal Itself," in the *Timaeus*, refers to *two* different intelligibles, and hence, presumably, Forms:

1. The generic character of being an animal.
2. The Form of a peculiarly gigantic species of animal which includes animals of other species as parts.

We can represent the situation as in Diagram 1. We can also say that since The Animal Itself$_2$ is such that any of its instances (of which it is best that there be only one) must include instances of the more humdrum species of animal as its "parts" in the ordinary sense of the term, there will be another technical sense of "part" (part$_2$) in which The Animal Itself$_2$ (i.e., The World Animal Itself) has The Lion Itself, The Tiger Itself as "parts." This relationship is represented in Diagram 2, where many Patterns are represented as parts of one embracing Pattern.

This structure will turn out to be of decisive importance when we come to interpreting what Plato has to say about the Idea of the Good (The Good Itself).

Let me sum up our results to date by drawing and explicating the following diagram (Diagram 3). The controlling analogy is that of a Pattern-cum-recipe which includes Patterns-cum-recipes and ultimately a list of basic ingredients. The things of which the *subordinate* Patterns are Patterns are (in the cases we have considered) raw material in their turn with respect to *superordinate* Patterns. As far as Diagram 3 goes, *the* superordinate Pattern is that of the body of The World Animal. In this respect, the diagram and the conceptual structure it represents call for a completion which will shortly be forthcoming.

In other words, the *Timaeus* presents the realm of Ideas or Forms under the aspect of a system of Patterns-cum-recipes-cum-ingre-

DIAGRAM II

(a)

Forms

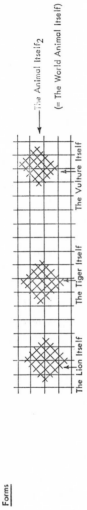

The Animal Itself₁

The Animal Itself₂

(= The World Animal Itself)

The Lion Itself   The Tiger Itself   The Vulture Itself

or, more abstractly and inclusively,

(b)

Forms

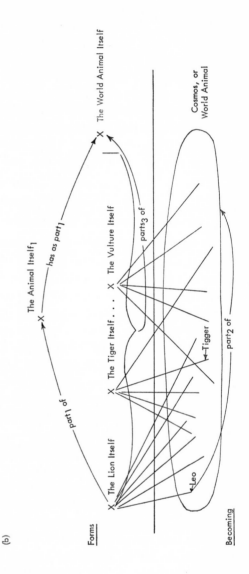

The Animal Itself₁

has as part₁

part₁ of

X The Lion Itself   X The Tiger Itself . . . . X The Vulture Itself

The World Animal Itself

parts₃ of

part₂ of

Leo   Tigger

Cosmos, or World Animal

Becoming

DIAGRAM III

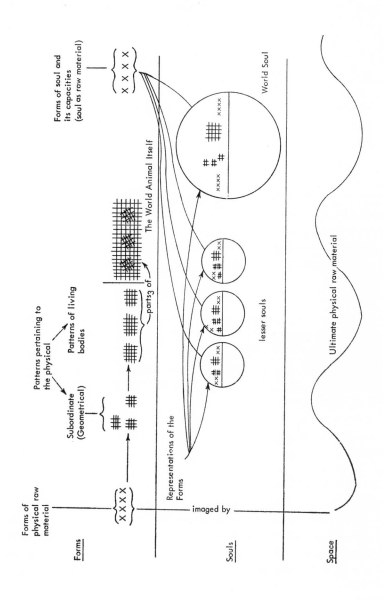

dients. Thus the realm of Forms has a structure which, while it may be viewed in terms of logical problems pertaining to genera and species, compatibilities and implications, ordinary Forms (The Circle Itself) and pervasive Forms (Being, Same, Other), first order Forms and higher order Forms (Formhood), etc., must ultimately be viewed as a system of *practical* truths in that broad sense in which "practical" truths concern how life is to be lived and how the raw materials which confront soul, including itself, can be shaped into instrumentalities for the good life.

The stress in the *Sophist* and other later dialogues on Collection and Division (that is, on the relation of kinds to subkinds) as tools of dialectic does not mean that Plato came to view the genus-species relation as the *only* relationship of Forms to one another (which it obviously is not), or even the most important relationship for philosophy. The dialectician must divide reality "at the joints" and the "joints" are not matters of the logically possible permutations and combinations of indivisible kinds, but rather of the blending and clashing of Forms—of the special relationships in which they stand to specific other Forms. And of these intelligible relationships, there are, broadly speaking, two kinds not easy to separate. There are, in the first place, those which lay down limits of possibility and compossibility as in geometry, for, as Mill pointed out, without such limits there is no craftsmanship. On the other hand, there are those intelligibilities which concern purposive action. The latter, for Plato, are primary. The intelligibilities of geometry would be as dust and ashes if there were no such thing as the intelligibilities of life.

III

Although the *Timaeus* presents the realm of intelligible Being as a complex pattern of artifacts to be realized in physical raw material and the raw material of the powers and propensities of soul, it highlights the role of the soul as *animator* of the body, as the craftsman which shapes and maintains its physical habitation. Thus the Pattern highlighted is the Pattern of the world's body which is realized as an orderly cosmos exhibiting to sight the power of reason to impose form on nonrational (and even irrational) materials. To get the full picture of the structure of the realm of Forms, we must look elsewhere—and, in the first place, to the *Phaedo* and the *Republic*.

The *Phaedo*, it will be remembered, presents the Forms as defining ideal standards which are only approximated to by physical becoming. One theme in this conception, also found in the *Republic*, is the inherited theme of the unreality—or at least lesser reality—of becoming. The problem of Not-Being (and change involves something's becoming what before it was *not*) laid a heavy burden on Greek philosophy which was first lightened, if not completely lifted, by Plato's *Sophist*.

A second theme, of greater relevance to our purpose, is the connection of this "approximating" with the concept of *striving*. With striving comes the possibility of failure, and the concept of striving mobilizes the role of intentional action as the paradigm of causing something to come to be.

But the fact that in the *Phaedo* Plato pictures equality, greatness and other geometrical Forms as objects of striving, but fails to discuss the structure of the realm of Forms beyond the minimum necessary for the culminating argument for immortality, and makes a casual reference to sticks and the life as the strivers, leaves most readers with the feeling that the idea that objects strive to realize or live up to geometrical Forms is to be construed as poetic license.

Nothing could be further from the truth. To be sure, the *point* of geometrical Forms is not to be the objects of blind, impulsive, sporadic striving by irrational strivers. On the other hand, their point, and the point of all Forms (as emerges in the *Republic*) is to be the objects of rational striving.

If we take seriously the idea that the Forms are *essentially* the objects of (or define the objects of) rational striving, then we get the doctrine of the *Republic*. (1) The Forms would have in common the character of being objects of such striving. (If we refer to this character as "object-of-striving-ness," we would have one meaning for "The Good Itself.") (2) The Forms would be objects of striving which were neither conventional nor arbitrary, but "by nature."

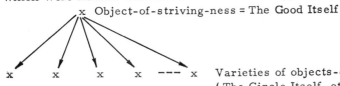

x Object-of-striving-ness = The Good Itself

x   x   x   x — — x   Varieties of objects-of-striving (The Circle Itself, etc.)

Initially this way of looking at the Forms suggests a mere side-by-side of desirables having in common the abstract character of being desirables ("by nature").

This, however, was the position we were in when, in our first look at the *Timaeus*, we considered The Animal Itself as a *genus* of which The Lion Itself, etc. are the species. There we saw that The Animal Itself was also an embracing whole in another sense, a Pattern which included the other animal Patterns as parts. In the terminology of nineteenth century Idealism, the ambiguous phrase "The Animal Itself" stands for both a "concrete" and an "abstract" universal. I suggest, then, that in addition to the Idea of the Good as abstract universal (to-be-realized-ness or object-of-striving-ness), there is also the Idea of the Good as a concrete universal—a "whole" which includes all the other Forms as relevant to one another in their various ways with respect to a non-arbitrary, unified object-of-striving. This would be the Idea of the Good as a "whole" in a sense akin to that in which The Animal Itself is a "whole."[2] (See Diagram 4.)

What to-be-brought-abouts or objects-of-striving exist "by nature"—in that inclusive sense in which the latter phrase connotes that which is non-arbitrary and can be explained and criticized with reason and truth? That, as in the case of man-made artifacts, an object which exists in this sense "by nature" may also exhibit conventional features which "flatter" rather than serve, does not impugn the validity of the concept. There is, therefore, a legitimate sense in which such physical artifacts as beds and shuttles exist "by nature." More obviously "by nature" is health which, literally crafted by the physician, is also crafted by the soul in a sense which becomes more and more analogical as the Platonic tradition moves through Aristotle to more recent

---

[2]Strictly speaking, the Idea of the Good *qua* abstract universal, as introduced above, would not be a *generic* universal, as is The Animal Itself, but a universal of *second order* which has universals rather than particulars for its instances. Thus the character of being an object of striving would be participated in by The Circle Itself rather than circular things in the World of Becoming. But the fact that The Good Itself and The Animal Itself as abstract universals are differently related to the Forms which fall under them is unimportant and simply points to another sense in which Forms can be "wholes" with "parts." It is The Good Itself as concrete universal which we will shortly find to be the heart of Plato's metaphysical doctrine. (That by the time of the *Sophist* Plato was aware of the distinction between generic and second level Forms is a story for another occasion).

DIAGRAM IV

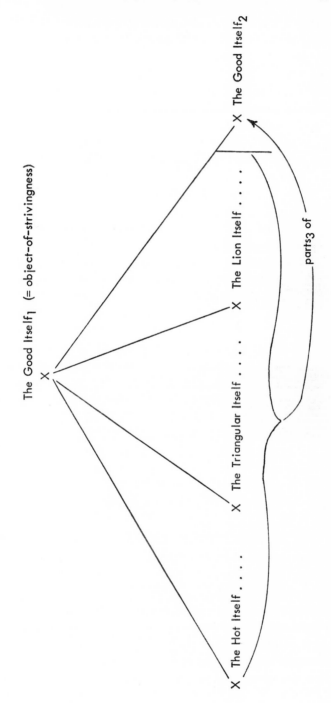

times. Then there is the weaving together of the products of the other crafts, which is the aim of the statesman. From this point of view, the world animal is the statesman writ large. Finally, there is the craft of the satisfying life (the "art of living"). This craft embraces all the others (1) as instruments and (2) as, in a sense, ingredients. From this point of view, the world animal is the philosopher writ large. And if, in the *Timaeus*, the World Soul is presented primarily in his cave as cosmic statesman, he is not denied the articulated vision of the Forms which lesser animals can only find by leaving theirs.

Thus, if there is a sense in which the craft of the statesman includes all of the crafts, there is a deeper sense in which the craft of living, of mixing a satisfactory life, includes all others—even that of the statesman.

To support the above summary remarks, I would call into play the argument against Callicles to show that the art of living, like the other arts, has rules; and the argument against Thrasymachus to establish the relative autonomy of the crafts. Plato anticipates, in a sense, the key feature of rule utilitarianism—the establishing of the non-arbitrariness of systems of rule-governed activity by exhibiting the place of these systems in a larger teleological scheme.

A soul's own happiness is, in a sense, its ultimate *end*; not, however, as a far-off event with respect to which each particular action is to be viewed as a means, but rather as a rationally ordered way of life which includes subordinate rationally ordered practices. As an analogy, one might use the relation of playing chess to happiness. It is not a mark of rational self-interest to make each move as a means to happiness, construed as a subsequent state of affairs. The same is true of engaging in a craft, including the craft of the statesman.

The relations of means to ends within a craft (formulated by the recipe) must be distinguished from the relations of the product to the purposes for which it is an instrument. The latter are in a sense external to the craft, but they are internal to the concept of its product. Thus a house is a physical structure of such and such a kind for the purpose of shelter. Again the means-end relationships within a craft and the purpose of the product must both be distinguished from the end to be achieved by *engaging in* the craft. It is this distinction which is highlighted by the contrast drawn

DIAGRAM V

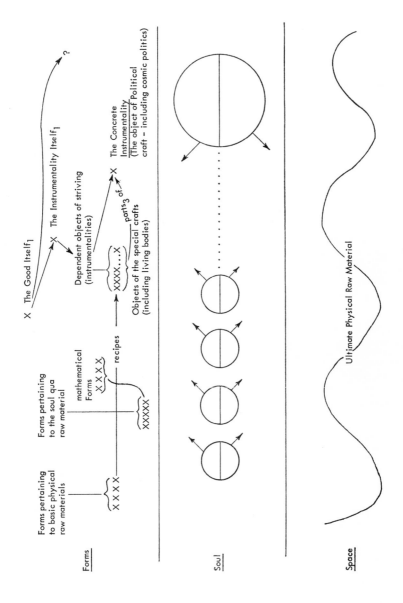

in *Republic* I between the physician *qua* physician and the physician *qua* practicing the art of taking pay.

We must thus distinguish between (1) the rationale of the recipe; (2) the rationale of the product, and (3) the rationale of engaging in the craft. Plato's point is that all these rationales are "by nature." They are non-arbitrary and can be reasoned out. There is, *pace* Protagoras, truth and falsity with respect to them.

V

If we look at the structure of the intelligible world from the point of view we have been developing, it presents itself first of all as in Diagram 5. But it is clear that even a cosmos of instrumentalities has a "point" which transcends it. The domain of objects-for-striving must include non-instrumentalities, and no mere side-by-side of these. Thus the structure of the Intelligible World must ultimately be represented by something like Diagram 6.

In its own way, the "life of reason" includes, as well as makes use of, the instrumentalities, recipes, and the Forms (including those of ultimate raw materials) which they involve. For an essential part of the life of reason is contemplating the intelligible structure we have been schematizing.

And if the above analysis is correct (at least in its general character), then we can say that the *Republic* lays down the general theme that the realm of Intelligible Being is to be understood in terms of a system of ends and instrumentalities having a complex structure to which violence is done when one claims that the connection between following rules and achieving happiness is an arbitrary one established by power and or convention. The *Timaeus* uses the ambiguity of the terms "part" and "whole" to highlight the idea of a fitting of artifact into artifact to make an embracing artifact. It is in the *Philebus*, however, that Plato comes as close as he does in his dialogues to giving us a lecture on the Good in its core aspect as the life of reason to which everything else contributes as raw material, instrumentality, or ingredient—not the least of which is the contemplation of how all these fit together.

> *Socrates:* ...to me it appears that in our present discussion we have created what might be called an incorporeal ordered system

DIAGRAM VI

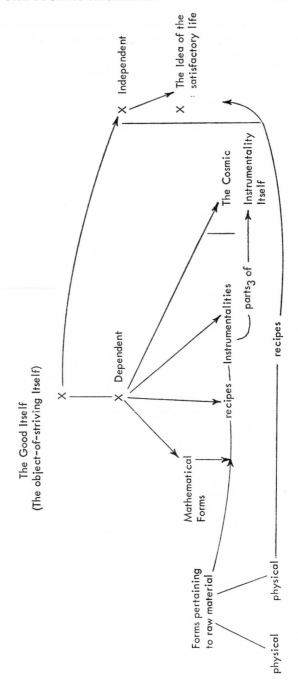

for rightful control of a corporeal subject in which dwells a soul.
Protrachus: You may assure yourself, Socrates, that my own conclusion is the same.
Socrates: Then perhaps we should be more or less right in saying
that we now stand upon the threshold of the Good and of that
habitation where all that is like thereto resides? (*Philebus,* 64B,
Hackforth translation.)

II

VLASTOS AND "THE THIRD MAN"

In his recent article on "The Third Man Argument in the *Paramenides*,"[1] Professor Vlastos raises anew the classic questions: "Is the Third Man Argument a valid objection to the Theory of Forms?" "Did Plato believe that it was valid?"[2] He reminds us that "one can find acute and learned critics on both sides of both these questions,"[3] and soundly concludes that "if any progress in agreement is to be made at this juncture, it must come from some advance in understanding the logical structure of the argument."[4] He proposes, therefore, to "pursue its analysis further than I think anyone has yet found it profitable to push it."[5] And he proceeds to give us what must be admitted to be a patient and painstaking reconstruction of Plato's argument. Furthermore, if this reconstruction is sound, and if we allow him one or two additional premises of reputable standing, Vlastos has struck a rich vein indeed. It not only yields clear-cut answers to the questions with which he began, but also reveals for our admiration and wonder a Plato who faced an intellectual, indeed spiritual, crisis in a manner "absolutely without parallel in the pages of Western Philosophy."[6]

There is much in Vlastos' paper with which I should like to take issue, for in the course of a rich and complex argument he takes a stand, to my mind not always a wise one, on many of the more exciting issues of Plato interpretation. On the present occasion, however, I shall limit myself to criticizing (1) his reconstruction of the Third Man Argument; (2) his conception of the place of what he calls "Self-Predication" (Triangularity is a triangle) in Plato's later metaphysics, and, consequently, (3) his interpretation of Plato's frame of mind when composing the first part of the *Parmenides*.

I

Vlastos opens his assault on this Everest of scholarship by quoting *Parmenides* 132a1-b1, which he translates as follows:

[1]*Philosophical Review*, LXIII:319-349, 1954. [2]*Ibid.*, p. 319.
[3]*Ibid.* [4]*Ibid.* [5]*Ibid.* [6]*Ibid.*, p. 349.

"I suppose this is what leads you to suppose that there is in every case a single Form: When several things seem large to you, it seems perhaps that there is a single Form which is the same in your view of all of them. Hence you believe that Largeness is a single thing."[7]

He calls this passage "the first step of the Argument"[8] and tells us that it "may be generalized as follows: (A1) If a number of things, *a*, *b*, *c*, are all *F*, there must be a single Form, *F*-ness, in virtue of which we apprehend *a*, *b*, *c*, as all *F*."[9] He explains the "generality" of (A1) by saying that " '*F*' stands for any discernible character or property."[10] He adds that "the use of the same symbol, '*F*,' in '*F*-ness,' the symbolic representation of the 'single Form,' records the identity of the character discerned in the particular ('large') and conceived in the Form ('Largeness') through which we see that this, or any other, particular has this character."[11]

Now (A1) as formulated by Vlastos tells us that the role of *F*-ness is that of making possible the apprehension of *a*, *b*, *c* as all *F*. But surely the point of the Theory of Ideas is that *F*-ness makes possible the *apprehension* of, say, *a*, *b*, *c* as *F*, because *F*-ness is that by virtue of which (i.e., by virtue of participating in which) *a*, *b*, *c* all *are F*. Thus, at the very least, (A1) should read "If a number of things, *a*, *b*, *c*, are all *F*, there must be a single Form, *F*-ness, by virtue of which *a*, *b*, *c* are all *F* and can be apprehended as such." But does a reference to our apprehension of *a*, *b*, *c* as *F* belong in (A1) at all? Granted that the text reads "when several things seem large to you, it seems perhaps that there is a single Form which is the same in your view of all of them," can we not take the "seeming" and the "viewing" to pertain to the *discovery* of the principle which is to function as a premise of the Third Man Argument rather than as constituent elements in the principle itself? Why does Vlastos think that the reference to apprehension belongs in the principle? The answer is that Vlastos, like Taylor before him, sees that even if the Third Man establishes an infinite series of Largeness as a consequence of the Theory of Ideas, this

---

[7] *Ibid.*, p. 320. At no point does my criticism of Vlastos' reconstruction hinge on a difference in translation. As a matter of fact, his translation avoids at least one pit into which others have fallen. See below, n. 22.

[8] *Ibid.*   [9] *Ibid.*   [10] *Ibid.*   [11] *Ibid.*

fact as such would not suffice to refute the Theory in the strict sense of showing it to be logically absurd.[12] For there is no logical absurdity in an infinite series as such. On the other hand, if this series could be shown to involve a *vicious regress*, the job would indeed be done. But would not Plato himself have regarded the infinite series as already unacceptable, and sufficient to refute the Theory if it could be shown to be a consequence of it? Vlastos recognizes that this is the case,[13] but since he thinks that Plato is anyway committed to an epistemological principle which, when combined with the infinite series of Largeness, does yield a vicious regress, he feels justified in putting it into the argument.[14] This principle, which Vlastos nowhere carefully formulates, is to the effect that we apprehend an item *as F* in virtue of apprehending the *F*-ness in which it participates *as being what it, in turn, is*. Thus, on the assumption that all *F*-nesses are *F*, the principle becomes: We apprehend an item as *F* in virtue of apprehending the *F*-ness in which it participates as also *F*. But while *F*-ness must indeed be apprehended to play its epistemological role, need it be apprehended *as being F*? There is an important distinction between the apprehension *of X*, and the apprehension of *X as so-and-so*. And if Vlastos sees this distinction, but is convinced that the former cannot take place without the latter, he has given no reason for foisting this conviction on Plato.[15]

But whether or not Plato (however "implicitly") mobilized an epistemic premise to insure the unacceptability of an infinite series of Largenesses, it is clear that it is not necessary to the establishing of the series itself. And in his reconstruction of *this* aspect of Plato's argument, Vlastos makes no use of this premise. Since it

---

[12]*Ibid.*, p. 328, n. 12.   [13]*Ibid.*

[14]*Ibid.*, p. 327. "We could thus get a *bona fide* infinite regress, logically vicious, since it is assumed that we discern *F* particulars in virtue of *F*-ness . . ., *F*-ness in virtue of *F₁*-ness . . ., and so on *ad infinitum*, the discernment of each successive Form being required for the discernment of its immediate predecessor, a requirement which can never be fulfilled, since the series is infinite."

[15]That Vlastos is on dangerous ground is shown by the fact that even a theory of Forms or universals which denies that *F*-ness is *F* (e.g., Russell's in *The Problems of Philosophy*) would yield a vicious regress when combined with Vlastos' epistemic principle. For even if *F*-ness is not *F*, it is at least changeless. And if in order to apprehend a particular as *F* one had not only to apprehend *F*-ness but also to apprehend it *as being what it is*, e.g., changeless, one would indeed be faced with a task that could never be begun.

is this reconstruction which I shall be criticizing, I shall, in the following, omit from (A1)—and later from (A2)—all reference to apprehension.

One other comment before we turn our attention to Vlastos' reconstruction of what he takes to be "the second step." In the passage which follows his formulation of (A1), Vlastos lays down a plausible procedural rule. He tells us that "Plato's argument professes to be a deductive argument and I propose to treat it as a formal structure of inference from premises, stated or implied. For this reason, I raise no questions about the Theory of Forms and presume no more information about it than I can extract from the text before me."[16] But whether or not this procedure is a viable one, Vlastos has already violated it by importing into his explication of (A1)—quoted above—a distinction between *large* as a "character or property" of large things and the Form *Largeness* in which they participate. Plato does, indeed, distinguish in the *Phaedo*[17] between a large thing, the large in the thing, and The Large Itself (Largeness), and he even recalls this distinction early in the *Parmenides* (130B), when Parmenides asks Socrates:

> Have you yourself drawn the distinction you speak of and separated apart on the one side Forms themselves, and on the other the things that share in them? Do you believe that there is such a thing as Likeness itself *apart from the likeness that we possess*, and so on with Unity and Plurality and all the terms in Zeno's argument. . . ?[18]

Nevertheless, while all this is true, the trichotomy in question just cannot be found in the passages which constitute the Third Man Argument. Vlastos asserts "that *F* and *F*-ness are logically and ontologically distinct is crucial to the argument."[19] But what he must mean is that it is crucial to his (Vlastos') explanation of why Plato offered the Third Man Argument which he (Vlastos) attributes to him, and of why he (Plato) failed to refute it. For this "crucial" thesis does not occur in the Third Man Argument itself, even as Vlastos reconstructs it. We will find it wise to interpret "large" not as "standing for" a "character" (whereas "Largeness" names a Form), but rather, more neutrally, as the

---

[16]Vlastos, *Op. cit.*, p. 320.   [17]102 ff.

[18]F. M. Cornford: *Plato and Parmenides*. London, 1939, p. 81. Italics mine.

[19]Vlastos, *Op. cit.*, p. 320, n. 5.

adjectival expression corresponding to the abstract noun "Largeness," which latter, according to Platonic theory, is the name of an Idea.

II

In the light of these remarks, let us reformulate (A1) to read:

(A1) If a number of things, a, b, c, are all F, there must be a single Form, F-ness, in virtue of which they are all F.

Let us now turn our attention to Vlastos' reconstruction of what he calls the "second step." This he translates as follows:

> What then if you similarly view mentally Largeness itself and the other large things? Will not a single Largeness appear once again, in virtue of which all these (*sc.* Largeness and the other large things) appear large? It seems so. Consequently, another Form of Largeness will appear, over and above Largeness itself and the things which participate in it.[20]

He then boils it down and "generalizes" it into the following principle, from the formulation of which, as before, we have omitted his reference to apprehension:

(A2) If a, b, c, and F-ness are all F, there must be another Form, F_1-ness, in virtue of which a, b, c, and F-ness are all F.

But why does Vlastos write "F_1-ness" instead of "F-ness$_2$"? By doing so, he introduces an unnecessary queerness into the argument, making it look as though Plato had in mind a principle of which the following would be an illustration: If a, b, c, and Red_0-ness are all red_0 (say scarlet), then there must be another Form, Red_1-ness (say, Harvard Crimson) in virtue of which a, b, c, and Red_0-ness are all red_0. But not only is there nothing in the text which requires him to attach the subscripts to the "F" in "F-ness,"[21] nothing in his formal reconstruction of the argument hinges on this placing of the subscripts. And while there would be no objection to so attaching them if it were clearly understood that it was to have no other force than if it were attached to the "ness," actually the temptation to construe "F_1-ness" and "F_2-ness" as standing for two different specific or determinate forms

---

[20]*Ibid.*, p. 321.

[21]It is interesting to note that Vlastos never writes "Large$_1$-ness," but always "Large-ness$_1$," even when it is intended as an illustration of "F_1-ness," e.g., p. 322, l. 14.

of a generic F-ness is so strong as to rule out this placing of the subscripts. Vlastos, indeed, lays great stress (e.g., in n. 7, p. 323) on the determinables and determinates which, as he sees it, are lurking in the Argument. He sees that the Theory of Ideas against which it is directed (and which he mistakenly believes to be the theory Plato actually held) involves that the Form F-ness is *superlatively* F, particulars being by contrast *humdrumly* F. He concludes that *being superlatively* F and *being humdrumly* F are two determinate ways of *being* F. It is doubtless this reasoning which underlies his choice of "F_1-ness" in the formulation of (A2). But it fails to justify the placing of the subscript after the "F" "F-ness." For these metaphysically different ways of being F are not, *in the usual sense*, specific or determinate ways of being F. The subscripts would belong to the "being" rather than to the "F" in "being F."

One more comment before we watch Vlastos rub (A1) and (A2) together. Even a casual reading of the passage which Vlastos boils down to (A2) shows that something is wrong. For the text (Vlastos' translation) actually gives us *two* steps: (1) When one views Largeness itself and the other large things, a single Largeness appears once again, in virtue of which all these are large. (2) *Therefore*, we discover a new Largeness which is over and above the Largeness already noted. And if we ask, What does the second of these steps add to the first? the answer is that the Largeness which "appears" in (1) is *other than* the Largeness previously discerned.[22] The significance of this point will emerge at the conclusion of our critique of Vlastos' reconstruction.

III

After reconstructing the text of the Third Man Argument into two steps, (A1) and (A2), and before he introduces the two additional premises which he finds implicit in the text, Vlastos pauses to make the following comment:

> Merely to compare (A2) with (A1) above is to see a discrepancy in the reasoning which, so far as I know, has never been noticed

---

[22]Note that there would be a radical redundancy if in (1) instead of "a single Largeness appears *once again*" the translation read (mistakenly) "*another* Largeness appears" (compare the translations of Fowler in the *Loeb Classical Library* edition and Cornford in his *Plato and Parmenides*.

before, though it leaps to the eye the moment one takes the trouble to transcribe the full content of the two steps in symbolic form. In (A1) we are told that if several things are all F, they are all seen as such in virtue of F-ness. But (A2) tells us that if several things are all F, they are all seen as such not because of F-ness, but because of a Form other than F-ness, namely F_1-ness. To be sure, there is a difference in the protasis of (A1) and (A2), and this is doubtless what has misled patrons or critics of the Argument: (A2) includes, while (A1) does not, F-ness, among the things which have the property F. The significance of the assumption which prompts this inclusion will be discussed directly, and will indeed remain the most important single issue throughout the whole of this paper. But if we simply stick to the logical form of the two statements, the disparity of reasoning as between (A1) and (A2) remains glaringly abrupt and unwarranted.[23]

Vlastos, in this comment, is pointing out that whereas according to (A1) the members of the class of F particulars, a, b, c, etc., are F by virtue of F-ness, according to (A2) *these same particulars* (and F-ness as well) are F by virtue of the *different* Form F_1-ness.[24] This, according to Vlastos, is a glaring inconsistency, [25] so that we can say straight away that if the Theory of Forms commits us to (A1) and (A2), we are in a position to reject it without waiting to derive further consequences (in particular, a regress) from (A1) and (A2).

Two comments are in order. In the first place, it must, indeed, be granted that the Third Man Argument, as formulated by Plato, involves that each large item, whether it be a particular or a Form, participates in an infinite number of Largenesses, and that it is large *many times over* by virtue of participating in these many Largenesses. But notice that as being large by virtue of participating in a given Largeness, an item is a member of a

---

[23]Vlastos, *Op. cit.*, p. 321.

[24]The soundness of this point is independent of the exact sense in which F_1-ness is different from F-ness—that is, if sound, the point would remain sound even if "F_1-ness" were replaced by "F-ness₁."

[25]That we have not misinterpreted the point which Vlastos is making is borne out by a reading of the footnote to this passage (n. 6) in which he offers a formal demonstration of the inconsistency by means of the propositional calculus. This demonstration, as he points out, rests on the assumption that "It cannot be true that x, y, z are seen as F in virtue of F-ness and also in virtue of a Form other than F-ness." It is this assumption that I am examining in the text above.

certain class of large items. Thus, *a, b, c*, etc., would be members of the class of large *particulars* by virtue of the fact that each participates in the *first* largeness. On the other hand, *a, b, c*, etc., *together with this first Largeness* are members of a more inclusive class by virtue of their common participation in the second Largeness, and so on. Thus it does *not* follow from Plato's premises that the members of *one and the same class* of large items, e.g., the class of large particulars, are members of *that* class by virtue of two different Largenesses. The latter would indeed be a gross inconsistency. Therefore, unless we are going to rule out of court as absurd the idea that a large item participates in many Largenesses, all we are entitled to do at this stage is note that the regress as Plato sets it up requires that it be incorrect to speak of *the* Form by virtue of which an item, *x*, is large, without going on to specify the class of large things [26] with respect to which it is being considered.[27]

If it is pointed out that the class whose members are large particulars can be different (as it must be) from the class whose members are large particulars *plus* Largeness, only if "large" connotes a *different* property in each case, whereas the Theory of Forms that is under attack clearly involves that "large" is not *ambiguously* applied to both large particulars and Largeness, this must indeed be granted. But must it also be granted that the difference between the *properties*, which is necessary to make the two *classes* different, is such as to entail that the word "large" is ambiguous *in the ordinary sense of "ambiguous."* (That the regress involves that "large" be ambiguous in an odd *metaphysical* sense is clear.) There is, indeed, an absurdity in the idea that large particulars are many times large *in the same sense* of "large."

---

[26]e.g., the class whose membership consists of large particulars; the class whose membership consists of large particulars, plus Largeness; the class whose membership consists of large particulars, plus Largeness, plus Largeness$_1$; . . .

[27]It snould be noted that the Third Man Argument can easily be set up in such a way as to avoid (at least *prima facie*) this participation of each large item in an infinite number of Largenesses. For instead of bringing in the second Largeness to account for the (presumed) fact that *a, b, c*, etc., and Largeness are all large, it can be brought in simply to account for the (presumed) fact that Largeness is large. Yet as soon as the question *is raised*, "Are not *a, b, c*, etc. and Largeness all large, and if so, must not *a, b, c*, etc., and Largeness participate in a common Form?" it would seem that an affirmative answer can be avoided only at the expense of denying that Largeness s large in the same sense of "large" in which *a, b, c*, etc., are large.

What I have been concerned to show is that the absurdity is no matter of a simple contradiction.

My second comment on this "discrepancy" is that Vlastos conceives of both (A1) and (A2) as *premises* of Plato's argument (though not of the one he reconstructs with premises mined from Plato's philosophical unconscious). He therefore finds it necessary to explain why Plato failed to notice this discrepancy. It is my purpose to show that (A2) is *not* a premise of Plato's argument, and therefore that Vlastos has not, as he supposes, given a good reason for holding that Plato was a puzzled spectator of his argument.

IV

If we now ask, "How does Vlastos conceive the role of (A2) in the argument?" the answer seems to be that it is the hypothetical from which, by *modus ponens*, we are to draw the conclusion, "There is another Form, F_1-ness," . . . From this point of view, two questions arise: (1) What authorizes the hypothetical? (2) What authorizes the affirmation of its antecedent?

Vlastos sees the first of these questions in terms of the problem, how to get from (A1) to (A2). And as it is immediately clear that (A2) does not follow logically from (A1) by itself, he looks for additional premises which, when combined with (A1), will do the job and which can reasonably be said to be implicit in Plato's formulation. But before "rummaging into other texts to discover what further assumptions Plato made about the Theory of Forms," Vlastos asks the purely logical question, "What are the simplest premises, not given in the present Argument, which would have to be added to its first step to make (A2) a legitimate conclusion?"[28]

He finds two additional premises to be necessary. The first of these is the Self-Predication Assumption, which he formulates as follows: "(A3) Any Form can be predicated of itself. Largeness is itself large. *F*-ness is itself *F*."[29]

Now the phrase "self-predication" is a misleading one. To begin with, there is the obvious point that it is not Largeness which is predicated of Largeness, but rather "large" or (material mode) *being large*. What is needed is, indeed, a principle of

---

[28]Vlastos, *Op. cit.*, p. 324.
[29]*Ibid.*

predication, but to speak of *self*-predication in connection with Forms is to run the risk (a clear and present danger) of confusing the principle needed with a principle of self-*participation*, (i.e., to confuse *Largeness is large* with *Largeness participates in itself*). Since the second additional premise required by the Argument will turn out to be a principle of *non*-self-participation, (i.e., the very denial of self-participation), it is clear that the above confusion would lead to the "discovery" of inconsistent premises in Plato's argument. Vlastos does, indeed, "discover" an inconsistency between the two additional premises required by the Argument, and it is confusion which leads him to do so. But it is a more radical confusion, in which the danger to which we have been calling attention plays at most an auxiliary role.

The assumption Vlastos has in mind would be formulated more correctly as "The adjective corresponding to the name of any Form can correctly be predicated of that Form." This might well be called the "*F*-ness is *F*" Assumption. However, there is enough appropriateness to the name "Self-Predication Assumption" to warrant its use, provided the above points are kept in mind.

Now (A3) seems more relevant to the question (2) above, "What authorizes the affirmation of the antecedent of (A2)?" than to the establishing of (A2) itself. Let us therefore turn our attention to the second of the additional premises. This he calls the Nonidentity Assumption, and formulates as follows: (A4) If anything has a certain character, it cannot be identical with the Form in virtue of which we apprehend that character. If x is F, x cannot be identical with F-ness."[30] I shall not comment specifically on this principle at this time, as what I should say about it is, in part, implicit in what I have already said about the other premises of Vlastos' reconstruction, and the rest is a matter of a fundamental flaw in all his formulations which will be pointed out in the next section.

V

Vlastos is clearly correct in saying that both Self-Predication and Nonidentity are essential to the Third Man Argument. Are they also sufficient, when joined with (A1) to generate (A2)?

---

[30]*Ibid., p. 325.*

Vlastos thinks so, though he qualifies this by adding "though in a very odd way."[31] And the reason for this is that he has just shown, to his own satisfaction, that these two additional premises are mutually inconsistent, "so that we should not be surprised to see them justify all kinds of contradictory conclusions."[32] Let us look at his demonstration of this inconsistency. He begins by giving a terse formulation of (A3), namely, "F-ness is F";[33] he follows this with a terse formulation of (A4), namely, "if x is F, x cannot be identical with F-ness," where x is a variable which includes not only particulars, but also Forms, in its range of values. He continues:

> Substituting F-ness for x in (A4) we get
> (A5) If F-ness is F, F-ness cannot be identified with F-ness.
> And since the consequent of (A5) is plainly false, because self-contradictory, at least one of the premises from which it follows—(A3), (A4)—must be false.[34]

Convincing? Yet this "demonstration" is a tissue of confusions. The passage which is most clearly diagnostic of these confusions is that in which Vlastos analyzes the way—the "odd" way—in which, as he sees it, (A1), (A3), and (A4) are jointly sufficient to establish (A2): "Since these premises warrant the proposition that F-ness is *not* identical with F-ness, they will warrant the proposition that F-ness *is* identical with F_1-ness, which *is* a Form not identical with F-ness, and (A2) will then follow from (A1)."[35] At this point Vlastos relegates to a footnote his formal analysis of this reasoning:

> For we know from (A1) that if a number of things are F there must be a Form, F-ness, through which they are apprehended as F. Whence it follows that
> (A2b) If a, b, c, and F-ness are all F, there must be a form, F-ness, through which they are apprehended as F.
> But if F-ness is identical with F_1-ness, we may substitute F_1-ness for F-ness in the second clause of (A2b), which will produce (A2).[36]

But notice the use that is made of (A1) in this argument! Whereas (A1) as initially formulated told us that if a set of *particulars*, a, b, c, etc., are F, there must be a form F-ness by virtue of which they are F, it is now being used as a more general principle to the effect

---

[31]*Ibid.*, p. 327.   [32]*Ibid.*   [33]*Ibid.*, p. 326.   [34]*Ibid.*   [35]*Ibid.*, p. 327.   [36]*Ibid.*, n. 11.

that if a number of "things" are F, there must be a Form, F-ness, where the "things" in question may be either particulars or Forms. Let us call this more general principle "(G)." Clearly something like the original (A1) results from applying (G) to the case where the "things" which are F are particulars. This suggests that (A2) might be the result of applying (G) to the case where the things which are F are F particulars together with the Form, F-ness, in which they all participate. Clearly, however, (A2) requires, in addition, the use of an Assumption of Non-identity.

But it is even more important to note the role played by the expression "F-ness" in (A1) as it is used in the above footnote. An expression such as "F-ness" may be a variable in either of *two* senses. (1) It can serve as a *representative symbol*. In this use, "F-ness" would represent the name of a Form. To assert a formula which includes a representative name is, in effect, to assert each and every sentence which results from the formula by replacing the representative name by a name. Consequently to formulate an argument in terms of "F-ness" where "F-ness" represents the name of a Form is, in effect, to propound a class of arguments in each of which there occurs *not* "F-ness," but the name of a single Form, e.g., "Largeness."

(2) "F-ness" can serve as a variable proper. The distinctive feature of a variable proper is that it makes sense to say "for all values of v," "for some values of v," etc. Thus, where "F-ness" is an variable proper, it makes sense to say "All F-nesses . . .," "Some F-nesses . . .," "The F-ness which . . .," "There must be an F-ness which . . .," etc. These contexts are improper for repre-sentative names.

Now, I wrote above that "an expression such as 'F-ness' may be a variable in either of two senses." I did not say "either *or both* of two senses," but it can readily be seen that, provided care is taken, these two modes of variability (*representative symbol* and *variable proper*) can be embodied in one and the same symbol. In this case a formula involving "F-ness" would *represent* a class of sentences in each of which there would occur, instead of "F-ness," one of the following: "Largeness," "Triangularity," . . ., where the latter, however, are to be construed *not* as names of single Forms, but rather as *variables*. In other words, the latter would be used in such a way as to admit of such contexts as "All Largenesses . . .," "There is a Triangularity . . .," etc. And the substituends for these variables, e.g., "Largeness," would be designated by some such device as the use of numerical subscripts, e.g., "Largeness$_1$," "Largeness$_2$," etc. Note that it would be obviously inappropriate to put the subscripts "inside" the variable, e.g., "Large$_1$ness," "Large$_2$ness."

If we now ask, "Which of these uses of 'F-ness' is appropriate to (G)?" the answer is obvious. "F-ness," here, must be a symbol which *represents* a class of *variables*. Indeed, (G), correctly formulated as

(G) If a number of entities are all F, there must be an F-ness by virtue of which they are all F,

is a formula which represents a class of propositions, one of which would be

(G-Largeness) If a number of entities are all large, there must be a Largeness by virtue of which they are all large.

And an application of this proposition to the case of large *particulars*, would yield

(H1-Largeness) If a number of particulars, *a*, *b*, *c*, are all large, there must be *a* Largeness by virtue of which they are all large.

This, in turn, must be carefully distinguished from

(L) If a number of particulars, *a*, *b*, *c*, are all large, they are so in virtue of a Form, namely Largeness.

For in the latter, "Largeness" appears as the name of a single Form, whereas in (H1-Largeness) it is a variable.

VI

If we approach the Third Man Argument in the light of these distinctions, puzzles and perplexities melt away like thawing ice. The movement of thought is from (L)—by "induction"—to (G-Largeness) and from (G-Largeness) to the series of hypotheticals which are its applications. These hypotheticals would be:

(H1-Largeness) as above.

(H2-Largeness) If a number of particulars, *a*, *b*, *c*, etc., and the

Largeness they jointly exemplify are all large, there must
be a Largeness by virtue of which they are all large.

(H3-Largeness) If a number of particulars, *a*, *b*, *c*, etc., the
Largeness they exemplify, and the Largeness exemplified
by all the preceding items are all large, there must be a
Largeness by virtue of which they are all large.

Indeed, since the Third Man Argument, though phrased in terms
of "Largeness," is intended to have a more general validity,
"Largeness" has a representative function and, at a certain stage
in the logical movement of thought, plays the role of "*F*-ness"
in the last paragraph of the preceding section. Much more, then,
than Self-Predication and Nonidentity must be found implicit in
Parmenides, 132a1 ff., if it is to embody a cogent argument.

But what of the charge that Self-Predication and Nonidentity
are mutually inconsistent? A quick review of these principles in the
light of the distinctions we have drawn exposes the groundless-
ness of this claim. For properly formulated, the Self-Predication
Assumption becomes

(SP) All *F*-nesses are *F*.

and the Nonidentity Assumption

(NI) If *x* is *F*, then *x* is not identical with *the F-ness* by virtue of
which it is *F*.

And a moment's reflection makes it clear that Vlastos found an
inconsistency, because he treated the "*F*-ness" in his formulations
as a representative *name*. Once it is realized that what is needed are
formulae in which "*F*-ness" functions as a representative *variable*,
it is seen that the Self-Predication and Nonidentity Assumptions
are to be formulated as above, and the inconsistency vanishes.

VII

What, then, does the Third Man Argument look like when all
these points have been taken into account?

Premises: (G); (SP); (NI); (P) = *a*, *b*, *c*, etc., particulars, are *F*.

(G)   (1) = (H1) If *a*, *b*, *c*, etc., are *F*, there is an
                       F-ness by virtue of which they are *F*.

(1), (P)   (2) There is an *F*-ness by virtue of which *a*, *b*,
                       c, etc., are *F*.

	(3) [Call this F-ness, "F-ness$_1$."]
(2), (3), (SP)	(4) F-ness$_1$ is F.
(4), (P)	(5) a, b, c, etc., and F-ness$_1$ are all F.
(G)	(6) = (H2) If a, b, c, etc., and F-ness$_1$ are all F, then there is an F-ness by virtue of which they are all F.
(6), (5)	(7) There is an F-ness by virtue of which a, b, c, etc., and F-ness$_1$ are all F.
	(8) [Call this F-ness, "F-ness$_2$."]
(NI)	(9) If F-ness$_1$ is F, then F-ness$_1$ is not identical with the F-ness by virtue of which it is F.
(4), (8), (9)	(10) F-ness$_1$ is not identical with F-ness$_2$.
(G)	(11) = (H3) If a, b, c, etc., and F-ness$_1$ and F-ness$_2$ are all F, then there is an F-ness by virtue of which they are all F.
(SP)	(12) F-ness$_2$ is F.
(12), (5)	(13) a, b, c, etc., and F-ness$_1$ and F-ness$_2$ are all F. ... ad libitum.

VIII

Is the argument we have just constructed to be found in the *Parmenides*? Certainly not "in so many words." Implicitly, then? But there are many ways in which formally complete arguments are "found" in arguments as actually propounded, and I would be willing to say that the above is "merely implicit" in the text of the *Parmenides* only if this phrase is so understood as to be compatible with the idea that this argument is a fair (albeit idealized) representation of Plato's thought, and, in particular, with the idea that its premises can be said to have been Plato's premises.[37] But it is not my aim, in this second part of my paper, to make a detailed case for the claim that the above is a satisfactory reconstruction of Plato's Third Man Argument. Indeed, I think that a careful reading of the complete argument as Plato gave it is sufficiently convincing. I say *complete*, because nowhere

---

[37] By "Plato's premises," I mean, of course, "propositions used by Plato as premises in the Third Man Argument," *not* "premises which Plato thought to be true." For, as I shall argue below, the whole point of the first part of the *Parmenides* is that the key premise of the Third Man Argument is false.

in his article does Vlastos reproduce, let alone analyze, what I suppose he would have called the "third step" of the Argument.

> I suppose this is what leads you to suppose that there is in every case a single Form: When several things seem large to you, it seems perhaps that there is a single Form which is the same in your view of all of them. Hence you believe that Largeness is a single thing. . . .
>
> What then if you similarly view mentally Largeness itself and the other large things? Will not a single Largeness appear once again, in virtue of which all these appear large. It seems so. Consequently, another Form of Largeness will appear, over and above Largeness itself and the things which participate in it. *And again, covering all these, yet another, which will make all of them large. So each of your Forms will no longer be one, but an indefinite number.*[38]

If Vlastos had devoted as much care and attention to bringing out the logical form of the "third step" as he did to the two other "steps," he must surely have been led to the distinction between a matrix of general principles and the specific steps in the regress constituted by their recurrent application. And this, in turn, must have led him to appreciate the diversity of roles played by "largeness"—failure to discern which is responsible for most of the confusions in his analysis.

It is Vlastos' diagnosis of Plato's philosophical frame of mind at the time of writing the *Parmenides* which is the target of this portion of my paper. This diagnosis occupies the second, and larger, part of his paper, and if Vlastos is right in his main contentions, then Plato could not have had in mind the argument with which we concluded Section VII above. Fortunately, this part of his paper rests on a few key premises in the discussion of which we can be quite brief.

Vlastos summarizes as follows the conclusions to be drawn from what he takes to be the fact that Plato presented the Third Man Argument with no clear indication of a refutation.

> If Plato had identified all of the premises which are necessary (and sufficient) to warrant the second step of the Third Man Argument, he would not have produced the Third Man Argu-

---

[38]I have used Vlastos' translation as before (*Op cit.*, pp. 320, 321), save for the italicized passage—which he neglects—in which I have followed Cornford: *Plato and Parmenides*, p. 88.

ment at all, unless he were simply pursuing a logical game for
its own sake, which is not what he is doing in the first part of the
Parmenides. In stating the Third Man Argument, and in leaving
it unrefuted, he is revealing (a) that he did not know all of its
necessary premises, whence it would follow that (b) he had no
way of determining whether or not it was a valid argument.[39]

The crucial step in this reasoning is the contention that if
Plato had realized that Self-Predication and Nonidentity are
indispensible premises of the Argument, he would have detected
their inconsistency, and would therefore, instead of playing with
a regress, have turned directly to the problem "Does my Theory of
Forms involve a commitment to these inconsistent principles? And
if not, what would remain if one or the other were abandoned?"
But we have undercut this step by showing that the idea on
which it rests—namely that Self-Predication and Nonidentity are
patently incompatible—is mistaken. Up to this point, therefore,
Vlastos has given no good reason for supposing that Plato had not
"identified all of the premises" and therefore "had no way of
determining whether or not it was a valid argument."

But Vlastos has another string to his bow. He claims to have
independent evidence—evidence, that is, which does not spring
from his analysis of the Third Man Argument—for the thesis that
Plato had not identified all of the necessary premises.[40] Specifically,
he proposes to establish (1) that Plato's Theory of Ideas, even in
its later form, is through and through committed to Self-Predication; but also (2) that Plato never came to an explicit recognition of this fact. (1) is clearly the crucial step, for unless it were
true, the fact—upon which Vlastos lays such stress—that Plato
nowhere explicitly formulates a Principle of Self-Predication[41]
could scarcely mean that Plato failed to recognize an essential
feature of his theory; nor could evidence be found in the fact

---

[39]*Ibid.*, p. 329.

[40]Thus, immediately following the passage just quoted he writes, "(1) can be
independently verified, and it will be in Section II."

[41]Vlastos himself points out, however, that Plato comes very close indeed to such
a formulation in the text of the Third Man Argument. Thus, after pointing out that
Self-Predication is essential to the Argument, Vlastos writes, "Plato's actual wording
of the second step comes as close to asserting it as one could without stating the Self-
Predication Assumption" (p. 325). And this is no understatement, as a glance at the
passage in question will confirm.

that Plato, in the later dialogues, arrives at conclusions about the Realm of Ideas—e.g., its genus-species structure; the existence of a Form of Motion (or Change)—which must have been seen to be incompatible with an *explicitly entertained* principle of Self-Predication. On the other hand, if Vlastos can establish that Plato's Theory of Ideas, even in its later form, *is* committed to Self-Predication, then one can hold that Plato was cognizant of the logical force of the Third Man Argument as we have reconstructed it, and therefore that he recognized that Self-Predication is its key premise, only at the expense of supposing that Plato believed either that the argument refuted his Theory of Ideas or that it could be saved by dropping the generalized Assumption of Nonidentity.

X

Vlastos has little difficulty in showing that the language of the earlier dialogues is fraught with Self-Predication. And it is scarcely plausible to discount the (familiar) evidence he brings forward by claiming that Plato's language was self-consciously metaphorical. For in what language would Plato have formulated to himself a distinction between the philosophical claims he was making, and the literal meaning of the language in which he was publishing these claims? Certainly it would be a mistake to suppose that when Plato began his philosophical speculations he found ready to hand a vocabulary whose *literal* meanings were the concepts and distinctions of the Theory of Ideas, a vocabulary which he could use *in foro interno* in the process of contriving the rhetorically more effective metaphors of the dialogues. Rather, the creation of the Theory of Ideas was identical with the creation of the language of the Theory of Ideas. The differences between the philosophical and the everyday meanings of words, as well as the awareness of these differences, was the slowly ripening fruit of philosophical argumentation about the Ideas, and of catch-as-catch-can wrestling with the perplexities they were introduced to resolve (as well as the perplexities which inevitably arise when everyday language is put to philosophical use).

I think it is fair to say that when Plato was writing the earlier dialogues, he had not yet been led to question the Self-Predicational force of the language of his Theory. But this is by no means equivalent to the idea that he was "implicitly" thinking of his Forms as Self-Predicational, (i.e., "taking" this [in Cook Wilson's sense] "for granted"). To establish this, we would have to show that significant features of the early Theory of Ideas, or of the arguments developed in connection with it, imply a commitment to Self-Predication. In other words, one would have to show that Self-Predication plays a role in the *philosophical* use to which Plato put the language of the theory. To do this is no simple task, and I shall not attempt to settle the matter one way or the other on the present occasion. I do, however, want to call attentio to at least two considerations which contribute to an explanation of the fact that Plato used language with Self-Predicational force, yet do not require us to say that he (even implicity) thought of the Ideas as Self-Predicational.

In the first place, there is the obvious fact that the names of the Ideas had to be formed from the roots of the class terms and adjectives, the applicability of which to particulars was to be explained by the Theory. Thus, *anglice*, the name of the Idea in terms of which statements of the form ". . . is triangular" or ". . . is a triangle" are to be explained, would be a noun or noun-phrase built from the root of "triangular" and "triangle." Only when the concept of a *universal* had been hammered out in philosophical debate would it come to be seen that there is something queer about the use of "The Triangle Itself" to designate this Idea. And until the concept of a *universal* had been hammered out, the distinctive expressions which philosophers use to designate them (e.g., "Triangularity," "Redness," etc.) did not exist. In short, Plato did exactly what we should expect. He took the existing noun "triangle" and put it to a new use. But the fact that by referring to the Idea as "The Triangle Itself," he was using language which implies that the Idea is a triangle, does not suffice to establish that Plato thought (even "implicity") that The Triangle Itself was a triangle. To show this, as we have pointed out, one must show that this implication of the language is put to philosophical use.

In the second place, the early dialogues stress the role of the Ideas as standards or norms which objects in the World of Becoming strive to realize, but necessarily fail to realize fully because of the inherent fuzziness of Becoming. Now, if *we* thought along these lines, we should carefully distinguish between the Idea or universal and the (nonexistent) *Ideal* which it specifies, e.g., between *Straight-Linearity* and a *perfectly straight line*. But this distinction was not a datum for Plato, and he could have been led to draw it only by the pressure of the perplexities which arise from a failure to draw it. Did Plato ever draw, in his own mind, this distinction between Ideas and Ideal Particulars? One immediately thinks of *ta mathematika*. Note, however, that, as usually conceived by those who find them in Plato, they are *existent* Ideal Particulars which are *other than* the Ideas they exemplify. As for a distinction between Ideas and *non-existent* Ideal Particulars, Plato was not in a position to draw it, until he had acquired the insight into "Not-Being," which is embodied in that most wonderful of the dialogues, the *Sophist*. Fortunately, the resolution of this problem is not my present concern. The point I wish to make is that to say that Plato's language embodies no distinction between The Circle Itself and an ideal circle, and, in general, between an Idea and the Ideal it specifies, is not the same as to say that Plato "implicitly" thinks of The Circle Itself as an Ideal Circle. The latter statement is much stronger in its force than the former. That Plato failed to draw an explicit distinction is, indeed, a *reason* for supposing that he "implicitly" thought of the Ideas as Ideal Objects. But it is not a *compelling* reason, as is made clear by the fact that we can conceive of considerations which would lead us to say that although Plato drew no such explicit distinction he "implicitly" distinguished between Ideas and Ideals. These considerations would spring from an examination of the different philosophical uses to which such expressions as "The Circle Itself" were put in the context of different problems.

X

But whether or not a careful examination of the evidence would lead us to the conclusion that in the early dialogues Plato thought of the Ideas as Self-Predicational, I am convinced that by the time he wrote the first part of the *Parmenides*, he had faced up to the question, "Is, e.g., The Large Itself large?" and answered it in the negative. This thesis is by no means a novel one. As Vlastos himself points out it is the orthodox view.[42] On what grounds does he reject it?

> If Plato never stated it (the Assumption of Self-Predication), what reason can be given for saying that he did make it after all? The reason is that it is certainly implied by various things he said and believed. It is implied, first of all, both by his Degrees of Reality Theory and by his Copy Theory of the relation of things to Forms.[43]

Postponing comment on the idea that Plato ever held a "Copy Theory of the relation of things to Forms," let us first take up the question of a Platonic "Degrees of Reality" theory. Vlastos approaches this topic from a number of directions. To begin with, he claims to find in Plato the "assumption"—"logically the costliest assumption that Plato made"—"that the verb 'is' and all its substantival, adjectival or adverbial variants have a *single* meaning."[44]

> What Plato means by saying...that "*x is,*" in the strict sense of "*is,*" becomes clear when we see that he understands this to entail:
>   (i) *x* is intelligible;
>   (ii) *x* is changeless;
>   (iii) *x* is not qualified by contrary predicates;
>   (iv) *x* is itself the perfect instance of the quality or relation which the word for *x* connotes.[45]

Now it is certainly true that we find no hint in the early dialogues that Plato is aware of the different meanings of "is" *and* also true that he thinks of the Ideas as the things that *are*, and also true that he is not yet able to give the reply direct to Parmenides, who *can* be said to have made the assumption in question. But this falls far short of establishing that Plato himself makes this assumption. Indeed, Plato's refusal to commit himself to Eleatic monism, as well as the elusive flexibility of his discussions of Becoming, and his willingness—noted by Vlastos[46]—to speak of objects in the World of Becoming as "beings" (*onta*), things that are, all indicate that Plato refused to postpone the solution of specific ontological

---

[42]Vlastos, *Op. cit.*, p. 337, n. 33; p. 346, n. 48.
[42]*Ibid.*, pp. 336-337.   [44]*Ibid.*, p. 334.   [45]*Ibid.*
[46]*Ibid.*, p. 335, n. 29.

problems until he had come to terms with the Parmenidean problem.[47] As for the later dialogues, surely a good case can be made for saying that once the Stranger of the *Sophist* has made it clear that "Being" has its puzzles no less than "Not-Being," and that we can scarcely hope to solve the latter until we have mastered the former, he embarks upon a course of reasoning the heart of which consists exactly in drawing distinctions between the meanings of the word "is" and its cognates as they occur in different contexts.

Vlastos nowhere clearly brings out what he conceives to be the relation of this "costliest assumption" to Plato's "Degrees of Reality Theory." As a matter of fact, it would seem obvious that if "is" had for Plato the meaning Vlastos says it did, then Plato could not, without inconsistency, have held such a theory. Vlastos tacitly acknowledges this, for immediately after ascribing this "costliest assumption" to Plato, he writes:

> Plato did not thereby revert to the Eleatic view that the sensible world is wholly unreal. His view was a Degrees-of-Reality theory *which permitted him, in compliance with his native tongue,* to say that sensible things are, as logical subjects of assertions of existence and ascriptions of properties and relations. They were halfway real, "between the purely real and the totally unreal" (*Rep.* 478d).[48]

Surely, however, this gives the show away. For to admit that Plato, in the discussion of particular problems, was willing to use "is" and related words "in compliance with his native tongue" is to grant that Plato's philosophizing was not limited by the strait jacket of the "assumption" that "the verb 'is' and all its substantival, adjectival and adverbial variants have a single meaning."

Yet there is, indeed, a connection between Vlastos' attribution of this assumption to Plato, and the Degrees of Reality Theory which he finds in the dialogues. For *if* "is" has one meaning, and *if* this meaning involves Self-Predication (item iv in the list quoted above) then degrees of "being" or "reality" could be expected to involve degrees of being F,—particulars being humdrumly F to

---

[47]And he was by no means the only philosopher who continued to philosophize in the shadow of "Being alone is, Not-Being is not."

[48]*Ibid.*, pp. 335-336. Italics mine.

various degrees, F-ness, however, being superbly F. That some such reasoning is at the back of Vlastos' mind is shown by the fact that he fails even to consider the possibility that Plato might have had a degrees of reality theory *without being committed* to Self-Predication.

We have not yet, however, plumbed the depth of Vlastos' thought. For if we ask "Why does Vlastos so confidently include the F-ness of F-ness in the very meaning of Plato's 'is'?" it strikes us that this inclusion would be a bald *petitio* unless there were at least the sketch of an argument to back it up. And clearly the argument would have to be more than a rehash of the evidence that Plato (implicitly) thought F-ness to be F. For what is needed is an argument which would show that Self-Predication is so intrinsic to Plato's conception of being, that he could not abandon the former without giving up the latter. And evidence that Plato at one time or another thought F-ness to be F would not serve this purpose.

There is indeed such an argument, and it is to be found in the following passage:

> Did not his Theory of Forms call attention, and for the first time, to the "reality" of universals as distinct from that of material existents? This of course is perfectly true. But what is no less true is that the Platonic ontology inadvertently blurs the very distinction it was devised to express. It compels Plato to think of the difference between empirical existents and their intelligible properties as a difference between "deficiently" real and perfectly real things (i.e., as a difference in degree between beings of the same kind, instead of a difference in kind between different kinds of being). To say that *the* difference between a white thing, like wool or snow, and the universal, Whiteness, is a difference in degree of reality, is to put Whiteness in the same class with white things, albeit as a pre-eminent member of that class, endowed in a pre-eminent degree with the character which its fellow members possess in various deficient degrees; it is to think of Whiteness as a (superlatively) white thing, and thus to assimilate it categorially to white things, instead of distinguishing it from them.[49]

Now, in reproducing this argument, I have italicized a certain little word. It plays so important a role that it deserves this

---
[49]*Ibid.*, p. 340.

distinction. For to say that *the* difference between an *F* particular and *F*-ness is a difference in degree of reality is indeed tantamount to saying that the *F* particular and *F*-ness are both *F*. For if they were not then this would be an additional difference between them over and above their different degrees of reality. On the other hand, if the *F*-particular and *F*-ness are both *F*, there must be some difference in the way they are *F*, for *F*-ness is not just another *F* particular. And this difference would be the difference in degree of reality which is *the* difference between them.

But why in the world should we suppose that (for Plato) *the* difference between *F* particulars and *F*-ness is a difference in degree of reality? And without this premise, the argument does not get off the ground. Let me emphasize that I have no objection to saying that Plato, throughout his philosophical career, divided the things that are into the more and the less real. I think it a serious mistake however, to suppose that the way in which Plato conceives of degrees or levels of reality involves a commitment to the Principle of Self-Predication. Indeed, as I have said before, I am convinced that the first part of the *Parmenides* is a deliberate and sustained critique of Self-Predicational interpretations of the Ideas.

One more comment on "is" before we turn to consider what would remain of a Platonic Degrees of Reality Theory if Self-Predication were dropped. After attributing to Plato the assumption that "is" has one single meaning, he writes, "The Aristotelian axiom that 'things can be said to be in many different senses' was not a commonplace in its day, but a revolutionary discovey."[50]

To this he adds as a footnote:

> [A discovery] which, among other things, offers a direct way of tracking down the source of the Third Man Argument, as Aristotle himself clearly saw. In his own language, the confusion of the sense which "is" has in the first category with its sense in one of the other categories is what "creates the 'third man.'" *Soph. El.* 178b37 ff; cf. *Met.*, 1038b34 ff.[51]

This is an ancient legend. It overlooks the sad extent to which Aristotle had to manhandle Plato's thought before he could convince himself that he had refuted it. It is indeed true that if you think of universals as substances in Aristotle's sense (which

---

[50]*Ibid.*, pp. 334-335.   [51]*Ibid.*, p. 335, n. 25.

they *obviously* can not be), then you are committed to thinking of them in Self-Predicational terms. For, let us face it, it is an analytic consequence of Aristotle's conception of substance that no universal can be a substance. Universals are necessarily *predicable of* something, otherwise they wouldn't be universals. (Primary) substances are not. Consequently, to suppose that a universal is a substance (always in Aristotle's sense) is to suppose that it is a particular. But to suppose that *F*-ness is a particular is tantamount to supposing that it is *F*, for clearly this particular has *something* to do with *being F*, and what could this something be but the particular's being itself *F*. To all this is suffices to reply that only the Plato of Aristotle's (and Vlastos') imagination thinks of *F*-ness as an Aristotelian substance.

Rather than saying that Platonists have thought of *F*-ness as *F because* they thought of *F*-ness as a substance in the Aristotelian sense, it would be more correct to say that when (if ever) Platonists have thought of *F*-ness as *F*, they have, in effect, treated *F*-ness as a substance in the Aristotelian sense (i.e., as a particular). But this reformulation amounts to abandoning the claim that Aristotle has traced the genealogy of the Third Man. Much more to the point is Vlastos' observation that the Greek language may trap the unwary into confusing the tautology "Justice is justice" with the absurdity "Justice is just." I think it can be shown, however, that *Protagoras*, 330c-d, "which, since first noted by Goblot in 1929, has become the star instance of Self-Predication in Plato," is capable of an interpretation (in the light of the dialectical structure of the dialogue as a whole) according to which Plato *uses* rather than *commits* this confusion. (And as for the claim that Plato must be guilty of the Assumption of Self-Predication because he has Socrates say [*Phaedo* 100c], "If anything else is beautiful, besides Beauty itself," and because "the whole point of Diotima's speech is that the Form of Beauty is superlatively fair,"[52] it is sufficient to reply that Plato thought of *all* the Ideas as beautiful to the contemplation of the philosophically trained mind, as have many other thinkers, including one of the many Bertrand Russells, who have *not* been guilty of the Assumption of Self-Predication.) However this may be, the point I wish to make

---

[52]*Ibid.*, p. 338.

is that the confusion in question is between the "is" of predication and the "is" of identity, rather than between two of the meanings distinguished by Aristotle, which are actually all special cases of the "is" of predication.

XI

What remains of Plato's hierarchial conception of reality if we omit the Assumption of Self-Predication? Items i-iii of Vlastos' list of what is entailed by "*x* is" in Plato's philosophy provide an excellent starting point. The Ideas are changeless, objects of mind, and consistent. In the early dialogues, Becoming is in constant flux, the object of sense perception, and, above all, inconsistent. Yet Plato didn't know quite what to say about the status of Becoming, for he had not yet reached to his own satisfaction the puzzles relating to "is not." In the *Republic* (478d) he places Becoming "between" Being (the Forms) and the utterly nonexistent. But there are, prima facie, two ways in which Plato could have interpreted this "intermediate" status. On the one hand, he could have viewed Becoming as somehow a *mixture* of Being (the Forms) and a Not-Being conceived as an ontological principle or, better, stuff. In favor of this interpretation would be the fact, emphasized by Plato, that to describe a change we must see both "is" (or "was") and "is not" (or "was not"). On the other hand, he could have taken Becoming to be an ultimate and irreducible mode of existence, one which, indeed, *depends on* Being (the Forms) but does not contain Being as an *ingredient*. On the whole it is the latter interpretation which comes closest to Plato's thought, even in the *Republic*. It finds its clearest expression in the Analogy of the Line, where the relation of Becoming to Being is compared to the relation (within the world of becoming) of shadows and reflections to physical things.

By the time of the *Timaeus* and the *Sophist* an important change has taken place. Becoming is no longer thought to be internally inconsistent. This revolution (and revolution it was) is signalized in the *Sophist* by the recognition of an Idea of Change. The failure of Becoming to be "truly real" could no longer be traced to its supposed self-contradictory character. Nor could the fact that it cannot be described without using "is not" suffice to give it a lower status, for the *Sophist* shows this to be equally true of the Ideas. It is, therefore, the categories of *dependence* and *independence* (or *self-sufficiency*) which now take over the major part of the job of ranking the levels of reality. Thus, although the Realm of Ideas and the World of Becoming are both *self-consistent*, the latter depends on the former (and on the Receptable or Place as well). The Ideas are taken to have an Olympian self-sufficiency. After all, if there were no Triangularity, there could be no triangles; but if there were no triangles, would there not still be Triangularity? To be sure, the Receptacle appears to be as self-sufficient as the Ideas, but this only means that its place at the bottom of the scale must be justified by other criteria. Again, to account for the place of Soul within the hierarchy would require a detailed analysis of the *Timaeus*.[53] But I have already said enough to vindicate the idea that the Great Chain of Being is possible without Self-Predication.

But, it will be said, it is exactly in the course of developing the Degrees of Reality Theory of the *Timaeus* that Plato most clearly commits himself to a Copy Theory of the relation of things to Forms. Does not Plato speak of the world of Becoming as consisting of "likenesses" of the Ideas? Do not both the *Sophist* and the *Timaeus* echo the assimilation, in the *Republic*, of the relation between Becoming and Being to that between image and thing, painting and subject, imitation and original? Once again it just won't do to jump from the fact that Plato uses language with Self-Predicational implications to the conclusion that Plato thought of the Ideas in Self-Predicational terms. "But can it seriously be maintained that Plato didn't think of things as likenesses or imitations of the Ideas?" One good question deserves another. What philosophical purposes could the language of imitation have been serving for Plato if he didn't think of the Ideas as Self-Predicational? And what advantages (and disadvantages) does it have as compared with the language of "sharing"? Until these questions have been answered, any discussion of the former quesion is premature.

I shall make the essential points briefly. The first and most obvious advantage of the copy-likeness-semblance-imitation ter-

---

[53]An excellent account of the status of Soul in the metaphysics of the *Timaeus* is to be found in Cornford: *Plato's Cosmology*, London, 1937.

minology is that it is admirably suited to give expression to the inferior status of the World of Becoming. Then there is the fact, of greater technical interest, that "likeness" does not, as such, imply an internal diremption of the F thing; whereas if we speak of F things as "sharing" in The F Itself, we confront a distinction within each F thing between a *sharer* and its *portion* of the *shared*.[54] Likeness is a two-term relation between copy and original. Sharing is a tetradic relation between *sharer, portion, shared item,* and *another sharer*. In this respect, "likeness" is much closer than "sharing" to such contemporary terms as "exemplifies" and "is an instance of."

The *Phaedo* is a key document in the interpretation of the language of the Theory of Ideas. There we find passages which, by speaking of the Ideas as Ideals which things strive to realize, suggest that it is the language of "likeness" or "imitation" which is appropriate to express the relation of things to Ideas. On the other hand, the final and most metaphysical argument for immortality is built on the distinction between *an F thing, the F in the thing* and *The F Itself*, which, at first sight, is the framework of "sharing," pure and simple. If we ask what there is to a thing over and above "the large in the thing," "the sweet in the thing," etc., we find, of course, no answer. The temptation is to read into the *Phaedo* a substratum theory[55] by something like the following line of thought. In the naturalistic philosophy of Empedocles, each object has its share of Earth, Air, Fire, and Water, yet contains no sharer over and above the shares. But Plato's shared objects are the Ideas; and since Becoming can scarcely be made up of shared Beings, there must be in things a substratum or sharer. We have already pointed out that until Plato made substantial progress in clarifying the puzzles of "is not," which were

---

[54]This must not be pressed too far; even as used by the man in the street, "sharing" does not always imply that the shared item is *divided* among the sharers. (Thus two people may share a common goal.) Whether this is also true of the corresponding Greek words I leave to the philologists. If so, the language of "sharing" gains an additional flexibility which makes it possible to use it cheek by jowl with the language of "likeness."

[55]On this interpretation, "the large in the thing" would be a reification of the *fact* that the substratum is related in a unique way to Largeness. Indeed, this interpretation calls for a conception of Largeness as a *component* of large things—a conception which entails that the Separation (*chorismos*) of the Platonic Ideas must be a mistake.

exploited by the Eleatics and Sophists alike, he was bound to be tempted, on occasion, to think of changing things as *mixtures* of Being and Not-Being—roughly Form and Non-Form.

Yet the fact remains that Plato drew no such conclusions. Nowhere do we find even a hint of a substratum analysis. And if we take this seriously and ask ourselves, "Can sense be made of the trichotomy 'F thing,' 'the F in the thing' and 'The F Itself,' without a commitment to a substratum?" we note that if "the F in the thing" were a *copy* or *reflection* or *imitation* of the F Itself, a substratum would no longer be necessary, since the thing could *consist of* these copies or reflections or imitations, namely the hot in the thing, or the sweet in the thing, without *consisting of* Forms (or "parts" of Forms). And it is a significant fact that as Plato's metaphysics of Becoming matured, it is the Heracleitean rather than the Ur-Aristotelian picture of physical things which prevails. Enduring things are constituted by a binding of the flux of Becoming to order and recurrence. Plato rejects in advance the Aristotelian dichotomy Form-Matter and replaces it by the dichotomy Process-Place.[56]

The distinction between "the F in the thing," and "The F Itself" is appropriate to both the "sharing" and the "likeness" terminologies. But clearly the Separation (*chorismos*) of the Forms —that is, the fact that Plato's Ideas are not constituents or parts in any sense (even "adjectival aspects") of changing things—is more adequately captured by the language of "likeness." It is essential to realize that "the F in the thing" is not a *universal*, (i.e., is not common to the many F things). By failing to appreciate this, Vlastos further confuses an imperceptive discussion of "the Separation Assumption"[57] He speaks (p. 342, n. 40) of "the F of F particulars" as a "predicate which attaches to particulars" and fails altogether to see that *the F in the thing* is, in effect, a subordinate

---

[56]Plato, indeed, places process in a context of active and passive powers from which they arise,—and this might make it seem as though process is being subordinated to the "causal" or "dispositional properties" of "continuants." But the powers of Plato's metaphysics—like those of Leibnitz centuries later—were not the austere "if's ..., then's ..." of contemporary philosophy of science. They were rather of the nature of desires or yearnings, and were really a deeper form of process. The *Timaeus*, in effect, compares the orderliness of the world process to the life of a man whose appetites are persuaded by his reason.

[57]*Ibid.*, p. 340 ff.

and component *particular* the whole nature of which is to be *F*. Interestingly enough, this conception of the *F* in the thing is echoed in Aristotle's *Categories* (1a24-b9) where, in effect, he distinguishes between *Whiteness* and *the white in the thing*, and tells us that while that which is individual is never *predicated of a subject*, it may be *present in a subject*.

To end this discussion of the comparative philosophical advantages of these two terminologies, it should be noted that "sharing" has the virtue that it does not imply Self-Predication. "*X* shares *y* with *z*" does not imply that *x* resembles *y*; though, of course, if The Hot Itself is construed as Empedoclean Fire, sharing in The Hot Itself would involve coming to resemble it. It is therefore interesting to note that it is "sharing" rather than "likeness" or "imitation" which plays the role of technical term for the relation of things to Ideas.[58]

XII

What, then, is the upshot of the first part of the *Parmenides?* The argument can be summed up as follows:

1. Obvious and insuperable difficulties arise if one construes the Ideas as the same sort of things as the "seeds" or "roots" of the Pluralists. For then sharing would be a matter of each thing having within it either the whole or a part of the Idea.

2. The temptation to construe the Ideas in this manner arises from supposing that in order for The Hot Itself to explain the hotness of hot objects, it must itself be hot (i.e., be the Fire of Empedocles). How, it is thought, can something make things hot, if it is not hot itself?

3. But this assumption can be shown to involve a regress (the Third Man).

4. On the other hand, Ideas are not mere thoughts. They are realities to which the mind is related in thinking, as physical objects are realities to which the mind is related in sense perception.

5. Shall we say, then, that things are imitations or likenesses of the Ideas? This would indeed avoid the difficulties arising in

---

[58] "It follows that the other things do not partake of Forms by being like them; we must look for some other means by which they partake. So it seems." *Parmenides* 133a, quoted from Cornford: *Plato and Parmenides*, p. 93.

connection with the first approach ([1.] above). But it doesn't avoid the regress (second version of the Third Man).

At this stage, we, in our modern sophistication, would like Plato to "come right out" and say something like the following: "The relation between particulars and universals cannot be identified with any relation which holds among particulars. Thus, any expression, e.g., "sharing" or "likeness," which mentions a relation which holds among particulars, must be at best a *metaphor*, the application of which to the relation between particulars and universals is to be justified with reference to certain formal analogies between the two relations." Yet it is obviously unrealistic to expect Plato to make any such statement. The decisive reason for this is that while Plato could say of a given property that it was "relative" (*pros ti*)—"with respect to something"—he had no general term for relations. In other words, he could say that *sharing* is *pros ti*, *likeness* is *pros ti*, but such an expression as "the relation between things and Ideas" falls outside his technical vocabulary. Thus, when he became aware of the limitations and dangers of the terminologies of "sharing" and "likeness," the limitations of his philosophical language precluded him from saying to himself, "let us use the word '. . .' for the relation between things and Ideas," and directed his search toward the discovery of another word in ordinary usage which might be more suitable than either "likeness" or "sharing." Thus we find Parmenides saying at *Parmenides*, 133a (quoted above, n. 58), "We must look for some other means whereby they partake."[59] In other words, these limitations led him to look for still another relation word or phrase in ordinary usage which might be an even more satisfactory metaphor, once its literal implications had been brought under strict philosophical control. We can imagine that he might have hit on some such phrase as "things are the children of the Ideas"—a metaphor which is actually to be found in the *Timaeus*—as the most useful expression for the relation between Becoming and Being.

The substance of the above remarks is that it would be a radical mistake to interpret Plato's search for another means whereby things partake of the Ideas as a failure to realize that no relation

---

[59]"Mode of partaking" would perhaps be a better rendering of the thought than "means whereby they partake."

among things can be identical with the relation between things and Ideas. For the fact that a philosopher makes a certain kind of philosophical use of those ordinary relation words which he applies to the Ideas can be good ground for saying that he recognizes the uniqueness of the relation between things and Ideas, in spite of the fact that nowhere does he "come right out and say this." And once this is realized, we are in a position to appreciate the subtlety and sophistication of Plato's later Theory of Ideas.

There are many who will feel, as apparently Vlastos does, that Platonic Ideas without Self-Predication have ceased to be Platonic Ideas; that without Self-Predication they are of merely logical interest and have ceased to define a metaphysics, a way of construing Man in the World. Nothing could be further from the truth. The heart of the Platonic tradition lies not in a picturesque realm where Horseness is a horse, Triangularity a triangle, and Courage a . . . (a what?), but rather in the conception of a domain of eternal (atemporal) objects which the human mind can "apprehend" or "see," and the interconnections of which, open at least in part to human inspection, constitute the fundamental principles of the World of Becoming. That one can speak in a logician's language of universals, particulars, and their mutual relationships and yet share this Platonic conception is made manifest by Bertrand Russell's "A Free Man's Worship." Platonism, thus widely conceived, is a metaphysical framework which admits of development in many different directions. And the direction taken by the early Russell (not to mention that taken by Santayana) has been taken by but few Platonists. The conception of the human mind as apprehending "abstract entities" has usually been construed (and, I think, reasonably so) to support a straightforward mind-body dualism,[60] and to fit harmoniously with a theistic cosmology. That it is a mistake has not prevented it from being one of the central threads around which have crystallized the values and attitudes of civilized Western man.

---

[60]For an elaboration of this point, see my essay "Empiricism and Abstract Entities" in *The Philosophy of Rudolf Carnap*, ed. by P. A. Schilpp, and published by Open Court (La Salle, Illinois), 1963.

VLASTOS AND "THE THIRD MAN": A REJOINDER

Professor Vlastos' reply[1] to my criticism[2] of his interpretation[3] of the Third Man Argument (TMA) in the *Paramenides* is divided into three parts.

I

The first part is devoted to a critique, indeed a refutation, of *my* interpretation of the TMA. "What he presents is a perfectly lucid and cogent deductive argument, and also a reasonably elegant one. The only trouble with it is that it is not Plato's."[4] He continues:

> The crucial difference occurs in its opening propositions, (1) and (2). Sellars' (1) reads "If *a*, *b*, *c*, etc. are *F*, there is *an F*-ness by virtue of which they are *F*." Substituting Plato's instance "large" for "*F*," the statement Sellars thinks Parmenides is making in the first step of the Argument is, "If *a*, *b*, *c*, etc. are all large, there is *a* largeness by virtue of which they are all large." I have italicized the word which makes all the difference in the interpretation...Thus "Largeness" in the TMA, Sellars thinks, is not to be construed as the proper name of an individual Form, but rather as a variable...Now let us look at the text: "I suppose this is what leads you to suppose that there is in every case *a single Form*: When several things seem large to you, it seems perhaps that there is *a single Form* which is the same in your view of all of them. Hence you believe that Largeness is *a single thing*."...Is there any suggestion here that the hypothesis which is being put forward is to the effect that wherever we find a set of things which have the same character there is a class of Forms, one member of which is the required one for this set of things, or, more simply, that there is at least one Form to serve this purpose? None at all. On the

---

[1]Addenda to the Third Man Argument: A reply to Professor Sellars, *Philosophical Review*, *LXIV*:438-448, 1955.

[2]Vlastos and "The Third Man," *Philosophical Review*, *LXIV*:405-437, 1955.

[3]The Third Man Argument in the *Paramenides*, *Philosophical Review*, *LXIII*:319-349, 1954.

[4]P. 438.

contrary, it is perfectly clear in the last sentence of the above text that "Largeness" is the name of a single Form that will do the job—not, as Sellars would have it, the name of a class of Forms some one or other of which will do the job.[5]

I have quoted this passage at length not only in order to ensure that Vlastos makes his point to the reader in his own words, but because it is a fresh embodiment of certain aspects of Vlastos' reading of the TMA, to the criticism of which I shall shortly return. Furthermore, it contains, in Vlastos' own translation, the passage from the *Parmenides* which, as he sees it, precludes my reconstruction of the Argument.

Now, it is certainly no easy task to show that the elaborate argument which I develop on pages 36-7 is an accurate representation of the thinking which found expression in *Parmenides* 132a1-b1. On the other hand, the negative task of showing that it does not achieve this purpose might well be quite easy. Vlastos, however, has *made* the task easy by assuming, in spite of everything I had written up to that point, and in spite of an explicit statement to the contrary, that step (1) of the deductive argument on page 36 was intended to be a reformulation of the first sentence of TMA, the sentence which Vlastos continues to call, as in the passage quoted above, "the first step of the Argument." But on page 35, I pointed out that the TMA includes an *inductive* as well as a deductive phase, the former supplying the premises for the latter. Thus, in spite of its low number, proposition (1) of the formal argument on page 36 is logically posterior to the premises listed in the first line of this argument (namely, (G), (SP), (NI), and (P)), which in turn, though the point was spelled out only in connection with (G), were represented as springing from the *inductive* phase of the Argument.

Thus, in my interpretation of the TMA, "Largeness" occurs *both* as a name *and* as a variable—as a *name* in the premise of the inductive phase, and as a *variable* in the premise of the deductive phase. On pages 35-6 I distinguished carefully between

(L) If a number of particulars, *a*, *b*, *c*, are all large, they are so in virtue of a Form, *namely* Largeness.[6]

---

[5]Pp. 438-439; Vlastos' italics.
[6]I now add the italics.

and

> (H1-Largeness) If a number of particulars, *a*, *b*, *c*, are all large, there must be a Largeness by virtue of which they are all large.[7]

which latter I characterized as the application of

> (G-Largeness) If a number of entities are all large, there must be *a* Largeness by virtue of which they are all large.

to the case of large particulars. The difference between (L) and (H1-Largeness) is exactly that in (L) "'Largeness' appears as the name of a single Form, whereas in (H1-Largeness) it is a variable"[8] which is existentially quantified. And while (L) belongs to the TMA in its inductive phase (which I shall shortly explore in greater detail), it is not a premise of the deductive phase which alone is represented on page 36. Thus I wrote:

> The movement of thought is from (L)—by "induction"— to (G-Largeness), and from (G-Largeness) to the series of hypotheticals which are its application.[9]

Step (1) of the deductive phase consists, therefore, not of the representative counterpart of (L), but rather of (H1), the representative counterpart of (H1-Largeness). And, on the other hand, if any single sentence in my reconstruction of the TMA as a whole captures the meaning of the first sentence of the text, it is (L), and not (H1-Largeness).[10] I do not think that anything in my paper can reasonably be construed as implying that *Parmenides* 132a1-b1 says that if a number of particulars are large, it is because there is a class of Forms, (i.e., a class of Largenesses), in one of which they share.

The above remarks suffice, I believe, to place the deductive argument developed on page 36 in its proper perspective. And having so placed it, I can now admit that it was a mistake on my part to introduce this deductive argument by asking, rhetorically, "What, then, does the Third Man Argument look like when all these points have been taken into account?"[11] thus implying that

---

[7]The "a" was italicized in the original.
[8]P. 418.
[9]P. 418.
[10]But see pp. 59 ff.
[11]P. 419.

the TMA consists of the deductive phase alone. This mistake had its source, undoubtedly, in the fact that my primary concern was to exhibit, *contra* Vlastos, the logical form of the regress in the TMA; but a mistake, none the less, it was. Having admitted this much, however, I would urge that it should not have misled anyone who followed the reasoning up to this point. And I would point out that since Vlastos has not yet noticed the inductive phase of the TMA, he could scarcely make *this* criticism without radically revising his reading of the Argument.

I shall now turn to Vlastos' second refutation of my reconstruction of the TMA. He writes:

> There is one thing more about the text to forbid Sellars' interpretation. Compare its opening lines, cited above, with its concluding text: "And *you will no longer have in every case a single Form*, but an infinite number (of Forms)." The initial hypothesis stands to the conclusions as p to not-p, and the logical form of the argument is, "if p [and . . .], then not-p; therefore not-p." Of this, the hypothetical, "if p, then not-p," is explicit in the argument and is the favorite device of Eleatic logic, the *reductio ad absurdum*. The conclusion, "therefore, not-p," is not stated as such, but is, of course, implied. For what is Parmenides doing here but going to work to refute Plato's Theory of Forms, and what conclusion is he bent on establishing except that the Theory is false?
>
> Where is all this on Sellars' formulation? His argument does not have the "if p, then not-p" form; nothing in its conclusion contradicts its initial hypothesis. On this account alone it would have to be ruled out, since the contradiction of hypothesis by conclusion is large as life in Plato's text.[12]

Now it is certainly true that Parmenides is arguing that the Theory of Forms must be false since it implies an absurdity, and that therefore, *in this sense*, the TMA has the dialectical form of a *reductio ad absurdum*. And it is equally true that the argument developed on page 36 of my paper does *not* have the form of a *reductio*. I believe, however, that the argument of my paper not only makes it clear what I conceive the dialectical structure of the TMA as a whole to be,[13] but shows conclusively that the

[12]P. 440; italics by Vlastos.

[13]It consists, as we shall see, not only of the inductive and deductive phases distinguished above, but of the *elenchus*, in which these are subordinate elements, and which is directed against a certain Theory of Forms.

reductio cannot have the form which Vlastos represents it as having in the passage quoted above.

Let me back into this point from a little distance. After all, the purpose of my original paper was polemical; and since my own interpretation of the TMA was expounded with an eye to its similarities and contrasts with that of Vlastos, its relationships to the text of the *Parmenides* stands out less clearly than would have been the case had it been developed as an independent commentary. Fortunately, given the background which has been built up, it will take but a moment (as these things go) to remedy this situation and to demonstrate how neatly the TMA falls into the framework of my reconstruction, hence it is approached without even a polemical nod at the Procrustean "steps" and "hypotheses" into which Vlastos so blithely cuts it up. Read in this spirit, it becomes obvious not only that a great deal more is going on in the first sentence than is formulated by Vlastos' (A1)[14]—which, of course, he would admit—but that what *is* going on is incompatible with the idea that it formulates a proposition p which is both a *premise* ("hypothesis") of the TMA *and* the *contradictory* of "you will no longer have in every case a single Form."

I can best bring this out by offering for the reader's consideration the following paraphrase of the first sentence of the TMA, which he will find (in Vlastos' translation) in the first lengthy quotation from Vlastos' *Reply.*

> I suppose that this is what leads you to *conclude* that there is in every case (i.e., the case of round things, the case of square things, etc.) a single Form. When you find several things to be, e.g., large, you find them all to share a single Form, namely Largeness. You *conclude* that Largeness is a single thing.

If this paraphrase is sound, the following remarks are immediately in order. (1) "That Largeness is a single thing" is represented not as a *premise*, but as a *conclusion* which Socrates draws from the idea that large things (i.e., large *ordinary* things, that is, large things in the World of Becoming, or, as we have called them, particulars) share a single Form. (2) That the *premise* from which Socrates is represented as drawing the above (comfortable) conclusion concerns large *particulars* only, is clear for two reasons:

---

[14]The Third Man Argument in the *Parmenides, Philosophical Review*, p. 320.

(a) the Theory of Forms developed by Socrates (and the younger Plato) was an attempt to explain what it is for large things in the 'visible world' to be large, and (b) the things that "seem large" in the first sentence are the "other large things" of the fourth sentence[15] which when "viewed" together with "Largeness itself" keep the dialectical ball rolling. (3) Socrates, in effect, is represented as arguing that since a single Form, namely, Largeness, is all that is necessary to account for large *particulars* being large, Largeness, as far as the Theory of Forms is concerned, is a single thing. (4) By representing Socrates as concluding that Largeness is a single thing, Parmenides is raising the question 'Is Largeness a single thing?' that is, 'Might not the Theory of Forms be committed to many Largenesses, or at least more than one?'

But if the *premise* from which Socrates draws his *comfortable* conclusion concerns the largeness of large *particulars* only, Parmenides now proceeds to bring out the fact that Socrates is prepared to assert of the members of *any* class of large items, particulars *or whatever*, that they must be large by virtue of sharing in a common Form. He does this by asking Socrates to consider the set consisting of large particulars together with Largeness.

> What then if you similarly view mentally Largeness itself and the other large things? Will not a single Largeness appear once again in virtue of which all these appear large? It seems so. Consequently, another Form of Largeness will appear, over and above Largeness itself and the things which participate in it.[16]

And, after all, it *would* be unreasonable for a person to (1) *agree* that Largeness, or, in the terminology of the earlier dialogues, The Large Itself, is large; (2) assert that large *particulars* are large *by virtue of* sharing a common Form, but yet (3) *deny* that the members of the set consisting of large particulars plus Largeness are together large by virtue of sharing a common Form. And to

---

[15]"What then if you similarly view mentally Largeness itself and the other large things . . . ." (*Parmenides*, 132a2, Vlastos' translation).

[16]*Parmenides* 132a3ff., Vlastos' translation. Indeed, Parmenides brings out in this passage not only that Socrates reasons in accordance with the more general principle "large whatevers are large by virtue of sharing in a Form of Largeness", but also that he reasons in accordance with two other general principles as well, namely Self-Predication and Non-Identity.

see that this is unreasonable is to have made the "Socratic induction" from (L) to (G-Largeness). I pointed out above (fn. 13) that the TMA has the dialectical form of an *elenchus* with inductive and deductive subordinate movements. Let me now add my conviction that in this terse argument Parmenides masterfully combines in a few sentences (*verbum sapienti sat*) all the ingredients which are to be found, spread out over many pages, in the refutations of the early dialogues.

That the role of this section of the TMA is to exhibit Socrates as reasoning in accordance with certain general principles,[17] and not to represent him as, so to speak, *running across* a Form of Largeness when he views mentally Largeness itself and the other large things—which, as far as I can see is what Vlastos conceives it to do—is brought out not only by the intrinsic absurdity[18] of the latter alternative, but by the fact that Socrates willingly trots down the regress which Parmenides, without further ado, proceeds to construct. By supposing that the two chunks of text which he freezes into his (A1) and (2) are successive "steps" in an "argument," Vlastos not only manhandles a subtle dialectical development, but cuts himself off from an understanding of the regress. As a result, he is led to invent a division of the TMA into *two* arguments, "the targets of [which] are Plato's ontology and epistemology respectively."[19] I shall be discussing this feature of his interpretation in a moment. The point I wish to make now is that while Vlastos may think that I make free use of "implicit" premises in my interpretation of the TMA, all my premises are at least as close to the surface as he conceives his versions of Self-Predication and Non-Identity to be. Whereas Vlastos himself, as we shall see, has but the smallest of fragments from which to reconstruct his Epistemological Third Man (the putative twin of the Ontological Third Man), a single use of the word "appears." And what would have been a masterpiece of philosophical paleontology, if only it had come off, turns out to be just another Piltdown Man.

[17]See fn. 16.

[18]That the idea that Largeness and large particulars share a common Form is a *conclusion* rather than a "discovery" is obvious to us, but, it may be asked, was it obvious to Plato? I think that a very heavy burden of proof lies on the shoulders of anyone who should seriously maintain the contrary. And if Plato recognized it to be a *conclusion* would the character of the *reasoning* have been so difficult to discover?

[19]P. 443.

What, then, is the form of the *reductio?* Is it, as Vlastos suggests, "if p [and . . .], then not-p, therefore not-p," where p is "the initial hypothesis 'that there is in every case a single Form'" and not-p "the concluding text: '. . .you will no longer have in every case a single Form. . .'"? If my argument is correct, the reduction *cannot* have this form. For (1), as we have already seen, p, thus understood, is not a *premise* ("initial hypothesis") of the TMA, but the comfortable conclusion which Socrates is represented as drawing from his interpretation of the largeness of large particulars; (2) if, on the other hand, p is construed as the proposition that there is in every case (the case of large particulars, the case of square particulars, etc.) a single Form *by virtue of which they are what they are* (large, square, etc.)[20] then, while it may, indeed, be said to formulate *a* Theory of Forms—and, of course, what is being reduced to absurdity is a Theory of Forms—it lacks, by virtue of its restriction to particulars, the generality it must have to involve, even when combined with Self-Predication and Non-Identity, a commitment to an infinite regress, and (3) though an adequate exposition of this point would require a restatement of the considerations advanced on pages 28-30 of my earlier paper, if "there is in every case a single Form" is interpreted as in (2) above, then it is *not* contradicted by the conclusion of the deductive phase of the Argument (i.e., the conclusion that in every case there must be an infinite number of Forms) whereas on my interpretation of the TMA, "there is in every case a single Form" means *exactly* what it says *and nothing more,*[21] and *is* contradicted by this conclusion.

Positively, I think that the dialectical structure of the *elenchus* can best be represented by offering the following paraphrase:

> You, Socrates, think that you are committed, in the case of large things, and all such cases, to only one Form, because on your Theory only a single Form, namely Largeness, is needed

---

[20] It is so easy to assume that "there is in every case a single Form" has the same meaning as "there is in every case a single Form *by virtue of which the particulars in question are, e.g., large.*" To see that this need not be the case, notice that on my interpretation of the former, it, but not the latter, would be contradicted by "there is in every case a series of Forms, only the first of which is the Form by virtue of which the particulars in question are, e.g., large."

[21] See fn. 20 above.

to account for the largeness of large particulars. But consider, now, the group consisting of large particulars, and Largeness itself. Are not all these things large? And if so, must not they, in their turn, share a common Form, a Form of Largeness? For is it reasonable to hold that large particulars are large by virtue of sharing a common Form without admitting that *sharing a common Form* is the reason why the members of *any group* of large items are large? And must it not be a *new* Form of Largeness over and above the large particulars and the Largeness which they share? for can a Form share in itself? But if we collect these admissions, do you not see that you are committed, in the case of large things (and all other such cases) not, as you have so comfortable supposed, to a single Form, but rather to an infinite number of Forms. And since, when submitted to scrutiny, your Theory turns out to have this absurd consequence, it cannot be true and must be abandoned.

II

Vlastos devotes the second section of his *Reply* to a defense of his epistemological interpretation of the regress in the TMA. I would have little to add to my earlier comments on this interpretation[22] were it not for the fact that in the course of this defense he attempts to show that Plato's text is incompatible with my merely ontological reading of the Argument. He admits that "in the first step...[the] references to 'seeing' and 'viewing' could be taken, as Sellars observes, 'to pertain to the discovery of the principle which is to function as a premise of the TMA, rather than as a constituent element in the principle itself.'"[23]

> But [Vlastos continues] look now at the text when it moves on to the second step (sic) of the Argument at 132a6-8: "What then if you similarly view mentally Largness itself and the other large things? Will not a single Largeness appear once again, *in virtue of which all these appear large?*" If Sellars has noticed the italicized words here, he says nothing about them. Don't they make it clear that Plato *is* thinking of the epistemological function of the Form in the course of this argument? For if not, why should he say that it is in virtue of this (second) Largeness that large things *appear* large, instead of just saying that in virtue of it they *are* large.

---

[22]"Vlastos and 'The Third Man,'" pp. 24-5 above.
[23]P. 442.

Now I am not prepared to deny that in this passage "Plato is thinking of the epistemological function of the Form," but I do want to deny that there is even the suspicion of an epistemological *premise*, let alone an epistemological *regress*, in the TMA. To begin with, let me remind the reader that the context of the passage quoted by Vlastos is one in which, from the beginning of the TMA, visual language has been used to present successive steps in Socrates' thinking about the Forms, steps, first of all, which he is represented as having taken before meeting "Parmenides," and, now, steps which he is about to take under the prodding of this wise old dialectician. Thus, Parmenides has just asked Socrates to *view* (i.e., consider) the group consisting of Largeness itself and the other large things, and when he continues by asking "will not a single Largeness *appear* once again. . .?" it is, in effect, as though he said "Do you not *see* that there must be a Largeness. . .?" So far, so good. But the text continues ". . .by virtue of which all these *appear* large," and it is *this* occurrence of "appear" on which Vlastos lays such stress. For if the purely ontological interpretation of the TMA were sound, would we not expect Plato to continue with ". . .by virtue of which all these *are* large?"

It clearly will not do to explain this second occurrence of "appear" as a mere continuation without reference to "the epistomological function of the Form" of the use of visual language to present the steps of Socrates' reasoning about the Forms. For that the items in question appear large by virtue of largeness is part of what Socrates "sees" and not of his "seeing." On the other hand, given that Socrates has been represented as *viewing* the items and, by implication, *seeing* that they are all large, is there so much difference between representing Socrates as "seeing that there is a Largeness by virtue of which all these *are* large" and representing him as "seeing that there is a Largeness by virtue of which *he sees that* all these are large?" There is, indeed, the difference in formulation to which Vlastos calls attention, but need this difference have the significance which he attributes to it? Let me make my point by means of a reasonably close parallel. Need the fact that someone says "Jones knows that his action was wrong because *he knows that it broke a promise*" instead of "Jones knows that his action was wrong because *it broke a promise*" indicate a greater concern for Jones' epistemological processes than if he had made the latter statement? Unless there were additional and less ambiguous reasons for supposing "the epistemological function of the Form" to be a premise of the TMA, the verdict on Vlastos' interpretation of this passage would have to be "not proven." But not only are there no additional, let alone less ambiguous, reasons for this idea, the text almost immediately takes a turn which rules it out of court. For, as Vlastos himself notes,[24] but does not linger to explain, when Plato makes what is obviously intended to be the parallel point about the set consisting of large particulars, Largeness itself and this new Form of Largeness, he writes, ". . .and, covering all these yet another, by virtue of which they will all be large."[25]

If Vlastos' interpretation of the TMA were correct, this sentence would surely *have* to read ". . .by virture of which they all *appear* large!" For if the epistemological function of the Form were the heart of the matter, it would scarcely appear and disappear like will o' the wisp. And remember that, according to Vlastos, the only reason why Plato, "husbanding his logical resources with the utmost economy,"[26] bothered to introduce this *third* Form of Largeness was for the sake of his epistemological argument.

Vlastos urges[27] that "the only way we can get an infinite regress out of the TMA is to include in all of its relevant statements'" which, as we have just seen, Plato himself did not, "a reference to F-ness as the Form by virtue of which we apprehend F-things as F." But, in the first place, as I carefully pointed out in my analysis of his argument [see pages 25-6 above], the epistemological premise necessary to establish a vicious regress is not "F-things are apprehended as F by virtue of F-ness," but rather "F-things are apprehended as F by virtue of apprehending the F-ness in which they participate *as also F*." The former without the latter leads at most to a potentially infinite series of apprehensions, and that only if an infinite series of Forms has been independently established on ontological grounds. And, in the second place, so far from it being true that

---

[24]"But a few lines later he does shift to an expression which does *not* contain this epistemological reference: 'and covering all these, yet another (Largeness) by virtue of which they will all *be* large.'" P. 442.

[25]Vlastos' translation. See footnote 24.

[26]P. 443.

[27]P. 443.

"we can get an infinite regress out of the TMA" only by including epistemological considerations, the epistemological regress Vlastos has in mind, and which requires the stronger premise mentioned above, *presupposes* the purely ontological regress. By this I mean that the premises necessary to establish the epistemological regress contain as a proper part of their logical force the purely onto-logical premises which are necessary and sufficient to generate the infinite series of Forms. In fact, all that the epistemological premise does is built the infinite series of Largenesses, established on ontological grounds, and which, though absurd, is not, perhaps, self-contradictory, into a *vicious* regress of apprehendings which is vicious because it can never get started. Vlastos suggests that for a purely ontological *reductio* "it would have been sufficient to prove that there are two [Largenesses]."[28] What he fails to see, as a result of his manhandling of the text, is that the premises *necessary* to establish *two* Largenesses are *sufficient* to establish an infinite number, so that the *reason* for the absurdity of the Theory of Forms which is being refuted would have been obscured if Plato had arbitrarily drawn the line at the second Largeness. Far from its being "uneconomical"[29] to go beyond two, it would have been false economy to stop there. In any event, Vlastos can scarcely be said to have made it clear exactly *how* the TMA generates an infinite series of Largenesses. For his analysis of the *ontological* phase ends with *two* Largenesses, while his cryptic account of the supposed epistemological phase makes free use from the very beginning of an infinite number of Largenesses which, as far as I can see, he has earned by no honest toil. For if one interprets the opening passages of the TMA as he does, then *no* admixture of epistemological premises, however seasoned with Self-Predication and Non-Identity (his versions, please!) will generate an infinite series of Largenesses, let alone a vicious epistemological regress.

III

In the third section of his *Reply*, Vlastos takes up our differences with respect to the role of Self-Predication in Plato's thought and

[28]P. 443.
[29]P. 443.
[30]"Vlastos and 'The Third Man,'" p. 31 above.

its relation to his "Degrees of Reality Theory." I shall limit my rejoinder to the main themes of his discussion.

Vlastos makes the following criticism of the passage[30] in which I discuss my own interpretation of the Principle of Self-Predication:

> What I do object to is his preceding statement, "that it is not Largeness which is predicated of Largeness, but rather 'large' or (material mode) *being large*," He says that this is "obvious," but it is not even true. Anyone who asserts that "justice is just" is predicating Justice of Justice.[31]

Now I must admit that I would have made my point more clearly if I had limited myself to pointing out that while it is correct usage to say that "x is large" *predicates largeness of x*, "largeness" in this context must not be equated with the "Largeness" of Platonic theory, nor the statement itself given any more force than "'x is large' says of x that it is large." To construe that the "largeness" of "predicates largeness of x" as the name of a Form is to equate "'x is large' predicates largeness of *x*" with the Platonic-theoretical sentence "'x is large' says that x participates in Largeness." And even if the Platonist believes the latter to be the *analysis* of the former, the logical structure of the TMA requires for its exhibition a neutral formulation of the principle of Self-Predication, one which restricts itself to the ordinary force of the expression "predicates largeness of x." Again, it is the very expression "Self-Predication" which was my target. For it suggests that Self-Predication is a relation between a Form and *itself*, and hence that Self-Predication is identical with Self-Participation (a conclusion to which the construction criticized above also leads). And, as I pointed out in the passage which contains the sentence Vlastos has singled out for criticism, if they *were* identical, then it *would* indeed, as Vlastos claims, be contradictory to combine, as Plato does in the TMA, a Principle of Self-Predication with a Principle of Non-Identity, for the latter is just another name for a principle of *Non*-Self-Participation.

Vlastos takes exception[32] to my claim "that the first part of the *Parmenides* is a deliberate and sustained critique of Self-Predicational interpretations of the Ideas."[33]

---

[31]*Reply*, p. 444, see footnote 1.

[32]P. 444.

[33]"Vlastos and 'The Third Man,'" p. 46 above.

He writes:

> But neither Sellars, nor those who would agree with him, would suggest (they could not with the least plausibility) that Plato ever so much as stated Self-Predication in his writings. Isn't this very odd? Why should Plato wish to conceal his target? Is there any parallel in Plato of such secretiveness? Is there any in the whole history of philosophy? . . . Where would we find a philosopher who, knowing that a certain misinterpretation of this doctrine was about, wrote a "deliberate and sustained critique" of it, but carefully refrained from mentioning it and tucked it away instead among the tacit premises of his Argument, where no one, so far as we know, was able to spot it until well over two millenia after his death?

Now I don't agree with any of this. A proper rejoinder would be another full-sized paper, however, so I shall limit myself to some supplementary remarks which will indicate the lines it would take. In the first place, the idea that Largeness is large is by no means "tucked away." It is "tacit" only to the extent that Mildred and other ladies swooned is "tacit" about Mildred's ladyship. And as for the more general premise that *all* Largenesses are large, it is indeed *implicit*, but, not "tucked away," for, as I have tried to show, not only is it essential to the regress, but Plato realized it to be such and intended the dialectically sophisticated reader (who else did Plato have in mind as potential readers of the *second* part of the Parmenides!) to appreciate it as such.

In the second place, I have emphasized that the TMA, properly construed, is an *elenchus* which contains, in compact and allusive form, all the features which, in the earlier dialogues, are fully explicit and spread out over many pages. Thus it is reasonable to compare the manner in which Plato conveys his philosophical purposes here with his earlier wont. Other philosophers may follow the speaker's maxim, "First tell 'em what you are going to say, then say it, then tell 'em what you have said," but Plato, as our students discover to their initial despair, never "calls his shots." For, like his recent contemporaries, he does not conceive of philosophy as the establishing or refuting of "theses" which can be fruitfully formulated apart from the dialectical development in which they are examined. He leaves it to the reader to add such editorial headings as he may wish *after* he has worked through the argument. Pondered before the argument is grasped, they would stand in its way. Put somewhat more strongly than Plato may have done, the dialogues are not a textbook of the Platonic philosophy.

Again, so far from its being true that Self-Predication was "tucked away...where no one, so far as we know, was able to spot it until well over two millenia after his death," I would have said that nobody who has read the TMA with any degree of comprehension has failed to appreciate that it is directed against a theory which seeks to explain the fact that ordinary things are humdrumly *F*, by postulating a domain of extraordinary things which are superlatively *F*. For this conception of the Ideas has been endemic among readers (and non-readers) of Plato since the dialogues were written. (That, on the other hand, the logical structure of the TMA has rarely been appreciated in all its detail is no cause for surprise when one remembers the hash that has been made of other arguments in the later dialogues, not to mention some of the simpler arguments of the early dialogues.) What Vlastos must mean is that if my interpretation of the first part of the *Parmenides* is correct, we must view Plato as having "carefully refrained" from expressing his conviction that whereas the Theory of Forms with Self-Predication leads to absurdity, we can keep the essentials of the Theory while discarding the latter and the absurdity it entails. And he must mean that it was *this* conviction which "no one was able to spot until well over two millenia after his death." But Plato does *not* refrain from expressing this conviction. He gives it philosophical (though not editorial) expression in the argumentation[34] of the later dialogues, the *Parmenides*, the *Sophist*, and even the *Timaeus*, for what is the first part of the *Timaeus* but a spelling out in less exacting and anachronistic garb of the revolutionary developments of the denouement of the *Sophist?* And when, in *Parmenides* 133a, he points out that "we must look for some other manner of participation," what, in the light of the arguments he has just offered, *can* this new manner of participation be but one which does *not* involve the

---

[34]For even though the later dialogues have lost the earlier drama of a clash of intellectual personalities, and one participant has been degraded to the status of "straight man" for the other, they continue to be *dialectical* in that the philosophy they contain is presented as a tissue of reasonings.

largeness of Largeness nor the equality of The Equals Themselves?

As for it taking two millenia for scholars to spot this conviction, will not Vlastos admit that most of these centuries are excess baggage? From the standpoint of any real insight into the later dialogues, only two brief periods are relevant. The first is the period which begins with Aristotle and ends with the decay of Neo-Platonism; the second begins with German scholarship in the early nineteenth century, and flourishes today as never before. I would be sincerely interested to learn what evidence Vlastos has accumulated concerning the former period. (Aristotle, of course, can be discounted for familiar reasons.) As for the latter, it is interesting to note that even Vlastos admits that in this short period the type of interpretation I defend has become "a well-known position," one which is "still" so widespread "that it may fairly be called 'orthodox'."[35]

On p. 445, Vlastos asks "Can a particular be 'like' a Form C-ness in respect of a given character C, unless C-ness *has* the character C?" He continues, "Sellars seems to think that it can. . .." But *of course* in the *ordinary* meaning of "like" x can't be like y "in respect of a given character, C" unless both x and y are C. My point was that since "Likeness" (or "Imitation," for that matter) is part of the vocabulary of a philosophical theory, it cannot be assumed either that it has *all* of its ordinary force, or indeed, that it has *any* of its ordinary force *in the same way*. In short, we must allow for the possibility—which I sought to establish as the actuality—that x can *in this sense* be "like" y (where the relevant fact is that x is large) *without y* being large. Vlastos argues that "Responsible exegesis of a historical system should follow rigorously the rule that every philosopher must be held responsible for the logical implications of his own statements, unless he gives definite evidence that these implications are adventitious features of his language."[36] But if by "gives definite evidence" Vlastos means that the author must *comment* to this effect, his rule is obviously much too narrow. If, however, he means merely that we should not conclude that a given implication does not belong to the philosophical use of a term *without good reasons* based on the text *in any of its dimensions*, then of course I agree. But it was exactly

---

[35]P. 438.
[36]P. 446.

good reasons of this broader kind that I was trying to give, and nothing Vlastos advances in his *Reply* persuades me that I did not succeed.

Vlastos finds that whereas I start out by "discounting" Imitation as "mere language," by the time I get to section XI "it becomes evident that Sellars himself does think Imitation a philosophical theory."[37] This time words almost fail me. I should have thought it evident that from the very beginning of my discussion of Plato's use of such terms as "sharing," "imitation," "likeness," that is to say, from section VIII on, I take them to be "technical" terms in a philosophical vocabulary by using which Plato says interesting and important things about the world and our knowledge of it. So far from taking these terms to be "mere language," by which, I suppose, Vlastos means taking them to be terms with a *stipulated* philosophical meaning, I expressed my conviction that they gradually and naturally came to have the sense I take them to have by being used in philosophical discussion for the sake of *these* implications, *those* being neglected, still *others* being added, so that eventually, by a cumulative but implicit alteration of their logical force nothing was left unchanged save only those general or formal features which lead *us*, though not the early Plato, to think of them as metaphors. In this connection I devoted considerable space[38] to an examination of the comparative advantages and disadvantages of "sharing" and "imitation" as candidates for the role of technical term for the relation of things to Ideas. *Of course*, if we want to put it that way, "Imitation is a philosophical doctrine." But what that doctrine is, and whether or not it involves the *f*-ness of *F*-ness, is not to be settled by an appeal to ordinary usage.

Finally, Vlastos misinterprets as "the substance of [my] objection to [his] view" (i.e., the view that Plato's Degrees of Reality Theory involves Self-Predication), an argument which I offered as a refutation of a specific argument which *he* used, or could be construed as having used to defend that view. He writes,[39]

> What then is the substance of his objection to my view? He states it at pp. 426, Section IX: "To say that *the* difference be-

---

[37]P. 446.

[38]"Vlastos and 'The Third Man,'" p. 51ff. above.

[39]P. 447.

tween an F particular and F-ness is a difference in degree of reality is indeed tantamount to saying that the F particular and F-ness are both F." But there is no reason to suppose, he continues, that Plato believed that this is *the* difference in question, "and without this premise the argument doesn't get off the ground." The reason is fallacious. To say that Self-Predication is implied by the foregoing Platonic doctrine does not require one to hold that *this* difference—difference in perfection of realization of a given character—is "the" (i.e., the only) difference between a Form and one of its instances, or the only difference that is asserted in Plato's Degrees of Reality Theory. There may be umpteen such differences. But if there is this one, the one asserted above, it would suffice to establish that Plato's Degrees of Reality Theory implies Self-Predication.

Now, if the reader will turn to page 340 of Vlastos' original paper, or to pages 46-47 (see page 45 above) of my critique, he will see that it was Vlastos, not Sellars, who introduced the idea that "the difference between a white thing...and Whiteness is a difference in degree of reality."[40]

Taking its point of departure from the passage just quoted, my argument had the following form: "Vlastos implies that Plato is committed to the idea that difference in degree of reality is *the* (i.e., the only) difference between F-particulars and F-ness. And it is indeed true that if he were so committed, he would be committed to the f-ness of F-ness and Vlastos would have an argument for the f-ness of F-ness which was not just a matter of stressing the everyday meaning of Plato's language. But not only does Vlastos offer no reason for supposing that for Plato their difference in degree of reality is *the* difference between F-particulars and F-ness, it isn't even so." To reply to this refutation by interpreting "difference in degree of reality" as "difference in perfection of realization of a given character" and pointing out that whether or not other differences are forthcoming, "if there is this one, the one asserted above [sic], it would suffice to establish that Plato's Degrees of Reality Theory implies Self-Predication" is to combine, in a truly economical husbanding of logical resources, an *ignoratio elenchi* with a *petitio principii*.

---

[40]The Third Man Argument in the *Parmenides*, *Philosophical Review*, p. 340.

III

ARISTOTLE'S METAPHYSICS: AN INTERPRETATION

IN A recent paper[1] I attempted to throw new light on the problem of the nature of Aristotelian forms and their relation to individual or "primary" substances on the one hand, and to the attributes which are the criteria for belonging to a thing kind or "secondary" substance on the other. I argued, in effect, that while it would be incorrect to say that in the Aristotelian system thing kind words are common names, and essential traits the criteria for their application, considerable light is thrown on the general tenor of Aristotle's treatment of substance by regarding it as some such thesis in the "material mode." I also argued that taken in conjunction with (1) Aristotle's use of the concept of artifact as the key to the understanding of changeable things, and (2) his theory of predication which derives from Anaxagoras *via* the Socrates of the *Phaedo*, it illuminates not only the sense in which the forms of individual things are themselves individuals (*thises*), but, which is more important, the sense in which for Aristotle, as for Plato, what living things primarily are is *souls*. Unfortunately, the brevity of the paper, required by the occasion for which it was prepared, made its argument almost intolerably compressed, and its character as excerpt from a longer study deprived it of those contextual aids to understanding which are provided by a unified treatment of a number of related issues. The aim of the present paper, which is a revised version of the latter study, is to remedy in some measure these defects, and to develop a more rounded account of the Aristotelian metaphysics of matter and form.

[1]Substance and form in Aristotle. *The Journal of Philosophy*, *54:*688-699, 1957. The paper as published was an excerpt from a longer manuscript, circulated in dittoed form, from which the present study has developed.

In the earlier paper I emphasized that Aristotle approached the problem of analysing concepts pertaining to changeable being in terms of a theory of predication inherited from the Academy. This theory takes as its paradigm the form "x is a Y"—thus "Socrates is a man." Under the influence of this paradigm, statements of the quite different form illustrated by "S is white" were construed as making a complex claim, one component of which, at least, was properly expressed by the paradigm form, thus "(q is present in S and) q is a white," where q is a *quale*[2] and *white* is the quale-kind to which it belongs. The theory is characteristically Platonic. Its most explicit formulation is to be found in the *Phaedo*, but it is also clearly present in other and later dialogues, including, in particular, the *Timaeus*. In the former dialogue (102ff.) Plato distinguishes between *the large thing*, *the large in the thing*, and *the large itself*, and tells us that while the large thing may become small (by losing the large which is "in it" and acquiring a small to replace it), the large in the thing can never become small nor the small in the thing large. There is, of course, an important difference between Aristotle and Plato in that the former refused to interpret either the fact that Socrates is a man or that the white in Socrates is a white in terms of a Platonic Idea (The Man Himself, The White Itself). The Socratic[3] conception of changing things as acquiring and losing particular hots, colds, whites, blacks, permeates the *Categories* and, if the argument of my earlier paper is correct, remained a presupposition of Aristotle's metaphysics throughout his career.

It is important for my argument that we take a somewhat closer look at the form this theory of predication takes in the larger context of Plato's theory of changeable things. Thus, in the *Phaedo*, such items as the large in Simmias and, in general, the *f* in an *f*-thing are, *in most cases*, dependent or second-class denizens of the world of becoming. We are told that when an *f*-thing ceases to be *f* and becomes its opposite, the *f* in the thing must either

---

[2]In the terminology I proposed, *qualia* are a variety of "abstract" or "dependent" particulars which "inhere" in "concrete" particulars (i.e., primary substances). On the radical difficulties which beset any attempt to carry through this approach to predication, see footnote 3 below.

[3]That it is more entitled to this description than most views put in the mouth of Socrates in the *Dialogues* is indicated by the kinship of this view to that of Anaxagoras, properly interpreted.

"go elsewhere" or "perish." *In most cases*, it would seem, it perishes. Thus it is undoubtedly implied that when a small thing becomes large, the small in the thing perishes, and presumably the same holds true of the white in a white thing which becomes black, and in other cases of this sort. There is, however, an exception which is the very heart of the metaphysics of immortality in the *Phaedo*. For the soul of a living thing is the alive in the thing[4] which can no more "become dead" than the large in a thing can become small. Surely, it is argued, it must "go elsewhere" rather than "perish" at the "approach of death."[5] In addition to this special exception, it may well be the case that Plato thought of the hot in a hot thing as (a portion of) fire, and believed (with Empedocles) that when a hot thing becomes cold, the hot in the thing "goes elsewhere" and does not perish, and similarly in the case of the other elements.[6] Yet he certainly came to think, if he did not think already, that the elemental opposites are perishable in a way in which soul is not. In the *Timaeus*, the likenesses of the elemental Ideas, which appear in the Receptable before the intervention of the Demiurge are ephemeral, and when the flux of becoming is stabilized by the imposition of geometrical form, they do not cease to be ephemeral; rather their appearance and disappearance becomes *orderly* and fitted to serve purposes.

Now the *Phaedo* throws little explicit light on the question,

---

[4] The transition in the *Phaedo* from treating "alive" as simply a predicate of individual living things to treating "alive" as *primarily* a predicate of souls and *derivatively* of living things as having souls within them which are alive in the *primary* sense, is of a piece with the interpretation of the sense in which white things are white as derivative from that in which the white in the white thing is white. On the former point compare Aristotle's statement that "a man is alive in virtue of himself, for the soul in which life directly resides is a part of the man" (*Metaphysics*, 1022a31-4).

[5] The argument, of course, rests on the idea that "*x* ceases to exist" (perishes) entails "*x* becomes dead" where *x* is a living thing. And, indeed, to speak of an animal (or person) as dead is equivalent to saying that it (or he) no longer exists. "Living" blends in an interesting way the bare notion of *existing* with that of possessing and exercising certain characteristic abilities and propensities. "Lives," so to speak, is "exists" as presupposing that the subject of predication belongs to the framework of living things. The intimate connection between the opposite predicates "alive" and "dead" and the contrast between "exists" and "no longer exists" explains both the plausibility of the argument and the fallacy it commits.

[6] A true Anaxagorean, of course, would have extended this principle to whites, all simple *qualia* existing in everlasting amounts, portions of which are variously mixed to form the objects which mortals think of as coming to be and ceasing to be.

"What is there to a thing—in Aristotelian terms, a changeable substance—over and above *the f_1 in the thing, the f_2 in the thing*," etc. Yet the major theme of the dialogue is that Socrates is a composite being consisting of soul and body, and if the alive in Socrates is "in" Socrates as a part (not, of course, a spatial part), may we not infer that Socrates' body similarly *consists of* the hot in Socrates, the white in Socrates? Indirect support for this interpretation (which finds a continuity of doctrine between the *Phaedo* and the *Timaeus*), according to which Plato did not conceive a substratum in which the various f's in the thing inhere, is found in the fact that Aristotle seems to have thought of the principle, central to his *Physics*, that opposite acts not on opposite but on a substratum qualified by its opposite as an original insight.

As I see it, then, the *Phaedo* construes changing things as a togetherness of whites, hots, larges, most of which are of short duration, coming into being (into becoming) only to perish and be replaced by opposites.[7] On the other hand, as we have seen, the *alive* in a living thing play a unique role. If Socrates continues to exist as a man, it is because at the heart of the ceaseless exchange of opposite for opposite, which is the body, the alive in Socrates remains self-identical. When the alive in Socrates moves elsewhere, the *man* Socrates ceases to be.

Furthermore, even certain *changes* of living things are derivative. Thus, whereas when Socrates changes from being white to being tan, it is because his body contains first a white (or whites) and then a tan (or tans); when Socrates changes from seeing green to seeing blue, it is only in a derivative sense that he as a man contains first a green-seeing and subsequently a blue-seeing. For *this* change is primarily a change in the soul and only derivatively in the composite of soul and body. Thus whereas fs in Socrates do not change, but constitute certain changes of Socrates by their evanescent presence, *the alive in Socrates* is itself a changing thing.[8]

---

[7]Since "opposites" in the broad sense includes any pair of contraries cut by reason from a qualitative continuum, as well as its extremes (cf. *Metaphysics*, 1018a25-30), Plato-Heracleitus construes these fs in the thing as so ephemeral that they never "are" but in one gesture both become and perish.

[8]Notice that the *Phaedo* insists that in its inmost being the soul (as contrasted, in particular, with the accretions which are connected with its sojourn in the body) is unchanging. This inmost being is its being *qua* knower. The notion that at the core of our being we unchangingly know the Ideas by having "images" of them in our

II

We shall be weaving other themes from Plato into our interpretation of Aristotle, but first let us take an initial look at Aristotle's account of changeable things against the above background. As a first approximation we can say that Aristotle replaces the idea that changeable things are leaky bundles of abstract particulars[9] by the idea that they are bundles of abstract particulars inhering in a substratum. Or, to put it somewhat differently, a changeable thing consists of a portion of matter in which inhere its attributes construed as abstract particulars and among which, as a privileged set, are those attributes by virtue of which it belongs to a certain thing kind. Thus, a shoe would be a piece of leather in which are found the traits essential to being a shoe.

I have chosen the foregoing example because the "root metaphor" of the Aristotelian system is the making of artifacts by skilled craftsmen who understand the purpose their products are to serve. Thus the logical form of the *recipe*, with its distinction between words for ingredients and words for finished products, and the teleological character of the explanation which a cookbook offers of the stages by which the ingredients are turned into the finished product, have been "ontologized" to become the very form of the world. Much of what I shall be doing in this paper can be brought under the heading of taking seriously the idea that the "logic" of recipes is the form of the Aristotelian world.

The first point to be made in this connection grows out of the contrast between

> x is a shoe (or statue)

and

> x is a piece of leather (or marble).

"Shoe" and "statue" are common names of artifacts. "Leather" and "marble" are expressions for kinds of material. Notice that the latter are not common nouns which apply to individuals.

---

souls—no mere cognitive propensities—is surely the counterpart and original of Aristotle's doctrine of the Agent Intellect. We shall ultimately be asking whether Aristotle thinks of the characteristic changes of living things as only derivatively that of the "composite" but primarily of the soul.

[9] This phrase does not do justice to the fact that souls (which differ from mere abstract particulars as capable of existing apart) and, in particular, the world soul hold things together—and apart—by persuasion.

One can, of course, speak of "a leather," but only to refer to a
kind of leather. It is a *piece* of leather, a *chunk* of marble, which is
the "individual." In these terms it is not too inaccurate, for our
present purposes, to say that in the Aristotelian picture of the
world, in so far as it consists of changeable things,[10] to be a *being*,
in the primary sense of the term, is to be an *artifact* or one of those
quasi-artifacts which are living things.[11] The status of raw materials,
whether for artifacts or living things, is more humble. One can
imagine someone asking a sculptor, "What is that thing in the
corner?" and getting the reply "It isn't anything; it's just a piece
of marble." In the Aristotelian philosophy, unless something is
an artifact[11] or a living thing, it is not a (changeable) *being*, but,
at best, material for beings.

This means, in effect, that those common names which refer to
artifacts[12] and which are "defined" in terms of the criteria (by
satisfying which an artifact is an artifact of a certain kind) have
a conceptual priority over other expressions which may, from a
purely grammatical point of view, share the status of common
noun. Thus, some common nouns are properly "reconstructed"
as *qualified* common nouns in the more basic sense. They are
already short for expressions of the form "*K* which is *f*" where
"*K*" is a *proper* thing kind expression as "cloak," to use Aristotle's
example, might come to be short for "man who is white" ("white
man"). Again, expressions of the form "piece of leather" and
"chunk of marble," though they function grammatically as com-

---

[10]It should be borne in mind that according to the Aristotle of Book IV of the
Metaphysics, "the sensible world which immediately surrounds us" and "is always
in process of destruction and generation . . .is—so to speak—not even a fraction of
the whole." (1010a30-1)

[11]The force which Aristotle gives to the analogy between artifacts and living things
will be explored in the concluding section of this essay. It should, however, be borne
in mind in all that follows that although artifacts are the *fundamentum* of the analogical
concepts (form, matter, the four causes) in terms of which we understand changeable
substances proper, they are not themselves substances proper. Substances proper are
living things, and artifacts are substances only by virtue of their analogy to living
things. That artifacts can be the fundamentum of the concepts through which we
understand substances proper, and yet be substances only through their analogy with
substances proper, emphasizes the subtile relationship in the Aristotelian tradition
between the order of being and the order of knowing.

[12]For the time being, I shall simply speak of artifacts, postponing until a later
stage the application of the distinctions now to be drawn to living things. See also
footnote 11.

mon nouns and could be replaced by single words, must not be assimilated to words like "shoe" or "table." To assimilate

x is a piece of earth

to the form

x is a K

where K is a *primary* common name, by reasoning that since a piece of earth is a clod, "x is a piece of earth" has the sense of "x is a clod" is to turn the Aristotelian analysis upside-down. To assimilate expressions for haphazard or pointless bunches of raw material to expressions for products is to miss the point that an Empedoclean world consisting of consecutive layers of earth, water, air, and fire would be as conceptually incomplete, from an Aristotelian perspective, as a recipe which ended with the list of ingredients.

We can sum up the above, again as a first approximation, by saying that for Aristotle the primary role of the form

X is a Y

is that in which "X" refers to an individual artifact, and "Y" is a common noun such as "shoe" or "house."

III

Before we follow up this line of thought, we must explore in somewhat further detail the logic of matter. For while the *primary* role of the form

X is a Y

is as characterized above, the description is capable of more than one interpretation, and the difference between them is of first importance to the understanding of Aristotle's conception of primary substance. We have already noted one secondary use of this form, that, namely, in which "X" refers to a piece of material and "Y" has the form "piece of M" where M is a kind of material, e.g.,

This is a piece of leather.

The question now arises, to what does "this" refer in the statement

This is a shoe?

We said above that in the primary use of the form "X is a Y," the referring expression X refers to "an individual artifact." But does it refer to the artifact *qua* artifact? *We* might be inclined to say that "X" refers to a logical subject qua identifiable. And there is no reason to think that Aristotle would object to this formulation. But the question remains, "What is it to be a logical subject of predication in the changeable world?" And Aristotle has two candidates: (1) primary substances, and (2) pieces of matter. Which of these, qua identifiable, is the referent of "this" in "This is a shoe?"

The decisive passage is *Metaphysics* 1049a19-b2, which goes as follows:

> For the subject or substratum is differentiated by being a "this" or not being one (i.e., the substratum of modifications is, e.g., a man; i.e., a body and a soul), while the modification is "musical" or "pale"...whenever this is so, then, the ultimate subject is a substance, but when this is not so, but the predicate is a form and a "this," the ultimate subject is matter and material substance.

The point Aristotle is making can best be brought out by contrasting the two statements

> This piece of leather is a shoe
> This man is musical.

In the first of these statements, the predicate has the form "a K," in the second the predicate is an adjective. What is the significance of this difference? Why should we say that the subject appropriate to the first type of predicate is (a piece of) *matter*, whereas the subject appropriate to the second type is a primary substance (i.e., a composite of form and matter)?

We are tempted to expostulate (1) that it is composites of form and matter which are shoes and (2) that even mere pieces of matter can be said to be white. If we can determine what Aristotle would reply to this comment, we will have the answer to our question. And as a matter of fact, it is easy to see what he would say. For while it is, indeed, "composites" which are shoes, so that it is correct to say, as we did, that given that the statement "X is a shoe" is true, "*X*" can properly be said to refer to an artifact, a "union" of form and matter. It must not be overlooked that the statement is an answer to the *question* "What is *X*?" *and this question does not presuppose that x is a "composite,"* for it is proper to give the answer

  X is (nothing but) a piece of leather.

Thus, even though x is a "composite," the statement "X is a K" does not refer to it *qua* "composite", but *qua* that which might be a composite (i.e., *qua* denotable piece of some stuff or other).

Again, although it is indeed true that pieces of matter can be said to be white (i.e., to be the subject of adjectival predication), the above expostulation is based on an *ignoratio*, for Aristotle's point concerns not adjectival predication generally, but the predication of those adjectives which presuppose that the subject of predication is more than a mere piece of matter. Thus the predicate "musical" presupposes that the subject is a man, as does, in its primary use "pale."[13] That we can properly make statements in which the adjectival predicate does not imply that the subject is a primary substance simply means that in these cases the subject, though it *may well be* a primary substance, is not being referred to as such. Thus when it is true that X is distant, X may or may not be more than a mere piece of matter (e.g., it is not *qua* more than a mere piece of marble—if *qua* this much—that a statue is distant), and if "Socrates is distant" implies that what is distant is a primary substance, it is because "Socrates" implies this rather than because it is implied by "distant." In this respect, "Socrates is distant" is akin to "This man is distant." If Socrates or a man is distant, it is not *qua* man or even *qua* living thing that he is distant, but *qua* a denotable something which may or may not be a living thing.

We can pull all this together by saying that the *primary* use of the form "X is a Y" is to say of something that may or may not be a primary substance that it is a primary substance of a certain kind. Clustering around this primary use are a number of related uses. Furthermore, the form

  X is a Y

in all its uses, is intimately connected with the form

  X is Y.

---

[13] It is interesting to note in this connection that whereas in the first edition of his translation of the *Metaphysics* Ross translated "leukos" in this passage as "white," he subsequently changed it to "pale."

It is essential to an understanding of Aristotle's ontology to realize that the various uses of these two forms can be ordered in no *single* dimension of priority. Thus,

> X is spherical

is "prior" to

> X is a ball

in the sense that being spherical is a necessary condition of being a ball; on the other hand, the latter is prior to the former in that the central role of (adjectival) characterization is to enable the identification of items as belonging to thing kinds, (i.e., to serve as criteria for the common names which carve the world at its joints by singling out items having a manifold of attributes and propensities unified in the service of either internal or external purpose), and this having been done to characterize the item in terms appropriate to the kind to which it belongs; thus, "This man is musical."

If the primary role of the form "X is a Y" is to say of a denotable that it is a primary substance of a certain kind, a living thing, or an artifact, its secondary roles, for there is more than one, are of two main types. The first of these is that in which a denotable is said to be, for example, a piece of marble or of leather or of earth. The second is that in which a denotable is said to be, for example, a surface or a triangle or, to pick up a thread from an earlier section, a *quale* or *quantum* of a certain kind.

To begin with the first of these secondary uses, it should be noted for future reference that pieces of material like primary substances fall into two groups, according to whether their teleology, such as it is, is internal or external. Thus a piece of earth is analogous to a living thing in that its teleological character, which is manifested in its motion towards the center of the earth, is "internal" ("by nature"), as contrasted with a piece of leather the purpose of which is external, and, indeed, derivative from the external purposes of such artifacts as can be made out of it.[14]

---

[14]That earth, air, fire and water (and aether) are externally teleological as the material for living things, and that this is, from the standpoint of metaphysics, their most significant teleological aspect has already been noted. Reflection also discloses that materials for artifacts (e.g., leather) have an internal teleology rooted in their chemical composition.

The point to be stressed here is that just as there are criteria which an item must satisfy in order to qualify as a primary substance of a certain kind, so there are criteria which an item must satisfy in order to be a portion of a certain kind of material, e.g., a piece of earth or a length of cloth. If we press the question "What is it which satisfies these criteria?" we are confronted with the problem of interpreting what Aristotle has to say about "first matter," a problem which takes us to the very heart of his metaphysics. A mistake here has repercussions throughout the interpretation of his system just as a twitch in the human heart sets the whole body in motion.[15]

We pointed out above that words like "marble," "leather," "cloth," and "salt" are words for kinds of material and that the context in which they belong is that of a recipe, thus:

> a cubic yard of marble
> twenty bricks of brick
> a piece of cloth 2 inches x 10 inches.

One speaks of a *dog* (a substance in the philosopher's sense) but not of a *cement* (a substance in the ordinary sense). Words like "cloth" and "brick" are ambiguous. Thus "cloth" in one sense means piece of cloth in the other, and "brick" in one sense means standard chunk of brick in the other. "Material" as a noun is the generic term which can take the place of words for specific kinds of material in the above contexts, thus

> a cubic yard of material
> twenty chunks of material
> a piece of material.

In English, the term "matter" does *not seem to* function as a synonym for "material." Thus we do not ordinarily speak of a piece of matter. Philosophers, however, bully this term to serve their purposes by using the phrase

> the matter of x

to have the sense of

> the material of which x consists or is made

"Matter" in this sense, of course, is not to be confused with "matter" as a collective term for material things. Nor should it

---

[15]The following paragraphs until the end of the section were presented at the University of Notre Dame symposium on "Matter," September, 1961, and published in its proceedings (South Bend, 1963).

be assumed that "material thing" means "thing made of (or consisting of) matter." For this is equivalent to construing "material thing" as "thing made of or consisting of a portion of some *material* or other," and to view the world in terms of the framework of raw materials, tools, and ends to be achieved.

A universe in which "matter alone is real," where this has the sense of "all individual things are simply portions of matter (material)," is as logically impossible as a wife without a husband. There must "be" the things for which the "matter" is the material. On the other hand, a universe in which "matter alone is real," where this has the sense of "all individual things are material things," is not in the same way absurd, if absurd it is.

A second recurrent theme in classical discussions of matter has its fundamental source in a mistaken interpretation of statements of the form "*S* is *P*." Consider the statement

A. Socrates is wise (courageous, snubnosed, etc.).

This is clearly logically equivalent to

A[1]. Socrates has (or is characterized by) wisdom (courage, snubnosedness, etc.)

It is only too easy to conclude that the former is not only logically equivalent to, but has the same sense as the latter.[16] This by itself would not suffice to generate the idea of a substratum. But suppose the argument continues as follows:

Socrates is not identical with the wisdom which he has, nor with the courage which he has, nor the snubnosedness which he has, etc."

This, of course, is true. Socrates is not identical with his attributes taken severally. At this stage, the temptation arises to ask "What does 'Socrates' refer to or name, if it is something distinct from all his attributes taken severally?" and to answer

It refers to a substratum which is neither wise nor courageous nor snubnosed, etc.

is surely false as stating in somewhat different terms a logical contrary of the original statement, (A), with which we began.

Put thus explicitly, the fallacy is so transparent that no one would be taken in by it. The step from

What "Socrates" refers to is not (i.e., is not identical with) wisdom

---

[16]This is the exact counterpart of supposing that because "p" and "It is true that p" are logically equivalent, they have the same sense.

to

> What "Socrates" refers to is not wise

is so obviously fallacious that no one would take it. But before adding a missing step which explains why philosophers have, on occasion, made this move, let me first sketch the final outcome of this line of thought. It is the thesis that what we refer to strictly or philosophically speaking is *bare substrata*, (i.e., substrata which are neither hot nor cold not white nor wise, etc.). Items which are hot or cold or white or wise, etc. are *wholes* consisting of a substratum and an adequate bunch of attributes. (The truth, of course, is that it is not *things* but *facts* which consist of individuals and attributes.)

The missing link which disguises the above howler is the role of such expressions as

> The greenness of this leaf
> the wisdom of Socrates
> the rectangularity of this table top.

These expressions obviously refer to *singulars*, that is to say, to "individuals" in that broad sense in which anything properly referred to by a singular term is an individual. But it can readily be seen, I believe, that these singulars or individuals are universals. Thus, consider the sentence,

> The greenness of this leaf is identical with (or different from) the greenness of that leaf.

Notice that whereas the expressions listed above are singular terms, the occurrences in them of "greenness," "wisdom," and "rectangularity" are *not*. Rather they are common noun expressions, "the greenness of this leaf" having the same form as "the owner of this house," and the above sentence the same form as

> The owner of this house is identical with (or different from) the owner of that house.

But it is easy to confuse the fact that *the greenness* of this leaf is an individual (in the *broad* sense, the sense in which formal universals as well as perceptible things are individuals or singulars) which is *a greenness* with the idea that the greenness of this leaf is an individual (in the *narrow* sense which connotes spatio-temporal location) which *is green*.[17]

---

[17]A note on the dangers of the use of color examples in discussing the problem of predication might not be out of place. Color words are radically ambiguous in a

Thus is born the widespread conception of changeable things as consisting of, or at least containing as ingredients, dependent or abstract particulars of which the greenness of this leaf, thus construed, would be an example. For, once one is committed to the idea that the greenness of the leaf is a spatio-temporally individuated green item, the inevitable conclusion is that green-nesses are the *primary* green items and that ordinary changeable things are green by virtue of *having greennesses*. And we can now appreciate how, thinking of the leaf as green in a derivative sense,

L is green = a greenness belongs to L

one inevitably either (1) concludes that there is a subject which is not a greenness or sweetness, etc., in which these qualia inhere, so that

L is green = a greenness inheres in L

or (2) takes the line that things are patterns of greennesses, sweetnesses, etc., in which case we have the formula

L is green = a greenness is a member of L.

The latter is a venerable position which has supporters even today. I shall limit myself to pointing out that Aristotle rejects the view that the elements could be hotnesses, coldnesses, moist-nesses, and drynesses on the ground that it makes interaction unintelligible. For, as Plato emphasized in the *Phaedo* (a dialogue to which Aristotle is closer than is the Plato of the *Timaeus*), a coldness cannot become hot without ceasing to be. But what else could a hotness *do* but warm that on which it *acts?* One must either abandon the very idea of interaction, or say that it is sub-jects qualified by opposites which interact rather than the opposites themselves. It is important to note that Aristotle need not have construed (if he did construe) these subjects as substrata in the dubious sense generated by the above described misinterpretation of predication. For to insist that interaction requires subjects qualified by opposites rather than the mere opposites themselves is to invoke substrata in a paradoxical sense only if this move is combined with one or other of the above misinterpretations of predication. (On the other hand, that Aristotle at least flirted with these misinterpretations seems clear.)

---

way which easily leads to serious confusion. Thus, "red" is (1) an adjective which applies to things, e.g., this apple is red; (2) a common noun which applies to *shades* of red, e.g., crimson is a red, and (3) a singular term (equivalent to "redness"), e.g., red is a color.

It is also interesting to note that the argument which Aristotle gives in *De Generatione* for a matter more basic than the elements rests on physical considerations pertaining to the transmutation of the elements. Yet it would be a mistake to construe the argument as physical *rather than*, in a broad sense, logical. The core of the argument is the idea that one's willingness to speak of water as *changing into* rather than as *ceasing to exist and being replaced by air* does imply an identical subject which is first moist and cold and then moist and hot. Once again it should be emphasized again that this subject need not be construed as a substratum which is neither hot nor cold not moist nor dry, though, of course, this is what one will be tempted to say if one is committed to the theory of predication examined above. It would suffice to say that the identical subject is capable of being at different times cold-dry, cold-moist, warm-moist, warm-dry, and is, at every moment, in one or other of these states.

Of course, if one already has as one's paradigm of qualitative change

This-X was f and is f'

where "X" stands for thing kind expressions (e.g., "man," "house") or, at a lower level, expressions of the form "portion of M" (e.g., "chunk of marble") which are the analogues of thing-kind expressions proper, then when one comes to the elements and tries to use the formula.

This portion of PM was cold-moist and is hot-moist

one runs up against the fact that whereas there are empirical criteria for being a dog or a piece of marble which are present both before and after qalitative change, there would seem to be no such criteria for being a portion of prime mater. To be sure, the *capacity* to be characterized (in sequence) by pairs from the list of fundamental opposites would persist through transmutation. But to accept this capacity as the criterion for being a portion of *PM* is, or so it might seem, to commit oneself to the idea that *PM* "as such" has no "positive" or "intrinsic" nature.

Notice, however, that if instead of the above, our paradigm of qualitative change were

S was f and is f'

where "S" is simply a referring expression, e.g., a demonstrative, then to grant that there are no "occurrent" (as contrasted with "dispositional") characteristics which persist through transmutation, e.g.,

    S was cold-moist and is hot-moist

is not to grant that S has no "positive" or "intrinsic" nature, unless one assumes that the nature of a continuant, if it is to be "positive" or "intrinsic" must include abiding "occurrent" qualities. One can, of course, stipulate a usage according to which this would be true *ex vi terminorum*—but then it does not seem that there must be anything particularly perplexing about subjects which do not have, in this stipulated sense, a "positive" or "intrinsic" nature.

    Certainly from the fact that S has no occurrent qualities which abide through transmutation one could infer neither that there were no empirical characteristics in terms of which it could be identified, nor that it has no empirical qualities. "S is not *abidingly* hot" does not entail "S is not hot." Thus, while transmutation would be a radical change, it would not lead us to speak of a qualityless substratum unless we were already doing so because of a faulty theory of predication.

    Suppose, now, we return to the idea that every proper subject of change must in principle be identifiable as either

        a K

where "K" is a thing-kind expression proper, or

        a portion of M

where "M" is a word for a kind of material. We now notice that where the context is one of craftsmanship, the immediate raw material for an artifact has and, it would seem (logically), *must* have "occurrent" qualities which abide through the changes involved in working it up into a finished product. (Compare processed leather before and after it is worked into a shoe.) Let us call these occurrent characteristics the "positive" or "intrinsic" nature of the material. From this standpoint transmutation would involve a "material" which "has no positive or intrinsic nature." But again, that this is so does not mean that in any paradoxical sense transmutation would involve a qualityless substratum. It would simply mean that the "M" of the procrustean formula

        S is either a K or a portion of M

(which presents the alternatives for answering the question "What is S?") is being used by analogy to cover what are now recognized as proper subjects of change which are not in the literal craftsman sense pieces of raw material. But that Aristotle's concept of matter, and of prime matter in particular, is a concept by analogy is scarcely news.

These considerations lend weight to the idea that the concept of prime matter, though rooted in the form "this portion of M," is simply the concept of the ultimate subject of predication with respect to changeable things in space and time,[18] the concept showing in its formula the traces of its analogical formation route, but having no correspondingly overt expression of the qualifications which, in effect, limit the analogy to the essential of an abiding subject of change.

But surely, it will be said, the qualifications do not remove the "indeterminateness" of prime matter, a trait on which Aristotle insists, and which gives it a richer metaphysical role than that of the bare concept of an abiding subject of change. There is *something* to this challenge, and it must be taken seriously; though it does not, in my opinion, militate against the essential correctness of the above interpretation. Let us examine the sense in which secondary matter is indeterminate. This indeterminateness is logically necessary, and is a consequence of the fact that words for materials belong in the context

Amount *x* of M.

A raw material which came in indivisible hunks which could not be put together would be a "degenerate" case of material. There would be no point in giving it a name with a grammar akin to that of "leather" or "marble." A common noun would suffice. The recipes involving it would read "...take a glub."

This indeterminateness belongs primarily to the kind, not to the individual. It is *marble* which is indeterminate, not (save in a derivative sense) this piece of marble. And marble is indeterminate only in the sense that "x is a piece of marble" does not entail "x is, say, one cubic foot in size." Clearly indeterminateness in this sense is a feature of the Aristotelian elements.

Now something akin to this indeterminateness is a feature of the ultimate subject of predication with respect to changeable things, even where the concept of such a subject has not been formed by analogy in the Aristotelian manner. For it is a necessary feature of the concept of such a subject that it have *some location or other* in space and time. The indeterminateness to which "some...or other" gives expression is, again, an indeterminateness pertaining to the "kind" and not to the individual. Now if "having some location or other in space and time" entails and is entailed

---

[18]For a discussion of the idea that the ultimate subject of predication is in some cases matter and in other cases primary substance, see the next section.

by "having some size or other," one can see how the formula

> This portion of PM (every portion of which has some size or other)

could have a philosophical force which was indistinguishable, save by its conceptual roots—a distinction which should not, however, be minimized—from the more familiar

> This ultimate subject of predication (every one of which was some location in space and time or other).

IV

I shall return to the topic of Aristotle's treatment of matter in the concluding section of this essay. But before the argument can advance, we must pick up some more threads from this theory of predication.

In *Categories* 2b4ff, Aristotle writes, "Everything except primary substance is either predicated of primary substances or is present in them, and if these last did not exist, it would be impossible for anything to exist." By "everything except primary substances," he presumably means, in this context, everything which is either a secondary substance or belongs in one of the other categories. And he is telling us that while some items other than primary substances may legitimately be said to exist, their existence is essentially bound up with the fact that they are either "predicated of" or "present in" primary substance.

What, exactly, does Aristotle have in mind by these technical expressions? Leaving "predicated of" aside, for the moment, let us note some distinctive features of his account of "present in," The expression is explained as follows: "By being 'present in,' I do not mean present as parts are in a whole, but being incapable of existence apart from the said subject" (1a24-5). He clearly intends to differentiate his use of "present in" from that in which the piece of wood which is a leg of his chair is part of the chair. For the piece of wood which is now a leg may later be separately existing in the corner of the room. On the other hand, not all ways of being incapable of separate existence are discussed in the *Categories*, and some of these *are* ways of being *parts* (in a broader or narrower sense)[19] of *wholes*. Thus, while the *piece of wood* is capable of separate existence, the (chair) *leg* is not, nor is an eye

---

[19]Cf. *Metaphysics*, 1023b12-1024a10; also 1034b32ff.

apart from an animal, nor a soul apart from its body. These remarks are designed to call attention to the fact that even though the language of the *Categories* is ontological through and through (however true it may be to say that it simply reflects in more or less adequate fashion the "logical grammar" of ordinary Greek). it makes no explicit reference to the concepts of *matter* and *form*, To make the essential point in terms of an example, it is not concerned (at least directly) to clarify the sense in which *a piece of leather* may be said to be *a shoe*, or "a hide, a bone and a hank of hair" *a man*, but rather with the sorts of things that the *shoe* or the *man* may be said to be. Any materiate substance of a given kind is a *subject* for its purposes, whether or not it in some sense contains another subject within it. It attempts, so to speak, no trans-level analyses.[20]

Having introduced *presence-in-a-subject* as incapacity for separate existence, Aristotle next tells us (2a26ff) that "with respect to those things which are present in a subject, it is generally the case that neither the name nor the definition is predicable of that in which they are present," to which he adds that "though the definition is *never* predicable, there is nothing, in certain cases, to prevent the *name* being used" (italics mine). He has just been pointing out that both the name and the definition of the species Man are predicable of the individual—thus "Socrates is a man" and "Socrates is a two-footed terrestrial animal." If we use the expressions "oblique predication" and "direct predication" to stand for the difference Aristotle has in mind, the question arises as to what sort of things are directly predicable of primary substances. The list includes not only the species, but also the genera, proximate or remote. *In a sense*, it includes the differentia, thus *two-footed* and *terrestrial* (but notice that these appear as qualifying the common noun "animal"). Aristotle continues the above passage by giving an example of something which is not included (i.e., an example of something which is "obliquely" rather than "directly" predicable of a primary substance). "For instance,

---

[20]Thus, whereas in the *Metaphysics* "substance" (i.e., secondary substance, the *kind*) is said to be predicted of *matter*, in the *Categories* it is said to be predicated of primary substance. The inconsistency is superficial since, as we have seen, the subject of which "shoe" is predicated is not a subject *qua* artifact; nevertheless, if the predication is true, it *is* an artifact, and the question "That is a what?" presupposes that it belongs to a thing kind, even though it can be answered by "It is nothing—only a piece of leather."

white being present in a body, (the word) 'white' is predicated
of that in which it is present; the definition, however, of white is
never predicated of the body."[21]

What Aristotle has in mind seems to amount to the following
doctrine: "*B*" is directly predicable of A if and only if A can be
said to be a B, where the statement that A is a B is at least a part
of the *primary* answer to the question "What (i.e., of what kind)
is A?" Thus "man" and "animal" are direct, or we may also
call them *essential*, predicates of Socrates because he can properly
be said to be *a man* or *an animal*, the former being the "whole"
and the latter a "part" of the answer to the question "What is
Socrates?" (i.e., "Socrates is *a what?*"). On the other hand, although
it is legitimate and proper to say that Socrates is white, it is not
proper to say that Socrates is *a white*.[22] Thus, "Socrates is white"
is a case of "oblique" predication, which might also be called
"derivative" predication, for "white" is, as Aristotle sees it, predicated of Socrates in a way which is derivative from its direct
or essential predication of another subject. For when "B" is
"obliquely" predicated of a subject, the predication expresses the
logical product of a direct predication of "B" in the form "a B"
and the relation of inherence or "presence in." Thus

A is B = x is *a* B, and x is present in A.

Thus when we say that a body is white, what we mean is that
a white (the white in the thing of the *Phaedo*) is present in the
body (i.e., that there is present in the body an item of which
"white" is directly or essentially predicable. The following passage

---

[21]The Oxford translation, which I have modified slightly, reads, "For instance,
'white' being present in a body is predicated of that in which it is present, for a body
is called white: the definition, however, of the color 'white' is never predicable of
the body." Notice that the specific point Aristotle is making here is valid independently
of his contrast between "predicated of" and "present in." Thus if he simply distinguished between "common noun" and "adjectival" predication, it is true that in
the former case the definition is predicable of the subject, while in the latter case it
is not; *if we construe the definiens as white in the sense of whiteness, rather than as the function,
x is white.*

[22]He can, indeed, be said to be *a white thing*, but this takes us back to "a thing
(subject) which *is white*" and hence presupposes rather than clarifies the form "*S* is *P*"
(as contrasted with "*S* is a *P*") which Aristotle, at least in the *Categories*, finds problematic. That in English we can say "Socrates is a white" (i.e., white man) is an
excellent illustration of the Aristotelian conception of a family of uses of a word, one
of which is primary.

from the *Topics* is illuminating in this connection:

> Next, then, we must distinguish between the classes of predi-
> cates in which the four orders in question (the reference is to
> the predicables) are found. These are ten in number: Essence,[23]
> Quality ... For the accident and genus and property and defi-
> nition of anything will always be in one of these categories;
> ...it is clear, too, on the face of it, that the man who signifies
> something's essence signifies sometimes a substance, sometimes
> a quality, sometimes one of the other types of predicates. For
> when a man is set before him and he says that that which is set
> there is "a man" or "an animal," he states its essence and sig-
> nifies a substance, but when a white color is set before him and he
> says that what is set there is "white"[24] or is "a color," he states
> its essence and signifies a quality....Likewise, also in the other
> case: for each of these kinds of predicates, if either it be asserted
> of itself (i.e., as "a man" is asserted of a man) or its genus be
> asserted of it (i.e., as "an animal" is asserted of a man) signifies
> essence; if, on the other hand, one kind of predicate is asserted of
> another kind (i.e., as when a man is said to be white), it does
> not signify an essence, but a quantity or a quality or one of the
> other kinds of predicate. (*Topics*, 103b20ff.)[25]

The above doctrine of predication which, though profoundly
illuminating with respect to central themes in his epistemology
as well as his metaphysics, is a more radical misperception of the
lay of the land than most of the fundamental distinctions he
draws, throws light on the fact that Aristotle seems to regard
the form

> X is (i.e., exists)

---

[23]"Essence" is here the translation of "ti esti" and has the sense of the "what it is"
or "identity" of something. To give somethings "ti esti" is to identify it as, e.g., "a man"
or "an animal," or, as becomes clear from what follows, "a white (quale)" or "a color
(quale)" x. In 102a32ff, Aristotle writes, "We should treat as predicates in the category of essence (ti esti) all such things as it would be appropriate to mention in reply
to the question 'What is the object before you?'"

[24]The translation should be "a white" to parallel "a man" as "a color parallels
"an animal."

[25]This is a fascinating passage which deserves more attention than I have time for
on this occasion. I shall limit myself to noting that the distinction between the first
class of predicates and the remaining nine drawn in this passage is not that between
substance and the various sorts of thing that can be said of substances, but rather
between the *identity*, the *what it is*, of an item of whatever category in the more familiar
sense, and the sorts of things that can be said of it.

as the primary use of the verb "to be." Thus he frequently contrasts *being* (or *to be* or *is*) with *being this* or *that* (e.g., *white* or
round), and draws similar distinctions in the case of *not being* and
coming to be. If we represent, for the moment, the two uses of
"to be," thus interpreted, by

    X is

and

    X is Y

respectively, we can call attention to the fact that even in the
Posterior Analytics Aristotle speaks (89b31ff.) of statements of the
form "X is Y" as stating "a part of the things being." Since the
implied contrast between stating a part of the being of something
and stating the whole being of a thing is correlated with the contrast between "X is Y" and "X is," we are apparently to conclude that statements of the form "X is" are properly used to
state the whole being of a subject.

    To all this one might be tempted to expostulate that to say
"X is" is to say *nothing* about X, save that it is. But to make this
remark is to misconstrue the significance of "X." If, indeed, "X"
were a pure referring expression, a demonstrative or a proper
name, the criteria for which were as thin as a spatio-temporal
location, then the statement "X is" would, indeed, *cover* the whole
being of a certain logical subject in that it referred to *all* of X,
and not just a *part* of it, but it could scarcely be said to *state* or
formulate the whole being of this subject. To see what Aristotle
has in mind, we must recognize that a paradigm example of the
form "X is" as he is using it would be not "This is," but

    This-man is

and that he thinks of the latter as having a sense closely related
to, but in an important sense more basic than

    This is a man.

If we focus our attention on the latter statement, we can see what
might be meant by saying that it formulates the whole being of a
certain subject. It does not do so, of course, in the sense that a
listener who understands the statement would be in a position
to infer the color, size, and shape of the item in question. For
though the statement formulates the whole being, it does so in

an *indeterminate* (ultimately disjunctive) way, only the thing kind criteria being specified to a relevant degree of determinateness (i.e., a degree sufficient to mark out an infima species under the category of substance).

Guiding Aristotle's thought in this connection is the fact that "man" as a common name is not the name of a part or an aspect of individual men, but the common name of individual men as wholes, just as "Julius Caesar" is the proper name of Julius Caesar and not of a part or aspect of Julius Caesar.[26] He also thinks of such common names as "man" and "animal" as belonging to a system of classification which coordinates a body of scientific knowledge pertaining to the substances to which these names are applicable. And while the criteria or defining traits of such a common name are only a sub-set of the attributes exemplified by any individual to which it is applicable, the common name itself covers the whole being of the individual, for it is a name of any individual to which it is correctly applied.

As "man" covers the whole being of *this man* (Socrates), so, according to Aristotle, "white" covers the whole being of *this white*.[27] On the other hand, the statement "This body is white" tells us that *a white* is present in *this body*, and, as present, is a part—an accidental part—of its being. *This body is* and *this white is*.[28]

I implied above that Aristotle attempts to understand "This is a man" in terms of "this-man is." To see *why* he does this is to penetrate to the very heart of his metaphysics and theory of

---

[26]But see below, pp. 107 ff.

[27]It is high time that the dangers of discussing predication in terms of color examples were taken to heart. Color words are notoriously ambiguous: thus, "red" is (1) an adjective ("This house is red"); (2) a common noun ("Scarlet is a red"), and (3) a proper name ("Red is a color"). In its use as a common noun, "red" is the name of *shades* of red, *not* particulars. Aristotle (by no means alone) has invented a use of color words in which they purport to be the common names of particulars which are not substances, but ingredients of substances. Whether or not this invention can be made to work is a question which falls outside the scope of this essay.

[28]The theses that "X is a Y" is the *primary* mode of predication, and that "X is Y" is to be understood in relation to it should not be equated offhand with the thesis that all predication is reducible to the form "X is a Y." Thus, to claim that "X is Y" has the form of "Something is a Y and *is present in X*" is self-stultifying, for the second clause of the latter contains the form to be "reduced." The construction of an ontology built around the form "X is a Y" is a more radical task involving (1) the analysis of "substances" into patterns of simple particulars, and (2) the introduction of "X is a Y" counterparts of relational statements, thus, "(x,y) is a greener than."

knowledge. To make the metaphysical point first, Aristotle not only construes kinds (to whatever category they belong) as dependent on individuals for their existence; he does so by insisting that the very sense in which kinds exist is to be explained in terms of the existence of individuals belonging to the kind. Thus, where S is a lion, S is not analyzable into the kind or sort *lion* in combination with some other factor. Matter is not something which combines with kinds or sorts to constitute the individuals which belong to them. He is insisting, rather, that the existence of the kind *lion* is derivative from the existence of individual lions.

A number of things come together here which must be separated. In the first place, it is a fundamental principle of the Aristotelian natural philosophy that unless there *are* lions, no lions can come into being in the future. If one thinks of the existence of a kind as the *possibility* of the existence of members of the kind, then this principle would make the existence of the kind dependent on the existence of members of the kind. Yet a Platonist could accept the above principle but distinguish between the sheer existence of a kind or sort (e.g., *lion*) as an eternal object, and the *effective* existence which accrues to it by virtue of the existence in the world of becoming of individual lions ready and willing to propagate. In Aristotle, however, we seem to find the stronger thesis that not merely the effective existence, but the sheer existence of the kind requires the existence of individuals belonging to the kind. And, indeed, it is not easy to absolve Aristotle from a confusion between the existence of lions and the existence of the kind or sort *lion*.

For even if it be granted that

Lions exist

is strongly equivalent to

Lion$_1$ exists or lion$_2$ exists or . . .

Where "lion$_1$," etc., are proper names formed from the common noun "lion" in such a way that the criterion for their application specify all the lions which the world *might* contain,[29] no such

---

[29] The difficulties in this notion are notorious (cf. Quine's query concerning the number of possible fat men in the doorway in his paper "On what there is," *Review of Metaphysics*, 1, 1948, reprinted in *From a Logical Point of View*). To develop it would also require a discussion of which type of modality—logical, physical, or epistemic— would be involved.

equivalence could provide the means of "reducing" the existence of the kind or sort *lion* to that of individual lions.

To appreciate this point more fully, it is necessary to notice an ambiguity in the phrase "the kind or sort *lion*." For there are several singular terms which pertain to lions in addition to singular terms referring to individual lions. Of these the two most directly pertinent to our investigation are (1) "lion kind" in the sense of "the class of lions," and (2) "the lion" as a distributive singular term (DST).[30]

The difference between (1) and (2) are crucial to our discussion, for if "the kind or sort *lion*," in the sense of "the class of lions" is confused with "the kind or sort *lion*" in the sense of "the lion," undeserved aid and comfort will be given to the idea that "the kind or sort *lion* simply *is* its members." For while, roughly speaking, the lion simply is lions, this is by no means true of the class of lions. The status of the lion is partly explicated by the following schema:

The K is f = Ks (as such) are f.

Needless to say, as the parenthetical comment indicates, not everything that is in point of fact true of lions generally is true of the lion. Yet of the things that are true of lions generally, some are true of the lion. As a first approximation, one can say that in the sense in which the average man is "reducible" to men *simpliciter*, the lion is reducible to lions. If we agree to call such terms as "the lion" DSTs[31] and the corresponding individuals *distributive*

---

[30]There is also (3) "lionkind" in a sense which might be expressed by the phrase "the family of lions," where to be a member of the family is to be related by blood ties to other lions. (I am *not* using this phrase to refer to a group of species, as zoologists do when they refer to the cat family.) If we use the suffix "id" to form common nouns which can be used to say of something that it is a member of a certain family, then in this usage

x is a lionid

would tell us that x was not only a lion, but a member of a relational system of lions. Notice that "id" terms formed from proper names (e.g., "Seleucid") presuppose the existence of at least one member of the family. This requirement could (but need not) be imposed on "id" terms formed from common nouns.

There is also (4) the spatio-temporal object, the primary parts of which are individual lions, but of which other parts are individual claws and fangs. The study of such *concreta* has been undertaken by Goodman and Quine.

[31]It should be noted that not all DST's involve the definite article. Thus "man" is functioning as a DST in "Man is rational." For an exploration of the logic of DST, see C. H. Langford: The institutional use of 'the.' *Philosophy and Phenomenological Research*, *10*:115-120, 1949.

individuals, we can put this point by saying that the distributive individual pertaining to a kind or sort is "reducible" to the non-distributive individuals which belong to it.

Carefully to be distinguished from the distributive individual is the kind or sort proper. I shall use the suffix "kind" to form the name of a kind or sort proper from the corresponding common noun, thus "lionkind" from "lion." The distinguishing feature of a kind or sort proper is that its name is appropriate to the context

x is a member of K-Kind

where "is a member of" stands for a relation and is to be carefully distinguished from the simple copula of

x is a K.[32]

Distributive individuals, such as the lion, are in a broad sense "abstract entities." But though the lion is not a concrete perceptible individual like Leo, it is, in its own way, in the real, as opposed to the conceptual, as is the average man. On the other hand, Lionkind and other kinds or sorts proper have the same ontological status as Triangularity and, like it, belong, for the Platonist, in the realm of Being or Essence. To show that the kind, *lion,* in the sense of the distributive individual, the lion, is reducible to individual lions is not to show that the kind, *lion,* in the sense of lionkind as just described is so reducible. Yet the confusion between the two senses of "the kind, *lion"* has often made it seem so.[33] Thus, if we return to the equivalence

Lions exist $=$ lion$_1$ exists or lion$_2$ exists or . . .

with which this digression began, to grant that it is true might well be to grant that

The lion exists $=$ lion$_1$ exists or lion$_2$ exists or . . .

but only the confusion noted above would make it seem to carry with it the truth of

---

[32]I have explored the philosophical importance of the distinction between "x is a K" and "x is a member of K-kind"—comparing it with the distinction between "x is f" and "x exemplifies f-ness"—in a number of papers, most recently: Abstract entities. *Review of Metaphysics*, *16*, June, 1963, and Abstract entities and the Russell paradox, *Review of Metaphysics*, *16*, September, 1963.

[33]This remark has called to memory G. F. Stout's ingenious but misguided attempt to solve the problem of universals. See his Hertz Lecture on "The Nature of Universals and Propositions," *Proc Brit Acad*, *X*, 1921-22.

Lionkind exists $=$ lion$_1$ exists or lion$_2$ exists or . . . .

Although the existence of qualities, relations, and kinds does not consist in their being exemplified by individuals in the spatio-temporal world, and there is no absurdity in the idea of a quality (even a simple one!) which does not have—indeed never has had nor ever will have—instances, or of a kind which does not have—indeed never has had nor ever will have—members; there is, indeed, a necessary, if more indirect, connection between the existence of universals and existence of spatio-temporal individuals. Thus, "Lionkind exists" has, roughly, the sense of "'lion' expresses a concept," and it is the fact that the existence of a conceptual framework, like the existence of a game, involves that it be *used* (played) which provides the link between the existence of universals (and other conceptual entities) and the world of Becoming.[34]

However this may be, and whatever the correct account of the less exalted status of universals in the Aristotelian system, whether or not in addition to losing the Olympian self-sufficiency they had for Plato, and in addition to being construed as "predicative" entities which are "stood for" but not "named" by such words as "white" or "lion," they have also been demoted to a conceptualistic status, the heart of the matter remains that Aristotle rejects the view that a member of a kind, e.g., Leo the lion, is a composite one element of which *is the kind*. This is not, of course, to say that for Aristotle there is no sense in which Leo is composite, nor, indeed, as we shall see, that he is not a composite of matter and *a leonine form*. It is simply to say that for Aristotle Leo is not a composite of matter and *lionkind*. Our present concern is to mobilize certain facets of Aristotle's epistemology which will prepare the way for, and support, the interpretation of Aristotle's metaphysics of matter and form to follow.

Yet Aristotle's claim is not simply, in contemporary terms, that facts about K-kind presuppose facts or possible facts of the form *that x is a K*, e.g., that the common noun "man" is presupposed by rather than presupposes the abstract singular term "Mankind," but rather the more radical claim that even common names, though they occupy for Aristotle (in the various categories) the primary

---

[34]The complications which arise when the possibility (and even the reasonableness) of playing a different conceptual game do not arise, of course, from the standpoint of the Aristotelian theory of concept formation.

place among predicates, have a derivative status. We may approach
the point gingerly by saying that it is as though he were analyzing
the common nature *lion* into the set of individual lions (i.e., attempting to derive the role of the common noun "lion" from that of
singular terms of the form "this-lion," thus reversing the actual
order of dependence, namely that of "this-lion" on "lion."[35] Let
us use the schema

$$x \text{ is a lion} = x \text{ is lion}_1 \; v \; x \text{ is lion}_2 \; v \; \ldots$$

to represent this attempt.

Now we have seen that Aristotle rejected the idea that universals are constituents of individuals. Unfortunately he went from
the sound idea that the *individual* which corresponds to the true
statement

This is a K

does not consist of a particular corresponding to "this" and a
universal corresponding to "K" to the mistaken idea that the
item which makes the statement true (in accordance with the
correspondence theory of truth) is a *nameable* (object) rather than
a *stateable* (fact).[36] Thus, even if he were prepared to say that in
a sense what *directly* makes the statement "This is a *K*" true is the
fact that this is a *K*, he would not stay here, but, thinking (correctly)
of the *fact* as a complex consisting of an individual and a universal,[37]
would go on to attribute to it a secondary status derivative from
a *nameable* and *primarily knowable* entity. This nameable (as opposed
to stateable) real which is the ultimate counterpart of the true
statement and which, *qua* nameable, is ultimately responsible for
its truth must show by its name that it *is* responsible for the truth.
The Aristotelian is thus led to the fiction that the referring expression "this-lion" or "lion₁," is prior to the predicative expression
"lion."

V

At this point it will be helpful to explore some of the preceding

---

[35]Thus "This lion is tawny" is explicated in terms of "This is a lion and it is tawny."

[36]Even if the nameable is complex as consisting in some sense of matter and form,
it does not consist of matter and a *universal*. It is essential to the argument that in this
context forms are not universals.

[37]Which, indeed, it is, as being the concatenation of items playing the role of "this"
and "is a K" in our language.

topics from the standpoint of epistemology. Here the guiding thread is that Aristotle's rejection of Platonism leads him to the idea that since the *fundamentum in re* of the truth of "This is a K" is the K itself (i.e., *this-K*), rather than the fact that it is a K, there must be a form of *knowing* which has the K *qua nameable* (rather than the fact that is is a K) as its object (i.e., which combines somehow the (incombinable) characters of being a grasping of this item *as a K* and of being prior to the idea of its being *a* K (as contrasted with other actual, or possible, K's). In other words, instead of recognizing that knowledge is *ab initio* the knowledge that *this is a K* (or *that this is f*), and is *ab initio* expressible by means of the statement "This is a K" (or "This is f"). Aristotle postulates (and he was not the last to do so) an ur-knowing which, if it had a verbal expression, would be properly expressed by a (fictitious) singular term of the form "This-K"[38] and supposes that the thinking expressed by "This is a K," which involves the multiple predicable "a K" is derivative from the direct, simple, and intuitive knowledge of *this-K*.

To put the matter somewhat differently, Aristotle conceives of statements of the form "This is a K," where K is an infima species, as viewing a single entity *this-K*—which can be known intuitively *as this-K*—in terms of a framework in which its resemblance to (indiscernability from) other *this-K's* appears as a K-entity *common to all this-Ks*. Only in this framework does the intuitive knowledge of *this-K* become the knowledge that *this-K* is a *K*. This framework plays an essential role in human knowledge, for something can be known as *this-K* only when it is *present* or *given* to mind as in perception. It is the fact that we can think of something as *a* K which makes possible, to borrow a term from H. H. Price, "thinking (or knowing) in absence."[39]

---

[38]Or, perhaps, by the statement "This-*K* is," which "posits" to use a Kantian term, this *K*.

[39]It is interesting to note that what the Aristotelian conceives of as the contrast between apprehending a manifold of resembling *this-Ks* and recognizing them to be so many members of the species K, is a mislocation of the contrast between "x,y,z, etc. are Ks" and "x, y, z, etc. are members of the species K." It is indeed true that "*x* resembles *y*" belongs to a level of discourse prior to that in which individuals are said to be related to universals. Aristotle's mistake was to suppose that "*x* is a *K*" says that *x* is a member of the species K," and hence to suppose that "resembles" belongs to a level of discourse prior to "x is a K."

Now it is the idea of such knowings which underlies (1) the characteristically Aristotelian theory of intuitive induction and (2) his resolution in the *Metaphysics* of the aporia presented by the "inconsistent triad":

1. What primarily is, is individuals and not universals.
2. The object of knowledge is what primarily is.
3. Knowledge is of the universal.

Each thesis has a claim on his allegiance.

Intuitive induction might well be described, in first approximation, as the transition from the intuitive knowledge that *this-K* is f to the intuitive knowledge that *being a K* entails *being f*. One comes to "see" that there is a connection between the abstract entities *being a K* and *being f*. A philosopher in the Platonic tradition need not be tempted to construe the knowledge which serves as the platform from which this cognitive leap is made as itself the knowing of a *requiredness*. The knowledge that this-K is f need only be construed as the context in which one comes to see a requiredness obtaining *not* between particulars (e.g., this trilateral and its three angles), but rather between universals (e.g., *being a trilateral* and *having three angles*). Aristotle, however, by the specific character of his treatment of the primacy of individuals and the knowledge of individuals, has committed himself to think of the knowledge of the requiredness pertaining to universals as not merely *occasioned by* the intuitive knowledge that this-K is f, *but as derivative from the knowledge of a requiredness which obtains at a level below that of universals, this-K requiring this-f*. It is reasonably clear what is going on. We saw above that Aristotle (mistakenly) believed himself to have located a level of knowledge more basic than that represented by "This is a K."[40] He therefore looks to this level for a knowledge of necessary connection which, as pertaining directly to *this-K*, might in its turn be prior to the knowledge that *universally* being a K necessitates being f. It was surely by some such route that he came to think of *this-K* as including *this-f* as "part of its being." This extension of the meaning of "part," which in its primary use *does* stand for a relation between *thises*, lends an unwarranted plausibility to the idea that there is a

---

[40]Aristotle seems to have interpreted "This is a K" as having the form "K is predicated of this" where "K" stands for the universal *K*.

relation of necessary connection prior to that which obtains between abstract entities.

The next step in our reconstruction of Aristotle's views concerning our knowledge of universal necessary truths and, in particular, his resolution of the "inconsistent triad," takes its point of departure from a contemporary view which, though Aristotelian in *spirit*, stops short of the commitments of his notion of intuitive induction. According to this view, to know, for example, that

Trilaterals necessarily have three angles

is to know that

Being a trilateral entails having three angles

the point of which is to be a principle authorizing inferences of the form

x is a trilateral

Therefore, x has three angles

where to know the principle is, at least in part, to have the propensity to infer, with respect to any given individual x, that it has three angles, given that it is a trilateral.

Aristotle would most assuredly have reacted sympathetically to the idea that knowledge of a connection between universals has its cash value in knowledge concerning individuals. I say "knowledge" because even where something is merely opined to be a trilateral, one knows that *if* it is a trilateral *then* it has three angles. And one knows this by virtue of the fact that the general principle

Being a trilateral entails having three angles

indefinitely implies many subordinate principles of the form

That x_i is a trilateral entails that x_i has three angles.

Notice that each of the latter formulates a relation between two abstract entities, namely *that x_i is a trilateral* and *that x_i has three angles*. These abstract entities have many interesting properties of which the one that is most immediately relevant to our purposes is that in addition to being *individuals* or *singulars* in the broad sense (logical subject), they *contain* and *pertain to* the concrete individuals x_i. That concrete individuals lie at their core, so to speak, gives rise to the temptation to confuse the abstract individuals (propositions) with concrete individuals, *and to misconstrue the necessary connection between the abstract individuals (propositions) as a necessary connection between concrete individuals, thus a trilateral and its three angles.*

But what stands behind these general inference licenses? How can we be said to *know* universal entailments unless we have good reasons to accept them? And where they are not derivable from other universal entailments, can the idea of intuitive induction be avoided?[41] One might be tempted to say that one comes to know that being a trilateral entails having three angles by coming to see in particular cases that

>   This has three angles *because* it is a trilateral

and, as will be developed below, there is *something* to this idea. As soon, however, as it is made more definite by interpreting "seeing that this has three angles because it is a trilateral" as "seeing a requiredness between *this* (which is a trilateral) *and its three angles,*" it runs aground. Such requiredness as *is* involved obtains between *that this is a trilateral* and *that it has three angles* and the "seeing" of it[42] is, in a sense to be qualified below, the knowing that whatever x may be, *that x is a trilateral* requires *that x have three angles,* or, more simply, that being a trilateral entails having three angles. Thus, to know that

>   This has three angles *because* it is a trilateral

includes, with qualifications to be noted, the knowledge that

>   Being a trilateral entails having three angles

and if so, it would be absurd to claim that one could come to

---

[41] I shall not attempt in this context an explication of the distinction between "analytic" and "synthetic" entailments, nor of the modes of "justification" appropriate to them. It is important to note, however, that if one means by an "analytic" truth one which is directly testable by explicit definitions and the principle of contradiction *alone,* then all interesting entailments are non-analytic. This fact obscured the essential distinction between "formal" and "material" entailments which was not substantially elucidated until the nineteenth and twentieth centuries.

[42] Granted, that is, as is the case in our example, that what is "seen" finds its appropriate expression in "This has three angles *because* it is a trilateral." The qualification is necessary because it is not true in general that where S is P entails that S be Q, being P entails being Q, for the entailment may essentially involve S.

know the former *before* coming to know the latter. *It would not,
however, be absurd to claim that one comes to know the latter in the very
act of coming to know the former.*

The truth in the conception of intuitive induction is two-fold.
(1) In the first place, there is the fact that entailments or principles
of inference pertain to language as a social institution—in Wittgenstein's phrase, a "form of life." As principles of inference they
concern the correctness or incorrectness of "moves," sequences of
statements. Given a rich enough framework of previous learning
a new principle can be learned by being told its abstract formulation. It is, however, clear on reflection that the framework which
makes this possible cannot itself be acquired in this way,[43] but
rather in that fundamental way in which one learns a game by
"playing" it under the guidance of a player. This involves making
particular "moves"—not yet fully *as* moves in the language—and
learning to think of them as correct or incorrect. This, in its
turn, involves learning—also by "playing"—the metalanguage of
"ought" and "ought not" as applied to language situations. Thus
we learn a language-cum-metalanguage as on Aristotle's conception we learn virtue (i.e., by first "going through the motions").
Thus, we progress from making such motions as

> This is a trilateral
> Therefore, it has three angles

to the *understood* drawing of the inference, which latter involves
knowing the universal truth that being a trilateral entails having
three angles.

If one does not understandingly draw the above inference unless
one knows this entailment, in what sense is (scientific) knowledge
primarily of the individual? The answer is that in so far as scientific
knowledge is of the real (extra-conceptual) order, it is always
knowledge that

> X_i is g (*because* it is f).

---

[43]In this respect, learning ones first language differs from learning a game. Given
that one knows a language—including its normative (metalinguistic) component—
one could, in principle, learn to play all games and live in all institutions (with the
interesting and important exception of morality and prudence by being given the
abstract formulation of their principles.

For the knowledge that

Being f entails being g

does not *directly* pertain to the real order, but rather to the conceptual order. It is, indeed, to the effect that

Statements of the form "x is g" may be inferred from statements of the form "x is f" (in our language)

and the realization of such principles in knowledge of the real order is knowledge of the form "X_i is g (*because* it is f)."[44]

If this account is correct, then while the knowledge that x_i is g *because* it is f contains the knowledge of a universal principle concerning being f and being g, the latter is simply the principle of *more* knowledge of this same form.

How do the above considerations relate to Aristotle's resolution of the inconsistent triad? They do so by showing that it makes sense to say that *actual* (scientific) knowledge is of the individual, while granting that scientific knowledge is of the universal. For the knowledge that being f entails being *g*, though it is itself *actual knowledge*, is the potentiality of knowledge of the form

X_i is g (*because* it is f)

given the perceptual knowledge that x_i is f. Individuals, which are the primary *beings*, are also the primary objects of scientific knowledge. But this is not all, for if our previous argument is correct, Aristotle regards the knowledge that being f entails being g as itself derivative from a *preconceptual* knowledge of a requiredness pertaining to concrete individuals. If he were right in thinking this, knowledge pertaining to individuals would be *doubly* prior to knowledge of the connection of universals:

1. Pre-conceptual knowledge that *this-f* requires *this-g* or that *this-K* "includes" *this-f* would be prior to the knowledge that being f entails being g or that being a K "includes" being f in that the latter are intuitively induced from the former.

2. The universal knowledge that being f entails being g (or that being a K "includes" being f) would be the potentiality of

---

[44]There is, however, a sense in which the knowledge that being *f* entails being *g* does "contain" knowledge of the real order which is not of the above form, for there is a sense in which it "contains" the knowledge that (x) fx — gx. But the exploration of the status about the real order is a long story. See my Truth and "Correspondence," *Journal of Philosophy*, 59:28-56, 1862, reprinted as Chapter VI in *Science, Perception and Reality*.

conceptual knowledge that x_i is g *because* it is f (or that x_i is f *because* it is a K).[45]

VI

Let us return to questions of "being" after this excursus into epistemology by reviewing the dimensions in which, according to distinctions we have drawn in previous sections, the being of items other than primary substances is dependent on the being of primary substances. In one dimension, which was stressed in the early sections of the paper, we find an asymmetrical relation between primary substances and the "abstract particulars" which we have called qualia and quanta, e.g., *this white*. The latter are "present in" the former and cannot exist apart from (i.e., as not "present in") the former. Changeable things, although they must have qualia and quanta present in them, and *in this sense* cannot exist apart from them, are not "present in a subject," and can exist apart in the specific sense in which abstract particulars cannot.

A *second* dimension is that in which universals in whatever category have a being which depends on the being of *thises* belonging to that category and hence depend *directly* (in the case of secondary substances) or *indirectly* (in the case of qualia and quanta) on the being of primary substance.[46]

---

[45]I leave out of account the possibility that Aristotle might have *equated* knowledge of universal principles with propensities to draw inferences pertaining to individuals (i.e., construed the "actuality" of universal knowledge as the actuality of a *habitus*— thus providing an additional dimension of meaning to the statement that knowledge pertaining to the individual is prior in its actuality to knowledge of the universal). Such an account would not do justice to the distinction between sequences of thought which are "in accordance with a principle" and those which are "obedient to a principle," though it would contain part of the truth, for unless there were propensities to think one thought on the occasion of another thought, there would be no such thing as inference. But it is not a sufficient condition. Rational processes in the *primary* sense essentially involve the occurrence of *thoughts of prescriptive principles*, principles which stand to thinking generally as moral principles to volition (and action). This fact is compatible with the short-circuiting of sequences which include second level practical syllogisms about how the sequences of (first level) thoughts should occur, into first level sequences which ape mere associative sequences, but differ from the latter in that the occurrence of certain danger signals would call the meta-level into play.

[46]Actually, as was suggested above, the dependence is indirect even in the case of secondary substance, for on the supposition to which Aristotle is, in the last analysis,

A *third* dimension is that in which forms, substantial forms, in the first place as *thises* and in the second place as universals, depend on primary substance. This dimension will be our chief concern in the present section, and our problem will be to distinguish the sense in which the form as *this* is "in" the substance (or is "in" the matter) from that in which abstract particulars are "in" (present in) a subject.

A *fourth* dimension is that in which secondary matter, though it can exist apart from changeable substances is "conceptually incomplete" apart from the latter. In this dimension we may also count prime matter, which is not only conceptually incomplete in this weaker sense, but is, in the Aristotelian scheme, incapable of separate existence.

It was argued above that the key to understanding Aristotle's conception of changeable substance is the realization that every substance belongs to a kind, and that expressions pertaining to them, such as "man" and "horse," are common names. It is exactly because it is a *name*, albeit a common name, that "shoe" or "man" can "cover the whole being" of a substance or thing. This insight also clarifies the problem of how attributes can be *prior* to substance as constituting *criteria* for belonging to a kind, without involving an equation of

$$X \text{ is a } K$$
with X is A_1 and A_2 ... and A_n.

The latter equation would omit the distinctive role of *kinds* (secondary substances), and, by doing so, would impoverish the logic of primary substances and, indeed, of *thises* generally. For the central question with respect to any this is "What is it?" in the sense of "It is a what?" And while we answer this question with reference to attributes, the question presupposes that the logical space of attributes is structured with reference to thing kinds for which certain attributes serve as the *criteria*, others being *properties*, and still others *accidents* with respect to (specific) kinds.

It is important for the subsequent argument, however, to note that it is not only changeable things which have common (and

---

committed that the *esse* of universals is *concipi*, their being depends directly on the individual intellects, and on the being of other *thises* in that the *esse* of certain concepts involves the perception of instances to which they apply.

proper names. We have already noted that "white" is not only an adjective "obliquely" predicable of a primary substance, but also (and primarily) a common name "directly" predicable of qualia. A given *quale* is a *this-such* as being *this-white*. To which we must now add that the immaterial beings, the intellects, which are the unmoved movers of those changeables which are rational, are also *thises* (indeed, the true firsts in the order of thises) which belong to kinds and are *this-suches*—even if (except in the case of men?) there is only one *this* to a specific (as contrasted with generic) kind.

How does what we have called "Aristotle's doctrine of predication" apply to these *thises?* If, as Aristotle recognizes, further qualities are predicable of what are already qualities of individual things, is this because further qualia are "present in" the qualia of the things? Do unchangeable things have attributes by virtue of the presence in them of abstract particulars? It is difficult to take seriously any answer other than "no," and, indeed, not only does the attempt to interpret predication in a substance framework as a matter of the "presence in" substance of abstract particulars notoriously break down in the case of relational predication (though its bankruptcy may be postponed by desperate expedients), Aristotle himself makes no serious attempt to apply it outside the category of quality, and then only to the qualities of changeable things.

Nothing, indeed, is clearer than that the doctrine of abstract particulars is the result of blending insights to make a confusion. One insight concerns the central role, with respect to any individual X, of the question "What (i.e., of what kind) is X?" The recognition of this central role leads to the idea of the primacy of the form "X is a Y." Now the idea that this form is in some sense "central" or "primary" does not require that all predication of individuals is reducible to it. Here is where the second insight makes its contribution. This insight is that in *some* sense the qualities of individuals are individuals. Thus we make such statements as

The color of this table is *a* red.

The phrase "the color of this table" is, of course, a description of a universal which is *per accidens* of this table by virtue of the fact that the table is qualified by it. Supposing the table to be crimson, then we can say

The color of this table is (i.e., is identical with) crimson.

Crimson is an individual in the sense of a singular logical subject
of which predicates can be affirmed. And though crimson is an
individual of type 1, when it is conceived *qua* color of this table,
it is easily misconstrued as an individual in the primary sense in
which individuals of type 0 are individuals, and the sense in
which it is secondary misconstrued as a matter of the second class
status of a "dependent" particular. An individual of type 1, the
universal *crimson*, which is per accidens "of" the table, is misconstrued as an individual of type 0 which is the table's own
private *instance of* crimson.[47]

One of our concerns will be to evaluate the role, if any, of this
confusion and the resulting doctrine of abstract particulars in
Aristotle's thesis that the forms of individual substances are themselves—in their primary mode of being—individuals or *thises*. That
Aristotle holds any such thesis is often denied, or, since a blanket
denial does too much violence to the evidence, it is denied that
it represents his mature and considered position. I shall subsequently argue that the thesis that the forms of individual substances are, in their primary mode of being, individuals is an
essential aspect of Aristotelian metaphysics. My present concern
is to define this thesis, and to determine whether or not it rests
on the doctrine of abstract particulars as found in the *Categories*.

We saw above that it is the changeable thing as a whole which
is the "primary substance," e.g., the shoe or the tiger. (We have
subsequently noted that such *changeable* things are "primary" only
as contrasted with (1) the kinds to which they belong and (2) their
modifications.) Now since these changeable things belong to kinds
by virtue of having certain attributes, it is tempting to suppose
that the form of a changeable thing is in some sense constituted
by the attributes which are the criteria for the kind to which it
belongs,[48] and that if Aristotle thinks that the form of a changeable

---

[47]The use of "crimson" as a singular term in this paragraph should be contrasted
with its use as an adjective in "The book is crimson" and its use as a common noun
in "Harvard red is a crimson." The philosophical dangers involved in a failure to
appreciate the systematic ambiguity of color words has been explored in Section III
above.

[48]That the form cannot simply be equated with the attributes is made evident by
the fact that the form of a substance has to make it not only a substance of *a certain*

thing is a *this*, he arrives at this by interpreting "x is A" as "There is an A which is present in x."

Instead of taking up this issue directly, I shall use an indirect strategy. I shall attempt to show that when Aristotle argues in Book Z for the view that the form of a changeable thing is, in its primary mode of being, an individual or *this*, from the premises (1) that the "substance of" a changeable thing is its *form*, and (2) that the "substance of" one thing cannot be the "substance of" another—and must, therefore, be a *this* as contrasted with a universal, neither his argument nor his interpretation of the conclusion involve a commitment to the doctrine of "abstract particulars" as developed in the *Categories*.

As a matter of fact, it will be sufficient to examine the distinction he draws between form and matter taken universally (i.e., as the form and matter of a species) and form and matter as *this form* embodied in *this matter* in terms of a much misunderstood example. *This bronze ball* is a spherical piece of bronze. Its matter is the piece of bronze—not, however, *qua* having the spherical shape it in point of fact has, but rather *qua* capable of a variety of shapes, one of which is the spherical. There is little difficulty, clearly, about the distinction between the matter of this bronze sphere, and the matter of this bronze sphere taken universally. The distinction is represented by the distinction between the referring expression

This piece of bronze

and the predicative expression

. . . a piece of bronze

which stands for a quasi-thing-kind. Bronze is a kind of matter and "piece of bronze" is an analogue of a thing kind, in the basic sense illustrated by *tiger* or *shoe*. Thus we can say, as a first approximation, that this bronze ball is this piece of bronze *qua* spherical, and, in general, that bronze balls are spherical pieces of bronze.

But what of the form? We have already abandoned the idea that the form of this bronze ball is the supposed abstract particular which is its shape ("this sphericity" it might be called, if there were such a thing). Is it, then, the universal *sphericity* or, perhaps,

---

kind, but a *substance* of a certain kind, and this the attributes as such cannot do. (*Categories*, 3B18-20).

sphere? To say that it is either is to run counter to explicit and
reiterated statements to the effect that the "substance of" a substance cannot be a universal. But if so, *what* is the alternative?
Part of the answer lies in distinguishing between the referring
and the predicative uses of the phrase "a sphere" as illustrated
by the statements

> That is a sphere
> A sphere is on the table.

We have been using such expressions as "this sphere" as equivalent
to "a sphere" in its use to refer to an individual sphere as a sphere.
In these terms we might say that the form of the bronze sphere
is the bronze sphere itself, not, however, qua *bronze* sphere, but
simply *qua sphere*. We might add that spheres can be made of
many materials and that while to characterize an item as a sphere
is to imply that it is made of some appropriate material or other,
to characterize it as a bronze sphere is to class it as a sphere and
to pin it down to one specific kind of material.

But while it is more accurate to say that the "individual form"
is *this sphere* rather than what we referred to as *this sphericity*, it is
still only an approximation to the truth. The final step is to distinguish between "a sphere" and "a ball." When they are carefully distinguished, the former concerns a class of mathematical
objects, the latter a class of material objects. Thus, "a sphere"
has a referring use in which it refers to a particular instance of a
certain mathematical kind, and a predicative use in which it says
that a certain region of Space (or Extension—*not* Extendedness)
is so bounded as to constitute a (mathematical) sphere. Space or
Extension plays a role analogous to that of matter in changeable
things, and can be called "intelligible matter." It is, of course,
a central Aristotelian theme that mathematical objects[49] and the
intelligible matter "in" which they exist are dependent beings.
Just how the dependence of this domain on that of material things
is to be construed is left somewhat of a mystery. As I see it, we
have here a prime example of Aristotle's ability to rest content
with partial insights, repressing the temptation to push them into
a "complete" but erroneous system.[50]

---

[49]The descendents of *ta mathematika* which hover around the Platonic dialogues.
[50]In a paper dealing primarily with Time, Time and the world order, *Minnesota*

While "sphere," then, marks out a class of mathematicals, "ball" marks out a class of physical things. It should not however be taken to mark out certain physical things merely *qua* having a certain shape. As a true thing-kind expression, or, more to the point, as a means of clarifying the status of true thing-kind expressions, it should be taken in the sense of "spherical material object serving a certain purpose," as, for example, "tennis ball." The reader is invited to think of a game in which a ball is used which might be made of any of a number of materials,[51] including bronze, thus "Pusho"; and in that context to distinguish between "a pusho ball" and "a bronze pusho ball."

In its predicative use, the expression "a bronze pusho ball" stands for a materiate thing kind in which *pusho ball* is the formal element and *bronze* the material. In its referring use, it refers to a *this qua* bronze pusho ball (i.e., *qua* a pusho ball and *qua* made of bronze). Thus the individual which is *a bronze pusho ball* is necessarily *a piece of bronze* which is *a pusho ball*. What it is *essentially* is *a pusho ball*. It is a pusho ball by virtue of the fact that being a piece of matter of a kind which can satisfy the criteria for being a pusho ball, it does in point of fact satisfy these criteria and even though "a pusho ball" refers to the individual in an *indeterminate* way in the sense that there is much that is true of the individual, including the material of which it is made, which we cannot infer from this referring expression, the reference is deter-

---

Studies in the Philosophy of Science, Volume III, Minneapolis, 1962, I have suggested that Space (and Time) are "metrical entities" related to the domain of physical objects by "correspondence rules" so designed that an object or event occupies a region determined by discounting not only error, but all physical forces pertaining to observed measurement. Though they share many of the logical features of theoretical frameworks with, e.g., atomic theory, this discounting, or division of labor, accounts for the *Unding*-ish character of Space and Time correctly stressed by Kant. The correspondence rules which take one from measurements to regions of Space (or Time) occupied are the counterpart of Aristotle's notion that mathematicals exist when boundaries are marked out by *physical* differences. Further elaboration of these points would bring out the essential truth of Carnap's contention that Space is an ordered set of triads of real numbers *qua* coordinated with a certain family of measuring operations.

[51]Even if *in point of fact* it can satisfy the purpose of the game only by being made of a specific material (e.g., as having a certain size and weight it must be made of bronze), the "logical possibility" remains—as long as the purpose does not specify that the ball be made of bronze (a topic for further exploration)—that it might be made of some other material.

minate in the sense that the criteria specify the material of which
the object is to be made with reference to a determinate purpose
which the object is to serve. Thus to refer to something as a pusho
ball is to refer determinately as one would not be doing if one
referred to it as *a ball played in some game or other*. For unless there
are varieties of the game of pusho ball, there is no more determinate *purpose* to which the materials for making pusho-balls are
to be selected. It is the *teleological* character of artifact kinds which
enables us to understand why

> bronze pusho ball

is not a species of

> pusho ball

as

> soccer ball

is a species of

> football.

The answer to our question, thus, is that it is *this piece of bronze
qua* pusho ball (i.e., *this pusho ball*), which is what *this essentially* is.
It is *this* bronze pusho *ball as a whole*, and not an abstract particular
in the sense of the *Categories*, which is an instance of the formal
element in the materiate universal *bronze pusho ball*. The sense in
which the form of the bronze pusho ball is a *this* which is "in"
the bronze pusho ball is *not* that in which a quale is a this which
is "present in" a substance. The form can indeed be said to be
an "abstract particular," but only in the sense of a particular
considered abstractly (i.e., a particular *qua* what it essentially is). To
consider it as a bronze pusho ball is, of course, also to consider it
abstractly, but as an instance of a *materiate* thing kind, rather
than as an instance of a thing kind *simpliciter*. Obviously, then, the
sense in which the form of a thing is "in" the thing is different
from that which the qualities of a thing are "in" the thing. But
this should surprise no one who has reflected on the multitudinous
uses of "in." And similar considerations obtain in connection with
the statement that changeable things "consist of" matter and form.

Before we consider the relationship between the sense in which
the form of a materiate substance is "in" the substance, and that
in which one of its *qualia* is "present in" it, let us tentatively apply

the above considerations to the case where the primary substance is Socrates and the secondary substance or thing kind is *man*. We can cut through the preliminaries by turning directly to the question "Is man *essentially* a being of flesh and bone?" To this question Aristotle's answer is that there is an essence *rational animal of flesh and bone* only in the sense in which there is the essence *bronze (pusho) ball*, which is to say that in that narrow sense of essence in which the essence of something is its form, flesh and bone do not belong to the essence of man. Here we must be careful, for there is a sense in which flesh and bone do belong to the essence of man, and, indeed, bronze to the pusho ball. For while being a pusho ball does not include being made of bronze, it does include *being made of some appropriate material or other*. Similarly being a man includes being made of some appropriate material or other, and hence includes being made of flesh and bone in that sense in which somebody includes *Smith*.

Thus the fact that the essence of Socrates is his form (i.e., his soul) is the parallel of the fact that the essence of *this bronze pusho ball* is *this pusho ball*. And if it be granted that we ordinarily use the name "Socrates" to refer to a certain substance *qua rational animal made of this mixture of flesh and bone*, the above suffices to show that the name would be more tidily used to refer to it *qua rational animal made of this piece of appropriate material*. Using it thusly we could say not only that the essence of Socrates is his form, but that *Socrates is identical with his essence* (i.e., with his form). And the above analysis makes it clear that we could do so without implying that Socrates is an immaterial substance. For in exactly the same way, given that a certain pusho ball is called "Beauty," we could say that the essence of Beauty is its form and that Beauty is identical with its essence (i.e., its form). The fact that Socrates is identical with his form no more implies that Socrates can exist apart from matter than does the similar fact about Beauty.

If this analysis of Aristotle's account of forms as *thises* is correct, we can say that he distinguishes between the primary mode of being of forms, which is to be, for example, *this bronze pusho ball* qua *this pusho ball*, and a secondary mode of being, which is to be, for example, the universal *pusho-ball*. Thus, while in the primary sense, forms are *thises*, there is a secondary sense in which they are universals. It is only to be expected, then, that in many passages

Aristotle clearly has universals in mind when he speaks of forms. That the forms of perishable things are individuals enables us to understand how *pure forms* or *immaterial beings* can be individuals. For if one thinks of the form of a perishable thing as a universal "in" a piece of matter, one will think of an immaterial substance as a universal which is not "in" a piece of matter.

Yet while the form in the primary sense, which is "in" the bronze ball, is a *this* or individual, Aristotle finds it appropriate to say that the universal *ball* is also "in" the bronze ball. For although he does not clearly distinguish between the ball (of which the universal is *not* a constituent) and the fact that the ball exists (of which it *is*), he does the next best thing by distinguishing between the sense in which the form as *this* is "in" the bronze ball from the sense in which the form as universal is "in" it.

That the forms of perishable things are *thises* in the sense analysed above is no mere incidental feature of Aristotle's metaphysics. For if the primary mode of being of forms were that of universals, then instead of being as perishable as the individuals of which they are the forms, they would be imperishable and eternal, and a central theme in Aristotle's theology would be lost. *It is just because the forms of perishable things are as perishable as the things themselves that beings which are pure forms and, therefore, imperishable individuals are required to be the real foundation of beginningless and endless time.*

I shall conclude this section by introducing a theme which will tie it more closely to what has gone on before as well as serve as a connecting link to what is yet to come. We have distinguished between a primary sense in which a form is a *this*, and a secondary sense in which a form is a universal. We must now note that there is yet another derivative sense of "form" in which the form of a thing consists of the *attributes* by virtue of which it belongs to a kind. Let me introduce this topic by calling attention once again to the passage in which Aristotle tells us that "modifications" are predicated of substance, whereas form is predicated of matter. Thus, "pale" or "musical" is predicated of, say, Socrates, whereas "a man" is predicated of a certain piece of matter. If we turn our attention to artifacts, we can contrast "worn" as predicated of a shoe, with "a shoe" as predicated of a certain piece of leather. Now although this piece of leather is a shoe by virtue of having certain attributes, having these attributes does not as such *con-*

stitute its being a shoe. It is only because these attributes are such as to make that which has them belong to a certain thing kind— which is, in the Aristotelian system, an ultimate kind of fact[52]— that the piece of leather belongs to the kind "by virtue of" having them. These attributes might, nevertheless, be said to be the "content" of the kind, for they serve as criteria for the predicability of the form or kind. It is only in the light of all the relevant distinctions that we can appreciate the coherence of his statements in the *De Anima* to the effect that the soul is the form of the body and that if an axe were a living thing, the ability to cut would be its soul, with his general account of form and matter in the *Metaphysics*.

If we view the above distinction in the light of the doctrine of the *Categories*, bearing in mind that the latter does not distinguish between those subjects which are substances proper, and those which, from a metaphysical point of view are "second class" subjects (i.e., mere pieces of matter), we can see that whereas form in the sense of the kind to which it belongs is "predicated of" but not "present in" a subject, form in the sense of criterion-attributes is both "predicated of" and "present in" the subject. Thus *man, shoe* and (mere) *piece of leather* would be predicated of but not present in appropriate subjects, whereas *rational, foot-shaped* and *tanned* would, presumably, be both predicated of and present in these subjects.

As I see it, then, the primary mode of being of a form, e.g., the form Shoe or the form Man, is its being as a *this* or individual, the individual form of this shoe or this man. As individual form it is, so to speak, private to the individual of which it is the form. For the form of an individual substance is, according to Aristotle, the "substance of" the substance, and, he insists, the substance of an individual cannot be common to many. We must, therefore, distinguish between form as individual and form taken universally, as we distinguish between individual matter and matter taken universally. It is essential to see that if a changeable thing is a (composite) or "whole," its "parts," in the primary sense, are an individual form and an individual piece of matter. It is only in

---

[52]One, of course, which expresses the central role in ordinary discourse of identifying things as belonging to a kind, which identification carries with it a knowledge of causal and other properties.

a derivative sense that the form taken universally is a "part" of the changeable thing.

But how is this "part-whole" relationship to be understood? Clearly a metaphor is involved. How is it to be interpreted? Are we to suppose that as in the *ordinary* sense the *spatial* togetherness of two individuals (the parts) constitutes a new individual (the whole), so in the *metaphorical* sense a nonspatial, metaphysial, togetherness of individual matter and individual form (the "parts") constitutes a new (and complete) individual (the "whole")? The answer, I submit, is no, for the simple reason that the individual matter and form of an individual substance are not *two* individuals but *one*. The individual form of this shoe is the shoe itself; the individual matter of this shoe is *also* the shoe itself, and there can scarcely be a real distinction between the shoe and itself.

What, then, is the difference between individual form and matter of this shoe if they are the same *thing*? The answer should, by now, be obvious. The individual form of this shoe is the shoe *qua*

(piece of some appropriate material or other—in this case leather) *serving the purpose of protecting and embellishing the feet.*

The individual matter of this shoe is the shoe *qua*

piece of leather (so worked as to serve some purpose or other—in this case to protect and embellish the feet).

Thus, the "parts" involved are not incomplete individuals in the real order, but the importantly different parts of the formula

(piece of leather) (serving to protect and embellish the feet)

projected on the individual thing of which they are true.

VII

I argued in the opening section that in the *Phaedo* Plato, drawing on a theme from Anaxagoras, construed changing things as "bundles" of whites, hots, larges, smalls, alives, etc., most of which are of short duration. One "f-in-Socrates" is replaced by a contrary f. In the *Timaeus*, we find a conception which, in spite of the greater sophistication and complexity of the framework, is essentially continuous with this account. The fs in f things have become the elemental powers, that is to say, hots, colds, moists, drys, etc., construed as powers—powers to act and be acted on.

Atoms of earth, air, fire, and water are not *things* which are *characterized by* their powers, but rather bundles of powers which the Demiurge has brought under discipline by the imposition of geometrical form—a discipline which is, presumably "continued" by the world soul. I shall not enter into the debate as to whether or not Cornford is right in suggesting that the Demiurge represents the rational part of the world soul, although I am strongly inclined to agree with him. I do think, however, that the elemental powers are to be construed as the "appetitive" part of the world soul. For these powers are not the "causal properties" of contemporary philosophy of science, but rather of the nature of *impulses*, or, since this has too momentary a ring, *urges* or, to use a thinner expression which, however, has analytic overtones, *abiding unreasoned intentions*—the sort of thing which would be an abiding resolve, if there had been a resolving. Paper burns in the presence of fire. Is there no temptation to think of the paper as having the settled intention to burn when and if fire approaches (though without having decided to do so)? or, perhaps, as "resigned" to burn in these circumstanes? or, even, glorying in the opportunity?

This conception of Greek philosophy as building its interpretation of *powers* on the model of conditional intentions (I shall do A when and if C) is, I believe, a valuable tool of historical analysis. Furthermore, the conception of elemental powers as simple conditional intentions can readily flower into the conception of living things as being what they are by virtue of having fixed intentions of that more complex type which might be referred to by the phrase "plan of life." But the point I wish to stress at the moment is that the logical necessity with which the *combustible* object burns in the presence of fire is matched by the logical necessity with which the intention to do A when and if C becomes the doing of A when, A being in the agent's power, he realizes that C obtains. In the case of intentions proper, of course, it is the *thought* that the circumstances are C rather than the circumstances themselves which immediately conditions the doing of A. But, then, one who attributes the burning of paper to an "intention" to burn if and when fire approaches is not likely to boggle at attributing to the paper a "perception" of the approaching fire.

Now the intentions and purposes which are fulfilled by artifacts *qua* artifacts are *extrinsic*. The intrinsic "intentions" which find expression in their behavior (i.e., their powers) are those of the material of which they are made. Chairs burn not *qua* chairs, but *qua* made of wood. And the "conditional intentions" of non-living matter are such that the "antecedent" is always satisfied by an *external* circumstance which the piece of matter "perceives." It does not, in other words, have a "source of motion or change in itself." Let us now turn our attention to Aristotle's interpretation of those materiate substances which exist by nature rather than by art, and have, *qua* being the kinds of things they are, a source of motion or change in themselves. The point I wish to develop and fit into the argument of this paper is the by no means novel one that although Aristotle clearly thinks that living substances are more truly substance than are artifacts, it is the latter rather than the former which serve as the basic model for his explanation of metaphysical concepts. He seeks to illuminate the metaphysical structure of living things by means of distinctions drawn in the context of craftsmanship and the products of craftsmanship. He draws a twofold analogy: (1) the soul and body of a living thing are to each other and to the living thing as the form of a shoe and the leather of which it is made are to each other and to the shoe; (2) the coming to be of a living thing out of a germinating seed is analogous to the making of a shoe by a shoemaker.

To bring out the proper force of these analogies in Aristotle's system, a terminological point will be helpful. Leaving aside, for the moment, the teleological element in the definition of the products of the various crafts, these artifacts can be regarded as portions of appropriate matter suitably shaped, arranged, and joined.[53] Let us call the set of attributes essential to a given artifact kind the "characteristic state" of the kind. (Clearly, the characteristic state pertaining to shoes is a determinable, a family of states the various dimensions of which have limits not independent of one another.) In these terms, a shoe exists as long as its leather (or rubber-cum-cloth) is in the appropriate characteristic state. Before it is in the state it is not a shoe, though it is *potentially* a shoe, as capable of being made into a shoe by a shoemaker.

Now although we have spoken as though the characteristic state

[53]Cf. *Metaphysics*, 1042b9 ff.

pertaining to shoes consists only of what would, in contemporary terminology, be called "occurrent" rather than "causal" properties, it is clear that it must include attributes falling under the latter heading; it must, in short, include active and passive powers. In the case of artifacts, however, these do not loom large in Aristotle's account, as these powers, generally construed, are characteristic of the proximate matter of the artifact. It is by virtue of being given the specific make-up of a shoe that the powers of leather are made available in that determinate mode which is suitable for warding off mud and stones. It is presumably for this reason that his account of artifacts stresses occurrent structural characteristics rather than powers (*Metaphysics*, 1042b9 ff.).

Consider, now, a flourishing, fully developed living thing "in full possession of its faculties," e.g., a carrot or a tiger, and conceive of a typical state in which it might be found as a "characteristic state" in the above sense. Here it will be necessary to lay more stress on *powers*, and *dispositions* for the essential powers and dispositions of carrots or tigers, unlike those of artifacts, are not determinate forms of powers and dispositions characteristics of their proximate matter.[54] However this may be, the point to which I wish to call attention is that whereas before this leather is in the characteristic state of a shoe, it is not a shoe—save potentially— and the form *shoe* is not "in" the leather, but there is a sense in which the form *carrot* or *tiger* is present in the germinating carrot or tiger seed even before the relevant matter is in the characteristic state of species in question.[55]

But before following through on this point, an apparent digression. In Book I of the *Metaphysics*, Aristotle makes the at-first-sight surprising claim that of the four causes, Plato had recognized only

---

[54]Aristotle might admit that the propensity to absorb nourishment could be defined in terms of the attributes of non-living matter (with a sufficient sprinkling of *ands*, *ors*, *nots*, *if-thens*, *alls*, and *somes*). He would nevertheless insist that this propensity is not found in the mixtures and compounds which are the matter for living save when they are in point of fact the bodies of living things. He would certainly insist that the power to have sensations and images are not even *definable* in terms of the attributes of non-living matter, though certain (roughly) correlative powers (cf. behavioristic constructs pertaining to discriminating behavior) might be.

[55]The recognition *that* there are, and *why* there are, no such forms as boy, acorn, etc., is essential to the understanding of Aristotle's philosophy of nature. For an example of the puzzles which arise when this recognition is lacking, see H. H. Joachim: *Aristotle on Coming to be and Passing Away*. Oxford, Clarendon Press, 1922, p. 260.

two, the material and the formal.[56] The surprise is occasioned primarily by the prima facie conflict of this claim with the patently teleological character of Plato's cosmology. Actually, of course, the point is quite simple. Plato attributed all purpose to soul. The everlasting existence of individual souls is one of their essential traits, whether or not it is to be interpreted, as in the *Phaedo*, as the undyingness of alives. They do not *come to be* and, *a fortiori*, do not come to be *to fulfill a purpose*. As for the coming to be of those things which do come to be, artifacts and (the bodies of) living things alike, it is attributed by Plato to souls (including the World Soul) acting as craftsmen. Souls "weave" material things (including bodies), as craftsmen weave baskets. Thus Plato's Ideas are the *final* causes of existence only by virtue of inspiring *souls* to shape the flux of becoming in their image.[57] For Plato, all realizing of ends is no mere analogue of, but simply *is*, craftsmanship.

For Aristotle, on the other hand, the level of purposiveness which *is* craftsmanship rests on a level which *is analogous to* craftsmanship. I pointed out above that Greek thought tended to construe *powers* on the model of *conditional intentions*. The point I wish to make in closing this paper is that Aristotle construes the presence of the form Carrot in a germinating seed *on the model of the presence of a goal in the mind of a craftsman*. The seed "is" a carrot as being appropriate matter aiming at assuming the characteristic state of a carrot. Since it is not yet "in its form" (*Metaphysics*, 1005a16), "is" a carrot only *qua* being (in a unique way) potentially a carrot a potentiality which requires only suitable "circumstances" to become realized. ". . . Man is prior to boy and human being to seed; for the one already as its form, and the other has not. . . everything that comes to be moves towards a principle, i.e., an end (for that for the sake of which a thing is, is its principle, and the becoming is for the sake of the end), and the actuality is the end, and it is for the sake of this that the potency is acquired." (*Metaphysics*, 1050a5ff.).

---

[56]988a7ff.

[57]"That for whose sake actions and changes and movements take place they assert to be a cause in a way, but not in this way, i.e., not in the way in which it is its nature to be a cause. For those who speak of reason or friendship class these causes as goods; they do not speak, however, as if anything that exists either existed or came into being for the sake of these . . ." (988b5ff.).

One might attempt to sum this up by saying that in this picture souls have two modes of being, one of which predominates in the seed and the young, while the other predominates in the adult. Of these modes of being the primary would be that of the "substance of" the actual adult living individual (i.e., the individual *qua* instance of the species defined with respect to *some appropriate matter or other*).[58] This mode of being would be *temporally prior* to the seed in its progenitor, and *temporally posterior* to the seed in its mature existence. The other mode of being would be that of an object of "aspiration" (the *natural appetition* of the schoolmen). This aspiration, in its turn, would have two modes: (1) the aspiration of seeds, and (2) the aspiration of the progenitor to make seeds. The being of objects of natural appetition would be analogous to the "intentional inexistence" of planned artifacts. This picture carries with it the implication that carrot seeds, as aiming at realizing the characteristic state of carrots, "know" (without deliberation, for nature, like art, does not deliberate[59]) the steps necessary to this end—"know," that is, the strategy with which to meet (when they can be met) the threats and opportunities presented by its possible environments.

Further, where a series has a completion, all the preceding steps are for the sake of that. Now surely as in intelligent action, so in nature; and as in nature so it is in each action, if nothing interferes. Now intelligent action is for the sake of an end; therefore the nature of things also is so. . . . If, therefore, artificial products are for the sake of an end, so clearly are natural products. . . . It is absurd to suppose that purpose is not present because we do not observe the agent deliberating. Art does not deliberate. If

---

[58]See the discussion of the *thisness* of forms in general and of souls in particular in sections VI, VII above. An important problem arises concerning the relation of the nature of a species of living thing defined with respect to some appropriate matter or other (the "immateriate form" it might, somewhat misleadingly, be called) and what we have called above the "characteristic state" of the species, one can appreciate the temptation to say, along Mortimer Adler's lines, that many of the features of the characteristic state are not necessary to the species as such, but are rather what the specific nature must make of the materials (ultimately the elements) which are in point of fact what is available. Thus, to use an image, the lordliness of lions might require a certain shape and tawny color given that it is to be realized in earth, air, fire, and water (as contrasted with other possible, but non-actual, elements). Adler, however, draws the mistaken conclusion that "the difference between an orchid and an onion is purely accidental."

[59]*Physics*, 199b25ff.

the shipbuilding art were in the wood, it would produce the same
results *by nature*. The best illustration (analogy?) is a doctor
doctoring himself; *nature is like that*. (*Physics*, 199a0-b30 *passim*,
query and concluding italics mine.)

What arouses this aspiration in the heart of a given piece of
matter and imparts this strategy? It is not The Carrot Itself, a
supposed separate eternal individual. "In the *Phaedo*, the case is
stated in this way—that the Forms are causes both of being and
of becoming; yet when the Forms exist, still the things that share
in them do not come into being unless there is something to
originate movement" (991b2-6). It is rather the action on *this
matter* by the parent carrot in accordance with its ultimate power
to originate new aspirants for the characteristic state of carrots,
and though the parent carrot is primarily a *form*, its being *qua*
form is not that of a Platonic Idea, but that of a perishable individual in the sublunary world, *this* portion of matter *qua* having
the attributes essential to carrots.

It is against this background that Aristotle's claim that Plato
failed to recognize the final and efficient causes of being is to be
understood. For Aristotle, the *existence* of souls, and hence of human
souls and craftsmen, is itself to be explained in teleological terms,
and Aristotle's forms (in their "intentional" mode of being) are
the *final* causes of *generation*, as well as of growth, by defining the
aims of the *efficient* causes which are actual individual forms. As
the form of a shoe is, in a certain sense, the shoe itself, so the soul
of a living thing is, in this same sense, the living thing itself, and
therefore comes into being and ceases to be. For Aristotle, the
craftsman is a soul. And while not all souls are in the literal sense
craftsmen, the existence of craftsmen—souls which conceptualize
ends and consciously strive to realize them in matter—rests on a
level of final and efficient causation which, though construed on
the model of conscious and conceptualized striving, is metaphysically more fundamental than the model in terms of which
we seek to understand it.

IV

SUBSTANCE AND FORM IN ARISTOTLE[1]

I

In *Categories* 2b 4 ff., Aristotle writes, "Everything except primary substance is either predicated of primary substances or is present in them, and if these last did not exist, it would be impossible for anything else to exist." By "everything except primary substances," he presumably means, in this context, everything which is either a secondary substance, or belongs in one of the other categories. And he is telling us that while items other than primary substances may legitimately be said to exist, their existence is essentially bound up with the fact that they are either "predicated of" or "present in" primary substances.

What, exactly, does Aristotle mean by these two technical expressions? Leaving "predicated of" aside, for the moment, let us note some distinctive features of his account of "present in." "By being 'present in a subject' I do not mean present as parts are in a whole, but being incapable of existence apart from the said subject" (1 a 24–5). He then tells us (2a 25 ff.) that "with respect to those things...which are present in a subject, it is generally the case that neither the name nor the definition is predicable of that in which they are present," to which he adds that "though the *definition* is *never* predicable, there is nothing, in certain cases, to prevent the *name* being used" (italics mine). He has just been pointing out that both the name and the definition of the species Man are predicable of the individual—thus, "Socrates is a man" and "Socrates is a two-footed, terrestrial animal." If we coin the expressions "nominal predication" and "full predication" to stand for the difference Aristotle has in mind, the question arises as to what sorts of things are fully predicable of primary substances. The list includes not only the species, but also the genera, proxi-

---

[1] I have found Joseph Owen's important book, *The Doctrine of Being in the Aristotelian Metaphysics*, Toronto, Pontifical Institute of Medieval Studies, 1957, and Ellen Stone Haring's analysis of *Metaphysics Z*, Substantial Form in Aristotle's *Metaphysics Z*, *Review of Metaphysics*, Vol. 10, 1957 helpful and suggestive, although I ran into the latter too late to give it more than a careful first reading.

mate and remote. It also includes the differentiae, thus *two-footed* and *terrestrial*. Does it include anything else? Aristotle continues the above quoted passage by giving an example of something which is *nominally* but not *fully* predicable of a primary substance. "For instance, white being present in a body, [the word] 'white' is predicated of that in which it is present; the definition, however, of white is never predicated of the body."[2]

In *Categories* 4a10ff., Aristotle tells us that "the most distinctive mark of substance appears[3] to be that while remaining numerically the same, it is capable of admitting contrary qualities." The question naturally arises, Is Aristotle contrasting materiate substances with items in other categories of being which, also remaining numerically the same, are *incapable* of admitting contrary qualities? And the answer to this is yes. "Thus," he continues, "one and the same color cannot be both white and black. Nor can the same action be both good and bad."

It should now be quite clear that by "one and the same color"— "a color which is numerically one"—Aristotle does *not* mean a shade of color, that is to say, a repeatable or universal which is common to many individual things, but a *particular*, an *instance* of a shade of color. If we call this particular "Tom," the idea is that Tom is, say, *a white*, as Socrates is *a man*, not as Man is an Animal. The doctrine is that of the *Phaedo*, where (102Dff.) distinguishing between the large thing, the large in the thing, and The Large Itself, Plato tells us that while the large thing may become small (by losing the large which is in it and, sharing in The Small Itself, acquiring *a* small to be *the* small which replaces it), the large in the thing can never be small, nor the small in the thing large.

The view which emerges from these passages is one according to which all predication is built on one fundamental form, namely

---

[2]The Oxford translation, which I have modified slightly, reads: "For instance, 'white' being present in a body is predicated of that in which it is present, for a body is called white: the definition, however, of the color 'white' is never predicable of the body."

[3]The "appears" is undoubtedly a tacit reference to the existence of unchanging, immaterial substances. Strictly speaking, however, it is probably incorrect to say that immaterial substances are substances in the sense of the *Categories* (i.e., in the sense in which substances are contrasted with the qualities, quantities, etc. by which they are characterized). They are, however, beings which "exist apart"—indeed, more truly apart than the primary substances of the *Categories*.

"X is a Y." If X is a primary substance, Y is a secondary substance or thing kind. But there are other examples of this form—
thus, "Tom is a white." Here Tom would be a quality in a "primary" sense which corresponds to the "primary" sense of "substance." A similar distinction is to be drawn in each of the other
categories.[4] We shall call items such as Tom, *qualia*, and primary
instances of the category of Quantity, *quanta*.[5]

There are, then, for Aristotle, at least two dimensions in which
the being of items other than primary substances is dependent on
the being of primary substances. In one dimension the "is" of
"This white is" stands to the "is" of "This man is" as "inseparable"
to "separate."[6] What they have in common can be represented by
saying that they share the form "X is a Y." A second dimension
in which beings other than primary substances are dependent on
primary substances is concerned with the being of universals.
This dimension is brought out by the formula

Man is = Some primary substances are men.

"Man is" is traced to "This (substance) is a man." In these terms
the significant difference between Plato and Aristotle is that whereas the former takes "man" to be *primarily* the *proper* name of a single
entity, Aristotle takes it to be primarily a *common* name of many
individual men (thus, *Categories*, 3b 15–17), and consequently re-

---

[4] Cf. Ross, *Aristotle*, Second Edition, p. 24.

[5] A no less explicit and, in certain respects, more interesting formulation of this
theory of predication is to be found in *Topics*, 102b20ff. Two points require to be made
about the translation: (1) "White" (in 103b32) should be "the (presented) white"
(*to ekkeimenon leukon*) to parallel "the (presented) man" (*to ekkeimenon anthropon*) which
the translator renders simply by "a man." (2) "Essence" is here the translation of
"*ti esti*" and has the sense of the "what it is" or "identity" of something. To give
something's *ti esti* is to identify it as, say, "a man" or "an animal"—or, and this is
the crux of the matter, "a white (quale)" or "a color (quale)." In 102a32ff., Aristotle
writes, "We should treat as predicates in the category of essence (*ti esti*) all such things
as it would be appropriate to mention in reply to the question 'What is the object
before you?'" Notice that the distinction between the first class of predicates and the
remaining nine which is drawn in this passage, is not that between *substance* and the
various sorts of thing that can be said of substances, but rather between the *identity*,
the *ti esti* of *an item of whatever category in the more familiar sense*, and the sort of things
that can be said of it.

[6] While changeable things must have qualia present in them, and in this sense
cannot exist apart from qualia, they can exist *apart* in the specific sense in which
qualia cannot, for primary substances are not *present* in a subject.

fuses to treat even its derivative use in, say, "Man is an animal" as that of a proper name.[7]

II

What light does the teaching of the *Categories* throw on Aristotle's analysis of changing substances into matter and form in the *Metaphysics?* One thinks right away of the fact that if anything is clear about an Aristotelian form it is that its primary mode of being is to be a *this*. Certainly the form of a materiate substance is not a *universal*, for, as Aristotle reiterates, the form is "the substance of" the composite, and the substance of a *this* must be of the nature of a *this* and never a universal.[8] Two questions obviously arise: (1) Is the form of a materiate substance not only a *this*, as contrasted with a *universal*, but a "primary substance" in the sense of the *Categories?*[9] (2) To what extent does the sense in which the form is present in either the composite or the matter correspond to the sense in which, e.g., the white-in-the-thing is *present in* the white substance?

That the form of a materiate substance is *in some sense* an "individual" or "this" is clear. Does it follow that since it is not a universal, it must be a "primary substance" in the sense of the *Categories?* No; for, as we shall see, it can be "substance" in a *derivative* sense as being the immanent principle or cause of a primary substance. It can be a *this* which is a substance as being that by virtue of which the substance in which it is present is a substance in the primary or underivative sense of the term.[10] In-

---

[7]The argument of the *Categories* implies that while we might begin to explicate "White exists" by saying "White is = Some primary substances are white," the analysis would not be complete until we said something like "White is = Some qualia are whites," though Aristotle nowhere explicitly undertakes this reduction.

[8]It is perhaps worth noting that the unmoved movers are with equal certainty not universals. Of what would they be predicated?

[9]As contrasted with the use of this and related expressions in other contexts. Thus in *Metaphysics* VII, 1032b1, 1037a5, and 1037b1, this expression is applied to the form of a materiate substance as the principle by virtue of which the latter is a substance. The form is "primary" as not itself consisting of matter and form, and as prior to the concrete individual which does consist of matter and form. Yet that the form of a materiate substance *in some sense* includes its matter will be argued below.

[10]It is essential to realize that the idea that the concrete individual is a substance in the *primary* sense of "substance" (as having separate existence) is *not* incompatible with the idea that there is an entity which though a substance in a *derivative* sense, is nevertheless *prior* to the concrete individual as a principle of its being.

deed, it can even be a *this* in a derivative sense *without being a universal*, which, after all, is the heart of the matter.

But if a form is a *this* which is a *this* and *substance* only in a derivative sense, what is it in its own character? To use Aristotle's own example, medicine is healthy *qua* capable of restoring health; but in its own character, it is, say, a concoction of juices. The answer which leaps to mind, though it won't do as it stands, is that the form is, in its own character, a quale (or quantum, or combination of these or other particulars from categories other than substance), but that it is a *form* not *qua quale*, but *qua* that by virtue of which the primary substance in which it is present *is a separate being of a certain kind*. We seem to find something like this account in Aristotle's treatment of artifacts. Of particular interest in this connection is a passage in the *Categories* where he writes (3 b 18 ff.):

> Yet species and genus do not merely indicate quality, like the term "white"; "white" indicates quality and nothing further, but species and genus determine quality with reference to a substance; they signify substance qualitatively differentiated.

To this passage should be related *Metaphysics* 1042 b 9 ff.—in which he tells us that the "principles of the beings of things" are to be found in the attributes with respect to which the various kinds of things or substances differ from one another. To this he adds the necessary reminder that the principle of the being of a substance cannot be found *simply* in a category other than substance, e.g., quality: "...none of these differentiae is substance, even when coupled with matter, yet it is what is analogous to substance in each case." This remark is, in the first instance, a reference to the view that the difference is to the genus as form to matter; that is to say, the genus is a determinable which the difference makes determinate much as *plane figure* is made determinate by *bounded by three straight lines*, and still more determinate by specifying that the lines are equally long. But of even greater significance is the fact that the difference is a *difference* of a kind of substance, as opposed to "a quality and nothing further," by determining *a way of being* a substance. For it clearly won't do to treat the category of substance as the highest determinable under which the difference falls, if the difference is construed simply as a quality, for then the category of substance would simply be the category of quality.

How is this to be understood? Aristotle, like all philosophers who take substance seriously, faced a dilemma. This dilemma concerns the relation of thing kinds or secondary substances to the criteria which things must satisfy in order to belong to these kinds. It is important to see that this dilemma depends in no way on the Socratic-Aristotelian distinction between qualities and qualia, quantities and quanta, etc., though failure to escape between the horns of the dilemma may suggest this multiplication of particulars.

On the one hand, there is a strong temptation to *identify* "S_1 is a K" with "S_1 is $Q_1 \ldots Q_k$," which identification might be expressed by the equation (where S_1 is an individual substance, $Q_1 \ldots Q_n$ its criterion qualities),

$$S_1 \text{ is a } K = S_1 \text{ is } Q_1 \ldots Q_n.$$

The violence this does to our conceptual framework is brought out by the fact that it doesn't make sense to say "S_1 is *a* Q_i." And no matter how "complex" we make the adjective "Q_i" it still doesn't make sense to say "S_1 is *a* Q_i." Even if "S_1 is Q_i" were equivalent in meaning to "S_1 is $Q_1 \ldots Q_n$," the question "What kind of thing is S_1?" (i.e., "S_1 is a *what?*" is no more answered by "S_1 is Q_i" (save by implication) than, as Urmson has pointed out, "Is this apple good?" is answered by "This apple is XYZ," where "XYZ" is the descriptive term which specifies the criteria for good apples.

In particular, it won't do to equate "S_1 is a man" with "S_1 is human," for, outside of the textbooks, "S_1 is human" means "S_1 is like a man" (cf. "Fido is almost human") or, more usually, like a good man (in some respect relevant to the discussion). Thus "S_1 is human," far from illuminating "S_1 is a man," presupposes it.

Since the question "S_1 is a what?" will not down, the attempt to reduce thing kind expressions to complex adjectives leads to the introduction of a new (and pseudo-) thing kind expression, namely "Substratum." It is "a substratum" which is $Q_1 \ldots Q_n$. The substratum is a "bare substratum" in that though "S_1 is a substratum" professes to answer the question "*Of what kind* is the object which is $Q_1 \ldots Q_n$?" it fails to do so. Clearly it is words like "man," "horse," "shoe," etc. which properly play this role.[11]

---

[11]The realization that "substratum" is a stone where there should be bread, combined with the fact that the question "S_1 is a what?" will not down, soon generates a more subtle scheme. By the simple expedient of coining a new usage according to

On the other hand (the second horn of the dilemma), the attempt to distinguish between the thing kind and its criteria may lead to equally desperate expedients. For if we insist that to say of S_1 that it is *a K* is to *characterize* S_1 in a way which does not amount to characterizing it as $Q_1 \ldots Q_n$, we are open at once to the challenge "Is it then *logically possible* for there to be a K which is not $Q_1 \ldots Q_n$ (although the latter are granted to be the criteria for being a K)?" While to take the line that "K," as distinguished from the criteria, simply *characterizes* S as "thingish" or "substantial" is to return to the "bare substratum" of the first horn.

Now the genius of Aristotle (as well as his limitations) is nowhere better illustrated than in his treatment of substance. This becomes clear once we discover how to run between the horns of the above dilemma. And, indeed, all we need to do is face up to the fact that thing kind words are *common names* and not a peculiar kind of adjective. Thus, while "S_1 is a K" *implies* that S is $Q_1 \ldots Q_n$, "K" is by no means "logical shorthand" for "being $Q_1 \ldots Q_n$." $Q_1 \ldots Q_n$ are criteria for the application of "K" without being "the meaning of 'K'" as XYZ, say, is the criterion for the application of "good" to apples without being *the meaning of* "good" as applied to apples. The point is not simply that there is "free play," "vagueness," or "open texture" in the connection

---

which the adjective "white" rests on a postulated common name "white" so that we can speak of "a white," and, in general, of "a Q," bare substrata are avoided by turning S_1 into a bundle consisting of $a Q_1$, $Q_2 \ldots$ and $a Q_n$. Since it is a fundamental feature of logic of a set of thing kind expressions belonging to a given universe of discourse, that no object belongs to more than one kind (unless these kinds are related as genus to species), the introduction of qualia soon leads to the feeling that no qulae can be of two kinds which are not related as determinable to determinate. I have trodden this road myself in Particulars, *Philosophy and Phenomenological Research*, Vol. 13 1952, and The logic of complex particulars, *Mind*, Vol. 58, 1949. My mistake was in thinking that in the language we actually use things are complex particulars, and "thing kind" words "abstract" references to sets of simple particulars. I remain convinced, however, that there is a sense in which an ideal description of the world would be in a language of this form. In any event, Aristotle's recognition of *whites* in addition to *white things* and *whiteness* is clearly not motivated by a desire to avoid substrata. Nor was his doctrine of prime matter motivated by logical puzzles relating to predication. That opposite (e.g., *a* hot) cannot act directly on opposite (e.g., *a* cold), but only qualified substratum on qualified substratum, is a fundamental principle of his *Physics*. And the very claim that first matter is, as such, "blank" and incapable of separate existence, rather than an empirical stuff such as fire or air, is argued on natural philosophical rather than narrowly logical grounds.

between *being a K* and the qualities $Q_1 \ldots Q_n$. The connection could be ever so tight, so tight that there is a definite set of conditions separately necessary and jointly sufficient to establish that something was a K and still "K" would play a unique role in discourse, a role which is quite other than that of a complex adjective. Words for thing kinds are no more shorthand for their criteria than proper names are shorthand for definite descriptions which serve as their criteria (cf. Wittgenstein: *Investigations*, §79).

I have emphasized that thing kind words are common names. By this I mean that they are common names of individuals, not proper names of universals, and, as I have already indicated, I believe that Aristotle saw this and saw it clearly. It is just because "man" is the common *name* of individual men that it can "cover the whole being of individual men." ("Man" is no more the name of a part of the individuals it names than "Julius Caesar" is the name of a part of Julius Caesar.) Also clearly reflected in his account is the fact that while a shoe may at one time be polished and at another time scuffed, which we may represent by the form

   S_1 is Q-at-t

thing-kind words do not have the form

   S_1 is a K-at-t.

A shoe is not *a shoe at a time*. Certainly there is a sense in which a piece of paper may be *now* a letter, *now* a (toy) aeroplane. But while the paper may come to be arranged in that way which makes it an aeroplane, and continue to be arranged in that way, and then cease to be arranged in that way, the aeroplane simply comes to be, exists throughout the stretch of time, and then ceases to be. To say that the paper is *now* an aeroplane is to say that the name "aeroplane" is *now* appropriately applied to the paper. And since "aeroplane" is the name of pieces of paper *qua* arranged in that manner, the name comes to be applicable to the piece of paper (the aeroplane comes to be) when the paper becomes so arranged, and ceases to be applicable (the aeroplane ceases to be) when the paper ceases to be so arranged.

We might put this by saying that *aeroplane* is predicable of the paper *qua arranged*, but the material mode of speech and the term "predicable" should not deceive us. We can, if we like, say that "aeroplane" means *the character of being an aeroplane*, and that this *character* is *attributable* to the paper *qua* arranged. The important thing is not to be misled by this manner of speaking into assimiating "being an aeroplane" to "being white."

But not only are thing kinds not reducible to the qualities which are their criteria, these qualities have, as criteria, their own logical peculiarities. We saw above that a shoe is not a shoe-at-*t*. It can now be pointed out that not only are animals not animals-at-*t*, but to be a two-footed animal is not to be an animal which is two-footed-at-*t*. Again when a certain quality, say white, is a criterion quality, its character as criterion for the thing-kind name is reflected in the fact that it has the form "white thing" or "white substance," where these phrases are *not* to be understood in terms of such contexts as "What is that white thing over there?" To refer to something as "a white thing" in the sense of this question is not to imply that the object would cease to be the thing it is if it ceases to be white. For the question has the force of

That thing over there, which is (now) white, of what
kind is it? it is *a what?*

On the other hand, as the form of the criterion-predicate, "white substance" indicates not only that to be white in this sense is not to be white-at-a-time, but implies that something which was not in this sense white would not be a thing of the relevant kind (i.e., that "being white" in this sense is a criterion for the applicability of the corresponding common name.

III

Let us apply these considerations to Aristotle's account of artifacts, for example, a shoe. "Shoe," then, is a common noun applicable to pieces of leather *qua* qualified by certain criterion qualities. "Shoe" is not a complex adjective, nor is it defined by qualities, but by qualities "determined with reference to substance." A shoe is a *this* in that it is *a shoe*. For to be a *this* in the primary Aristotelian sense is to be not simply *not a universal*, but to be an instance of a thing kind.[12]

---

[12]In *Metaphysics* 1049a19-b2, which begins with the familiar characterization of prime matter as "that which is no longer with reference to something else called 'thaten,'" Aristotle distinguishes between predication in which the subject is a "this" (a concrete individual) and predication in which the subject is not a "this" but, rather, matter. He writes: "For the subject or substratum is differentiated by being a 'this' or not being one; i.e., the substratum of *modifications* is, e.g., a man, i.e., a

It is against this background that we can understand Aristotle's denial that matter is (save in a derivative sense) a *this*. For while the matter of which a shoe is made is a particular in a broad sense as contrasted with a universal, it is not a *this* in the sense of "a K." Notice that we speak of "a shoe" but of "a *piece of* leather"; "a statue" but "a *chunk of* marble," and so on. "Leather," "marble," "bronze" are not thing kind words, and Aristotle's distinction between *thises* and *the matter for thises* reflects an important distinction. What Aristotle has in mind is that when you have said of something that it is a piece of leather, you have not classified it under a secondary substance, and that even when you say "a piece of leather of such and such a size and shape," you have not yet characterized it as a *this*, though you will have done so *by implication* if by virtue of being a piece of leather thus qualified, it conforms to the criteria for a thing kind, e.g., shoe.[13]

Now if the shoe "as a whole" is the instance of the secondary substance *shoe* (a fact which reflects the role of "shoe" as a common name), what is the *form* of the shoe as contrasted with its matter? Among the conditions to be met by an answer are the following: (1) The form is not a universal, yet it is not *simply* a *this* or primary substance. (2) The form is not a quale, quantum, etc., nor

---

body and a soul, while the modification is 'musical' or 'pale'. . . . Wherever this is so, then, the ultimate subject is a substance; but when this is not so but the predicate is a form and a "this," the ultimate subject is matter and material substance." The concluding sentence is likely to be misinterpreted and to lead to unnecessary puzzlement unless it is realized that "the predicate is a form and a 'this'" has the sense of "the predicate is 'a K' (e.g., 'a man," 'a shoe,' etc.)."

[13]It might be thought that "piece of leather" is a thing kind expression, even if "leather" is not. Let me indicate, in an Aristotelian mood, why it is only "in a sense" that this is so. Artifacts are purpose servers. The purpose of shoes, for example—to protect and embellish the feet—is part of the very "meaning" of "shoe." But pieces of leather *as such* are purpose-servers only by being raw material for direct purpose-servers. The context "piece of . . .," "chunk of . . .," etc., so characteristic of *recipes*, turn words for kinds of material ("leather," "marble," etc.) into expressions which, as far as purpose is concerned, imply at most that their designata can be the material cause of items which, as correctly designated by a proper thing kind expression (in the universe of discourse of artifacts), are direct purpose-servers. A shoe can, indeed, be part of the matter for, e.g., a store window dummy; yet, it remains a purpose-server in its own right. But something which is *merely* "a piece of . . ." is *only* a purpose-server in a derivative sense. The fact that leather is *made* doesn't mean that pieces of leather are artifacts in the *primary* sense of this important Aristotelian expression. Aristotle views even the elements in the context of craftsmanship (including the "craftsmanship" of living things). It is for this reason that he views pieces of earth, air, etc., as *thises* only in a derivative sense.

any combination of these, for it is that by virtue of which the shoe is a primary *substance;* yet, it cannot be explained without reference to categories other than substance. The answer, as far as I can see, is to be found by a more careful analysis of the secondary substance *shoe*. We have been representing it (in the material mode, so to speak) as *such and such qualities determined to substance*. Would we not, however, better reflect the above analysis if we represented it by *such and such qualities determined to substance in leather?* If so, it springs to the attention that shoes, after all, can be made of other materials, for the attributes which justify the application of the name "shoe" to a piece of leather can, at least in principle, be present in these other materials. Thus, the form of shoes taken universally is the secondary substance *shoe* as represented immediately above ("leathern shoe") without the specification of the material in which the criterion qualities are to be present. On the other hand, the form (taken universally) is not these qualities *simpliciter*, but these qualities determined with reference to substance (i.e., as criterion qualities for a thing kind name) *in some appropriate material or other*. Thus Aristotle can say that the form of *this shoe* is, in a certain sense, the shoe itself. For, to follow up the above line of thought, the form of *this shoe* is the shoe itself *qua* a foot-covering made of *some* appropriate kind of matter. The form is *in this disjunctive sense* (indicated by "some") more "abstract" than the shoe, but it is not for this reason a *universal*. Furthermore, the form, in this "abstract" (disjunctive) way includes the whole being of the individual shoe. The form *qua form* is incapable of separate existence as disjunctive facts are incapable of existing apart from "basic" facts, but it is not "present in" the shoe as a quale is present in a primary substance. For the form taken universally is fully predicable of the subject. S_1 is not only a covering for the feet made of *leather*, it is a covering for the feet made of *some appropriate material or other*. The sense, therefore, in which the form of the shoe is present in the shoes and is an *incomplete* entity incapable of separate existence, is not to be simply identified with the sense in which qualia and quanta are present in primary substances, nor is it to be identified with the sense in which universals are incapable of separate existence.[14]

---

[14]That the form component of the materiate universal (secondary substance) *man* might also be found in other materials is suggested by *Metaphysics* 1036a31ff.

It is, I think, clear that something like the above distinction, can be drawn without a commitment to the theory of prediction of the *Categories*. As far as I can see, however, Aristotle remained committed to this theory throughout his career.[15] And this is the occasion to admit that Aristotle sometimes seems to think of the form of a materiate substance as a substance which is more truly substance than the substance of which it is the form—particularly in the case of living things, where Human Soul, for example, seems at times to be a thing kind which is more truly a thing kind than the materiate universal Man; the soul of Socrates to be in a *primary* sense a *this*, and Socrates a *this* in a derivative sense as having a primary *this* within him. To be sure, the soul of Socrates would not be primary substance in the full sense of the *Categories*, for it is incapable of separate existence. But, then, is any being truly capable of separate existence save those incorporeal intelligences which everlastingly think on thought?

That Aristotle *could* think along these lines was made possible by the fact that his theory of predication provides a built-in way of going from "this matter is (. . .)" to "a (. . .) is in this matter." Is not this the key to Aristotle's claim that whereas "'to be man' is not identical with the essence of man, 'to be soul' *is* identical with the essence of soul?" For the latter treats souls as items which are not only the essence of the living things to which they belong, *but themselves have an essence*. What essence? Do we not have here an echo of the *Phaedo*, of the idea that souls are essentially alive, and, as alive, make the composites to which they belong derivatively alive?[16]

---

[15]See, for example, *Metaphysics* 1077b5 and 1087a17; also 991a14.

[16]The *Phaedo* interprets the soul of a living thing as *the alive in the thing*. As the white in the thing is white, so the alive in the (living) thing is alive. At the "approach of death," it, like every *f*-in-the-thing at the approach of its opposite, must either "withdraw" or "perish." It is argued that unlike, say, the white in a white thing at the approach of black, it cannot "perish," and hence must "withdraw."

V

RAW MATERIALS, SUBJECTS, AND SUBSTRATA

I

The "matter" of the Aristotelian system is raw material for changing things or substances, the fundamental model of the system being that of the craftsman who brings ingredients together in terms of a recipe to produce an artifact which serves a purpose. Substances proper, living things, are characterized by internal teleology. They are self-developing and self-regulating agencies, the activity of which is to be understood in terms of the analogical conception of a craftsman who consciously and deliberately enlarges his body, regulates its activity, and makes copies of himself.

Whereas living things are artisan-analogues, artifact-analogues, goal-analogues, and means-analogues all rolled into one, and are *beings* in their own right, artifacts-proper, as such, have being only in relation to the purposes of men. Thus the *fundamenta* of the analogy whereby we understand beings proper are themselves beings or substances in a derivative sense.

The elements, like living things, have an internal teleology. For their motion, like the growth of plants, is conceived by analogy with the pursuit of goals. But they are more like slaves than craftsmen, for they are essentially raw material for living things, and are therefore essentially characterized by an external teleology which is conceived by analogy with the status of a list of ingredients in a recipe for, say, a cake.

But my aim is not to explore the familiar structure of the Aristotelian system as a whole. I shall limit myself to some logical features of the role played by matter as raw material in this system, with particular reference to the theory of predication.

II

Words like "marble," "leather," "cloth," and "salt" are words for kinds of material. The context in which they belong is that of a recipe, thus:

a cubic yard of marble
twenty bricks of brick
a piece of cloth 2 inches x 10 inches.

One speaks of a "dog" (a substance in the philosopher's sense) but not of a "cement" (a substance in the ordinary sense). Words like "cloth" and "brick" are ambiguous, thus "cloth" in one sense means piece of cloth in the other, and "brick" in one sense means standard chunk of brick in the other. "Material" as a noun is the generic term which can take the place of words for specific kinds of material in the above contexts, thus,

a cubic yard of material
twenty chunks of material
a piece of material.

In English, the term "matter" does not seem to function as a synonym for "material." Thus we do not ordinarily speak of a piece of matter. Philosophers, however, bully this term to serve their purposes by using the phrase "the matter of *x*" to have the sense of *the material of which x consists or is made*. "Matter" in this sense, of course, is not to be confused with "matter" as a collective term for material things. Nor should it be assumed that "material thing" means "thing made of (or consisting of) matter." For this is equivalent to construing "material thing" as "thing made of or consisting of a portion of some *material* or other," and to view the world in terms of the framework of raw materials, tools, and ends to be achieved.

A universe in which "matter alone is real," where this has the sense of "all individual things are simply portions of matter (material)," is as logically impossible as a wife without a husband. There must "be" the things for which the "matter" is the material. On the other hand, a universe in which "matter alone is real," where this has the sense of "all individual things are material things," is not in the same way absurd, if absurd it is.

III

A second recurrent theme in classical discussions of matter has its fundamental source in a mistaken interpretation of statements of the form "*S* is *P*." Consider the statement:

A. Socrates is wise (courageous, snubnosed, etc.).

This is clearly logically equivalent to:

A'. Socrates has (or is characterized by) wisdom (courage, snub-nosedness, etc.).

It is only too easy to conclude that the former is not only logically equivalent to but has the same sense as the latter.[1] This by itself would not suffice to generate the idea of a substratum. But suppose the argument continued as follows:

Socrates is not identical with the wisdom which he has, nor with the courage which he has, nor the snubnosedness which he has, etc.

This, of course, is true. Socrates is not identical with his attributes taken severally. At this stage, the temptation arises to ask "What does 'Socrates' refer to or name, if it is something distinct from all his attributes taken severally?" and to answer:

It refers to a substratum which is neither wise nor courageous nor snubnosed, etc.

is surely as false as stating in somewhat different terms a logical contrary of the original statement, A, with which we began.

Put thus explicitly, the fallacy is so transparent that no one would be taken in by it. The step from:

What "Socrates" refers to is not (i.e., is not identical with) wisdom

to:

What "Socrates" refers to is not wise

is so obviously fallacious that no one would take it. But before adding a missing step which explains why philosophers have, on occasion, made this move, let me first sketch the final outcome of this line of thought. It is the thesis that what we refer to strictly or philosophically speaking is *bare substrata* (i.e., substrata which are neither hot nor cold not white nor wise, etc.). Items which *are* hot or cold or white or wise are *wholes* consisting of a substratum and an adequate bunch of attributes. (The truth, of course, is that it is not *things* but *facts* which consist of individuals and attributes.)

The missing link which disguises the above howler is the role of such expressions as:

---

[1] This is the exact counterpart of supposing that because "p" and "It is true that *p*" are logically equivalent, they have the same sense.

the greenness of this leaf
the wisdom of Socrates
the rectangularity of this table top.

These expressions obviously refer to *singulars*, that is to say, to "individuals" in that broad sense in which anything properly referred to by a singular term is an individual. But it can readily be seen, I believe, that these singulars or individuals are universals. Thus, consider the sentence:

The greenness of this leaf is identical with (or different from) the greenness of that leaf.

Notice that whereas the expressions listed above are singular terms, the occurrences in them of "greenness," "wisdom" and "rectangularity" are *not*. Rather they are common noun expressions, "the greenness of this leaf" having the same form as "the owner of this house," and the above sentence the same form as:

The owner of this house is identical with (or different from) the owner of that house.

But it is easy to confuse the fact that *the greenness* of this leaf is an individual (in the *broad* sense—the sense in which formal universals as well as perceptible things are individuals or singulars) which is *a greenness* with the idea that the greenness of this leaf is an individual (in the *narrow* sense which connotes spatio-temporal location) which *is green*.[2] Thus is born the widespread conception of changeable things as consisting of, or at least containing as ingredients, dependent, or "abstract" particulars of which the greenness of this leaf, thus construed, would be an example. For, once one is committed to the idea that the greenness of the leaf is a spatio-temporally individuated green item, the inevitable conclusion is that greennesses are the *primary* green items and that ordinary changeable things are green by virtue of *having greenness*. And we can now appreciate how, thinking of the leaf as green in a derivative sense,

$$L \text{ is green} = \text{a greenness belong to } L$$

---

[2] A note on the dangers of the use of color examples in discussing the problem of predication might not be out of place. Color words are radically ambiguous in a way which easily leads to serious confusion. Thus, "red" is (1) an adjective which applies to things, e.g., this is red; (2) a common noun which applies to *shades* of red, e.g., crimson is a red, and (3) a singular term (equivalent to "redness") e.g., red is a color.

one inevitably concludes either that there is a subject which is not a greenness or sweetness in which these qualia inhere, so that

$$L \text{ is green } = \text{ a greenness inheres in } L;$$

or one takes the line that things are patterns of greennesses or sweetnesses, in which case we have the formula

$$L \text{ is green } = \text{ a greenness is an element of } L.$$

It is not my purpose to examine the view that changeable things are "patterns" of greennesses or sweetnesses. It is a venerable position, and is certainly to be found in Plato. I shall limit myself to pointing out that Aristotle rejects the view that the elements could be hotnesses, coldnesses, moistnesses, and drynesses on the ground that it makes interaction unintelligible. For, as Plato emphasized in the *Phaedo* (a dialogue to which Aristotle is closer than is the Plato of the *Timaeus*), a coldness cannot become hot without ceasing to be. But what else could a hotness *do* but warm that on which it acts? One must either abandon the very idea of interaction, or say that it is subjects qualified by opposites which interact, rather than the opposites themselves. It is important to note that Aristotle need not have construed (if he did construe) these subjects as substrata in the dubious sense generated by the above described misinterpretation of predication.

It is also interesting to note that the argument which Aristotle gives in the *De Generatione* for a matter more basic than the elements rests on physical considerations pertaining to the transmutation of the elements. Yet it would be a mistake to construe the argument as physical *rather than*, in a broad sense, logical. The core of the argument is the idea that one's willingness to speak of water as "changing into" rather than as "ceasing to exist and being replaced by air" does imply an identical subject which is first moist and cold and then moist and hot. Once again it should be emphasized that this subject does not have to be construed as a substratum which is neither hot nor cold nor moist nor dry, though, of course, this is what one will be tempted to say if one is already committed to the theory of predication examined above. It would suffice to say that the identical subject is capable of being at different times cold-dry, cold-moist, warm-moist, warm-dry, and is, at every moment in one or other of these states.

Of course, if one already has as one's paradigm of qualitative change:

$$\text{This-}X \text{ was } f \text{ and is } f'$$

where "X" replaces thing kind expressions (e.g., "man," "house") or, at a lower level, expressions of the form "portion of M" (e.g., "chunk of marble") which are the analogues of thing kind expressions proper, then when one comes to the elements and tries to use the formula:

$$\text{This portion of } PM \text{ was cold-moist and is hot-moist}$$

one runs up against the fact that whereas there are empirical criteria for being a dog or a piece of marble which are present both before and after qualitative change, there would seem to be no such criteria for being a portion of primary matter. To be sure, the *capacity* to be characterized (in sequence) by pairs from the list of fundamental opposites would persist through transmutation. But to accept this capacity as the criterion for being a portion of PM is, or so it might seem, to commit oneself to the idea that PM "as such" has no "positive" or "intrinsic" nature.

Notice, however, that if instead of the above our paradigm of qualitative change were:

$$S \text{ was } f \text{ and is } f'$$

where "S" is simply a referring expression, e.g., a demonstrative, then to grant that there are no "occurrent" (as contrasted with "dispositional") characteristics which persist through transmutation, e.g.,

$$S \text{ was cold-moist and is hot-moist}$$

is not to grant that S has no "positive" or "intrinsic" nature, unless one assumes that the nature of a continuant, if it is to be "positive" or "intrinsic" must include abiding "occurrent" qualties. One can, of course, stipulate a usage according to which this would be true *ex vi terminorum*—but then it does not seem that there must be anything particularly perplexing about subjects which do not have, in this stipulated sense, a "positive" or "intrinsic" nature.

Certainly from the fact that S has no occurrent qualities which abide through transmutation, one could infer neither that there were no empirical characteristics in terms of which it could be identified, nor that it has no empirical qualities. "*S* is not *abidingly* hot" does not entail "*S* is not hot." Thus, while transmutation would be a radical change, it would not lead us to speak of a qualityless substratum unless we were already doing so because of a faulty theory of predication.

Suppose, now, we return to the idea that every proper subject of change must in principle be identifiable as either a "*K*," where "*K*" is a thing kind expression proper, or a portion of *M*, where "*M*" is a word for a kind of material. We now notice that where the context is one of craftsmanship, the immediate raw material for an artifact has and, it would seem (logically), *must* have "occurrent" qualities which abide through the changes involved in working it up into a finished product. (Compare processed leather before and after it is worked into a shoe.) Let us call these occurrent characteristics the "positive" or "intrinsic" nature of the material. From this standpoint transmutation would involve a "material" which "has no positive or intrinsic nature." But again, that this is so does not mean that in any paradoxical sense transmutation would involve a qualityless substratum. It would simply mean that the "*M*" of the procrustean formula

$$S \text{ is either a } K \text{ or a portion of } M$$

(which presents the alternatives for answering the question "What is *S*?") is being by analogy to cover what are now recognized as proper subjects of change which are not in the literal craftsman sense pieces of raw material. But that Aristotle's concept of matter, and of primary matter in particular, is a concept by analogy is scarcely news.

These considerations lend weight to the idea that the concept of primary matter, though rooted in the form "this portion of "*M*," is simply the concept of the ultimate subject of predication with respect to changeable things in space and time,[3] the concept showing in its formula the traces of its analogical formation route, but having no correspondingly overt expression of the qualifications which, in effect, limit the analogy to the essential of an abiding subject of change.

But surely, it will be said, the qualifications do not remove the

---

[3]For a discussion of the idea that the ultimate subject of predication is in some cases matter and in other cases primary substances, see the next section.

"indeterminateness" of primary matter, a trait on which Aristotle insists, and which gives it a richer metaphysical role than that of the bare concept of an abiding subject of change. There is *something* to this challenge, and it must be taken seriously; though it does not, in my opinion, militate against the essential correctness of the above interpretation. Let us examine the sense in which secondary matter is indeterminate. This indeterminateness is logically necessary, and is a consequence of the fact that words for materials belong in the context:

Amount x of M.

A raw material which came in indivisible chunks which could not be put together would be a "degenerate" case of material. There would be no point in giving it a name with a grammar akin to that of "leather" or "marble." A common noun would suffice. The recipes involving it would read ". . .take a glub."

This indeterminateness belongs primarily to the kind, not to the individual. It is *marble* which is indeterminate, not (save in a derivative sense) this piece of marble. And Marble is indeterminate only in the sense that "x is a piece of marble" does not entail "x is (say), one cubic foot in size." Clearly indeterminateness in this sense is a feature of the Aristotelian elements.

Now something akin to this indeterminateness is a feature of the ultimate subject of predication with respect to changeable things, even where the concept of such a subject has not been formed by analogy in the Aristotelian manner. For it is a necessary feature of the concept of such a subject that it have *some location or other* in space and time. The indeterminateness to which "some . . .or other" gives expression is, again, an indeterminateness pertaining to the "kind" and not to the individual. Now if "having some location or other in space and time" entails and is entailed by "having some size or other," one can see how the formula:

This portion of PM (every portion of which has some size or other)

could have a philosophical force which was indistinguishable, save by its conceptual roots—a distinction which should not, however, be minimized—from the more familiar:

This ultimate subject of predication (every one of which has some location in space and time or other).

IV

The above remarks need to be supplemented by some comments on the notion of an ultimate subject of predication. The contrast between ultimate and "non-ultimate," which I have in mind, does not concern the distinction between individuals and universals. I would, indeed, defend the thesis that individual things and persons in space and time are the ultimate subjects of predication. Also the more radical thesis that they are the *only* subjects of predication. But that is a story for another occasion. The contrast I now have in mind is developed by Aristotle in *Metaphysics*, 1049a 19–b2. He writes:

> For the subject or substratum is differentiated by being a "this" or not being one, i.e., the substratum of modifications is, e.g., a man, i.e., a body and a soul, while the modification is "musical" or "pale." Whenever this is so, then, the ultimate subject is a substance; but when this is not so, but the predicate is a form and a "this," the ultimate subject is matter and material substance.

Aristotle is here contrasting predication which can be represented by the formula:

1. /substance/ is /modification/

with that which can be represented by the schema:

2. /matter/ is /substance/

In (1), the substance in question is an individual substance, a *synholon* consisting of form and matter, thus an individual man. In (2), the word "substance" is place-holding for a substance-kind expression, e.g., "man." To be a "this" in the sense of the passage quoted is to be an instance of a thing kind. Indeed, Aristotle uses "is a this" as we might use "is a K" where "K" is a representative expression for thing kind words such as "man." Thus the conclusion of the passage quoted could be written: ". . .but when this is not so, but the predicate is a form and a K, the ultimate subject is matter and material being." Now it is important to see that while Aristotle is committing himself to the thesis that whenever a statement classifies a changeable subject under a thing kind expression, the subject is matter, he is *not* committing himself to the thesis that where the predicate is not a thing kind expression, the subject is a substance consisting of both matter and form (a synholon). In other words, he is not committing himself to the thesis that the *only* predication in which matter is the ultimate subject is predication in which the subject is brought under a thing kind.

Rather, what he is claiming is that whereas all thing kind predications have matter as their ultimate subject, *some* non-thing kind predicates presuppose that their subject is a *substance* (i.e., falls under a thing kind). The examples he gives are essential. He could not have used "heavy" instead of "musical" or "white" instead of "pale."[4] The point he is making could be put by saying that a sentence which classifies a subject under a thing kind is an answer to the question: "What is *x*?" This question cannot presuppose that the subject is a *synholon*, for the answer could very well be (for example): "*x* is (nothing but) a piece of marble." Thus even though *x* is in point of fact, a *synholon*, the statement, "*x* is a *K*," does not refer to, it *qua synholon*. It refers to it *qua* something which may or may not be a *synholon* (i.e., *qua* denotable portion of some matter or other).

V

In conclusion, I want to touch briefly on the nature of Aristotle's distinction between form and matter, and on the question whether a "real distinction" exists between the form and the matter of an individual substance. As I see it, the primary mode of being of a form, e.g., the form Shoe or the form Man, is its being as a *this* or individual, the individual form of this shoe or this man. As individual form it is, so to speak, private to the individual of which it is the form. For the form of an individual substance is, according to Aristotle, the "substance of" the substance, and, he insists, the substance of an individual cannot be common to many. We must, therefore, distinguish between form as individual form and form taken universally, just as we must distinguish between matter as individual matter and matter taken universally. It is essential to see that if a changeable thing is a *synholon* or "whole," its "parts," in the primary sense, are an individual form and an individual piece of matter. It is only in

---

[4]It is interesting to note that in the first edition of his translation of the *Metaphysics* Ross translated "leukos" as "white" instead of the "pale" to which he subsequently changed it.

a derivative sense that the form taken universally is a "part" of the changeable thing.

But how is this "part-whole" relationship to be understood? Clearly, a metaphor is involved. How is it to be interpreted? Are we to suppose that as in the *ordinary* sense the *spatial* togetherness of two individuals (the parts) constitutes a new individual (the whole), so in the *metaphorical* sense a nonspatial, metaphysical togetherness of individual matter and individual form (the "parts") constitutes a new (and complete) individual (the "whole")? The answer, I submit, is no, for the simple reason that the individual matter and form of an individual substance are not *two* individuals, but *one*. The individual form of this shoe is the shoe itself; the individual matter of this shoe is *also* the shoe itself, and there can scarcely be a real distinction between the shoe and itself.

What, then, is the difference between the individual form and matter of this shoe if they are the same *thing*? The answer should, by now, be obvious. The individual form of this shoe is the shoe *qua:*

> (piece of some appropriate material or other—in this case leather) *serving the purpose of protecting and embellishing the feet.*

The individual matter of this shoe is the shoe *qua:*

> *piece of leather* (so worked as to serve some purpose or other—in this case to protect and embellish the feet.)

Thus, the "parts" involved are not incomplete individuals in the real order, but the importantly different parts of the formula

> (piece of leather) (serving to protect and embellish the feet)

projected on the individual thing of which they are true.

VI

It is important to see that although Aristotle flirted, in the *Categories* and elsewhere, with the Platonic doctrine that changeable things have dependent or abstract particulars as ingredients, neither his argument for, nor his interpretation of, the thesis that the forms of individual changeable things are themselves, in their primary mode of being, individuals, depends on this doctrine. I believe that the real nature of Aristotle's thought on this topic can be brought out most effectively by a careful re-examination of a much misunderstood example.

This bronze ball is a spherical piece of bronze. Its matter is the piece of bronze—not, however, *qua* having the spherical shape it in point of fact has, but rather *qua* capable of a variety of shapes, one of which is the spherical. There is little difficulty, clearly, about the distinction between the matter of this bronze sphere, and the matter of this bronze sphere taken universally. The distinction is represented by the distinction between the referring expression: "This piece of bronze," and the predicative expression "...a piece of bronze," which stands for a quasi thing kind. Bronze is a kind of matter, and "piece of bronze" is an analogue of a thing kind in the basic sense illustrated by Tiger or Shoe. Thus we can say, as a first approximation, that this bronze ball is this piece of bronze *qua* spherical, and, in general, that bronze balls are spherical pieces of bronze.

But what of the form? We have already abandoned the idea that the form of this bronze ball is the supposed abstract particular which is its shape ("this sphericity" it might be called, if there were such a thing). Is it, then, the universal *sphericity*, or, perhaps, *sphere*? To say that it is either, is to run counter to explicit and reiterated statements to the effect that the "substance of" a substance cannot be a universal. But if so, *what* is the alternative? Part of the answer lies in distinguishing between the referring and the predicative uses of the phrase "a sphere" as illustrated by the two sentences: "That is a sphere," and "A sphere is on the table." We have been using such expressions as "this sphere" as equivalent to "a sphere" in its use to refer to an individual sphere as a sphere. In these terms we might say that the form of the bronze sphere is the bronze sphere itself, not, however, qua *bronze* sphere, but simply *qua sphere*. We might add that spheres can be made of many materials and that while to characterize an item as a sphere is to imply that it is made of some appropriate material or other, to characterize it as a bronze sphere is to class it as a sphere *and* to pin it down to one specific kind of material.

But while it is more accurate to say that the "individual form" is *this sphere* rather than what we referred to as "this sphericity," it is still only an approximation to the truth. The final step is to distinguish between "a sphere" and "a ball." When they are carefully distinguished, the former concerns a class of mathematical objects, the latter a class of material objects. Thus, "a sphere" has a referring use in which it refers to a particular instance of a certain mathematical kind, and a predicative use in which it says that a certain region of Space (or Extension—*not* Extendedness) is so bounded as to constitute a (mathematical) sphere. Space or Extension plays a role analogous to that of matter in changeable things, and can be called "intelligible matter." It is, of course, a central Aristotelian theme that mathematical objects[5] and the intelligible matter "in" which they exist are dependent beings. Just how the dependence of this domain on that of material things is to be construed is left somewhat of a mystery. As I see it, we have here a prime example of Aristotle's ability to rest content with partial insights, repressing the temptation to push them into a "complete" but erroneous system.[6]

While "sphere," then, marks out a class of mathematicals, "ball" marks out a class of physical things. It should not however be taken to mark out certain physical things merely *qua* having a certain shape. As a true thing kind expression, or, more to the point, as a means of clarifying the status of true thing kind expressions, it should be taken in the sense of "spherical material object serving a certain purpose," as, for example, "tennis ball." The reader is invited to think of a game in which a ball is used which might be made of any of a number of materials,[7] including bronze, thus "pusho"; and in that context to distinguish between "a pusho ball" and "a bronze pusho ball."

---

[5] The descendants of the "*ta mathematika*" which hover around the Platonic dialogues.

[6] In a paper dealing primarily with Time, I have suggested that Space (and Time) are "metrical entities" related to the domain of physical objects by "correspondence rules" so designed that an object or event occupies a region determined by discounting not only error, but all physical forces pertaining to observed measurement. Though they share many of the logical features of theoretical frameworks with, e.g., atomic theory, this discounting or division of labor accounts for the *Unding*-ish character of Space and Time, correctly stressed by Kant. The correspondence rules which correlate operationally defined metrical properties with the occupation of regions of Space (or Time) occupied are the counterpart of Aristotle's notion that mathematicals exist when boundaries are marked out by *physical* differences. Further elaboration of these points would bring out the essential truth of Carnap's contention that Space is an ordered set of triads of real numbers *qua* coordinated with a certain family of measuring operations.

[7] Even if *in point of fact* it can satisfy the purpose of the game only by being made of a specific material (e.g., as having a certain size and weight it must be made of bronze). The "logical possibility" remains—as long as the purpose does not specify that the ball be made of bronze (a topic for further exploration)—that it might be made of some other material.

In its predicative use, the expression "a bronze pusho ball" stands for a materiate thing kind in which *pusho ball* is the formal element and *bronze* the material. In its referring use, it refers to a "this" *qua* bronze pusho ball (i.e., *qua* a pusho ball and *qua* made of bronze). Thus the individual which is *a bronze pusho ball* is necessarily *a piece of bronze* which is *a pusho ball*. What it is *essentially* is *a pusho ball*. It is a pusho ball by virtue of the fact that being a piece of matter of a kind which can satisfy the criteria for being a pusho ball, it does in point of fact satisfy these criteria. And even though "a pusho ball" refers to the *individual* in an *indeterminate* way in the sense that there is much that is true of the individual, including the material of which it is made, which we cannot infer from this referring expression, the reference is determinate in the sense that the criteria specify the material of which the object is to be made with reference to a determinate purpose which the object is to serve. Thus to refer to something as a pusho ball is to refer determinately as one would not be doing if one referred to it as *a ball played in some game or other*. For unless there are varieties of the game of pusho ball, there is no more determinate purpose to which the materials for making pusho balls are to be selected. It is the *teleological* character of artifact kinds which enables us to understand why *bronze pusho ball* is not a species of *pusho ball* as *soccer ball* is a species of *football*.

The answer to our question, thus, is that it is *this piece of bronze qua* pusho ball (i.e., *this pusho ball*, which is what *this essentially* is). It is *this* bronze pusho ball *as a whole* and not an abstract particular (in a sense of the *Categories*) which is an instance of the formal element in the materiate universal *bronze pusho ball*. The sense in which the form of the bronze pusho ball is a this which is "in" the bronze pusho ball is *not* that in which a quale is a this which is "present in" a substance. The form can indeed be said to be an "abstract particular," but only in the sense of a particular *considered abstractly* (i.e., a particular *qua* what it essentially is). To consider it as a bronze pusho ball is, of course, also to consider it abstractly, but as an instance of a materiate thing kind, rather than as an instance of a thing kind *simpliciter*. Obviously, then, the sense in which the form of a thing is "in" the thing is different from that in which the qualities of a thing are "in" the thing. But this should surprise no one who has reflected on the multi-

tudinous uses of "in." And similar considerations obtain in connection with the statement that changeable things "consist of"
matter and form.

Before we consider the relationship between the sense in which
the form of a materiate substance is "in" the substance, and that
in which one of its *qualia* is "present in" it, let us tentatively apply
the above considerations to the case where the primary substance
is Socrates and the secondary substance or thing kind is *man*. We
can cut through the preliminaries by turning directly to the question: "Is man *essentially* a being of flesh and bone?" To this question
Aristotle's answer is that there is an essence, *rational animal of flesh
and bone* only in the sense in which there is the essence *bronze* (*pusho*)
ball, which is to say that in that narrow sense of essence in which
the essence of something is its form, flesh, and bone do not belong
to the essence of man. Here we must be careful, for there is a sense
in which flesh and bone do belong to the essence of man, and,
indeed, bronze to the pusho ball. For while being a pusho ball
does not include being made of bronze, it does include *being made
of some appropriate material or other*. Similarly being a man includes
being made of some appropriate material or other, and hence
includes being made of flesh and bone, in that sense in which
somebody includes *Smith*.

Thus the fact that the essence of Socrates is his form (i.e., his
soul) is the parallel of the fact that the essence of this bronze pusho
ball is this pusho ball. And if it be granted that we use the name
"Socrates" to refer to a certain substance *qua rational animal made
of this mixture of flesh and bone*, the above suffices to show that it
would be more tidily used to refer to it *qua rational animal made of
this piece of appropriate material*. Using it thus we could say not only
that the essence of Socrates is his form but that Socrates is identical
with this essence (i.e., with his form). And the above analysis
makes it clear that we could do so without implying that Socrates
is an immaterial substance. For in exactly the same way, given
that a certain pusho ball is called "Beauty," we could say that the
essence of Beauty is its form and that Beauty is identical with its
essence (i.e., its form). The fact that Socrates is identical with his
form no more implies that Socrates can exist apart from matter
than does the similar fact about Beauty.

If this analysis of Aristotle's account of forms as "thises" is correct, we can say that he distinguishes between the primary mode of being of forms, which is to be, for example, this bronze pusho ball *qua* this pusho ball, and a secondary mode of being, which is to be, for example, the universal *pusho ball*. Thus, while in the primary sense, forms are "thises," there is a secondary sense in which they are universals. It is only to be expected, then, that in many passages Aristotle clearly has universals in mind when he speaks of form. That the forms of perishable things are individuals enables us to understand how "pure forms" or "immaterial beings" can be individuals. For if we think of the form of a perishable thing as a universal "in" a piece of matter, one will think of an immaterial substance as a universal which is not "in" a piece of matter.

Yet while the form that is "in" the bronze ball is, in the primary sense, a "this" or individual, Aristotle finds it also appropriate to say that the universal ball is "in" the bronze ball. For although he does not clearly distinguish between the ball (of which the universal is *not* a constituent) and the fact that the ball exists (of which it *is*), he does the next best thing by distinguishing between the sense in which the form as "this" is "in" the bronze ball from the sense in which the form as universal is "in" it.

That the forms of perishable things are "thises" in the sense analyzed above is no mere incidental feature of Aristotle's metaphysics. For if the primary mode of being of forms were that of universals, then instead of being as perishable as the individuals of which they are the forms, they would be imperishable and eternal, and a central theme in Aristotle's theology would be lost. It is just because the forms of perishable things are as perishable as the things themselves that beings which are pure forms and, therefore, imperishable individuals are required to be the real foundation of beginningless and endless time.

VI

MEDITATIONS LEIBNITZIENNES [1]

I

My purpose in this paper is to explore the thesis, so central to Leibnitz' philosophy, that the world in which we live is but one of many possible worlds, decidedly more numerous than blackberries. The exploration I have in mind is partly historical, concerned with the questions "How exactly is Leibnitz' thesis to be understood?" and "How did he defend it?" I also have in mind the question, "Is this thesis, or something reasonably like it, true?" My starting point will be Leibnitz' contention—so bruskly rejected by Arnauld in his first letter—that "the individual concept of each person includes once for all everything which can ever happen to him."

Now the phrase "individual concept" will be at the center of the stage, once the argument is fully under way. For the moment, it will suffice to characterize the individual concept of a substance as the sense of God's proper name for that individual; thus, the individual concept of Julius Caesar is the sense of the divine name for the individual substance we refer to as Julius Caesar. Although Leibnitz insists that we have a confused grasp of this sense, which consists of our *petites perceptions* in so far as they represent Julius Caesar, this confused grasp of the individual concept is not, of course, *our* concept of Julius Caesar. For the sense of the term "Julius Caesar," as we use it, is not, strictly speaking, an individual concept at all but—one is tempted to say—a peculiar kind of general concept which applied to many *possible* individuals, though only to one *actual* individual. And, indeed, one is tempted to say

---

[1] A shortened form of this essay was read as the opening paper in a symposium on Rationalism at the May, 1958, meeting of the American Philosophical Association. In preparing the manuscript for publication, I have limited myself to stylistic changes and, where matters of substance were involved, to the omission of less fortunate passages. I have, however, added a brief discussion (Section III) of Leibnitz' general theory of relations to provide a background for the more specific discussion of causality.

that for Leibnitz, the "names" we use are not really names at
all, but a peculiar kind of general term.

But more about names, divine and human, individual concepts,
and possible individuals later. For our present purposes, the important thing about the individual concept of an existing substance is that though as *concept* it exists in the *divine understanding*,
it exists *in re* as the *nature* of the substance. This gives us a second
formulation of the contention which so startled Dr. Arnauld, to
wit, "*the nature of each individual substance includes once for all everything which can ever happen to it.*"

The notion of the nature of an individual substance is a venerable one, though not without its puzzles. But this notion has
obviously taken a new twist in Leibnitz' hands. Leibnitz was not
the first to conceive of the *nature* of an individual substance as
accounting for its individuality. He was, however, the first to see
clearly that the individuality of a substance can only be understood in terms of *episodes* in its history, and to conclude that if
the nature of a substance is to account for its individuality, it
must account for episodes, and not merely the capacities, powers,
dispositions—all, in principle, repeatable—which were traditionally connected with the natures of things.

If we meant by the *nature* of an individual, the criteria in terms
of which we identify it as that individual, there would be no
puzzle to the idea that natures individuate. But, of course, this
is not how we use that expression. We may identify a certain
automobile as the one owned by Smith, but in no ordinary sense
of the term is to be owned by Smith the nature of the automobile.
However difficult it may be to make the notion of the nature of a
thing precise, this nature is not that in terms of which we identify
it, but that in terms of which, *if we but knew it*, we could explain
why it behaves as it does in the circumstances in which it is placed.

Now if we take as our model for interpreting the physical conception of the nature of the substance the kind of account we find
in Broad,[2] we can by suitable over-simplification construe the
nature of a substance S in terms of facts of the form "if at any
time S were to be involved in an episode of kind E_1, it would be
involved in an episode of kind E_2." Thus, suppose that on a cer-

[2] C. D. Broad: *Examination of McTaggart's Philosophy*, Cambridge University Press,
1933, Vol. 1, pp. 264-278.

tain occasion S is found to have been involved in an episode kind E_2, then the nature of S would account for this fact in the sense that if we knew the nature of S and if we were to discover that S had obviously been involved in an episode of kind E_1, we would be in a position to say

> S was involved in an E_2 because it was previously involved in an E_1.

If one accepts the above as a crude model for the classical account of the nature of the thing, the first thing one is tempted to say about Leibnitz' conception of the nature of a substance is that it not only provides the general hypotheticals, but the episodic premises as well. Such a nature would, in Hegelian terms, be a set of syllogisms *in re*.

II

How are we to account for this strange twist, in Leibnitz' hands, to a familiar notion? It might be thought that the explanation is to be found in his denial of interaction. If the explanation of what goes on in a substance is not to be found in what goes on in another substance, must it not be found in that substance itself, and hence in its nature? Now there is indeed a connection between his conception of the nature of the substance and his denial of the reality of relations between substances. But the latter by itself does not account for the pecularity of his view as can be seen when we notice that Spinoza is in his own way committed to the idea that the nature of a substance provides not only the hypotheticals (laws) but *affirms the antecedents* as well. For, conceived under the attribute of extension, the nature of Spinoza's one substance specifies not merely that if the physical world were at any time to be in a certain state, it would subsequently be in a certain other state, but specifies whether or not, at a given time, it is in the former state. The nature of substance not only provides the *if* but turns it into *since*.[3] At the heart, then, of Spinoza's conception of the nature of substance is the demand that the occurrence of

---

[3]Hegel did well to point out that the central concept of traditional rationalism was that of syllogisms *in re*. He also saw that the argument *in re* which, according to a thoroughgoing rationalism, has as its conclusion the reality of *this* natural order rather than another—let alone the reality of *any* natural order—cannot itself be syllogistic in form.

any *episode* has (in principle) an explanation which is not simply
of the form

This episode because that episode.

Such an explanation is, of course, legitimate as far as it goes. It
is, however, a *relative* explanation of one episode in terms of
another. Spinoza demands, in Kantian terms, that the series of
other-grounded episodes must have its ground in something, obviously not an episode, which accounts for its own existence. This
self-explainer is substance (*Deus sive Natura*); and, of course, in
thinking of it as a self-explainer, he is thinking of an argument
in re of which one premise says that substance *can* exist, another
premise says that what *can* exist *must* exist if there could be nothing
incompatible with its existence, and another premise, itself a conclusion from a prior argument, says that nothing could be incompatible with the existence of substance. Let us be quite clear that
whatever rationalists may have said about abstractions, they were
precluded from holding that the *esse* of possibilities is *concipi*.

Now Leibnitz makes exactly the same demand with exactly the
same result. Reality provides the principle and affirms the antecedent of an argument *in re*, which proves the existence of any
episode which belongs to the history of the actual world. But,
unlike Spinoza, he offers a complicated story which makes some
sense of the idea that this might be the way things are—whereas
Spinoza ultimately rests in the assurance that it *must be so* if the
world is to be intelligible.

But, of course, the idea that the actual course of events in the
world is the only possible course of events is *prima facie* so absurd
that the principle of sufficient reason on which it rests would have
no plausability at all unless some meaning could be given to the
idea that other courses of events are possible—even if *in the last
analysis* they are not really possible. Leibnitz offers such an account.

A useful way to get the hang of this account is to conceive of a
philosopher who is a blend of Leibnitz and Spinoza; let us call
him Leibnoza. Leibnoza, unlike Leibnitz, is happy about the
interaction of finite substances. He conceives of the universe as a
set of interacting substances whose natures are *hypotheticals*. He
also conceives of the universe as involving a temporal series of
world-wide episodes in which these substances participate. The

hypotheticals provide explanations of each such episode relative to another. But Leibnoza, by accepting the principle of sufficient reason, demands in addition that every truth be either analytic or a necessary consequence of analytic truths.

Leibnoza, as a good Christian, believes that the world of interacting finite substances was created by God. And this means to him that God chooses to create *this* world rather than any of the other possible worlds which he might have created instead. It also means that this choice is in a relevant sense free. This freedom, however, must be compatible with the idea that there is a logically valid argument *in re* with a *logically necessary* premise which proves the existence of this world. An impossible combination? Not for Leibnoza. He simply asks us to conceive of a set of possible Creators, each one freely choosing sub specie possibilities to creat a different possible world. He then points out that one of these possible Creators must be the most perfect and necessarily exists. To use a Leibnitzian (and Spinozistic) turn of phrase, the possible has a *nisus* towards actuality in the sense that an *unimpeded* (or an insufficiently impeded) possibility is *ipso facto* actual. In short, what is logically necessary is not *the choosing*, but *that the chooser of this choosing exist.* It is indeed logically necessary that the choosing exist, but no *existent* which is not defined in terms of the choosing logically implies the choosing. The existence of God necessitates the existence of the choosing choice, but God is defined in terms of the choice. In short, Leibnoza (like Leibnitz) applies to God the latter's solution of the free will problem as it applies to Julius Caesar.[4]

Caesar's decision to cross the Rubicon was free in that (1) the objective of the decision is internally consistent in the way in which the objective of an (impossible) choosing to stand and sit simultaneously is not, and (2) the choosing is not a logical consequence of any fact about Caesar which does not include the choosing; in particular, it is not a logical consequence of his prior state of mind. It is, however, a logical consequence of his nature, for his nature is simply a set of states of affairs which *includes* the state of affairs which is choosing to cross the Rubicon, and in no other sense can be said to constrain or necessitate the act.

---

[4]*Discourse on Metaphysics*, Section XIII.

As the existence of Caesar entails the existence of his free acts, so the existence of God entails the existence of His free acts. The difference is simply that Caesar exists by virtue of a choice made by God—whereas God exists as being the most perfect of a set of possible Creators. If we transfer Leibnitz' attempted reconciliation of freedom with the principle of sufficient reason to Leibnoza, we get the following account of how the existence of this world can be logically necessary and yet be one of many possible worlds. For according to Leibnoza, this world necessarily exists because the possible God who freely chooses it *sub specie possibilitatis* necessarily exists. From this perspective, we can see that the important difference between Leibnitz and Spinoza is not that Spinoza thinks that Carsar's crossing of the Rubicon is a necessary consequence of possible being whereas Leibnitz does not, but rather that Leibnitz thinks that the relation of possible being to the crossing of the Rubicon is of the form:

> The possible God who freely chooses to create
> the possible substance which freely chooses
> to cross the Rubicon necessarily exists.

III

A brief excursus on the classical problem of relations will set the stage for the next step in the argument. Suppose one thinks that the truth of

> This leaf is green

requires that there be an item inhering in this leaf which is its greenness in the metaphysical sense of a dependent particular numerically different from all other greennesses, even of exactly the same shade, which inhere in other substances. Then relational edication immediately generates a puzzle. Consider

> S_1 is R to S_2.

If we treat this proposition as a special case of

> S_1 is P

thus,

> S_1 is R-to-S_2

and attempt to introduce a dependent particular which corresponds to this predicate as a particular greenness corresponds to "This leaf is green," we are faced by a dilemma:

1. Is the dependent particular an R-to-S_2? This would seem to require that S_2 inhere in S_1 as being a part of the R-to-S_2 which inheres in S_1.

2. Is the dependent particular an R rather than R-to-S_2? If so then it inheres in either (a) S_1 alone, or (b) both S_1 and S_2 or (c) neither S_1 nor S_2. But not (a), for then the fact that S_1 is R to S_2 would be unaccounted for; furthermore, it would imply that S_1 could stand in the relation without having a relatum. And not (b), for "an accident cannot have its feet in two subjects." Even if S_1 and S_2 could share an R, S_2 might cease to exist (thus, be destroyed by God) and we would be back with the absurdity of the previous alternative. And not (c) for particulars other than substances are *dependent* (i.e., necessarily inhere in substance).

Leibnitz found an interesting way out of this dilemma. In effect, he adopts a modified form of the first horn. He accepts the principle that

$$S_1 \text{ is } R \text{ to } S_2$$

is true, then there must be an R-to-S_2 inherent in S_1, and he accepts the consequence that S_2 must be *in* S_1. But he reinterprets these commitments in the light of the cartesian (ultimately scholastic) distinction between "representative" (or "objective") and "formal" being. Thus, the R-to-S_2 inherent in S_1 is interpreted as a representing of S_2 inherent in S_1, and Leibnitz, therefore, interprets the sense in which S_2 is a "part" of the R-to-S_2 inherent in S_1 as a matter of its being that which has objective or representative being in the representing which is the R-to-S_2. According to this analysis, the truth of statements of the form

$$S_1 \text{ is } R_i \text{ to } S_2$$

where R_i is *prima facie*, a real relation rests on facts of the form

$$S_1 \text{ represents (in specific manner } M_i) S_2$$

where, needless to say, the manner of representation M_i which *corresponds* to R_i and makes this relational fact a phenomenon *bene fundatum*, is not what common sense has in mind when it uses the term "R_i."[5]

If it is objected that on the above account

S_1 is R to S_2

could be true even though S_2 did not exist, since non-existent substances can be represented, Leibnitz would welcome this objection, but turn its edge by agreeing that the truth of the relational statement requires the actual existence of both S_1 and S_2, and hence that the mere fact that S_1 represents a substance in the appropriate manner does not make the corresponding relational statement true. The substance represented must have formal as well as objective being in order for this to be the case. After all, his problem was to resolve the classical puzzle about relations, and this he has done, to his own satisfaction, by giving phenomenal relations between substances a metaphysical underpinning in which they have as their real counterparts acts of representing and mobilizing the distinction between the two modes of being which representables may have. Roughly, a true representation is one the subject matter of which is a representable which, in addition to having "objective" being in the representation has "formal" being in the world.

IV

If we apply these considerations to causality, we can understand why Leibnitz believes himself forced to interpret the fact that

S_2 is acted on by S_1 (e.g., S_1 by being in state ϕ *causes* S_2 to become ψ)

as involving, among other things, facts of two radically different types:

1. S_2 representing the fact that S_1 is in state ϕ
2. S_2 being caused by representing this fact to become ψ.

---

[5]Thus the statement, in the phenomenal framework of material things in space,
  S_1 is linearly between S_2 and S_3
might have as its real counterpart something like
  S_1 represents S^2 and S_3 more directly than S_2 and S_3 represent each other
where a representing of S_i is indirect if it is a representing of a representing of S_i.

The first type of fact is a matter of the ideal relation of *truth* between a judgment and the actual state of affairs which makes it true. That in most, if not all, cases of the action of one substance on another the judgment is "confused," is a complication which can be overlooked for our present purposes. What *is* important for our purposes is that the ideal relation between a judgment and the fact which makes it true and, in general, between "ideas" and their "ideata" was conceived to be the logical product of two relations, one between the idea and a content, the *being* of which was its *being represented*, and the other between this content and the "external" object or state of affairs.

Notice, in the light of the preceding brief exposition of Leibnitz' general theory of relations, that although

S_1 by being in state ϕ caused S_2 to become ψ

implies that both S_1 and S_2 exist, so that it would be nonsense to say "S_1 caused S_2 to become ψ but that there is no such thing as S_2," Leibnitz can argue that the existence of S_1 and its being in state ϕ is *causally* irrelevant to S_2's being ψ and is relevant only to the *truth* of the representation which is the *vera causa* of S_2's being ψ. Thus S_2 is, as far as the *relation* grounding each of its episodes in other episodes is concerned, as self-contained as Leibnoza's world of interacting things. Both, however, are contingent and require a self-affirming premise as their sufficient reason. It is, at least in part, the fact that truth is a perfection, which rules out the possibility that the universe might consist of S_2 and God, S_2's representation of S_1 being a representation of something that does not exist.

V

We can sum up our results to date by saying that one line of thought which underlies Leibnitz' thesis that the nature of an individual substance entails episodic as well as hypothetical facts about it, stems from his commitment to the principle of sufficient reason. Yet the argument is incomplete, for granted that episodes have a sufficient reason, and granted that this sufficient reason does not involve the actual being of other substances, it could still be argued that although hypothetical facts and episodic facts alike are grounded (not, of course, independently) in the First

Cause, we are not thereby forced to count the episodic facts as elements in the nature of the substance. Why not continue, with Broad, to identify its nature with the hypotheticals, while granting that both episodes and hypotheticals are grounded in Necessary Being?

Part of the answer lies in the fact that we have been guilty of an anachronism in attributing to Leibnitz the contemporary distinction between causal properties as general hypotheticals and occurrent states as the categoricals which cooperate with the former in generating further categoricals in an ontological two-step. The truth of the matter is that Leibnitz, like most of his predecessors and many of his successors, interprets causal properties on the model of desires, plans, personal commitments. Thus, whereas *we* might be inclined to interpret the statement "Jones has a strong desire to go to New York" in terms of conditional facts about Jones, Leibnitz thinks of a strong desire as a continuing series of episodes which tends to develop into a going to New York and will continue to develop if not impeded. Thus, to be more precise, he tends to think of the fact that S_2 would become ψ if S_1 were to become ϕ as a matter of S_2 having the plan of becoming ψ if S_1 were to become ϕ. For becoming ϕ is (*realiter*) doing something. And, having, *the plan* of doing A if B is (though the *plan* is hypothetical in character) itself a categorical fact about S_2.

Actually, then, there is a sense in which for Leibnitz all the fundamental facts about a substance are episodic facts. And, consequently, the notion of the nature of a substance as the law-like hypothetical which would provide an explanation of each episode relative to another episode, is ultimately replaced by the notion of the nature of a thing as that which *logically* explains each single episode. And, of course, the only way it can do this is by duplicating in some way the set of episodes which it is to account for.

If we were to press Leibnitz with the question, "What is the mode of existence of the nature of a substance," and "How is it related to the substance?" I think that he would answer somewhat as follows. The nature of a substance is to be construed as its life-plan, and as such it has *esse intentionale* as the content of an abiding aspiration which is the core being of the substance. This connecting of *truths* about what a substance will do with an abiding plan of life raises in an acute form the problem of the relation of time to truth.

VI

That problems pertaining to truth play a central role in Leibnitz' metaphysics is a familiar fact. Thus he supported the ideas that the nature of a thing includes once for all everything which can happen to it, and that the individual concept of a thing includes once for all everything that can happen to it—which so startled Arnauld—by considerations pertaining to truth. Like the argument from explanation, the argument from truth purports to show that there are entities, the sort of thing that would usually be called facts, themselves without dates, (though they are *about* dates), which account for the truth of true ideas about individual substances.

Thus, suppose the following statements, made today, are true:

1. S_1 was ϕ_1 in 1957.
2. S_1 is ϕ_2 now.
3. S_1 will be ϕ_3 in 1959.

To make these statements is to say that one and the same individual subject was ϕ_1 is ϕ_2 and will be ϕ_3. On the assumption of a correspondence theory of truth, each of these statements corresponds to a fact; thus:

1. Corresponds to the fact that S_1 was ϕ_1 in 1957
2. Corresponds to the fact that S_1 is now ϕ_2
3. Corresponds to the fact that S_1 will be ϕ_3 in 1959

and indeed (always on the assumption of the truth of the original statements) it *is* a fact that S_1 was ϕ_1 in 1957; it *is* a fact that S_1 is ϕ_2 now; it *is* a fact that S_1 *will be* ϕ_3 in 1959.

We say of an episode that it took *place, is taking place,* or *will take place.* But if something is a fact, it *is* a fact—not *was* a fact nor *will be* a fact. This is not quite true, for there are contexts in which "was a fact" and even "will be a fact" do make sense. But these are derivative uses in which, roughly, we are viewing someone else in the past or in the future as thinking of something as a fact. Where it is *we* who are thinking of something as a fact, the proper expression of this thought is always by the use of the *present* tense of "to be a fact."

Now it is easy to move from the impropriety, in non-oblique contexts, of "it will be a fact..." and "it was a fact that..." to the idea that the "is" of "it is a fact that..." has to do with a timeless mode of being. (After all, one does not say "two plus two will be four" or "two plus two was four." Are not facts like numbers?) In effect, Leibnitz makes this move. To make it is to suppose that there is a timeless set of entities (i.e., facts) which are about what happens to a substance at different times, and such that it is by virtue of corresponding to these entities that our statements and judgments about the substance are true.

Before we take a closer look at this ontology of truth, let us notice that even if it were illuminating to say that every true statement is true because it corresponds to a timeless fact, this by itself would give no aid or comfort to the idea of the nature of a substance as a set of facts which make statements about its history true. For unless one has already denied the reality of relations, there would be many facts (i.e., relational facts) which have more than one substance as constituents. In the absence of Leibnitz' theory of relations, therefore, the ontological version of the correspondence theory of truth would support at most the idea that the only thing which has a nature, strictly speaking, is the universe as a whole. But, of course, Leibnitz does have his theory of relations, and so his theory of truth does dovetail with the argument from explanation. It is important, however, to note that even in combination with his theory of relations the argument from truth provides in and of itself no reason for calling the timeless set of facts about a substance its "nature."

Returning now to the idea of the nature of a substance as the abiding life plan of that substance, we note that to say that the statement

$$S_1 \text{ will be } \phi_3 \text{ in } 1959$$

is true, because to say S_1 *now* plans to be ϕ_3 in 1959 is to lose the *prima facie* advantages of the simple ontological theory and embark on an uncharted course. On the other hand, the notion of a timeless aspiration would seem to be nonsense. But even if Leibnitz was guilty of the category mistake of conflating the notions of timeless facts and life plans, the former notion undoubtedly guided his thinking. It is therefore appropriate to make the point, scarcely a surprising one, that this notion will not do at all. To see that this is so, one simply needs to see that the "is" of

> it *is* a fact that S_1 *will be* ϕ_3 in 1959

is exactly what it seems to be, namely the present tense of the verb "to be," and that the "will be" of the that-clause is exactly what it seems to be, namely "will be" in relation to the present tense of the main verb.

But surely, it may be said, this "is" can be in the present tense only if it *could be* a "was"—which you have denied. But I have not denied it. I have pointed out that "was" is appropriate, but only where we are indirectly expressing someone else's point of view. And this is the heart of the matter. For

> It is a fact that S_1 will be ϕ_3 in 1959

is, in a very important sense a counterpart of

> "S_1 will be ϕ_3 in 1959" is a true statement

(not, of course, as Strawson has pointed out,

> "S_1 will be ϕ_3 in 1959" is a true sentence.)

To refer to the statement "S_1 will be ϕ_3 in 1959" is always to refer to the relevant sentence as used at a certain time. And when I say

> "S_1 will be ϕ_3 in 1959" *is* a true statement

the time in question is *now*. If I say

> "S_1 will be ϕ_3 in 1959" *was* a true statement,

the reference is to the use of the sentence at a time before now; and if I say

> "S_1 will be ϕ_3 in 1959" *will be* a true statement,

the reference is to the use of this sentence at a time later than now. We can now see why, if we limit ourselves to fact statements which express our own point of view *hic et nunc*, there is no place for

> It *was* a fact that S_1 *will be* ϕ_3 in 1959.

The point can be made by supposing someone to ask Why doesn't

> It *was* a fact that S_1 will be ϕ_3 in 1959

correspond to

> "S_1 will be ϕ_3 in 1959" was a true statement

as

It is a fact that S_1 will be ϕ_3 in 1959

corresponds to

"S_1 will be ϕ_3 in 1959" is a true statement.

The answer is, of course, that to use the expression "*that* S_1 will be ϕ_3 in 1959" is to imply a reference to the *present* use of the sentence "S_1 will be ϕ_3 in 1959," whereas,

"S_1 will be ϕ_3 in 1959" *was* a true statement

explicitly refers to a past use of this sentence. Thus, if we limit ourselves to fact statements which express our own point of view, that is, if we limit ourselves to fact statements which do not occur in indirect discourse, all fact statements will be counterparts of statements of the form

X *is* a true statement

and will imply a reference to a *contemporary* use of the sentence represented by "X."

There is an obvious comeback to this argument. It runs as follows: you have been considering the sentence "S *will be* ϕ_3 in 1959" and it must be granted that this sentence is used to make different statements at different times. And it is reasonable to argue that given a that-clause constructed from this sentence (i.e., a *tensed* that-clause), the "is" of "it is a fact that that" must be in the *present* tense. But this reasoning no longer holds if we turn our attention to the sentences "S is ϕ_1 in 1959," "S_1 is ϕ_2 in 1958," and "S_1 is ϕ_3 in 1957" where these sentences have been de-tensed. These sentences, the objection continues, make the same statement whenever they are used, and, consequently, the statements

1. It is a fact that S_1 is ϕ_3 in 1959
2. It is a fact that S_1 is ϕ_2 in 1958
3. It is a fact that S_1 is ϕ_1 in 1957

no longer need to be construed as being in the present tense, save in that "timeless" use of the present found in "two plus two is equal to four." The answer to this objection consists in showing that the *contrived* sentence "S_1 is ϕ_3 in 1959" makes sense only as introduced in terms of tensed sentence-forms and amounts to the disjunction

S_1 was ϕ_3 in 1959 or S_1 is ϕ_3 in 1959 or S_1 will be ϕ_3 in 1959.

Now for the purpose of my present argument, it will be useful to lay down an over-simplified thesis to the effect that statements of the form

It is a fact that-p

are simply another way of saying that

"P" *is* a true statement in *our* language

and, to get down to fundamentals, that statement of the form

That-p is a proposition or state of affairs

is simply another way of saying

"P" is a statement of our language.

Now if these theses be granted, it follows that to say that

The statement "S_1 will be $\emptyset_3$ in 1959" is true *because* it is a fact that S_1 will be $\emptyset_3$ in 1959

is like saying

We're here because we are here.

The "because" is out of place because nothing is explained. There is indeed a proper because-statement in the neighborhood, but it must be formulated, rather, as follows:

The statement "S_1 will be $\emptyset_3$ in 1959" is true because S_1 *will be* $\emptyset_3$ in 1959.

If the truth of statements about substances requires no ontology of *facts*, the argument from truth collapses. Furthermore, the implication is unavoidable that insofar as the concept of the nature of the thing is a legitimate one, it can be formulated in such a way that it requires no use of "fact" which is incompatible with the schema

It is a fact that-p if and only if "p" *is* a true statement of our language.

This, I believe, can be done. Of more immediate concern, however, is what might be called the promissory note character of the idea that things have natures. This promissory note character is a pervasive feature of the statements we are in a position to make about the world. But before I expand on this schema, there is one more strand to be disentangled from the thinking which

finds expression in the thesis that the individual concept of a substance includes once for all everything which had ever happened
to it. This I will call the argument from proper names.

VII

Before exploring the cluster of reasonings which I propose to
sum up by the phrase "the argument from proper names," I shall
set the stage by some informal remarks which will show how the
land lies with respect to my own view on the matter. As I see it,
proper names of things and persons play an indispensible role in
discourse. Although essentially related on the one hand to definite
descriptions, and on the other to demonstratives, they are reducible
to neither. The fact that any *single* name can be dropped and
replaced by a descriptive phrase, at least in a specific context,
should not deceive us into thinking that all names can be dropped
from the language in favor of definite descriptions.

Again, the use of demonstratives presupposes that the speaker
locates himself and his hearers in a common world of objects in
space and time; and the framework in terms of which this locating
is done is constituted by the use of names and definite descriptions
of abiding things. But if the use of demonstratives presupposes the
use of names and descriptions, the use of names and descriptions
in their term presupposes the use of demonstratives. The meaning
of names and descriptions alike requires that I be able to recognize
a named or described object as *this* object. No one of these modes
of references is, so to speak, the foundation of reference, the Atlas
which supports all the rest.

That proper names presuppose definite descriptions is scarcely
controversial. To use a name "N" is to purport to be ready to
make at least one statement of the form

N is the f-thing.

Thus names presuppose the statement form "Something is f." But
in their turn statements of the form "Something is f" presuppose
that we have some way of referring to objects other than by making
general statements. The idea that the Atlas of reference is bound
variables is as mistaken as the once popular idea that it is demonstratives. The statement

Something is red: (Ex) x is red

is a functioning part of language only because there are names and demonstratives to function in determinate singular reference.

It is not, however, my purpose to *argue* that descriptions and demonstratives presuppose names (and vice versa). I shall simply assume that this is so. For my concern is with the question, "Granted that names are an irreducible mode of reference, what are the implications of the idea that every individual thing is *nameable?*" For if anything is a central fact in Leibnitz' metaphysics, it is that he clearly assumes that every substance is nameable, and I believe that the recognition of this fact throws a flood of light on his system.

Let us call the idea that every substance is nameable the "Principle of Nameability." The first thing to note about this principle is that it stands in a certain interesting relation to the principle of the identity of indiscernables (or the dissimilarity of the diverse). To begin with, if names were shorthand for definite descriptions (which they are not), to stipulate that every individual is nameable would be to stipulate that

$$(x)(Ef)(y) \; fy \rightarrow y = x$$

from which it follows that

$$(x)(y) \; x \neq y \rightarrow (Ef) \; fx \text{ and } \sim fy$$

The important thing to see is that even if one does not *equate* names with definite descriptions, the same conclusion follows from the principle of nameability if one makes the related claim that every name has a *sense* which consists of one (or more) definite descriptions. For one can hold that *being the f-thing* is a *criterion* for being correctly called N without holding that "N" is *shorthand* for "the f-thing."

It is sometimes thought that the reason why it is incorrect to characterize names as shorthand for definite descriptions lies in the precariousness of our beliefs about the world which makes it advisable to avoid pinning a name down to only one definite description. In short, it is thought that there are *practical* reasons independent of vagueness, open-texture and the like for refusing to equate names with descriptions—for one can grant that the use of names rests on a fallible inductive footing which warrants a looseness in the connection of names with descriptions, without construing this connection on the model of logical shorthand.

In any event, I am going to stipulate for the purposes of my argument that names have definite descriptions as their senses, in that definite descriptions serve as the criteria for the application of names. Statements about named objects, then, presuppose (in Strawson's sense) the truth of statements affirming the existence of a unique descriptum. Because, thus construed, names presuppose states of affairs, one can appreciate why those who seek an ultimate mode of reference which involves no commitment to something's being the case either deny (with Wittgenstein in the *Tractatus*) that names have a sense, or equate the sense with the referent, or, with Quine, deny that naming is an ultimate mode of reference and seek to reduce it to the use of bound variables. But this notion of a presuppositionless mode of reference is but another manifestation of the idea that empirical knowledge has a foundation, other facets of which I have explored in "Empiricism and the Philosophy of Mind."

Now I am implying that Frege's conception of proper names—though not his theory of definite descriptions—is not only sound, but closer to the tradition than certain modern alternatives. In particular, I am implying that it is in close harmony with Leibnitz' treatment of names, though the latter nowhere develops an explicit theory of names along these lines. Assuming this to be so, the first point I wish to make is that Leibnitz is clearly committed to the idea, indeed takes for granted, that every individual substance is *nameable*, and that this acceptance of the Principle of Nameability carries with it the principle of the Identity of Indiscernibles. For according to the above theory of names, the name of each properly (and not merely putatively) named substances will have as its sense a criterion which distinguishes its nominatum from all other substances. Let us call this *sense* the "individual concept" which the name "stands for."

Now this is exactly the sort of thing Leibnitz means by the phrase "individual concept." But whereas *we* would think that the individual concept for which a name stands need specify only a few facts about the nominatum; for we think that a few facts suffice to single it out from other things, Leibnitz interprets the individual concept associated with the name as specifying everything that the nominatum does or suffers throughout its entire career.

Why should Leibnitz think that the sense of a proper name must include a complete description of the nominatum? The answer to this question is surprisingly simple once one realizes that Leibnitz is concerned not with *our* names for substances— indeed as we have already pointed out he thinks that the so-called names we use are not really names at all but a peculiar kind of general term—but with *God's* names for things. Thus the principle of nameability is the principle that every individual substance is nameable by God. If, now, we bear in mind the argument that the sense of a name must serve to distinguish its nominatum from all other substances, we see right away what is going on. For Leibnitz simply takes it for granted that it makes sense to speak of naming possible substances! And it is by no means implausible that, though an incomplete description of an object may serve to distinguish it from all other *actual* things, only a complete description which pins the object down in all conceivable respects in accordance with the law of excluded muddle can distinguish it from all other *possible* things. If it were to be granted that God has names for all possible substances, it would seem indeed that the individual concepts for which these names stand must be as Leibnitz characterizes them.

Now even before we turn the cold light of analysis on the idea of names of possible substances, we can put our finger on an ambiguity in this conception. We have pointed out that the sense of a name serves to discriminate its nominatum from the other members of a set of mutually discernible substances. Now, granted that the set of all logically possible substances is a mutually discernible set, the question arises "Is the mutually discernible set *which is relevant to the naming of a possible substance* the set of all *logically* possible substances?" The point is an important one, for it is only if the former is the case—only, that is, if the names of possible substances are prior to any *more restrictive* principles of compossibility which build logically possible substances into possible worlds—that it would be true that their "individual concepts" must describe them exhaustively. If the set of mutual discernibles relevant to the naming of a possible substance coincides with the more restricted notion of a possible world having extra-logical coherence, the individual concept of a possible substance could discriminate it from other substances in its world without having to describe it completely; and its distinguishability from all possible substances in other possible worlds would follow from the distinguishability of the worlds. To take this line in applying the principle of nameability is to deny that there are any possible substances apart from possible worlds.

Now it seems to me quite clear that Leibnitz actually thinks of the individual concept of each possible substance as specifying its place in a system of mutually adjusting substances which develop in the orderly lawful way characteristic of a possible world. In so doing, I shall argue, he has undercut his demand, insofar as it is based on the idea of a name, that the individual concept of a possible substance selects that substance in terms of a *complete* description. Instead, however, of supporting this criticism directly, I shall do so indirectly by turning my attention to the question, What sense is there to the notion of the name of a possible substance?

VIII

Are there such things as possible substances? That question is best approached by considering a familiar case for the negative. It rests on the idea that the primary use of the term "possible" is in such context as

It is possible that Tom will get well.

It rests, in short, on the idea that it is states of affairs rather than things which are said, in the first instance at least, to be possible or impossible. And, it is argued, the statement that such and such a *state of affairs* is possible presupposes the actual existence of the *things* with respect to which this possibility obtains. Thus the possibility that Tom will get well presupposes that there actually is such a person as Tom.

It might be thought that this argument is self-refuting. How can one properly argue that there are no *possible* things on the ground that possible states of affairs concern *actual* things? Surely to speak of "actual things" is to imply that it makes sense to speak of "non-actual" or "merley possible" things. But of course, the argument did not say that in order for there to be the possibility that Tom will get well, Tom must be an actual thing, but only that there must actually be such a person as Tom.

Having made plausible the idea that the primary use of "possible" is in connection with *states of affairs,* the case for the negative now grants that a derivative use of "possible" might be introduced in which one would speak of possible *things* in accordance with the following schema

> There is a possible man in the corner = it is possible
> that there is a man in the corner.

In this stipulated sense, there would be possible things—for to deny it is to deny that sentences such as "It is possible that there is a man in the corner" can ever be used to make a true statement.

Now I take it to be common ground that such sentences as "It is possible that Tom will get well" and "It is possible that there is a man in the corner" are often used to make true statements. I also take it to be common ground that these statements are the blood brothers of *probability* statements and as such are statements in the *present* tense which imply a reference to evidence now "at hand" or "available." Just as the probability statement

> Tom will probably get well

has roughly the force of

> There is a balance of evidence at hand in favor of
> the statement "Tom will get well"

so the possibility statement

> It is possible that Tom will get well

has the force of

> There is no conclusive evidence at hand against the
> statement "Tom will get well,"

and just as when more evidence becomes available, it may become proper to say

> It is still very likely that Tom will get well

so, if the evidence is unfavorable, it may become proper to say

> It is no longer possible that Tom will get well

or

> The possibility that Tom will get well no longer exists.

IX

Now if we have reason to believe that there is a man in the corner, we can properly say "let's call him Jack." In this case,

"Jack" has as its sense "the man in the corner." As long as we have reason to think that there was a man in the corner at that time, we have reason to think that "Jack" is our name for a man. On the other hand, as soon as we have reason to think that no man was actually there, we have reason to think that in the use we gave to it, the word "Jack" does not name anything. For a word in a certain use, say "Jack," to be a name for something there must be such a thing as is specified by the sense we have given to the word—there must be such a thing as Jack. This is the insight contained in the slogan: A name is not a name unless it names something. If, therefore, we discover that there was no man in the corner, we are no longer entitled to regard "Jack" in that use as a name. To be sure, we can *now* use it as *short for* "the man who was in the corner." But if we do so, we are no longer using this descriptive phrase as the criterion of a *name*, and we can no longer say that this phrase gives the sense of a name. In short, we cannot say that "Jack," as we are *now* using it, is a name.

It would be obviously absurd to say

> It is possible that there is a man in the corner: Let's call him Jack.

If, however, we have made the move from

> It is possible that there is a man in the corner

to

> There is a possible man in the corner

we may not see the absurdity. For if it makes sense to say

> There is a tall man in the corner, let's call him Jack

why shouldn't it make sense to say

> There is a possible man in the corner, let's call him Jack

The mistake is obvious, but the latter simply repeats the absurdity of

> It is possible that there is a (unique) man in the corner; let's call him Jack.

In short, it is only if one construes "naming" as introducing an abbreviation for a definite description that one will regard it as proper to speak of naming in this connection. For one would then construe

> It is possible that there is a man in the corner; let's call him Jack

as a paradoxical way of saying

> It is possible that there is a unique man in the corner; let's use "Jack" as short for "the man in the corner."

Notice, however, that even this could not be construed as naming a "possible man" whose status as possible was independent of epistemic vicissitudes. For if "Jack is a possible man" has the sense of "It is possible that there is a (unique) man in the corner," as soon as new available evidence about the status of the corner at that time requires us to say "It is not possible that there was a man in the corner," we would have to say "Jack is an impossible man."

X

This last point reminds us that the case for the negative has been built on what might be called the "epistemic" sense of the terms "possible" and "impossible." This sense is not, of course, independent of the "nomological" senses of these terms, but must not be confused with them. In the epistemic sense, statements of possibility are relative to evidence available to the speaker. They pertain to the world not as it is "in itself," but to the world as known by someone in some circumstances at some time. And, as a first approximation, we can say that the more evidence that is available concerning a spatio-temporal region, the fewer possible objects and states of affairs it will admit.[6]

If we mobilize the Peircean idea of an inductive community, a community consisting of ourselves and those who join us, and suppose that our remote descendants in this chain have evidence and principles which enable them to decide with respect to every earthly spatio-temporal region whether or not it contained a man, we could imagine them to say

---

[6]If one allows that "there is a man in the corner" entails "it is possible that there is a man in the corner," where possible is used in the epistemic sense—which does some violence to ordinary usage—then one should say " . . .the fewer *merely* possible objects and states of affairs it will admit."

> At such and such places and times there were men;
> at such and such other places and times there were
> no men,

and, by way of epistemic commentary on the latter statement,

> It is not possible that there were men at the latter
> places and times

or, by an extended usage,

> There were no possible men at those places and times.

The truth of these future statements is no more incompatible with
the truth of *my*

> It is possible that there is a man in the corner

or

> There is a possible man in the corner

(given that there is no man in the corner) than the truth of the
croupier's statement

> It is impossible that the dice showed seven

is incompatible with the truth of my prior statement

> It is probable that the dice showed seven

(given that I know my dice to be loaded).

It is worth pausing to note that the philosophers who argue
that determinism implies that the possible coincides with the
actual are guilty of two confusions:

1. they are telescoping epistemic and nomological possibility
   into one concept, and
2. they are fallaciously supposing that because it would be true
   for a demon who knows a cross-section and the laws of a
   LaPlacian universe to say (with respect to any time t) "it is
   not possible that the state of object O at time t should have
   been other than S," my statement "it is possible that O is
   not S at t" must be false.

The fact that determinism implies that an ideal knower could
make no true statement of the form "both p and not-p are possible,"
where the *epistemic* sense of "possible" is involved, does not imply
that it cannot be true for imperfect knowers to say "both *p* and
not-*p* are possible." If, speaking as convinced determinists, *we* say

that "when you come right down to it, only what *actually* happens is *really* possible," this simply expresses our sense of community with those ideal members of the republic of investigators, the concept of which is the regulative ideal of the life of reason.

XI

At this stage, we may imagine the opponent of possible-but-not-actual things to grant that the epistemic sense of "possible" permits the truth of statements of the form "it is possible that-*p*" where not-*p* is, in fact, the case; and also that correctly construed, sense can be made of such statements as "there is a possible man in the corner." But, he adds, it is only if indeterminism is true that these possible-but-not-actual things are anything more than expressions of human ignorance. And even if there are possible-but-not-actual things (in the epistemic sense) which are *not* relative to ignorance, they presuppose the actual existence of the known evidential context (objects and statement of affairs) which fail to pin them down. Mere possibilities in the epistemic sense cannot, in the nature of the case, be prior to actual existence in the sense required by Leibnitz' system.

All this, however, would be readily granted by Leibnitz. For he is committed to the view that *in the sense of the previous discussion* there are no possible-but-not-actual substances save in relation to human ignorance. For, according to Leibnitz, God creates one of the possible worlds (in a sense of possible to be explored) and each possible world being a maximum set of *compossibles*, it follows that there are no states of affairs compossible with, but not included in, a given possible world to be the careers of substances which are possible-but-not-actual relatively to that possible world. Consequently, whichever possible world is the actual one, it could only be in relation to incomplete evidence that a knower in that world would be entitled to say "It is possible that there is a man in the corner" when in point of fact there is not.

Now given a set of qualities and relations and supposing all simple qualities and relations to be compatible (i.e., supposing no extra-logical limitations on compossibility), it is not possible to define more than one maximum set of compossible objects. In short, it is not possible to define more than one possible world involving these qualities and relations. (And what a queer world that would be!) This means that in order for there to be more than one possible world of compossible substances, an additional restriction must be introduced. And this additional restriction pertains to the lawfulness of possible worlds. The way in which Leibnitz introduces this additional restriction is instructive. He introduces a reference to the decrees of the Creator into the defining traits of the possible world. After all, since the proximate possibility of a possible world is the possibility of the act of creation by which it would come into existence, the intrinsic consistency of the world is but the possibility of this proximate possibility. Leibnitz tells us that the possibility of *choosing* to perform a certain act presupposes that the description of the act is not self-inconsistent. The following is an illustration: the impossibility of *choosing* to stand and sit simultaneously stems from the impossibility of standing and sitting simultaneously. On the other hand, simply because a state of affairs is self-consistent, it does not follow that it is possible that I choose it. If we suppose that God chose at LaPlacian world, it follows that a non-LaPlacian world, in Leibnitz' terms, is not *really* possible.

XII

We have seen that Leibnitz' notion of possible-but-not-actual things cannot be justified in terms of the inductive or epistemic use of "possible." And this for two reasons: (1) there is no such thing as naming possible objects in any sense of "possible" springing from this use, and (2) a commitment to determinism involves a commitment to the idea that "the *really* possible coincides with the actual."

Is there any other line of thought which enables us to understand what was at the back of Leibnitz' mind? The answer lies in the fact that it does make sense to speak of the *actual* world, and, by contrast, possible-but-not-actual worlds. Now it might be thought that to speak of "the actual world" is to refer to the actual course of *the world*, as contrasted with possible-but-not-actual courses of *the world*. If this were the case, the possibility involved would be analogous to the possibility that Tom will get well, and would be either the inductive possibility expressed by

> It is (on the evidence at hand) possible that Tom will get well;

or it would be a misnomer for the *contingency* of the state of affairs (i.e., the fact that the idea that Tom will get well is neither analytic nor self-contradictory). But as we have seen, both the possibility that Tom will get well and the contingent character of this state of affairs presuppose the existence of Tom and of the world which includes him.

But what can the contrast between the actual world and possible-but-not-actual worlds amount to if it is either of these? The general lines of the answer emerge if we remember that to think of the *actual* world is to think of what it would be *known as* by our ideal inductive descendants, that is, by ideal members of *our* scientific community. *This* world is essentially *our* world. *This* is what I am perceiving and can talk about with *you*. What, then, does it mean to conceive another world? It means to conceive not only a different set of substances than those which make up this world, but a set which does not include *us*.

Now if to think of an object is to use an expression which refers to it, we can not think of these other substances by using the referring expressions of the language we actually use. *Ex hypothesi*, they refer to the objects of the actual world. It would seem, then, that to think of the objects of a non-actual world we would have to use a language we do not have. Again, one cannot specify what object a referring expression refers to save by *referring* to it by means of another referring expression. And this referring expression would be one which belongs to the language we use and which talks about "actual things."

Fortunately there is a simple model at hand for talking coherently about non-existent things, and using names which do not really name anything. This model is fictional discourse. Thus, to "imagine" that there was such a person as Oliver Twist is to do what we would call purporting to describe an actual person, if the description did not occur in a rubric ("once upon a time") which brackets discourse in a way which frees it from responsibility to inductive confirmation.

Thus to imagine a possible but not actual world is to place discourse which, if *seriously* intended, would purport to describe *this* world, in a rubric which marks it as fiction. And, of course, the "names" in this fictional discourse are only *fictional* names, and the sentences which constitute their *principia individuationis* are fictional sentences. The referring expressions in this fictional discourse do not translate into the language we seriously use. Language about a possible world is not a *different* language simply in the sense in which Italian is different from English—for *Parigi* does translate into Paris, and we can say that *Parigi* refers to Paris.

To say what a language of a possible world is about, we have to make *fictional* use of another language into which the *fictional* object language translates.

Furthermore, *to imagine* a possible world is to imagine that "I" belong to this world and am a member of an inductive community ferreting out its secrets. For the concept of *actuality* includes a reference to us and ultimately—if ungrammatically—to "I." Consequently, imagined actuality involves a reference to an imagined "I."

Is it not self-contradictory to speak of imagining that I am in a different world? Am I not, by definition, in *this* world? No, for to imagine that I am in a different world is simply to suppose that the states of affairs by virtue of which the general criteria associated with the term "I" are satisfied are other than they actually are; it is to suppose that these states of affairs are among those which belong to the fictional rubric.

But this is not the place to ferret out the truth in Kant's conception of the transcendental unity of appreception as the fundamental form of experience. Our task is rather to illuminate Leibnitz' conception of the actual world as one of an infinite number of possible worlds. What I am suggesting is that at the back of Leibnitz' mind is the picture of God as making use, within the fictional rubric, of alternative languages, and by so doing conceiving of alternative sets of individual substances.

According to this picture, the model for *creation* is obviously the removing of the fictional rubric from one of these languages; the move, on God's part, from "Suppose that there were such and such things" to "There are such and such things," *via* "Let there be such and such things."

XIII

Now it is obvious that if the *esse* of possible worlds like the *esse* of Oliver Twist consists in fictional discourse about them, we have a new sense in which *actuality* is prior to possibility—roughly that in which Dickens is prior to Oliver Twist. This accords with Leibnitz' contention that the Divine Understanding is the locus of possible worlds. How, then, can he extend the notion of possibility to God Himself? For God is that Being who necessarily exists if He is possible. And God *qua* possible can scarcely have a being which is dependent on God's Understanding. I shall limit myself to two points:

1. When Leibnitz tells us that the Divine Understanding is the locus of the possible, he seems, in the whole, to have the contingently possible in mind, and to be telling us that the *real* or *proximate* possibility of the contingently possible lies in the possibility of its intended Creation, and hence involves a reference to God's thought of it. This is compatible with an account of possible substances which make them prior to the actuality of God.

2. If my positive argument is correct, the actuality of God, as of anything else, would presuppose *our* existence as discoverers of God.

PART TWO

VII

PHYSICAL REALISM

A discerning student of philosophy, familiar with the writings of Sellars *père*, who chances to read Sellars *fils*, and is not taken in by the superficial changes of idiom and emphasis which reflect the adaptation of the species to a new environment, will soon be struck by the fundamental identity of outlook. The identity is obscured by differences of terminology, method, and polemical orientation, but it is none the less an identity. How natural, then, and, in a sense, how true to say that Critical Realism, Evolutionary Naturalism, and all that they imply, are part of my paternal inheritance. How tempting to explore the network of stimulus and response, or perhaps the depth-psychological forces that gave one mind the shape of another. This, however, I am not going to do, at least on the present occasion. The psychologist in the laboratory who locates his subject in a gapless, if incompletely envisaged, network of stimulus-response connections, intervening variables and theoretical constructs, locates himself in that everyday "space" in which observations are carefully made, evidence is weighed, connections seen, and purposes achieved. If, on occasion, and with one part of his mind, he locates himself in the former network, outside the laboratory, he places not only himself, but also his human subjects in the "space" defined by the categories of thought and action. And, as my purpose in this essay is philosophical, not psychological or biographical, I, too, shall locate myself and my subject in this latter "space" and shall view our identity of philosophical outlook as but one more example of agreement reached (I cannot say independently!) by two minds who have made the same observations, weighed the same evidence, seen the same connections, and drawn the same conclusions.

I

Physical Realism, like most of the synoptic frames of reference developed in the early decades of the twentieth century, devotes what must seem to the contemporary student a disproportionate amount of space and attention to problems relating to sense perception. The reasons, however, are not far to seek. The great speculative systems which then towered above the philosophical scene had succeeded in turning what might be thought to be an Achilles heel into one of the strongest points in their armor. Sense perception, ostensibly, to use Plato's suggestive metaphor, an intercourse between man and a co-real physical environment, had been "proved" to point "inward" to a source in "mind," and to find its "significance" in its "internal relations" to others, more obviously "mental" "contents." But even after this table has been re-turned, there remains the evident fact that sense perception is one of the two activities in which the mental is most intimately related to the physical, so that any serious attempt to come to grips with the "mind-body" problem must give it careful attention. And it is clear that for no attempt at a philosophical synthesis is this a more crucial problem than for Physical Realism—which claims to continue and revitalize the great naturalistic and materialistic perspectives of the past.

II

Physical Realism, as the previous sentence implies, is historically conscious, and is proud to measure itself against competing visions of man and his destiny. This historical orientation, the patient scrutiny of battles lost and won in the war between the gods and the giants, which is an integral part of this new attempt to rebuild an ancient vision, makes it not only appropriate, but even necessary, to approach the Philosophy of Physical Realism in its temporal setting.

The historian who seeks to locate the revolt against Idealism in the broad secular trend of philosophy is struck by the fact that the initial attack on the *esse-percipi* approach to the objects of sense perception went hand in hand with an attack on the *esse-concipi* approach to the "objects of thought." Now, the central theme of the conceptualistic tradition was the notion of an "intentional" or (in the traditional sense of the term) "objective" mode of being which is possessed by the objects of thought *as objects of thought*, and by virtue of which they are "immanent in" or "contents of" the act of thought. This framework was developed with particular reference to thought about "abstract objects," but the distinction drawn between "actual" and "intentional" being was also applied to our thought of particulars. Thus, the moon has intentional being as the content of my thought of the moon, and actual being as a reality independent of thought. The moon as actually existing is the "transcendent object," the moon as intentionally existing the "immanent object" of the thought. When, on the other hand, I think of the loneliest centaur, my thought has an immanent object, but no transcendent object. Conceptualism as an attempted solution of the problem of abstract entities added to the above framework, which it shared with "realistic" theories, the claim that abstracta have only *esse intentionale*. It denied that there corresponds to the Triangularity which has intentional being as the content of my thought, a Triangularity having actual being; being, that is, which is not being-for-thought. There is, indeed, an archetypal Triangularity, but its *esse*, too, is *concipi*, the being-conceived by God.

Now the difficulties lurking in Conceptualism were not immediately seen, for "abstract entities do not have actual being (as opposed to being-for-thought)" tended, for historical reasons, to be confused with "abstract entities are not things or substances: Man is not the common substance of Socrates and Plato; nor a whole of which they are parts." In short, the clumsiness of early medieval realism, which gave straightforward realism a bad odor which not even the more subtle realism of high scholasticism was able to overcome, and the tendency of "Moderate Realism" to look very much like Conceptualism on close scrutiny, made it possible for Conceptualism to thrive for a considerable period before becoming sensitive to the seriousness of its own predicament.

Perhaps the simplest way of describing the conceptualist's predicament is by calling attention to the fact that he is torn between two ways of speaking of the relation between the immanent and the transcendent objects of thought. On the one hand, there is Scylla, the language of "identity." There is somehow one and the same entity which has two modes of being—*the moon* is one entity which exists actually in nature and intentionally (or "objectively") in thought; Triangularity is one entity which has intentional being in my thought and also in God's archetypal Thought. Obviously, however, an explicit recognition of such identical entities would be an embarrassment to Conceptualism, threatening a collapse of immanent and transcendent objects into one. On the other hand, there is Charybdis, the language of "representation." My idea of the moon is a "representation" of the moon, my idea of Triangle is a "representation" of the archetypal Triangularity. This way of talking avoids the above collapse, but at the expense of threatening to turn *aboutness* or *reference* into *similarity*, by turning the idea of Triangularity into a triangular idea, and the idea of the moon into a private *replica* of the moon.

Now, I hope to show that the conceptualist's predicament is the key to the understanding both of the Idealistic movement, and the realistic reaction. (We all know how troublesome a term "realism" is; there is, however, as we shall see, historical method in its madness.) To begin with, let us remind ourselves that Conceptualism sought to explain the relation between thought and its objects *in rerum natura* as the logical product of two relations: (1) the relation between thought and its immanent object or content, and (2) the relation between the latter and the transcendent object. In short, "transcendent aboutness" is the logical product of "immanent aboutness" and "correspondence." Now it seemed clear that a thought could have immanent aboutness without having transcendent aboutness, as in the above example of *the loneliest centaur*. And there is no inspectable difference in authenticity between the thought of the moon and the thought of the centaur. "Correspondence" began to look more and more like a *de facto* relation accidental to the nature of thought.

But what of my thought of myself? Here the pre-Kantian conceptualist was just inconsistent. He dodged the responsibility of giving an account of consciousness of self which would be consistent with his general analysis of aboutness, and postulated a consciousness of one's own mind and mental acts which was unmediated by *intentionalia*. This inconsistency made possible the temptation to suppose that the world of nature exists merely as the immanent object of thought, and that the only items which have an existence other than existence-for-thought, in short which have existence *an sich*, are minds and mental acts.

But would not the conceptualist have granted that the colors we see and the sounds we hear have an existence other than existence-for-thought? that our consciousness of them is as unmediated by *intentionalia* as they took our consciousness of our present mental acts to be? The answer, of course, is that the seeing of colors was assimilated to the thinking of abstractions. The by no means implausible thesis that the *esse* of colors is *percipi* was assimilated (and by assimilation, falsified) to the thesis that the *esse* of abstracta is *concipi*, in that the distinctions developed for the latter were transferred to the former. Instead of the colors we see and the sounds we hear providing clear evidence that the *an sich* is not limited to minds and mental acts, they were degraded to the status of "contents of sensation," sensation being conceived as a low grade mental act belonging to the same continuum as conceiving.

Kant's contribution to the evolution of Idealism was twofold. To begin with, he was (as we have already suggested) the first to realize that it is impossible, consistent with the principles of Conceptualism, to hold that the self has a knowledge of itself which is unmediated, i.e. which does not involve a distinction between the self and its acts as transcendent object (*an sich*), and the self and its acts as immanent object (*fuer mich*). With respect to colors and sounds (the manifold of sense), Kant seems to have rejected the traditional assimilation of them to *intentionalia*, but he by no means faces up to the problem of how, if they are *not intentionalia*, they can play a role in the consciousness, fundamentally judgmental in character, of objects.[1] The fact that the colors we see are in *some* sense *fuer mich* was sufficient to bridge the gap. And certainly he insists that our consciousness of how it stands with colors and sounds is consciousness of a state of affairs which exists *fuer mich*— though only as a philosopher does one come to realize this.

In his reflection on the categories, Kant was led to abandon the traditional view of them as *summa genera*. He distinguished between the *form* and the *content* of our concepts of objects, and while he

---

[1]Kant's vagueness concerning the status of the manifold of sense is paralleled by an equal (and related) vagueness concerning the status of Space (and Time). By saying that we have an *intuition* of Space, Kant often seems to mean no more than that our consciousness of Space is the consciousness of an individual (as opposed to a class)—which is, of course, compatible with its being a *thinking* of Space. Indeed, Kant later seems to grant that our consciousness of Space and Time is a function of the Understanding (even Reason). Our consciousness of particular regions and configurations in Space is bound up with our consciousness of colors and sounds, but our consciousness of Space is *pure* in that none of the properties of Space arise out of the properties and laws of its contents, as is made clear by the "fact" that we can conceive of Space being empty of content.

granted to the empiricist that somehow the matter is derived from the manifold of sense (though one would very much like to discover a Kantian essay on how this was done), the form is underived and unlearned. It is never quite clear whether Kant is denying that the unschematized categories are the sort of thing that *could* be exemplified by the *an sich*, or whether he is limiting himself to the assertion that they are not exemplified by the manifold of sense. Clearly he agrees with Hume on the latter point.

We can now sum up the Kantian position as follows. Reality must consist of existence *an sich* as well as existence *fuer mich*, if only because the act of which the *fuer mich* is the immanent object must itself be *an sich*. But since the relation between thought and any *an sich* is the logical product of immanent aboutness and a *de facto* relation of correspondence, so that we can never compare the immanent and transcendent objects even where a transcendent object *does*—in some measure[2]—correspond to an immanent object, we can have no knowledge, only "faith" concerning the *an sich*.[3]

The Hegelians questioned Kant's idea that the empirical aspects of the content of thought are somehow taken up into thought from without and added to a categorial scaffolding. Nothing "within" thought comes from "outside" thought, and nothing "within" thought is merely juxtaposed with the rest. They also tended to turn Conceptualism into a pan-objectivism by (1) refusing to draw a sharp and ultimate distinction, within the *contents* of thought, between particulars and universals, and, by this refusal, identifying objects as known with internally related systems (in the last analysis one system) of universals, and (2) failing in any

---

[2]It will be remembered that Kant believed himself to have proved (in the *Transcendental Dialectic*) that the thought of a spatio-temporal world *an sich* is internally inconsistent.

[3]To know, as we do, that it includes thoughts of which the spatio-temporal world is the content, is not to know how it stands with these thoughts *qua* existences *an sich*. Nor can the causal principle take us from the *fuer mich* to the *an sich*. The causal principle, specifying, as it does, a formal character of the *fuer mich*, enables me to infer from this *fuer mich* to that *fuer mich*, but never to the *an sich*. And even if one knew that acts of thought *an sich* conform to the principle of sufficient reason, what principle would relate the character of the immanent object of a thought to the character *an sich* of the "cause" of the thought? Descartes laid it down that the cause of a thought must be at least as real as what the thought is about; but even if Kant could accept this, it would be of little help unless he was prepared to go the rest of the way with Descartes' proof of a material world *an sich*.

consistent way to distinguish the *act* of thinking of an internally related set of universals from the latter as the immanent object or *content* of the act.[4] But to fail to draw this distinction amounted, in their case, to abandoning Conceptualism for a Platonic Realism which includes the World of Becoming as the most specific Idea of which both what they think of as *parts* of the world, and what we think of as *kinds* and *categories*, are generic or determinable features.[5] But while the latter position would be "idealistic" only in that sense of this ambiguous term in which it connotes a realistic theory of universals, and would be, in effect, a peculiar and extreme form of realistic rationalism, the Hegelian movement made no such *explicit* break with the conceptualistic tradition, and continued to think of the *esse* of universals as *concipi* (though by the Absolute Mind, thus turning the World of Becoming into an expanded version of the Divine Intellect of Plotinus), and of the *esse* of sensible objects as *percipi*.

III

In Moore and in the Russell who was under Moore's influence, we find a radical abandonment of the conceptualistic tradition. The distinction between the immanent and the transcendent objects of thought is abandoned. Thought is not directly about "contents" (*intentionalia*) which may or may not correspond to realities *an sich*. Thought is directly about existence *an sich*. Even though existence *an sich* does not include a present king of France, our thought about the present king of France is about existence *an sich*. And since the direct objects of thought are no longer "contents" or *intentionalia*, it is no longer correct to say that the direct object of thought is *as such* "in the mind." The object of thought is no longer *mental* unless it is (as, for example, in introspection) itself a mental act. The contrast between the mental and the non-mental is traced to the contrast between items which are *acts of awareness*, and items which are not. Since the colors we

---

[4]No bald statement can be anything but misleading. The point at which I am driving is that the Hegelians abandoned the traditional (conceptualistic) account of the aboutness of (finite) acts of thought. They attempted to deal with this aboutness in terms of *ontological* categories (e.g., the "act" is *about* the "object" = the former would *be* the latter if it were "fully developed").

[5]For a penetrating account of Hegel's metaphysics along these lines, see W. T. Stace: *The Philosophy of Hegel*, New York, The Macmillan Co., 1924.

see and the sounds we hear are not acts of awareness, they fall
on the side of the non-mental. Thus, the philosophers who explored
this vein assured us that merely to be aware of colors, sounds,
etc., or, for that matter, of numbers and logical relations, is already
to be "outside the circle of our ideas."

To appreciate the dynamics of the controversies which soon
began to divide the developing realistic movement, we must note
that the early realists tended to take our (supposed) "awareness"
of colors as paradigmatic of "awareness" in general. This led to
the "problem of error." After all, it does not seem possible to be
mistaken about the colors we see; so that if *thought about x* involves
awareness of x, it would seem impossible for thought to be mistaken.
Let us also note that as soon as colors and sounds were classified
as "non-mental," the problem arose as to how these non-mental
items are related to *material* things. It would clearly have been
contrary to the whole spirit of the earliest stage of the realistic
movement to maintain that material objects constitute a domain
of entities of which we have no awareness, but which are responsible
for the existence of colors and sounds of which we are aware. We
should be as shut up in the circle of the latter as we would be if
they were mental. A domain which awareness cannot reach would
be, for these realists, a domain which thought and knowledge
cannot reach. Sooner or later they were bound to choose between
saying that we are aware of material objects as well as colors
and saying that "material objects" do not constitute a domain
additional to colors and sounds. It is interesting to watch Russell's
development in this connection. He seems to have shied away at
the very start from the idea that we are aware of colors *and* material
things. His initial line was that while we are aware of colors, etc.,
our consciousness of material objects requires for its explication
the logical form of the definite description, thus, "the *x* such that
x is material...." He argued that the awareness of a *proposition*
(itself a non-mental entity) concerning a material *descriptum* need
no more involve the awareness of a material object than the
awareness of a proposition concerning the present king of France
need involve the awareness of a king of France. And, since consciousness of a material object is not *awareness of* a material object,
there is no reason to suppose that error about material objects is
impossible.

But while it was plausible to suppose that "there is an *x* such that..." has the property of enabling reference to items which are not "given," it seemed too much to ask that it enable reference to items in a domain of entities *none* of which are *ever* objects of awareness. Thus, Russell soon turned to the attempt to "construct" material things out of *sensibilia*. And this enterprise, of course, was soon followed by the attempt to "construct" both mental and material things out of neutral entities.

IV

Such, then, are the essentials of the historical context in which the Sellarsian outlook began to take form. I have said nothing about the ingenious theories which can be lumped under the heading "Objective Relativism," partly for reasons of space, but mostly because they missed the nub of the problem faced by early realism—namely, if the fundamental relation between mind and its objects is *given-ness*, how is error possible? No amount of pointing out that in some sense snow is yellow to the jaundiced eye (as in *some* sense it is) throws any light on *this* question. In bypassing those labyrinthine by-ways of the realistic movement, I am only following in my father's footsteps, and, indeed, for much the same reason. For the central theme of his divergence from the Moore-Russell line was (and is) a consistent refusal to equate the fundamental *aboutness* with which thought is about its objects, with the *awareness* with which we are aware of the colors we see. In short, he attacked (and continues to attack) the equation of aboutness (or reference) with acquaintance or given-ness.[6] He returns to this theme again and again in his writings, and makes it clear that he regards this mistaken equation (and surely it is a mistake) as the root error of the positivistic-phenomenalistic tradition of which Russell was the (sometimes proud, sometimes puzzled) father.

Another way of putting this is by saying that a perceptual judgment can be about a physical object without the object being referred to as *the such-and-such*, and yet also without the object being in consciousness as the colors we see are in consciousness.[7]

---

[6]See, for example, *The Philosophy of Physical Realism*, New York, The Macmillan Company, 1932, pp. 56-60 *passim*, 76-82, *passim*, 94, 140.

[7]See, for example, pages 194 and 199 of his essay Knowledge and its categories

Thus, when Jones sees a chair, although his "perceptual experience" is *founded on, guided* and *controlled* by his sensations, there is nothing in the nature of aboutness or reference which requires us to say that his "experience" is *primarily* about the sensations, and only about the chair in some more complicated or derived sense of "about." His perception is "mediated by" the sensations, but his perception is not *about* the sensations.[8] It is about the chair. "Critical Realism keeps the directness of natural realism *but explicates its mechanism.* That is why I am not fond of the expression epistemological dualism."[9] Certainly, the concepts in terms of which Jones classifies the chair are concepts the acquiring of which involves having sensations of certain kinds in certain kinds of circumstances. But although the sensations Jones has control (in part) his classification of the object,[10] he is neither attributing his sensations to the object (logical nonsense) nor judging that the items, which in point of fact are his sensations, are related in any way to the object.[11] "[Sensory data] are points of departure for predicative interpretation of objects and not themselves such predicates. When I assert that an object is blue, I am not assigning it my sense-datum as such. Rather am I characterizing it in terms of a property thought by means of a specific predicate founded on the sense-datum....Things appear in my data and I think them categorially as things having properties."[12] Nor is he attributing to the object a property exemplified by his sense data;[13] he may classify an object as "blue," when he is actually having a sensation of green. I would add that not even when he judges that a chair *looks green* is his judgment about the item which is his sensation. (We do not suppose that objects cease to look green when we turn away.) Nor should the way in which such judgments are "controlled" by sensations be interpreted as a matter of the sensations

in Durant Drake *et al.: Essays in Critical Realism*, New York, The Macmillan Co., 1920; also *PPR*, pp. 63, 78 ff., 122 ff., 219 ff.

[8]*PPR*, pp. 75 ff., 138 ff.

[9]*PPR*, p. 104. (Italics in text.)

[10]*PPR*, pp. 77, 139.

[11]*PPR*, pp. 149, 193.

[12]*PPR*, p. 154.

[13]Of this point I am less confident; see, for example, *PPR*, pp. 92, 102, 148. "Predicate founded on the sense-data," seems sometimes to mean "predicate which applies to the sense data."

being *used as evidence* for the judgments. The closest we come at the common sense level to judgments which are about our sensations is in such judgments as "I am seeing yellow."

Now, it must, of course, be granted that there is a sense in which Jones' sensations on looking at the chair are more intimately related to his perceptual experience than is the chair.[14] But this does not mean that the perceptual experience is *of* the chair in a second class sense of "of." For the sense of "conscious" in which we are conscious of the colors we see, *as seeing them*, is not the sense of "conscious" in which to be conscious of something is to be cognitively disposed toward it. *Being conscious* in the sense in which this is contrasted with *being unconscious* is not a cognitive fact at all, let alone the basic relation between mind and existence. To feel a pain is not to know a pain.[15]

Let us sum up the above by saying that while our sensations mediate and control our perceptual knowledge of the physical world, this knowledge is not a second-class knowledge built on a first-class knowledge of colors and sounds. Certainly, when we do make such judgments as "I see red," we are less likely to be mistaken (indeed, the sense in which we *can* be mistaken is not the usual sense of "mistake") than when our concern is with physical objects. *But it should not be assumed that thought must be less directly about that concerning which we are more liable to error.*

It is not the primary purpose of this paper to discuss technical points in my father's Critical Realism. Yet, as we have already noticed, the problem of perception occupies a central position in his thinking, and a glance at the divergence between his Critical Realism and that of the "essence wing" of the movement (Drake, Santayana, and Strong) will provide a useful clue to his basic philosophical commitments. The latter philosophers continued the radical anti-conceptualism of the original realistic impetus, but combined this with a staunch refusal to make the colors we see and the sounds we hear constituents of physical objects. The sensations caused by the object, and the sets we have acquired from past

---

[14]*PPR*, pp. 138 ff.

[15]For an elaboration of this point, see my paper on A semantical solution of the mind-body problem, *Methodes*, 1953. I might point out that the solution of the "mind-body problem" offered in this paper is thoroughly in the tradition of Physical Realism.

experience, focus the mind, so to speak, on a certain propositional[16] *meaning* (e.g., the meaning of "There is a chair two feet away from me") so that the mind comes to apprehend this meaning. Now this propositional meaning is not a *mental* or *subjective* entity. Its *esse* is not *concipi*. It is, in effect, a possible state of affairs. If it is a *mere* possibility, the perceptual experience is "unveridical"; if it is an *actualized* possibility, the experience is "veridical." Thus, in veridical perception, the mind is acquainted with a meaning *in re* which is identical with a state of affairs in the physical world.[17]

Now this account certainly had the virtue of making the perceptual experience directly about the physical state of affairs itself. Indeed, since the propositional meaning is apprehended by the mind, indeed "given"[18], the essence wing insisted that it, rather than our sensation, is the *datum*. The sensation itself is not part of what is known in perceptual experience; it is the "vehicle" of the datum rather than the datum itself.[19] Thus, in veridical perception, the physical state of affairs itself is the datum—though not *qua* actual, rather *qua* possibility.

There are many interesting questions that can be raised concerning this approach to perception. Thus, how does it avoid the problem of error? If a possibility is given, must not its constituents be given? and how can error arise concerning what is given? The answer to this seems to be that particular physical objects are *not* constituents of the datum, for the latter is either a *kind* (in which case the essence is not a propositional meaning) or else a proposition having the general form illustrated by *there is a tree....* A more interesting question concerns the account to be given of the meaning of such terms as "here," "me," "over there," etc., which seem unavoidable in the verbal formulation of perceptual judgments. But the main point I wish to make is that the objections

---

[16]I am tidying up the position a little, since it was not always recognized that the meaning or essence must be propositional in character. Thus in his essay On the nature of the datum, in *Essays in Critical Realism*, C. A. Strong writes, (p. 242) "...on our view knowledge requires two things: the given-ness of an essence, and affirmation—that is, acting as if the essence were embodied in a real object...."

[17]In many respects the best presentation of the views of the "essence wing" is to be found in Durant Drake: *Invitation to Philosophy*, Chicago, The Houghton Mifflin Co., 1933.

[18]See, for example, the passage quoted from Strong's essay in fn. 16 above.

[19]Strong, *op. cit.*, p. 234.

of the non-essence wing to the above account were primarily of an *ontological* character. In effect, all that kept them from wholehearted agreement was the conviction that while at a certain level it is all very well to speak of the "mind" as being led to "apprehend" an "essence" which, if "realized" is identical with a physical state of affairs, this way of talking is a philosophical "short cut" and must be replaced by a more penetrating analysis.

> I would contrast this approach with the essence-theory developed by Santayana and adopted by Strong and Drake. This theory has its fingers on an important point, *viz.*—that in veridical perception, or conception, knowledge can only mean a disclosure of the nature of the object. But, to me, this principle does not carry with it the solution of the mechanism of knowing. It has seemed to me that the term, essence, was something of a verbal short-cut....In short, I felt that there was a multitude of problems, and that we were only at the beginning. (*PPR*, p. 60.)

> It is my feeling that universals have been the expression of a short-cut in philosophy. It has been so easy in epistemology to speak of the essence before the mind as *embodied* in veridical perception in the object known. It has been so easy to account for contentual sameness in ideas by an *entity* which recurs. It has been so easy to think of two minds as overlapping in a universal, and to disregard the whole genetic growth of these minds. Surely we must push our analysis deeper into the constitution of the world, and the mechanism of knowing. (*PPR*, p. 159.)

What divided the Critical Realists was not so much the problem of perception as the problem of *meaning*, the problem as to the nature of "mental acts," the "relation" of aboutness which obtains between mental acts and their objects, and the status of such entities as "universals," "truths," "realized essences," "unrealized essences"—in short, the issue was a more general form of the age old problem of universals.

Now, as we have already pointed out, the Physical Realist holds that perceptual experience is directly about the physical object itself. Thus my father insists again and again[20] that the perceiver "denotes," "refers to," "selects for characterization" the physical object itself.

The point wherein I differ from Russell is with respect to the

---

[20]See, for example, *PPR*, pp. 77 ff., 219 ff.

application of demonstratives. It seems so evident to me that
these are used in connection with acts of reference to external
objects of perceiving, objects which are regarded as common.
Critical Realism can quite agree with the outlook of natural
realism. It is the existent which is known and referred to by such
acts as pointing. And the verbal demonstratives follow the direction of the act of perceiving.... Critical Realism differs from
natural realism only in knowledge of the mechanism involved.

This divergence is important, since I am convinced that much
of the so-called modern logic has not done justice to the real
employment of the intellect and to referential judgments of the
categorical type....

I take it that, in such knowing, there are always two poles to
judgment, *reference* and *characterization*....

...Just as descriptions do not necessarily describe anything,
so references do not necessarily involve an existent as a terminus
of the reference. The analogy would be that a pointing does not
imply *something* pointed at. An act of knowing has a direction and
intention, but may be mistaken.... Minds are local and reach out
precariously to other things.

It is relevant to recall that my denial of a cognitive relation
had this ontological situation in mind. Even in the case of a true
judgment, the fact seems to be that there is a referent corresponding to the reference, and that it is correctly characterized,
but that there is no unique relation between the mental act and
the object.... The analogy is that of throwing at a mark. An act
of cognition is an intentional cast through denotative and characterizing meanings. The success of our cast must be judged by
its foundation and by applications and implications. (*PPR*, pp.
219–221, *passim.*)

One other point. Knowing is an act while knowledge is the
achievement which the act claims to contribute. It is for this
reason that I speak of all acts of cognition as cognitive-claims.
It is always possible that they will not achieve knowledge. (*PPR*,
p. 79.)

He calls attention to the behavior characteristic of reference,
and denies that reference is a supposed unique act or "cognitive
relation" over and above the behavior and behavioral sets involved.[21]

---

[21]*PPR*, pp. 78, 81-82, 126-127. Although I agree that *in some sense* all there is to
reference is behavior, I do not agree that "x refers to y" can be *analyzed* in terms

I have long denied the validity of speaking of a cognitive relation in the knowing of external things. But it has been my impression that other thinkers did not grasp the point I had in mind. And yet it is fairly simple. If the knowing of external things begins with organic attention and passes to denotation by means of a mechanism of intelligible reference, we must not think of the mental act as actually impinging upon the thing selected as its object. Referring is an activity and not a relation. It is an activity of selecting what is being thought about. Here we have a property of the organic mind which emerges from organic *attention towards*. This is a behavior attitude or, more accurately, a response-direction. . . . It is so easy to fall back on a generic term like relation and then to be misled by it. It is an aiming, a pointing, a selecting, a referring, a denoting. These terms are less misleading. (*PPR*, pp. 126–127.)

But perception is not a mere matter of selecting or referring to an object. It involves the "judging" or "affirming" that the object has such and such properties and stands in such and such relations. Thus, the perceiver, in some sense, "selects" not only an object, but also certain properties and relations, and "characterizes" the former in terms of the latter. Indeed, even the selection of the object presupposes the ability to classify and relate.[22] But how is all this to be understood? The platonistically oriented Realist is happy to speak in terms of an irreducibly mental activity or relation of apprehending abstract entities. The apprehending may be brought about by, guided by, or accompanied by bodily states, sensations and imagery, but is not to be identified with the latter with however rich a sprinkling of subjunctives. The sophisticated Platonist finds less and less of our thinking to be actual apprehendings of abstract entities, and emphasizes dispositions to apprehend; but the heart of the matter is still apprehensions of abstracta.

But what is the alternative? We have already looked at the havoc wrought by Conceptualism. How can we interpret such a statement as "Jones sees that the table top is rectangular" without postulating the existence of a unique mental relation between Jones and Triangularity, between Jones and *that the table top is rectangular*? Positively put, how interpret this statement in terms of

---

of behavior. See my "Note on Popper's Argument for Dualism," *Analysis*, 15, 1954.

[22]*PPR*, p. 220.

habits, associations, stimulus-response connections, behavior and dispositions to behave, imagery—in short, categories other than the "irreducibly mental" categories of aboutness, reference, "apprehension"? Now, like all radically naturalistic thinkers, my father is convinced that this can be done. That is, he is convinced (and, I think, rightly so) that what goes on when *Jones sees an automobile coming rapidly towards him* can, in principle, be exhaustively described without speaking of Jones as apprehending universals, possibilities, or essences.

> . . . What I have been trying to do is to do justice to what are called essences and abstract universals without falling back on the mythology which goes with the usual theories about them. These are not mysterious timeless entities which exist nowhere but which are yet intuitable and may happen to be intuited by my mind at the same time as they are embodied in external things. Rather are they meanings in experience connected with the operation of interpretation and associated with symbols. Their ontological foundation is a cerebral pattern which integrates with cognitive responses. In this sense, meanings are always potential predicates. . . ." (*PPR*, p. 194.)

But although I think that his heart is definitely in the right place, I do not think that he has sufficiently clarified the relationship which such an ideal description would have to the statement "Jones sees an automobile coming rapidly towards him."[23]

It might be thought that the best way to attack the Platonist's *apprehension of redness*, is by attacking the idea that "there is an identical characteristic which red things exemplify," or even the idea that "two things can have the same quality." This, of course, won't do.[24] My father places a great deal of emphasis on his selection of "similarity" rather than "identity" as an "ontological category,"[25] and he might seem open to the charge that he has made this mistake. An examination of the relevant passages shows, however, that what he is concerned to deny is, in the first place,

---

[23]For an analysis of the sense in which intentionality is reducible to behavior, see my paper: A semantical solution of the mind-body problem, *Methodes*, 1953. A condensed presentation of this argument can be found in my Mind, meaning and behavior, *Philosophical Studies*, 1952.

[24]For a nice discussion of this point, see Arthur Pap: A semantical examination of realism. *Journal of Philosophy*, 1947.

[25]*PPR*, p. 126.

that objects *consist*, in whole or in part, of entities which are identically parts of other objects. Here he is surely right. Plato himself realized that The Triangle Itself is not a *part* of triangular objects. Furthermore, my father wishes to deny not only that two red patches have a common "part," but also that knowing that two red patches are similar involves "apprehending" a common entity to which they are "related," and, in general, that neither the formation of concepts nor their application involves a transaction between the "mind" and a realm of "essences," "universals," or "eternal objects." On the other hand, it must be admitted that he does not clearly distinguish this latter point from the (mistaken) idea that "*a* and *b* are both red" can be *analyzed* in terms of "*a* resembles *b*." Yet his treatment of "*a* resembles *b*" indicates that he is not guilty. For although he often speaks of similarity as an "ultimate ontological category," he interprets this claim in such a way as to give it a more complex and acceptable meaning than it might seem to have. Thus, the full sentence partially quoted above reads:

> Similarity rather than identity is the ultimate ontological category and...*similarity is epistemic if we think of it as a relation.*"
> (*PPR*, p. 126; italics in the original.)

Thus, he is not saying that the state of affairs *in re* which justifies Jones' statement "*a* and *b* are both red"[26] is *a* and *b* standing in a certain relation of similarity, but rather *a* and *b* being such that it is proper for Jones to apply to both the concept or predicate "red."[27] And he never implies that the correct answer to the challenge "How are they such that...?" must be in terms of similarity *rather than*, say, "They are both red," or "They both have the color (or even quality) we call 'red.'" For this would be to take similarity to be an ontological relation. In effect, then, the purely *ontological* side of his replacement of "identity" by "similarity" is the rejection of identical entities which are either common parts of things, or enter into transcations with the "mind."

Evolutionary Naturalism is distinguished from certain other contemporary naturalisms by its avowedly *realistic* character. But

---

[26]It is assumed throughout this discussion that red is a most determinate shade of color.

[27]*PPR*, pp. 161 and, especially, 172.

what is "realism"? Perhaps the most useful answer is in terms of its contrast with "radical empiricism." For the approach of the naturalistic realist to the problems of knowledge and meaning is as unlike that of radical empiricism as an approach can be without renouncing all claim to the term "empiricism." And, indeed, we find that in *The Philosophy of Physical Realism*, my father points to the radical empiricism of C. I. Lewis as the most challenging formulation of the anti-realistic point of view.[28] The issue between these two empiricists finds its focus in the phrase "transcendent reference." My father insists, in *PPR*, that to think of a state of affairs in the physical world is not to think of actual or conditional future experiences, even though future experience is in some sense the ultimate court of appeal for claims concerning physical states of affairs.[29] How can experience testify to the occurrence of a certain physical state of affairs, unless that state of affairs has *implications* for actual or conditional future experience? But *of course* physical states of affairs have implications, in *some* sense of "implication," for experience. We can truly say such things as "If this is sugar in the spoon, than if I put it in my mouth, I will taste a sweet taste," "If there was sugar in the spoon, then if I had put it in my mouth, I would have tasted a sweet taste," and "If there is sugar in the spoon tomorrow . . . ." Our commerce with physical objects is responsible for our perceptions of colors and sounds, in ways with which we are already familiar at the common sense level, though we have gained additional insights with the advance of physical and psychological theory. Certainly, if all the basic physical properties of the common sense world (e.g., red, sweet, square) were "secondary qualities" in Locke's sense (powers to yield perceptions), then to assert the presence at a certain time and place of an object possessing these properties would be to formulate subjunctive conditionals about perceptions. But that not all the properties which common sense attributes to physical objects can be analyzed in terms of subjunctive conditionals about perceptions becomes clear once we note that subjunctive discourse of the kind that is relevant to our problem embodies our consciousness of the laws of nature. (Some subjunctive

---

[28]*PPR*, pp. 150 ff., 185 ff.

[29]*PPR*, p. 128.

conditionals, of course, embody our consciousness of the laws of logic.) Thus, common sense subjunctive conditionals about perceptions would embody our common sense consciousness of the laws of sense perception. But it is evident, on reflection, that this consciousness relates sense perception to bodily and physical occurrences. Consequently, a vicious circle lurks in the attempt to analyze common sense physical properties in terms of perceptual subjunctives—for the analysis of the latter leads right back to physical terms.

And it is by no means clear that *any* of the above properties are powers. The conviction that, for example, the (common sense) physical property *red* is a power, definable in terms of the "sense quality" *red*, can be traced to two things. In the first place, (1) it arises from the fact (if it is a fact) that we can introduce into sophisticated sense-quality talk a dispositional predicate "red" which is applicable whenever the common sense term "red" is applicable. But this (supposing it can be done) must no more be confused with giving an *analysis* of the common sense property *red*, than sophisticated talk about sense data with the analysis of what is meant at the common sense level by "seeing colors" or "hearing sounds."

A second source lies (2) in the idea that since we *learn the meaning of* the common sense word "red" by seeing such and such colors in such and such circumstances, the word must *mean* the power of causing a person to see such and such colors (illegitimately identified with "have such and such sense data") in such and such circumstances. (A parallel mistake on the part of those who stress "appearing" talk leads to the conclusion that "red" means the power of appearing thus and thus in such and such circumstances.) To be sure, "x is red" has implications of the form "I would see ————, if I looked at x in such and such circumstances," as well as of the form "x would look . . ., if I saw it in such and such circumstances," and "I see *red* when I look at x" has implications of the form "It would be true that x is red, if the circumstances were thus and such." And it may even be correct to say that these implications exhibit, in part, the correct use of the expressions "x looks red," "x is red," and "I see red." But only if one has swallowed some version of the radical empiricist dogma concerning meaning and the given will one know *ab initio* that *red* as a property of physical objects is *analyzable into* hypotheticals.

According to the Physical Realist, then, when I judge, at the common sense level, that the book is red, I am not judging that the book has a certain power (or set of powers), although the Physical Realist would grant that from the fact that something is red it *follows*, for example, that it would look red in daylight. But, it will be said, if I am not judging that the book has a *power*, I must be judging that it has an *occurrent property*. But what is it? The sense quality red? No. The occurrent property science discovers to accompany the power to cause perceptions of red in daylight? No. "Red" is a common sense term the use of which must not be identified with that of any term in scientific or quasi-scientific theory. Science has not shown our common sense judgments to be false; it gives us new truths in terms of new concepts which correlate with our common sense truths and concepts.

Now I am not certain just how far my father would go along with all of this. Thus, on the one hand he writes:

> Perceiving...is a level of knowing which should be criticized only when taken in its natural context. (*PPR*, p. 92.)
>
> The deepening of this cognitive [perceptual] act by scientific method and reasoning should never be regarded as a rejection of it. (*PPR*, p. 94.)

On the other hand,

> ...perceptual judgments are valid only for their level and must be reconstructed at the level of science. That is, things do not have color as a quality nor the visual size they appear to have.... (*PPR*, p. 95.)
>
> We have argued that many of the predicates assigned to objects of perception must be relinquished and substitutes made for them. Thus, the scientist refuses to regard color as a proper predicate of physical things and takes the sensuous quality of a visual datum as, instead, a clue to the frequency of the light sent to the eye from the object. (*PPR*, p. 102.)

V

But we have not yet come fully to grips with the problem of "transcendent reference"; though we have been beating around the neighboring bushes. At bottom, the problem is the relation of meaning to immediate experience, and we have been pointing out that the Physical Realist rejects the radical empiricist account of concept formation lock, stock, and barrel. We have been pointing out that for the Physical Realist there is no such simple connection between meaning and the "immediacy" of sensation as is as-sumed—almost as an *a priori* thesis—by this account. He grants, of course, that the process of acquiring concepts of physical objects essentially involves the occurrence of patterns of sensations arising from our commerce with physical objects, and that these sensations are more intimately related to the go of the organism than are their external causes—but he warns against drawing the conclusion that knowledge and meaning must be more intimately *about* these patterns of sensations than about their external cause. It no more follows from the fact that sensations are essentially involved in physical concept formation that physical concepts must be concepts of sensory patterns, than it follows from the fact that symbolic manipulations are essentially involved in mathematical concept formation, that mathematical concepts are concepts of symbolic manipulations. Indeed, not even the common sense concepts of *seeing a color, hearing a sound,* or *feeling a pain* are concepts of sensuous immediacy. To acquire empirical concepts is (in part) to learn to respond to one's environment with these concepts. But the relation of a sensation of red to the judgment *that book is red* must not be confused with the relation of *I am seeing red* to *that book is red*. *I am seeing red* is a *reason* for *the book is red*. The sensation of red is not a *reason* even for *I am seeing red*. Having sensations is having *causes of* judgments, not *reasons for* judgments. Or, better, in view of the ambiguities of "having a reason," *having sensations* is not *knowing premises* from which one *draws inferences*. Needless to say, however, the process whereby Jones acquires concepts guar-antees that when his environment evokes from him the judgment *that book is red*, he is, in all probability, confronting a book, and it *is* red.

Lewis admits that statements about the past are genuinely about the past, and not exclusively about the actual and conditional future experiences which would confirm them.[30] He insists, how-ever, that unless statements about the past *imply* conditional

---

[30]*An Analysis of Knowledge and Valuation*, p. 197 ff.

future experiences, the occurrence of the latter would not confirm
them. The conditional future experiences are, so to speak, the
testable or *cashable* meaning of the statements. They do not, however, *exhaust* their meaning. Why, then, is it not open to the
Physical Realist to claim that the same is true of statements about
contemporary physical situations. Why can he not say that these
statements imply conditional future experiences; but that these
implications no more exhaust the meaning of the statements in
question than do the corresponding implications of statements
about the past? But what kind of implication is this? he will be
asked. And it is clear that to the physical Realist it can be nothing
more nor less than "causal implication," the implication to which
we appeal when we argue from the existence of a situation of one
kind to that of another kind not tautologically contained in it.
In short, what our common sense statements about physical
objects imply in the way of experience is a matter of what we have
discovered, at the common sense level, about the ways of things,
including, in particular, the ways of sense perception.

> In opposition to this positivism, the critical realist argues that
> knowing is, in intention, the interpretation of physical things as
> these in some measure appear, or are manifested, in sensory
> presentation, and that, in critical knowing, we achieve a complex
> content which is regarded as revealing the independent, physical
> thing. On this basis we can justify Lewis' predictive hypotheticals
> by giving their ground and, at the same time, satisfy the cate-
> gorial meanings of antecedent reality which the pragmatist is
> aware of but which he rejects on the negative ground that no
> theory of knowledge has as yet done justice to it. (*PPR*, p. 152.)

The reader who is at all familiar with this controversy will have
anticipated Lewis' reply. It is that the implication in question
must be an "analytic" implication in the sense that it is a matter
of the *very meaning* of the statement in question. For if no set of
conditional predictions of future experience *analytically* implied
the existence or probable existence of some physical state of affairs,
and if statements about physical objects did not *analytically* imply
statements about conditional future experiences, physical objects
(supposing that we could form such concepts) would be *dinge an
sich*, otiose, and barren.

Now I think that Lewis has his finger on a very important

point. But I think that he is overly hasty in assuming that "analytic" *as he uses the term* excludes "causal." I do not have the space to develop this point, but the following remarks will serve to indicate the lines along which I would reconcile the claims of Phenomenalism and Realism. Lewis insists that statements about the past must *imply* statements about future conditional experiences. He also insists that the implication must be *analytic*. He points out that the fact that "Yesterday was Monday" analytically implies "Tomorrow will be Wednesday" and does not require that the time slab which is yesterday be a part of the time slab which is tomorrow.[31] He concludes that "Caesar died" can *analytically* imply certain conditional future experiences without being itself in the future. Very good. But whereas the relation between "Yesterday was Monday" and "Tomorrow will be Wednesday" obviously holds by virtue of the meanings involved, surely "Caesar died" implies conditional future experiences only in conjunction with auxiliary historical propositions *and a framework of laws of nature.* Is Lewis willing to hold that the relevant laws of nature are *analytic?* Certainly they are not *tautological,* but for Lewis the "analytic" is broader than the "tautological."[32] I would argue that unless Lewis can develop such a position, he is not entitled to criticize Physical Realism for failing to appreciate that the relation between physical object statements and conditional predictions of future experiences holds *ex vi terminorum.* If, on the other hand, he can successfully develop such a position (and I think it can be done[33]) the Physical Realist can equally agree that the relation is a meaning relation while continuing to deny that statements about physical objects are *translatable* (even in principle) into conditional predictions of future experience. Indeed, I would go further and say that only a philosophy which, like Physical Realism,

---

[31]*AKV*, p. 199.

[32]See my discussion of this point in Is there a synthetic a priori?, *Philosophy of Science,* 1953, reprinted, with alterations, in *Science, Perception and Reality.*

[33]Indeed, that our consciousness of the *ways* of things is "analytic of" (to use a Deweyan phrase of which I am not overly fond) our consciousness of the *kinds* and *properties* of things, is something that I have argued in a whole series of papers from Realism and the new way of words, *Philosoophy and Phenomenological Research,* 1948, to Inference and meaning, *Mind,* 1953, and, most recently, Some reflections on language games, *Philosophy of Science,* 1954, reprinted, with alterations, in *Science, Perception and Reality.*

has abandoned the dead end road of immediacy, while yet main-
taining a broadly empirical orientation, can hope to combine the
insights of the coherence theory of meaning ("a concept is an
intersection in a network of implications") with the empricist's
contention that it is always proper to ask for an "inductive"
justification of any proposal to revise the framework of law-like
sentences (and, hence, of meanings) in terms of which we approach
our environment. But while such justification involves an "appeal
to observation," not even observational meanings are immune to
criticism and revision.[34] There is no "sky hook" of *given* meanings
to serve as a fulcrum for moving the world of ideas. And by the
same token, the process of revision must be compared to repairing
a ship at sea, rather than to reconstructing a building on the same
old solid foundation.

---

[34]I have sketched the general lines of a philosophy of inductive reasoning which
embodies these features in the concluding sections of the paper on language games
to which reference is made in the preceding footnote.

VIII

THE INTENTIONAL REALISM OF EVERETT HALL

I

EVERETT HALL's intentional realism is an example of systematic philosophy at its best. It is no myopic sequence of small scale analyses strung together like beads on a string. Yet its foundation was laid over the years by painstaking and scrupulous probings into the many problems and puzzles with which a systematic philosophy must deal. Again, though it is rooted in a sympathetic and perceptive interpretation of the philosophical classics, it is as contemporary as the latest issues of *Mind*. Few philosophers have taken as seriously the obligation to keep in touch with the best work of their contemporaries. He recognized that it is only by submitting ideas to the constant challenge of other lines of thought that philosophers can gain assurance that their speculations are not sheltered idiosyncracies. Everett Hall's philosophy is thoroughly empiricist in temper, but completely lacking in the procrustean urge which has marred so many recent empiricists. Above all, it is in a most important sense self-conscious or self-referential in that it concludes as an essential component a theory of the philosophical enterprise, a theory which faces up to the ultimate challenge which any systematic philosophy must face: What is the status of your philosophical claims, and what are the criteria by which you distinguish them as true from the false and unacceptable claims made by rival philosophies? Thus, by no means the least important of his achievements is the way he found between the horns of Hume's dilemma, which, in modern dress, reads as follows:

> Philosophical statements are *either* analytic (in which case they tell us nothing about the world) or synthetic (in which case they fall within the scope of empirical science).

Inspired by this dilemma, Hume was willing to throw all distinctively philosophical statements into the flames. (One wonders whether he would have done so with his own.) The Wittgenstein of the *Tractatus* denied that there *are* any distinctively philosophical statements. What purport to be such he found to be therapeutic devices which can be cast aside, perhaps into the flames, once they have served their purpose. Hall offers instead a conception of philosophy as "neither *a priori* nor empirical."[1] By "empirical" he has in mind, I take it, the inductive methods of the empirical and theoretical sciences. He argues for "a third kind of knowledge" which he calls "categorial" (Hall, p. 6). The test of claims falling within this "third enterprise" is to be found "in the forms of every-day thought about everyday matters in so far as these reveal commitment in some tacit way to a view or perhaps several views about how the world is made up, about its basic 'dimensions'" (Hall, p. 6). "We find," he continues, "these forms of everyday thought chiefly in the grammatical structures (in a broad sense) of daily speech, in what may be called the resources of ordinary language, although they are also present in the ways in which we personally experience things.... The latter," he adds, "reflect, to a great extent, the formative influence of our mother tongue," (Hall, p. 6) a theme to which I will return.

This characterization of the philosophical enterprise illustrates once again the catholicity (i.e., the universal sweep), of Everett Hall's philosophy, for, in my opinion, this conception of philosophy is the truth to which both the descriptive phenomenology of Husserl and the conceptual analysis of the developing phase of Oxford philosophy are halting approximations.

But my concern in this essay is not the Hallian metaphilosophy, but with certain specific theses in his philosophy of mind—theses pertaining to his realistic analysis of perception. The central theme of Hall's intentional realism is his interpretation of perceptual acts as sentence-events in a natural language (i.e., as items which are *analogous* to sentence-events in conventional languages). This move enables him to put such concepts as *meaning, reference, predication, ascription, truth* to effective use in clarifying the relation between the act of perceiving and the object perceived. It must be emphasized in this connection that although sentence-

---

[1]Everett Hall: *Our Knowledge of Fact and Value.* Chapel Hill, 1961, p. 5. References made solely by page number will be to this work.

events in natural language are conceived by analogy with sentence-events in conventional langauge, this does not mean that the meaning, reference, and truth which pertain to natural language are derivative from the meaning, reference, and truth which pertain to conventional language. We must distinguish here, following Aristotle, between priority in the order of knowledge and priority in the order of being. We come to understand the nature and function of natural language through conceiving of it by analogy with conventional language. But in the order of being, natural language is prior. As Hall sees it, if there were no such thing as natural language with its modes of meaning, reference, predication, and truth, there could be no such thing as conventional language.

Hall's conception of natural language is in the tradition of William of Ockham and revitalizes insights which were lost in the heyday of British Empiricism. A glance at Hume will be instructive, for although, like all empiricists, Hall has learned much from Hume, the guiding thread of the intentionality of the mental (i.e., of those features of mental acts by virtue of which they are analogous to conventional speech) enables him to avoid a key confusion which occurs at the very beginning of the *Treatise* and infects the argument on almost every page.

It will be remembered that the human mind, according to Hume, is a system of impressions and ideas. If we leave aside the impressions and ideas which constitute the life of feeling and emotion and concentrate on those which pertain to our experience of the physical world, we can take as our paradigm of a Humean impression *a visual impression of a red triangle*. Now a careful study of the *Treatise* makes it clear that there are two incompatible themes in Hume's account of the sort of item referred to by the italicized phrase:

1. An impression of a red triangle is a red and triangular item which is immediately and non-inferentially known to exist and to be red and triangular.

2. An impression of a red triangule is a knowing that a red and triangular item exists.

According to (1), the impression is an *object* of knowledge. It is literally red and triangular, and is directly known to be so. It is an object of knowledge, but scarcely, it would seem, a *knowing*. For even if a knowing could be literally red and triangular, its character as a knowing could not *consist* in its being red and triangular. Furthermore, if there were such a thing as a red and triangular knowing, it could scarcely be its own object. The object known must surely be other than the act by which it is known.

According to (2), the impression is a knowing rather than a known, and it is the known rather than the knowing which is literally red and triangular.

Alternative (1), by using the term "impression" for *objects* of immediate knowledge, has no category for the *acts* by which they are known, and hence no place for the intentionality of perception. Alternative (2), by using the term "impression" for *acts* of knowing, has no category for the objects of immediate knowledge. The conflation of these two alternatives provides both knowings and objects to be known, but at the expense of a radical ambiguity in the use of the term impression, and a confusion, which Hall points out, of the relation between a perceiving and a certain attribute—e.g., triangularity—by virtue of which the perception *signifies or intends* the attribute, with the relation which holds between something which is literally triangular and the triangularity it *exemplifies*.

Against the background of this radical confusion, the strategy of Hall's intentional realism stands out in bold relief. What Hall calls perceptions correspond by and large to Hume's impressions in those respects which take intentionality into account. With this in mind, we can draw up the following points of similarity and difference:

1. Hall's perceptions—like Hume's impressions—are states of the percipient which are causally evoked by the action of external objects on his sense organs.

2. Hall's perceptions—unlike Hume's impressions—are not the *objects* of perceptual knowledge. They can, indeed, be known in what is misleadingly called introspection. But they are not perceived. They are perceiv*ings* rather than perceiv*eds*.

3. Hall's perceptions—unlike Hume's impressions—are not *knowings*. The term "know" in its primary use implies (a)

truth (i.e., to say that a sentence (conventional or natural) expresses knowledge is to endorse the sentence as true) and (b) conclusiveness or certainty. But on Hall's analysis perceptions can be false, and even true perceptions are usually only highly probable, supported by their consilience with other perceptions.[2] Hall's perceptions might well be called perceptual *convictions* about physical objects and processes. They are perceptual convictions *that* something is the case, e.g., *that* a certain object is red and triangular.

Before continuing with our enumeration, it might be noted that there is a strand in Hume's treatment of impressions according to which they would be *knowings* only in a weakened sense of this term in which it amounts to "convictions." According to this strand, "impressions" are intrinsically indistinguishable from very vivid "ideas." Hume's account of "ideas" is at least as confused as his account of "impressions," thus sometimes the "idea" of a red triangle is a red and triangular item deserving the name "impression." But, as in the case of impressions, the theme of intentionality is not lacking. Here "ideas" are *thoughts* which, according to their degree of forcefulness, range from "merely thinking of," e.g., the existence of a red triangle, through various degrees of belief in the existence of a red triangle, to the *conviction*, indistinguishable from an impression, that a red triangle exists. The fact that impressions are located in a continuum with ideas suggests that when impressions are described as knowings, the latter term is to be construed in a way which does not imply endorsement, or certainty in any other than the subjective sense of *conviction*. This, of course, would be the point of view of Hume within his study; outside the normative overtones of the credibility and authority of perception would reappear.

4. According to Hall's account, the perception of a red triangle is neither red nor triangular. That is to say, it does not literally *exemplify* either of these attributes. On the other

---

[2]One of the most interesting moves Hall makes is to argue that each perception, merely by virtue of the fact that it occurs, has a certain intrinsic probability, to which additional credibility can be added by the mutual support of perceptions in accordance with principles of perceptual confirmation. These principles, as well as the principle of intrinsic probability, are given a metaphilosophical defense by pointing out that they are framework features of perceptual experience.

hand, the attribute is present in the perception in another manner (i.e., a manner other than that of being exemplified). As Hall sees it, one of the primary sources of skepticism and phenonemalism is the idea that "the only way properties are present in the world" (Hall, p. 37) is by being exemplified.

5. Since perceivings, on Hall's account, are perceptual convictions about physical objects and processes, the problem of skepticism is *not* that of what authorizes an inference from impressions as directly known objects to their putative causes—a source of skepticism which is rooted in the first strand of Hume's account of impressions. The problem is rather: Are impressions as perceptual convictions (i.e., the impressions of the second strand in Hume), capable of being true? And if so, can we have reason to suppose that any of them are? The Hume we were sketching a moment ago would say, on Berkeleyan grounds, that they are not capable of being true, and would add that even if these Berkeleyan grounds were mistaken and they could be true, we could have no reason to suppose that any of them are. Hall's answer to both these questions is categorically affirmative.

II

Let me now develop a second background against which it will be helpful to view Hall's intentional realism. I have in mind the Cartesian distinction, derived from Scholasticism, but given a distinctive twist, between formal and objective reality. This distinction concerns two modes of being or reality which entities can have:

1. Things and their attributes can have "formal" being; things, including minds, by existing in the world, and attributes by being exemplified by things.
2. Things and their attributes can have "objective" being in acts of thought. Thus Socrates has objective being in any mind that thinks of him, and wisdom in any mind that thinks of something as being wise.

Notice that an object, e.g., Socrates, which has objective being in a certain mind is not in that mind in the sense of being a part or aspect of the mind—let alone being spatially within it. The object is not, as the metaphor has it, "bodily present" in the mind. Succinctly put, *objective* presence is not *bodily* presence. Again, an attribute, e.g., triangularity, which has objective being in a certain mind which is thinking of something as triangular, is not in that mind in the sense of being *exemplified* by the mind. Obviously the thought of something as triangular is not a triangular thought.

This distinction between the "objective" presence of things and attributes in thought and their formal presence in the world permits the formulation of a simple theory of the truth of at least certain kinds of thought. Roughly, a thought to the effect that a certain object O has a certain attribute A is true if and only if the object O, which is objectively present in the thought, is formally present in the world, and the attribute A, which is objectively present in the thought, is exemplified by O.

Now, in the case of the attributes involved in perceptual conviction, this distinction between "objective" and "formal" presence corresponds to Hall's distinction between "present as experienced" and "present as exemplified" (Hall, p. 35). Thus, if I have a perception of a red object and the perception is veridical (i.e., there really is a red object before my eyes), then red is *present as experienced* (i.e., objectively present) in the perceiving and this same attribute, red, is also *present as exemplified* in the object perceived. Again, Hall emphasizes that the objects of perception are not "bodily present" in the act of perception, but only present as experienced (Hall, pp. 72, ff.). In Cartesian terms, the objects of perception as well as the attributes they are perceived to have are only objectively present in the act of perception. All this is compatible, as Hall emphasizes (Hall, pp. 35-36, 74 ff.). with the idea that perceptual and other mental acts *exemplify* attributes, e.g., temporal and spatial relations, and even neurophysiological propeties, in their own right.

III

The Cartesian also distinguishes between the act of thought *qua* having things and attributes objectively present in it and the act of thought *qua* existent exemplifying attributes in its own right. His account of acts of thought in the latter respect, however, is remarkably thin. Acts of thought exemplify temporal relations, and they exemplify the relation of belonging to or occurring in a mind as well as such attributes as tending to be followed by certain other thoughts. They exemplify the derivative attribute of having certain items objectively present in them. But, one wonders, what is their qualitative character in their own right? Here one runs up against the puzzling view that *qua* acts of thought, though they may differ in their *relations* and in their *derivative* attributes, are *intrinsically indistinguishable*. One is put in mind of the diaphanous character which G. E. Moore ascribes to awareness—though Moore's general approach is quite different.[3]

Hall avoids this puzzling conception by rejecting the classical interpretation of self-awareness on a perceptual model (Hall, p. 16). To construe direct self-knowledge as akin to sense perception is to look for qualitative features in mental acts as the objects of introspection which would correspond to colors as qualitative features of things seen, and sounds as qualitative features of things heard. Since no such qualities are to be found, the fictitious quality of "diaphanousness" is invented to fill the gap. This generates the classical problem of how mental acts with their diaphanousness are related to non-diaphanous states of the body. By refusing to construe self-knowledge on a perceptual model, Hall is enabled to suggest that in their intrinsic being perceptual acts are neurophysiological events. For since self-knowledge does not assign them *any* qualitative character, let alone a diaphanous quality inconsistent with the qualitative character of neural events, it is open to us to hold that their qualitative character is that of a neural event.

Notice that although perceivings would be neural episodes, which requires that they have properties which we do not ordinarily think of them as having, this identification also requires that certain neural episodes have properties which we do not ordinarily think of them as having. For the neural episodes in question would have the property of having objects and attributes objectively present in them in the mode of *being experienced* as contrasted with that of *being exemplified*. Hall, as far as I know, explicitly applies this analysis only to perceivings and bodily feelings (i.e., to mental acts which belong to the natural language

---

[3]For an elaboration of this point see the opening sections of my Being and being known, *Proceedings of the American Catholic Philosophical Association*, 1960, reprinted in my *Science, Perception and Reality*, London, 1963.

of perception and feeling). It is, however, readily extensible to all mental acts without exception, and so extended would construe them as neural events which "have" the derivative property of having objects and attributes of various kinds and types objectively present in them. This would raise the interesting question of what correlation might exist between these derivative properties of neural events and what might be called the *natural* characteristics of neural events (i.e., their character as objects of scientific description and explanation).

IV

We are now in a position to examine more closely Hall's conception of a perceptual act, or perceiv*ing*. We have seen that although perceivings are neural events, they are perceivings by virtue of the objective presence in them of objects and attributes (i.e., the presence of the latter *as experienced*). Let us relate this to our earlier account of them as sentence-events in the natural language of perception. The reference to sentence-events reminds us of Peirce's distinction between linguistic types and their tokens. (The word "the" as *type* is a repeatable; there are many tokens of "the" on this page.) Hall refers to a sentence-type in natural language as an *intention* (Hall, p. 74). Thus a sentence-event in perceptual language is, so to speak, a token of an intention. Intentions, he tells us, "are like properties in being incomplete, by nature dependent on something else, and universal in the sense that the same one may belong to several events" (Hall, p. 74). He distinguishes the sense of "intention" he has in mind from the sense which pertains to action by calling them "references" (Hall, p. 74). This, however, is misleading in that it suggests that intentions are the natural language counterpart of referring expressions rather than sentences. Not only is this not the case, but one of our problems will be to see in what sense there are any referring expressions in natural language as construed by Hall.

Intentions, he tells us, have a "certain inherent complexity. They may be said to include ordinary properties" (Hall, p. 75). Thus the intention tokened by the perception that an object is triangular includes the attribute triangularity.

Now it is clear that if the intention were simply a complex property, as being-red-and-triangular is a complex property, its relation to the mental act could not be that of exemplification. For if the intention were a complex property of which triangularity were a part, and if the perceiving exemplified the intention, then the perceiving would *a fortiori* be in part literally triangular—which is exactly the thesis he is most concerned to reject. At this point, Hall could make either of two moves: (1) He could hold that an intention is a complex property but deny that the relation between the perceiving and the property is that of exemplification; (2) He could hold that the intention is a unique kind of complex which, although it *includes* properties, is not a complex property. Actually he makes both moves. He characterizes the relation between an act and the intention which it "has" or which "belongs" to it as analogous to but not the same as exemplification. And he emphasizes that intentions are analogous to properties but unlike them in key respects. Finally, he stresses that although "they may be said to include ordinary properties," they do so "neither as exemplified by themselves (i.e., the intentions) nor by what has them (i.e., the neural events), but, instead, by their objects." He concludes that "intentions can themselves be called natural or radical signs, identical with their objects (in veridical perception) in the quality or character of those objects' properties, but non-identical in the factor of exemplification (in place of exemplification intentions have ascription)" (Hall, p. 75).

This important passage is rather cryptic, but I take it that the term "ascription" characterizes the inner structure of the intention, and is intended to differentiate the place of triangularity in an intention from its place in a complex property.

Perceptions, then, ascribe properties to objects. How is this to be understood? We might begin by construing a perceptual intention as a perceptual sentence of the form ·(object) exemplifies (property)· where the dot-quotes indicate that the intention is analogous to a sentence in conventional language, while the fact that they are special quotes indicates that after all it is not a sentence in conventional language. If we assume provisionally that the intention contains an expression which refers to an object and an expression which refers to a property, then for the intention to ascribe the property to the object is for the intention to consist of three items uniquely related: a natural word for the property, a natural word for the object, and a natural word which means *exemplified*.

Now Hall emphasizes that in the natural language of perception, "red as experienced names, designates, means, immediately the red as exemplified; the red of the perception refers to the red of the sunset, the red in one capacity or status means the red in the other" (Hall, p. 35). Here, he tells us, "we have the basis of designation, designation as it occurs originally, prior to conventional rules" (Hall, p. 35). Thus the intention includes in a unique way the property itself and the nexus of exemplification. If we assume that the intention includes in the same unique way the object itself, then we could think of natural *words* as the objects and attributes themselves *as occurring in intentions*. Intentions, then, would be unique wholes of which objects and attributes would, in a unique way, be parts. I suppose that this is true enough, for the term "unique" is elastic enough to cover a great deal of ground. Yet, at least as far as objects are concerned, we run into the difficulty that an intention may contain an object, even though—as in the case of hallucination—there is no such object. But I shall not press these points, since they lead to some of the most intricate issues in ontology. Suffice it to say that Hall is well aware of this difficulty (Hall, p. 75), and that the above remarks are not intended as a criticism.

But there are other aspects of perceptual intentions as characterized by Hall which I find quite puzzling, and which lead me not to doubt the truth of his intentionalistic analysis of perception, but to wonder if his natural language is rich enough to do the job.

To bring this out, it will be helpful to explore the structure of perceptual intentions by scrutinizing the conventional sentences which give them expression. In this connection, Hall draws a most important distinction between "perception proxies" and "perception depicters" (Hall, pp. 38 ff.). Failure to observe this distinction he finds to be another source of subjectivism and skepticism. Perception depicters are biographical statements which assert the occurrence of a perceiving—e.g., "First X saw a bright red flash, then X heard a rumbling noise." Notice that although perception depicters can be about anybody at any time or place, the most important subset for our purposes consists of those which concern *myself here and now*—for it is these which can be confused with perception proxies.

Perception proxies are, in the first instance, translations (Hall, p. 38) of selected features of the total perceptual experience into conventional language. They are, indeed, the closest conventional counterpart of sentences in the natural language of perception. An example might be; "*This* is red and triangular."

Now perception proxies have several features which are not present in the perceptions they translate. Thus, to begin with, perceptions, unlike perception proxies, "contain neither demonstratives nor proper names" (Hall, p. 42). This raises the question: How is the reference of a perception to its object to be understood? Surely, we are tempted to expostulate, there must be expressions in natural language which are the counterparts of *referring expressions* in conventional language, as properties-as-experienced are the counterpart of conventional *characterizing expressions*.

One might be tempted to suppose that, lacking demonstratives and proper names, natural language contains the counterpart of definite descriptions. Perhaps the perception which translates into "The book over there is red" has a natural language definite description as its subject. But Hall rejects this move on the ground that Russell's analysis (and, for that matter, Strawson's) shows definite descriptions to involve such notions as "all," "identical with," "if . . ., then . . .," in short, all the conceptual apparatus of propositional and functional logic, and these, as we shall see in a moment, are also not present at the perceptual level proper, but belong exclusively, as Hall sees it, to conventional language.

Hall emphasizes that conventional language, once we have it, blends with natural language, so that perceptual experience proper is enriched with "in the head" use of conventional expressions. But, he writes:

> [Pure perception] contains neither demonstratives nor proper names. This is perhaps partly just a verbal specification. When I meet with perceptions containing demonstratives or proper names, I refuse to call them "pure." But it is in part observational also. *I find that I have perceptions which are descriptive or predicative or predicative throughout and are in fact quite devoid of conventional symbols.* (Hall, p. 42, italics mine.)

What puzzles me about this is how a pure perception can be a *sentence*, and yet be "predicative throughout." Are not predicative expressions the correlatives of referring expressions? Must not pure perceptions contain expressions referring to an object in order to be able to characterize an object? Hall writes:

> In pure perceptual experience, we have batteries of predications, so to speak. These are "of" individuals; and one individual is selected in perception for predication simply by the whole battery of predications made of it, the "it" being that which is asserted by the perception to exemplify them all together with an indefinite number of unspecified other properties from which the perception has selected just the ones whose assertion constitutes that perception (Hall, pp. 42-43).

This suggests that while perceptions contain neither demonstratives nor proper names, they do contain expressions which are the natural language counterparts of an indefinite "it," and have the form

· It exemplifies /properties/ ·

Yet it must be granted that this interpretation is not easily reconciled with the above claim that pure perceptions are predicative throughout. On the other hand, it is confirmed by such statements as the following:

> Although I have no way of getting at [the chair] perceptually save through properties I experience it as having, still it is not these properties. *My experience is of the properties as exemplified.* . . . (Hall, p. 44, my italics.)
> Perception is the predication of these properties, the ascription of them to an object (Hall, p. 73).
> . . . Perceptual experience . . . always affirms that there is something that exemplifies the multiplicity of its groups of predicated properties . . . (Hall, p. 47).

The last of these would have to be construed as a misleading formulation of the above analysis, for taken as it stands it suggests that perceptions have the form

· (Ex) x exemplifies /properties/ ·

which is ruled out by the absence, on which Hall insists, of logical connectives and quantifiers from natural language.

To sum up this first comparison of perceptions with perception proxies, Hall thinks of pure perceptions as containing a primitive or rudimentary mode of reference, though his account is not unambiguous. On the other hand, the sophisticated devices of demonstratives, proper names, and definite descriptions are lacking at the level of pure perception, and make their way into perceptual experience only through the blending of pure perceptions with conventional language.

V

What, then, of logical connectives and operators (i.e., such expressions as "not," "if..., then...," "all," etc.)? Hall insists, as has already been pointed out, that these are not to be found at the level of pure perception. He claims, however, that their use in conventional language does have perceptual underpinning. Let us begin our exploration of this contention by considering the case of "not." Here the thesis is by no means lacking in plausibility, for surely, as Hall puts it, "to all appearances our perceptual experience is positive throughout" (Hall, p. 49). Whether or not this is actually the case, and if so in what sense the phrase "perceptual experience" is being used, are questions for subsequent exploration. But certainly there are many who would agree with Hall on this point. Let us grant, then, at least for the moment, that we see that a certain object is red, but do not see, at the level of pure perception, that it is *not* green.

Yet, as Hall points out, singular negative perception proxies do occur. Consider the perception proxy, "This is *not* green." Now that something is not green can be *inferred* from the fact that it is red, for these attributes are incompatible. But how do we know this? As a staunch empiricist, Hall replies—by generalization. Of course, the generalizations—roughly, "(x) red $x \to \sim$green x" and "(x) green $x \to \sim$red x"—cannot be from pure perceptions by the route

O_1 is red, round, not green...

O_2 is red, square, not green...

O_3 is green, oval, not red...

for there is no pure perception of objects as *not green* or *not red*. Rather, as far as I can make out, the generalizations take their point of departure from positive perception depicters, and instead of being instantial inductions are of the nature of hypotheses to explain the fact that we never perceive green objects which are red or red objects which are green. I suspect that lurking in this ingenious solution is a corresponding problem about negative self-knowledge, thus "I am not perceiving a red object which is green," but it is certainly an interesting move and far more penetrating than most discussions of the subject.

But even granting the success of Hall's move with respect to "not," there are other problems to be met. Thus while philosophers since the time of Parmenides have been bothered by the little word "not," they have paid less attention to "or," and far less to "and." Yet it is a familiar feature of modern logical theory that "and," "or" and "not" are the same sort of word. Thus one would expect that if there are no negative pure perceptions, there are also no conjunctive pure perceptions. What would this involve? To come immediately to the point, it would seem to conflict with the account of perceptual "sentences" at which we arrived in the preceding section. It will be remembered that according to this account, these sentences are of the form

0 exemplifies /properties/

But surely this must be interpreted as

0 exemplifies P_1 and P_2 . . . and P_n

which is equivalent to

0 exemplifies P_1 and 0 exemplifies P_2 . . . and 0 exemplifies P_n.

Hall speaks on p. 44 of a "group of predications about a single individual." On p. 42 he equates a "battery of predications" being made of an individual with the object's being "asserted to exemplify them all together." But this identification is debatable, to say the least, for it amounts to identifying a set of sentences with the single sentence which is their conjunction. The point at which I am driving is, in Kantian terms, that the perception of a manifold must not be confused with a manifold of perceptions. Thus, if we leave "and" out of the language of pure perceptions, one could not pure-perceive an object to exemplify a number of properties all together. This conjunctive togetherness would, on Hall's account, have to be grasped through conventional language. The perception proxy

(0 is P_1 and P_2...and P_n)

would have to be interpreted as involving a move from the more basic perception proxies, "O is P_1," "0 is P_2," etc., which *do* translate pure perceptions, *via* what logicians call "Conjunction Introduction;" schematically,

p,q

p and q

Another apparent consequence of the denial that the logical connectives are present in pure perception would be the restriction of the attributes which could be ascribed to objects in pure perception to what Aristotelian's call the "proper sensibles." It would exclude not only negative and conjunctive attributes, but also disjunctive attributes. Since I think that determinable or generic attributes are a special case of disjunctive attributes, this would mean that no pure perception could be generic. I believe that this consequence would disturb Hall, since I know from personal conversation that at one time (1955) he thought they could.

That the exclusion of logical connectives from pure perception would also exclude the pure perception of causal attributes, dispositions, and propensities is obvious, but would not disturb Hall, since he would regard all concepts of this kind as involving inductive generalization, and hence as derivative from basic perceptual experience. Thus the fact that we perceive objects as stones, pieces of paper—classifications which clearly involve reference to causal properties—would simply highlight the pervasive role played by conventional language in sophisticated perceptual experience. We have already noted that he emphasizes on many occasions that although the *core* of perceptual experience is the innate natural language of pure perception, as soon as the child learns a conventional language, the latter becomes almost seamlessly intertwined with the former. It becomes a second-nature language of perception.

> ...Now that we have this sharp distinction [between natural and conventional language] it is necessary to admit that in everyday situations we frequently have mixtures and cases that are difficult to classify. I remember witnessing a floating piledriver capsize in the harbor of our yacht club and, while seeing a man scrambling down the scaffolding, suddenly hearing myself

exclaim, "Why, it's Ivan Thorp and he can't swim!" Now it would be easy enough to separate this into two parts, one in the natural language of perception, the other in conventional English, and this would be justified. But such a procedure is not wholly fair to the situation. My perceptual identification of the man was in part effected by my uttering of his name; the latter was not just a translation of a recognition of him that had already occurred. Indeed, most of us talk to ourselves most of the time, so that pure perceptions, perceptions devoid of all conventional expressions, are very rare (Hall, p. 33).

VI

Let me pull some of these considerations together. As I see it, they add up to something like the following. While I wholeheartedly agree with the fundamental thesis of Hall's intentional realism, the thesis that perceivings are to be regarded as tokens of inner or mental sentences, I doubt that the language to which these sentences belong can do the job required of it unless it contains the fundamental logical apparatus found in conventional language. I think that this point would stand out even more clearly if Hall had developed an account of self-awareness in terms of an inner language of what, for lack of a better word, I will call introspection. Kant's decisive point about the unity of apperception or self-consciousness, namely that the consciousness that

> I who have experience A am identical with I who have experience B

requires *not* just the occurrence of the two self-awarenesses

> I have experience A
> I have experience B

but the single "combinative" awareness

> I have experience A *and* (I have) experience B.

It is around this (and related) points that Kant built his transcendental deduction of the logical forms of judgment. In this general respect my position *vis-a-vis* Hall is analogous to that of Kant *vis-a-vis* Hume.

Thus it is my conviction that even the most basic "inner" or "mental" language must contain the logical operation of conjunction, and once this is granted, there is no place for boggling at the remaining logical forms.

It is important to note, however, that to allow that the inner language of perception contains logical expressions does not *require* one to say that negative, conjunctive, disjunctive, or quantified perceptions are completely on a footing with singular, affirmative perceptions. It is *compatible* with the claim that there is a sense in which *rock-bottom* perception is a matter of singular, affirmative sentences which attribute perceptible attributes in a *strict* sense to objects. Thus it *could* be argued that conjunctive perception involves a "conjunction introduction move" from the component perceptions. The important thing would be that the inner language of perception proper contained the logical apparatus for making this move, so that the move could occur *in it*, rather than after the translation of the conjuncts into another language ("conventional perception proxies").

Again it might be true that although the inner language of perception contained quantification, no "rock-bottom" perception is quantified, quantification coming in as a move from the perception $\cdot$ 0 is red $\cdot$ to $\cdot$(E x) x is red $\cdot$; but as I see it, these "rock-bottom" perceptions would simply be the ones we have when our mental set is cautious and skeptical. When less cautious, we simply perceive in richer terms without "making moves from rock-bottom." (We see that there is no cheese in the refrigerator, to use a well-worn example.)

Thus it is my conviction that the inner language of perception and, I would add, self-awareness is a language in the full-blooded sense; it requires the presence of logical expressions and principles of inference, and I must confess that I do not understand why Hall committed himself too thoroughly to the opposite position. I have two suggestions to make.

Perhaps something like the classical Aristotelian dictum ("Nihil in intellectu . . . ") was operating in the form "Nothing in the basic inner language of perception that is not to be found in the world as perceptible by the senses." Thus Hall might argue that every feature of the basic language of perception must be something which is *formally* present in the world and derivatively capable of being objectively present in percipient organisms (i.e., present as experienced). Add to this the premise that logical words do not stand for anything in the world and the thesis would follow.

But logical words function so differently from referring and characterizing expressions that the principle

No feature can be objectively present in the basic language of perception which is not formally present in the world (i.e., "bodily" in the case of objects; "as exemplified" in the case of attributes)

might well be restricted to objects and attributes. In any case, to put logical words into the basic inner language of sense perception is not to commit oneself to the absurd idea that logical words can be defined in terms of words for perceptible qualities and relations.

Incidentally, Hall is, in my opinion, absolutely correct in attacking (Hall, p. 48) those who regard logical words in conventional language as (in principle) dispensible. My contention is that they are equally indispensable features of even the most basic inner language of sense perception—and, I would add, of introspection.

Is there any other reason why Hall would have felt uneasy about locating logical words in the inner language of perception? I think that there is, and I also think that it highlights one of the central problems in the philosophy of mind. It concerns the *innateness* of the basic inner language of perception. Hall emphasizes that this language is a natural language the use of which requires no *learning*, only *maturation*. The grasping of logical connections, on the other hand, is conceived by Hall as the sort of thing that *does* involve learning and, indeed, is acquired in the course of learning to use a conventional language.

We can sketch the situation in terms of an inconsistent triad:

1. The understanding of logical words requires learning.
2. The basic language of perception does not require learning.
3. The basic language of perception involves logical words.

Hall accepts (1) and (2) and therefore rejects (3). I, on the other hand, accept (1) and (3) and, therefore, reject (2). Thus, whereas Hall sees the basic language of perception as an innate language which is the *original* on which the richer conventional language of interpersonal communication is based, I see "inner language" in general, and perceptual inner language in particular, as nothing other than conventional language itself. It is conventional language as it exists in what Hall refers to as "talking to oneself," but which

I prefer to think of as truncated thinking-out-loud. As we have seen, the notion of the occurrence of conventional language in "talking to oneself" is central to Hall's interpretation of perceptual experience as it exists in people who have learned to use a conventional language. But the very difficulty Hall finds (Hall, p. 33) in distinguishing between the natural language of pure perception and the conventional enrichment which is so seamlessly entwined with it suggests that there is something wrong with Hall's linguistic dualism.

On the other hand, it must be granted that perceptual experience does involve abilities which *mature* and are not *learned*. The abilities I have in mind enable the perceptible qualities and relations of physical things to be *present* in a unique way—a way other than by exemplification—in perceptual experience. But whereas Hall sees only *two* ways in which qualities and relations can be present in something,

> present as exemplified
>
> present as *signified, meant,* or *intended*

I think that there are three modes of presence,

> exemplification
>
> signification
>
> representation by sense impressions,

and that the innate abilities involved in perception involve the third of these modes, a mode which is *not* to be construed by analogy with language, and does *not* constitute an innate natural language of perception.[4]

But important though this difference between us may be, it is a minor difference compared to the major issue between realism on the one hand and skepticism, subjectivism, and phenomenalism on the other. For the essential thesis of Hall's intentional realism is that perceptions are to be construed as inner sentence events which refer directly to external objects and predicate perceptible qualities and relations of these objects themselves—not copies or replicas of them. And this I think to be the very heart of a sound theory of perception.

---

[4]For a constructive account of sense impressions along these lines, see the chapter on Phenomenalism in my *Science, Perception and Reality*, London, 1963; also The identity approach to the mind-body problem, *Review of Metaphysics*, 1964, and the *Proceedings of the Boston Colloquium on the Philosophy of Science*, Second Series, New York, 1964.

IX

ABSTRACT ENTITIES

I

I have argued in a number of papers[1] over the past decade or so that the abstract entities which are the subject matter of the contemporary debate between platonistic and anti-platonistic philosophers—qualities, relations, classes, propositions and the like[2]— are linguistic entities. They are linguistic expressions. They are *expressions*, however, in a rarified sense, for they are distinguishable from the specific linguistic materials (sign designs) which embody them in historically given languages. Redness, as a first approximation, is the word ·red·[3] construed as a linguistic kind or sort which is capable of realization or embodiment in different linguistic materials, e.g., *red*, *rot*, and *rouge*, to become the English word "red," the German word "rot," and the French word "*rouge*." Expressions in this rarified sense I have called— borrowing Peirce's term but putting it to a different, if related, use—linguistic *types*. Thus ·red· is a type which is shared by the

---

[1] Realism and the new way of words, *Philosophy and Phenomenological Research*, vol. 8, 1948 (reprinted in *Readings in Philosophical Analysis*, edited by Herbert Feigl and Wilfred Sellars, New York, 1949); Quotation marks, sentences and propositions, *Philosophy and Phenomenological Research*, vol. 10, 1950; Grammar and existence: a preface to ontology, *Mind*, vol. 69, October, 1960, reprinted in *Science, Perception and Reality*.

[2] The medieval problem of universals, as is well known, was primarily the problem of genera and species in the category of substance, though solutions were extended by analogy (and with little success) to other categories. More recent discussion, for a number of reasons of which the most obvious—the temporary eclipse of the category of substance—is scarcely more than a restatement of the phenomenon to be explained, locates the problem primarily in the categories of quality and relation and extends solutions to genera and species of *things* and *events* in a fairly cursory manner and with equal lack of success. The present paper, as I see it, provides a perspective within which the medieval and the modern problems fall into place and show themselves to be different facets of a more embracing issue.

[3] I shall use dot quotes to form the names of the expressions—in the sense to be explicated—which is realized in English by the sign design illustrated between them. I shall use asterisk quotes to form the name of the sign design illustrated between them, thus *red* is the name of the design which in English is the written word "red." These conventions will be clarified and made more precise in the course of the argument.

English word "red," the German word "*rot*," and the French
word "*rouge*."

Now the thesis that the universal redness is the linguistic type
·red· has the ring of absurdity. There are several ways in which
this discomfort can be expressed. ("What is the type ·red·—if
there is such a thing—but a universal? And granted that there
are linguistic universals, is it not obvious that redness is a non-
linguistic universal?") I shall open my argument by formulating
an objection which, by cutting deeper than most, leads to a firm
foundation for a restatement and defense of the thesis.

To prepare the way for this objection, let us suppose that the
thesis to be defended is properly formulated as the claim that
abstract entities are linguistic types, where a linguistic type is a
kind or sort of expression in the sense adumbrated above. The
objection opens by granting, for the sake of argument, that there
are such things as linguistic types which can be embodied in
different linguistic materials in different languages. It then argues
that to construe the abstract singular terms which are the source
of so much philosophical perplexity as referring to linguistic types
is not only wrong-headed, but obviously so. It is open to an immediate *reductio* in Barbara.

> All abstract entities are linguistic kinds
> All kinds are abstract entities
> *Therefore*, all kinds are linguistic kinds.

The conclusion is obviously false. Man, for example, is a kind,
but scarcely a linguistic kind. (That "man" is a linguistic kind is
another matter.) On the other hand, surely the minor premise is
true. Is there a fallacy of ambiguity? Or must it not be granted
that the major premise is false and with it the interpretation of
qualities, relations, propositions, etc. as linguistic types?

Before facing these questions, some beating about in the neighboring bushes is in order. Thus, if the conclusion is false, and the
minor premise true, we can construct the following syllogism with
the denial of the original conclusion as its major premise:

> Some kinds are not linguistic kinds
> All kinds are abstract entities
> *Therefore*, some abstract entities are not linguistic kinds.

What might these abstract entities be? And how are they referred to? How is their abstractness to be understood? Obviously, if the thesis that universals (in the sense of qualities, relations, classes and the like) are linguistic kinds is to stand, the abstractness of the abstract entities which are *not* linguistic kinds cannot be explained by saying that they are universals. Perhaps some light on the nature of the abstract entities which, putatively, are not linguistic kinds, can be thrown by exploring the kinds which, according to our new major premise, are not linguistic kinds.

Consider, for example, the various pieces in chess. A familiar dialectic unfolds. Pawns, for example, are a concrete many. Over and against this many is the pawn as a one. This encounter with an old friend (the One and the Many) would normally be a source of rejoicing to any philosopher worth his salt. But to one who attempts to interpret sorts and kinds as linguistic types, it must occasion a sense of *malaise*. It will certainly do so if he has been assuming that the problem of universals in the modern sense (i.e., the problem of the status of qualities, relations, sorts, kinds, and classes as over and against their instances or members) is *the* problem of "the one and the many." For if the pawn as one is a kind or sort to which the many individual pawns belong, then we are confronted by the syllogism,

> All universals are linguistic kinds
> The pawn is a universal
> *Therefore*, the pawn is a linguistic kind

which restores the original tension. For surely the conclusion is false. Shall we deny the major and thus abandon the thesis which was to be defended? Or is the minor premise vulnerable? To highlight the latter possibility, let us once again form a new syllogism, taking the denial of the above conclusion as our new minor premise, thus,

> All universals are linguistic kinds
> The pawn is not a linguistic kind
> *Therefore*, the pawn is not a universal.

Can this conclusion be defended? It requires us to hold that not all *ones* over and against *manys* are universals (i.e., qualities, relations, sorts, kinds or classes), and, consequently, to conclude that the problem of "the one and the many" is in fact broader than the problem of universals (in the specified sense).

But how are we to understand the idea that we can refer to the pawn as a one over and against the many pawns without referring to it as a universal of which the latter are instances? The key to the answer lies in working out the implications of the idea that to refer to such a *one* we need a singular term other than the singular terms by which we refer to individual pawns, and yet which does not refer to a universal of which they are instances. At first sight, however, this line of thought is stymied by the fact that the pawn *is* a kind or sort of chess piece, which seems to imply that the singular term ("the pawn") which we have been using to refer to the *one* which is not to be a universal, does, after all, refer to a universal. It is only if this singular term has another use in which it does *not* refer to a universal that the above move can be made.

Now "pawn" is a common noun, and it will prove helpful to explore the logic of common nouns to see if there is a more general phenomenon of which the desired result is but a special case. Thus, consider the common noun "lion." Is there a singular term, which we might represent by S_L, by the use of which true singular statements of the form

> S_L is. . .

can be made where it would be incorrect to prefix these statements by "the universal. . ." thus

> The universal S_L is. . .?

To ask this question is to answer it. For it must have been immediately clear that "the lion"[4] serves exactly this purpose. For we can make the true statement,

> The lion is tawny

whereas it would obviously be incorrect to say

> The universal, the lion, is tawny.

The example is instructive, for it calls our attention to the fact that a distinctive feature of this use of "the lion" is that what can be said of the lion also be said of lions, thus

---

[4] The use of "the" in such contexts has been called the "institutional" use by C. H. Langford. For an invaluable study of some of the problems which arise in this connection, see his paper, The institutional use of "the," *Philosophy and Phenomenological Research*, vol. 10, 1949, pp. 115-120. I should add that the idea of a distributive singular term and the light it throws on the problem of abstract entities was developed independently of Langford's paper.

The lion is tawny

Lions are tawny.

If, therefore, we can understand the relation of *the lion* (one) to *lions* (many) without construing *the lion* as a universal of which lions are instances; and if the looked-for singular term pertaining to pawns can be construed by analogy with "the lion"—indeed, as "the pawn"—then we would be in a position to understand how *the pawn* could be a one as against a many, without being a universal of which pawns are instances. This in turn would enable a distinction between a generic sense of "abstract entity" in which the lion and the pawn as well as triangularity (construed as the ·triangular·) and that two plus two equals four (construed as the ·two plus two equals four·) would be abstract entities as being ones over and against manys;[5] and a narrower sense of abstract entity in which qualities, relations, sorts, classes, propositions and the like are abstract entities, but of these only a proper subset, universals but not propositions, for example, would be *ones* as over and against *instances* or *members*. This subset would include the kind *lion* and the class of pawns, which must not be confused with *the lion* and *the pawn* as construed above. But all this will be given a more careful formulation in what follows.

Such is the agenda. It is readily carried out. The first task concerns the relation of *the lion* to *lions*. Here the fundamental theme is the equivalence schema

$$\text{The } K \text{ is } f \equiv \text{All } Ks \text{ are } f\dagger$$

where this represents an identity of sense, the dagger indicating that the righthand side is a "non-accidental" truth about Ks (i.e., [roughly] that *being f* is either one of the criteria for *being a K* or is implied by the latter on inductive grounds.[6] Notice particularly that although the commentary represented by the dagger is

---

[5]The manys corresponding to triangularity (in this context) and to that two plus two equals four would be *linguistic* manys. According to the convention I shall follow in this paper, dot quotes are used to form the common nouns which refer to the items which play the role played in our language by the design illustrated between them.

[6]The logic of such statements as "the lion is tawny" requires to be spelled out with care, otherwise the lion may have to suffer paradoxical indignities not unlike the wig which Russell removed from the present king of France. A minimal condition is that "Not (the K is f)" not be equated with "The K is not-f." This echoes the requirement that "All Ks are f" be a nonaccidental truth about Ks to support "The K is f."

in the metalanguage, the two sides of the equivalence and, specifically, the expression "the K" and "Ks" are at the same level of discourse—discourse about the lion being at the same level as discourse about lions.

Now if we reflect on the two statement forms

1. The K is a one
2. Ks are a many

we note that they are in the material mode, the former having (in first approximation) the sense of

"The K" (in English, our language) is a singular term, the latter (and it will be noticed that the plural verb is an unperspicuous consequence of surface grammar) having the sense of

"Ks" (in English, our language) is a plural term.

The second of the above statements (2) must be carefully distinguished from "Ks are a many" in the sense of "There are many Ks," which is why it would be more perspicuously represented by

2' Ks is a many.

The contrast between *the K* as a one and Ks as a many is obviously independent of how many Ks there are, if any.

I propose to call expressions of which "the lion" is a paradigm example "distributive singulars." Notice, however, that distributive singulars need not contain the institutional "the." Thus "man" in "Man is rational" is a distributive singular, and the statement is equivalent to "All men are (of necessity) rational."

We have therefore unearthed a sense in which *ones* are *reducible* to *manys*, *the lion* to *lions*, and, in general, *the K* to Ks. This reduction, however, must not be confused with a reduction of qualities, relations, kinds, or classes to their instances or members. The latter (i.e., qualities, etc.) are, indeed, reducible to particulars in accordance with the schema

The K is f
Ks (of necessity) are f

but the particulars in question are not the lions and tigers, the flashes and thunderclaps of the world *tout court*, but that rule-governed subset, linguistic (and conceptual) episodes—the "logical order"—in terms of which the "real order" is pictured.

The above conclusion is implicit in what has already been said.

For to construe "triangularity" as having, albeit less perspicuously, the sense of "the ·triangular·" is to imply that triangularity as a *one* is reducible to a many which is not *triangular things*, but rather ·triangular·*s*, as *the pawn* is reducible to *pawns*. Thus, "·triangular·" would be the common name of items which play the role played in our language by *triangular*s where the asterisk quotes form the common name of the design tokens of which one is found between them—as "pawn" is the common name of items which play the role played in our game of chess by pieces of wood. And "triangularity" would be the singular term which stands to the role played by ·triangular·s as "the pawn" stands to the role played by pawns, and "the lion" pertains to the class of lions or lionkind. Notice, however, that in the use which we have in mind neither "the pawn" nor "the lion" is the name of the role or kind to which the common noun pertains. This, however, is not to say that these expressions may not have a further use in which they do function as names of universals. This question will come up for review at a later stage of the argument.

It is, perhaps, worth a moment's digression to note that attempts have not been wanting by nominalistically oriented philosophers to avail themselves of the contextual definition of *ones* in terms of *manys* to reduce universals to particulars: thus

$$\text{Triangularity is } f =_{df} \text{triangles are } f$$

(with more or less commentary on the right hand side). An interesting virtue of this solution is that if it were correct, the temptation to hold a doctrine of self-predication would be simultaneously explained and rendered harmless. For

Triangularity is triangular

would be tautologically true, having the sense of

Triangles (as such) are triangular.

That the theory is false is a consequence not of a mistaken approach to the problem of the one and the many (for such a singular term as "the triangular thing" could be introduced by this procedure), but rather of a failure to appreciate the *normative force* of the contexts in which expressions referring to universals and propositions belong. It is by reflection on these contexts, and, in particular, on the necessary equivalence between

F-ness *implies* g-ness

and

That something is *g* *may be inferred from* that it is *f*

that one comes to appreciate the kinship of such expressions as "triangularity" and "that *a* is triangular" to the "pawn." Both the idea that qualities, relations, kinds, and classes are *not reducible to manys*, and the idea that they *are reducible to their instances or members* are guilty of something analogous to the naturalistic fallacy.

II

Let us take a closer look at the way in which *the pawn* is bound up with the rules of chess, in the hope that it will help us understand what it means to speak of universals, propositions, individual concepts and other abstract entities in the narrower sense of the term as linguistic types.

The fundamental point is reasonably straightforward. Just as the equivalences

The K is f $\equiv$ Ks are f†

which pertain to thing kinds, rest on the more basic relationship between the common noun "K" and its criteria of application, which can, for our purposes, be represented by the schema

x is a K $=$ x is $\varphi_1 \ldots \varphi_n$

so the corresponding equivalences pertaining to pieces in a rule-governed system

The R is f $\equiv$ Rs are f†

$$\left.\begin{array}{l}\text{The } R \text{ is (correctly)}\\\text{positioned and moved}\\\text{thus and so}\end{array}\right\} \equiv \left\{\begin{array}{l}R\text{s are (correctly)}\\\text{positioned and moved}\\\text{thus and so}\end{array}\right.$$

rest on the relationship between the common noun "R" (e.g., "pawn") and its criteria, expressed by the schema

$$x \text{ is an } R \equiv \left\{\begin{array}{l}(x \text{ is } f_1 \ldots f_n) \text{ and}\\(x \text{ is in } C_1 \rightarrow \text{ permitted } [x \text{ is moved thusly}]).\end{array}\right.$$

Notice that the criteria have been split into a descriptive and a prescriptive component. It is the latter which is essential to the character of the equivalence as defining a "piece." For while it is possible and, indeed, usual to specify the empirical characteristics of the pieces beyond what is implied by the description of the moves to be made with them, and beyond what is implied by the fact that pieces of the same kind must be discernibly similar and pieces of different kinds discernibly different, this need not be done.

The division of the criteria into descriptive and prescriptive components is, potentially, the drawing of a distinction between a "piece" in a narrower sense (the criteria of which are specified by the prescriptive component) and what might be called a recognized "embodiment" or "materialization" of the piece. Thus,

x is an $R \equiv D(x)$ and $P(x)$

can generate (where "$D(\text{x})$" contains more than is implied by "$P(x)$")

x is a DR'

where "D" is an adjective belonging to the vocabulary of the game which is derived from the function "$D(x)$," and "R'" is a common noun the criteria of which are summed up by "$P(x)$."

Again, the empirical criteria for what is to count as a "move" or a "play" and for what is to count as a "position," perhaps on a "board," from which it is to be made, can be specified in more or less generic or determinable terms. Thus, if (with an eye to chess as a paradigm) the moves of a game are specified in relatively generic terms, the potentiality exists for a similar distinction between the move as specified in terms of permissions relating to these generically characterized alterations of the *status quo*, and the various recognized "materializations" of the move. The latter would usually go hand in hand with the specification of what were to count as the different kinds of pieces and, if one is necessary, what was to count as the board.

Since the empirical criteria for pieces, positions and moves are always, of necessity, to some degree generic, the potentiality for a distinction between these pieces, positions, and moves, and a plurality of recognized "embodiments" of them in empirically different "materials" and, hence, of different "materializations" *of the same game* is always present. Notice that we have been concerned with "recognized" varieties, as contrasted with ad hoc variations, e.g., "let's use pieces made of candy, so that when captured they can be eaten!"

Again, the fact that although the empirical criteria associated with the move-, piece-, and position-words of the game vocabulary may be quite generic, it is always possible—save in the limiting case of the *summa genera* defined in terms of the mathematical theory of structures[7]—to modify the connection between the distinctive vocabulary of the game and their criteria by associating the vocabulary of the game with more generic forms of these criteria, thus opening the way to new ways of playing the game ("Let's play chess with Cadillacs for queens, Volkswagens for pawns...and counties for squares") and to the possibility of acknowledging ways of playing the game which would have been ruled out by the more specific criteria.[8]

What is it to come to see that two games of independent origin are different ways of playing one and the same game? Surely it is in the first instance to see that a common game vocabulary could be introduced and associated with generic empirical criteria of which the two sets of criteria for the two game vocabularies would be determinate forms. To see this *from outside*, as it were, is to see that they could be regarded as different ways of playing one and the same game. To put such an embracing game vocabulary to actual use is to see them *from inside* as different ways of playing the same game.

Thus, if Texans had independently developed a game played with automobiles and counties called "Tess," with its own distinctive vocabulary for its pieces and moves, we might have come *first* to appreciate isolated similarities between Tess and chess, and *then* to see that they could (along the above lines) be regarded as different ways of playing a game which chess would be another way of playing. At this stage, instead of coining a new vocabulary for the "same game," we would probably raise the criteria for being a "pawn," a "king," a "board," and consequently for being a game of chess, to a higher degree of abstraction, and begin to contrast "Texas chess" with "conventional chess" as (materially)

---

[7]Think of what games of chess played by bringing about appropriate changes in the most radically different materials would have in common!

[8]The distinction between what might be contrasted as "formal" and "material" varieties of a game is an important one. Chess played with conventional pieces differs "materially" from Texas chess described above. Chess without capture *en passant* differs "formally" from chess with such capture. My concern is to highlight the concept of materially different forms of the same game.

different varieties of chess. Before this move, we could speak of two similar games, and, even, of two games "so similar that they could be regarded as different ways of playing one and the same game." Only after this step could we speak, without qualification, of two forms of the same game.

The point of the above remarks is clearly to suggest that it is fruitful to regard human languages of approximately the same degree of sophistication as materially different varieties of one and the same "language game"; thus, to compare the difference between German, say, and our language, which I shall suppose to be English, to that between Texas chess and conventional chess. More particularly the point is to suggest that as both small objects of the familiar shape and Volkswagens can be pawns, the former in conventional chess, the latter in Texas chess, so both *triangular*s and *dreieckig*s can be ·triangular·s, the former in English, the latter in German.[9]

But, as should be clear from the above discussion, it is one thing to say that English and German, granting that they can be usefully compared to games, *can be regarded as* different ways of playing one and the same game, and, as a result, to coin a "game vocabulary" which, *if it came to be used,* would structure the situation as one in which one and the same game (Human Language) is played in a number of materially different ways. It is quite another to say that the conception of our language as one way of playing a game with more generic descriptive criteria of which there are other materially different varieties is already implicit in the conceptual framework we actually use. Thus, it might be said, "granted that English and German can be regarded, etc., and that

> ·triangular·

"could be introduced" to be a common noun which stands to *dreieckig*s (in German) and *triangular*s (in English) as

> pawn

stands to Volkswagens (in Texas chess) and the familiar pieces of material (in conventional Chess), is there any expression *in actual*

---

[9]It will be remembered that asterisk quotes are used to form the common noun for the designs illustrated between them.

use which embodies this conception of the situation? Are you not claiming that there is? Or are you?"

This challenge immediately calls attention to the fact that what I have actually claimed to find *in actual use* is an expression which corresponds *not* to the contrived common noun

·triangular·

but, rather, to the contrived singular term

the ·triangular·.

For I have been proposing (as a first approximation) a "rational reconstruction" of *Triangularity* as *the* ·*triangular*·. The question, therefore, immediately arises, "Is there, in actual use, a common noun related to 'triangularity' in a way which can be compared to the way in which 'pawn' is related to 'the pawn'? And if not, why not?" The challenge and the question can be summed up by asking,

> Granted that
>
> > *dreieckig*s (in *G*) and *triangular*s (in *E*) stand for triangularity
>
> can be compared to
>
> > Volkswagens (in Texas chess) and the familiarly shaped pieces of material (in conventional chess) embody the pawn.
>
> Why is there no common noun in actual usage such that, representing it by "*R*," we can say
>
> > *dreieckig*s (in *G*) and *triangular*s (in *E*) are *R*s
>
> as we can say
>
> > Volkswagens (in Texas chess) and the familiarly shaped pieces of material (in conventional chess) are pawns?

The answer to this challenge and the related questions is to be found by reflecting (1) on the comparative rarity of inter-linguistic comparisons, and (2) on the advantages and disadvantages of the ready availability of samples of pieces when the game in question is a linguistic one. If we follow the first line of thought, we notice that when it is a question of two expressions in one and the same language, we do find common nouns which admit of radical differences in the designs to which they apply. Thus we can say not only (instances of) sound$_i$ and shape$_j$ stand for triangularity

but

(instances of) sound$_i$ and shape$_j$ are "triangular"'s.

Thus it would be a mistake to say that the quoted expression
    "triangular"

simply refers to the script design sampled between the quotes *qua* playing a role in the language. Nor will it do to argue that the sample represents a class conceived in quite generic terms, for to stretch "generic resemblance" to cover what written and spoken "triangular"'s have in common is to conceal vital differences between different ways in which linguistic designs can have something in common.

Nor will it do to argue that
    "triangular"

refers to the disjunction of written and spoken designs. For to do this is to misinterpret the looseness of the connection between *being of a certain shape* and *being a "triangular"* as a matter of a tight connection between the latter and the disjunctive character of *being of a certain shape or of a certain sound*. It is better, all things considered, to say that quotation is a flexible device which *only at one extreme* (in certain contexts) implies that the expressions referred to by an expression in quotes are of the sampled design, and that where it applies to items of other designs, the guiding thread is *not* similarity of design.

Shall we say that the guiding thread is similarity of office or role? Before we attempt to do so, we must pay due attention to the fact that although the expressions formed by the use of quotation marks (and their counterparts in speech) do have a range of application which extends beyond the design they illustrate, the additional designs to which they most obviously extend (written designs in the case of spoken quotation; spoken designs in the case of written quotation)[10] are tied to them by the user's language habits. If we put this by saying that whatever the *potential* scope of the reference of quoted expressions may be, their *actual* reference is limited to designs which are more intimately related to one

---

[10] I leave aside for separate treatment on another occasion the whole topic of the use of quotation to quote *thoughts*, but see Chapter 2 of *Science, Perception and Reality*.

another than by similarity of office or role, then we can imagine
someone to argue as follows:

> We *actually do say* of an inscription in another language, thus
> *dreieckig*'s in German, that it stands for triangularity. We do
> not actually say of an inscription in another language that it is
> a "triangular"; nor do we have any other role common noun by
> which to make such a statement. Therefore "triangularity" as
> we actually use it can scarcely be construed as having a sense
> of the form "the *R*."

This argument, however, makes a basic mistake. It overlooks the
fact that the use of "triangularity" in *inter*-linguistic contexts is
an extended use which has developed from its use in *intra*-linguistic
contexts. Thus, instead of contrasting the appropriateness of

> *dreieckig*'s (in *G*) stand for triangularity

with the oddity of

> *dreieckig*'s (in *G*) are "triangular"'s

we should reflect on the equal appropriateness of

> *triangular*'s (in *E*) stand for triangularity

and

> *triangular*'s (in *E*) are "triangular"'s

and ask ourselves

> Why, granted that in the limited horizon of reference to our
> own language game, "triangularity" can be correlated with
> common noun ""triangular,"" is the *extended* use of "triangularity"
> in inter-linguistic contexts not paralleled by a similarly extended
> use of ""triangular""?

To do so is to notice that within the limited horizon, the abstract
suffix "-ity" can be regarded as a form of quotation, thus

> triangularity

and

> "triangular"

would be parallel constructs. The chief difference (of a non-
superficial kind) would be that whereas ordinary quotation yields
expressions which, though they serve primarily as singular terms,
thus

> "Triangular" is an adjective

can also serve without undue violence as common nouns, thus

There were three "because"s and four "whereas"s in the resolution

expressions formed with "-ity" are singular terms only. But although "-ity" adding and ordinary quoting build linguistic designs into expressions referring to linguistic expressions with which these designs have *something* to do, the references of expressions formed with "-ity" is clearly less tightly tied to the illustrated design than is the reference of expressions formed by ordinary quotes. This is shown by the fact that whereas we can always take an adjective and form a singular term from it by the use of an appropriate suffix, the result is often stilted and artificial, and competes with a standard expression involving such a suffix, but of which the stem is no longer an adjective in actual use.[11] From our point of view this means that whereas singular terms with these suffixes refer to linguistic types with which the design preceeding the suffix has a reasonably close connection (sufficiently close in one way or another to mobilize relevant linguistic dispositions for rehearsal), the connection need not be so direct that we can say

"... .-ity" refers to the type embodied in our language by *...*s

let alone

"... .-ity" refers to *...*s *qua* playing the role they do in our language.

Direct quotation, on the other hand, is less free to wander from its primary use in which it forms expressions which refer to linguistically functioning designs which are either of the kind illustrated in the quotation or are intimately related to them in the nexus thought-speech-writing. Thus, when it is a matter of putting existing resources to use in speaking of foreign expressions, singular terms formed by adding suffixes to relevant designs are better suited to the task of referring to designs which have only a similarity of role to connect them with the designs they illustrate. This is not to say that expressions formed by ordinary quotation are never given a parallel extension. They are, but, typically, in

[11] Though it must not be too unfamiliar, for when it fails to be recognized as an archiac (or classical) counterpart of an adjective in current use, it will be replaced by a singular term formed from the latter.

contexts in which the import of particular historical (or fictional) utterances is being given, and in which quotation can without too much violence be regarded as occurring in the rubric,

/that which corresponds in the speaker's language to/ . . .
thus,

Julius Caesar said /that which. . ./ "The die is cast."

The above remarks, I believe, throw some light on the fact that whereas, within the horizon of one language (a situation which can be compared to one in which we chess players have not yet encountered Tess) we find common nouns formed by ordinary quotes which parallel singular terms of the same design in such a way that it is reasonable to "reconstruct" their relationship in terms of the perspicuous relationship between "a K" and "the K," when it is a matter of foreign expressions these parallel singular terms and common nouns formed by ordinary quotation are not available. We must use singular terms (formed by suffixes and other devices) to which there are no corresponding common nouns. This, of course, is not to say that the "logical space" of inter-linguistic role or office common nouns is lacking. Implicit in such singular terms as "triangularity," it can be brought to the surface as a quantified variable in explicating the translation rubric. Thus, consider

"dreieckig" (in G) means *triangular*.

It would be clearly incorrect to construe this as stating that

*dreickig*s (in the German variety of the human language game) are "triangular"s.

It would, however, be equally incorrect to equate it with

*dreieckig*s (in G) stand for what *triangular*s stand for in our language (i.e., triangularity).

For the identity of role implied by the original statement can be given explicit recognition by construing it as

*dreieckig*s (in G) *are* what *triangular*s are in our language[12]

which has the form (using "R" as a common noun variable)

*dreieckig*s (in G) $\subset$ ($^{\iota}R$) (*triangular*s [in E] $\subset$ R).

Let us, therefore, continue to use expressions formed by means

---

[12]To which we with our contrived role common noun, can add . . . (i.e., •triangular•s).

of dot quotes to refer to linguistic types, which latter, though identifiable (by virtue of the name-forming practice) as the types realized in our language by the designs within the quotes, do not have *being of these designs* among their criteria. Thus, a ·triangular· need not be a *triangular* (written *or* spoken). It can be a *dreieckig*. The most useful way to put this at the present stage of the argument is by the proportion

$$\frac{\text{expression formed by dot quotes}}{\text{expression formed by ordinary quotes}} = \frac{\text{``pawn'' as applying to the appropriate pieces in any game which can be regarded as a different embodiment of chess}}{\text{``pawn'' as applying to the familiarly shaped pieces used in ordinary chess}}$$

If we bear in mind our earlier discussion of the criteria for application of common nouns, we can say that dot quotation corresponds to ordinary quotation where the latter practice has been modified in such a way that the descriptive component of the criteria for the application of the common noun formed by quoting has been reduced to that which is implied by the prescriptive component, and the latter has been given its most generic formulation.[13]

It should also be noted that whereas ordinary quotation forms an expression which, depending on context, functions as a common noun or as the corresponding singular term, we shall give our dot quotes the job of forming an expression which must be preceded by "the" to form the corresponding singular term. It will be remembered that it is expressions of the latter kind which we are offering as our "rational reconstructions" of abstract singular terms, thus

---

[13]That the prescriptive component of the criteria of linguistic role or office common nouns pertains to intra-linguistic syntax (including "material" as well as "formal" transformation rules) and what I have elsewhere called language entry and language departure transitions, will not be argued in this paper. See Some reflections on language games, *Philosophy of Science*, *21*:204-228, 1954. Also Truth and "correspondence," *Journal of Philosophy*, *59*:29-56, 1962. Both these papers are reprinted in *Science, Perception and Reality*.

Triangularity = the ·triangular·

That it is raining = the ·it is raining·.[14]

At this point it might be asked, "How do expressions in dot quotes translate into other languages?" The answer is to be found by reflecting on the above distinction between being a criterion for the application of a name, and being an implication of a name-forming practice. Thus, given that Germans use dot quotes as we are using them, English

the 10th inscription was a ·triangular·

becomes

die 10te Inskription war eine ·Dreieckig·.

It is worth noting, however, that this assumes that the generic rules with reference to which the expression "·triangular·" is to be understood are serving directly as prescriptive criteria for the common noun. In this event, the connection of the design *triangular* with the role ·triangular· is a purely nominal one—is a matter of a name-forming practice. The design, however, can play a more substantive role without thereby becoming a criterion of application in the sense that to be a ·triangular· an item must be a *triangular*. For "·triangular·" might be so used that a ·triangular· is *directly* an item playing the role played in our language by *triangular*s. Clearly, in this event, a reference to the design would be involved in the criterion of application (without, however, requiring that ·triangular·s be *triangular*s). We might say that in this case the *ultimate* criteria for being a ·triangular· are indirectly specified by definite description in the *immediate* criterion, whereas in the former case, the ultimate and immediate criteria coincide. In the present case, the translation of "·triangular·" into "·dreieckig·" would be a translation of an expression into its counterpart in another language, without being a translation in that stricter sense in which a noun translates into another noun only if the immediate criteria of each mentions nothing which is not mentioned by the immediate criteria of the other. In the case we are considering, the immediate criteria of "·tri-

---

[14] As has already been implied, these equations, and particularly the former, are but a first approximation to an adequate reconstruction. A finer-grained analysis will be given in a subsequent section.

angular·" would refer to *triangular*s, and the immediate criteria of "·dreieckig·" to *dreieckig*s. Our concern, however, is with the *ultimate* criteria of the expressions pertaining to linguistic types, and these would be identical, and such that if they were used as immediate criteria as in the case envisaged at the beginning of this paragraph, the German and English expressions pertaining to linguistic types would be inter-translatable in the strictest sense.

The point of the above remarks is to suggest that "triangularity" (which we are comparing to the contrived English "the ·triangular·") and "Dreieckigkeit" (which we are comparing to the contrived German "die ·dreieckig·") can be construed as translatable merely in the weaker sense without requiring that to express triangularity an item must be a *triangular*. On the other hand, since even if we so introduce dot quotes that the resulting expressions have *immediate* criteria which, mentioning specific designs, are appropriately translatable only into counterparts mentioning other designs, the ultimate criteria would be strictly translatable. And it is this strict translatability of ultimate criteria which we have in mind when we say that "triangular" (in *E*) and "dreieckig" (in *G*) stand for one and the same abstract entity, triangularity.[15]

It will therefore be a pardonable oversimplification if we interpret abstract singular terms by comparing their formation with the use of dot quotations so construed that the criteria of application of the quoted expressions are directly and simply what from a more subtle point of view are their indirect and ultimate criteria. The latter must, in any case, be available, even though it is by rehearsing in imagination prescriptions pertaining to the use of designs in our language that we become aware of them.

---

[15]That few English words translate exactly into German raises other interesting and important questions relating to various ways in which languages can resemble or differ. Our attention has been directed to abstract entities as the sort of thing that *can* find expression in other languages than our own. We can regard the pawn as the sort of thing that *could* be embodied in all sorts of material and moved in all sorts of ways, provided that the relevant prescriptions are determinate forms of the same maximally generic prescriptions. A universal is the sort of thing that could find expression in a number of languages. We are, of course, primarily interested in universals which are expressed in a living language (i.e., our own). It is important, however, to reflect on possible abstract entities, and, as an aid to this reflection, on possible games.

IV

Before developing the above analysis into a more articulated theory of universals and propositions, let us put it to use in connection with a familiar problem.

Query: What light does the above analysis throw on the fact that both the following statements are true:

> (a) Triangularity is a universal
> (b) Triangularity is an individual

or, to rephrase these statements in ways which highlight the paradox,

> (a¹) Triangularity is an attribute
> (b¹) Triangularity is a subject

also

> (a²) Triangularity is a concept
> (b²) Triangularity is an object.

If we replace "triangularity" by its proposed reconstruction, the original statements become

> (a³) The ·triangular· is a universal
> (b³) The ·triangular· is an individual.

Both of these have distributive singular terms as grammatical subjects, and both of them might seem, therefore, to be reducible without further ado in accordance with the schema

> The K is f = Ks are (of necessity) f

explored in an earlier section. Actually, however, the situation is not quite so simple, for although it turns out that both of these statements do have distributive singular terms as their subjects, *it is not the same distributive singular term*. To appreciate this, consider the statements

> (c) Socrates is a man
> (d) Socrates is an individual.

The latter has as its rational reconstruction

> (d¹) The ·Socrates· is an individual constant[16]

and reduces to

---

[16]It would be misleading to say that (d) is to be explicated as

> The ·Socrates· is an individual

(i.e., to change only the subject when passing to the formal mode of speech), for there is no provision in ordinary usage for reducing statements of the form (d²)   ·Socrates·s are individual constants.

Thus the context
—— is an individual

is an unperspicuous representation of the context
The ·——· is an individual constant.

If so, then, whereas
(a³)   The ·triangular· is a universal

reduces directly to
(a⁴)   ·triangular·s are universals¹⁷

i.e.,
(a⁵)   ·triangular·s are predicates

in order to reduce
(b⁴)   The ·triangular· is an individual

we must first see it as
(b⁵)   The ·the ·triangular·· is an individual constant

which becomes
(b⁶)   ·the ·triangular··s are individual constants.

According to this analysis, in (a) *triangularity* plays its basic role, whereas in (b) it is playing a secondary role in which it is equivalent to *the ·triangularity·* (in a hybrid of English and our analytical contrivance), and to *the ·the ·triangular··* in the pure form of the latter. The secondary role might also be signalled by use of italics or underlining, in which case we would have as correct formulations of the original statements,

(a)   Triangularity is a universal
(b⁷)   *Triangularity* is an individual

and, correspondingly,

—— is an individual
to cognate statements of the form
——s are individuals
in accordance with the above reduction schema. For an elaboration and generalization of this point, see the next footnote.

¹⁷Again it would be misleading to say that (a) has the same sense as (a³). It must be borne in mind that a rational reconstruction is neither a report of an identity of sense between two expressions in actual use nor a simple reproduction of the use of a given expression in new verbal materials. The point I am making in this and the previous note stands out more clearly if we change our example to "triangularity is a quality," for "universal" is a philosophical term to which philosophers *give meaning* (or meanings—often inconsistent), whereas the meaning of "quality," like that of

  (c)   Socrates is a man
  (d³) *Socrates* is an individual.

V

We have been emphasizing the distinction between such common nouns as "lion," "pawn," etc., and the corresponding distributive singular terms "the lion," "the pawn," etc. Consider, now, the following statements:

  (e)   The lion is an abstract individual

  (f)   (The) lion is a kind

  (g)   The lion is a kind

  (h)   (The) lion is an abstract individual.

It is, I take it, clear that in all of these statements the expression "lion" is being used *not* to refer to lions, but to refer or to be a component of an expression which refers to an abstract entity. As a crude sizing-up of the situation, we might say that "lion" is being mentioned rather than used. But what of the definite article? Here there are two possibilities: (1) it is the phrase "the lion" which is being mentioned, and (2) the definite article "the" is being *used* rather than mentioned. The second construction is indicated in the above statements by placing the definite article in parentheses.

Thus (e) has the form

  (e¹) *The lion* is an abstract individual

which, on our analysis, becomes the true statement

  (e²) The ·the lion· is a distributive singular term

"relation," is to be reported (and analyzed). Thus whereas
     The ·triangular· is one-place predicate
can be reduced to
     ·triangular·s are one-place predicates
there is no provision in ordinary discourse for reducing statements such as
     Triangularity is a quality
to statements of the form
     ——s are qualities.
Although it is philosophically illuminating to reconstruct such material mode of speech categories as "individual," "quality," "relation," etc., as classifications of linguistic types, ordinary discourse does not provide for a reduction of statements involving them which would parallel the straightforward reduction of their formal mode of speech counterparts.

which reduces to

(e³)   ·the lion·s are distributive singular terms.

It will be noticed that although (e³) shares the form "—s are distributive singular terms" with

(b⁸)   ·the ·triangular··s are distributive singular terms

the latter can be expanded to

(b⁹)   ·the ·triangular··s are *metalinguistic* singular terms

whereas (e³) cannot. The significance of this latter fact will be pointed out shortly.

Turning our attention now to (f), we notice that in accordance with our convention it construes the role of the definite article as a matter of use rather than mention, "lion" alone being mentioned. This amounts to construing it as

(f¹)   *Lion* is a kind

and the role of the definite article as that of avoiding the appearance of using a common noun as a singular term. On this interpretation (f¹) is to be reconstructed in first approximation as

(f²)   "lion" is a common noun

and, in terms of our finer-grained analysis, as

(f³)   The ·lion· is a common noun

(which brings out the deeper appropriateness of the definite article). This in turn reduces to

(f)   ·lion·s are common nouns

and we see that on this interpretation (f) shows itself to be a sibling of "Triangularity is a quality," for the latter reduces, on our analysis, to "·triangular·s are (one place) predicates."

What, then, are we to make of (g)? Here, it will be remembered, the phrase "the lion" as a whole, rather than just the common noun "lion," is being mentioned. The essential point to notice is that if this construction is to make sense, the word "kind" must have a different sense than it does in (f). Indeed, it must be equivalent to "distributive individual." For whereas in the context of (f) "kind" is the material mode counterpart of "common noun," in the context of (g) it would have to be the material mode counterpart of "distributive singular term" (DST). For in the formal mode (g) gets under way as

"The lion" is . . .

and, appropriately, completed becomes

   (g¹)   "the lion" is a DST[18]

or, in terms of our finer-grained analysis,

   (g²)   The ·the lion· is a DST

which reduces to

   (g³)   ·the lion·s are DST's.

The possibility that the word "kind" might have these two senses
throws light on Russell's erstwhile distinction between classes as
ones and classes as manys. Or, with an eye to Frege, we can say
that in contexts such as (g) kinds are *distributive objects*, whereas
in (f)-like contexts they are concepts or functions.

Let us finally turn our attention to (h) which though verbally
similar to (e) differs by being construed as using rather than
mentioning the definite article, using it, indeed, (as in f) to avoid
the appearance of grammatical absurdity. Does (h) make sense?
To see that it does, we must first note that instead of using the
definite article to this end in (f) we could have used, instead, one
of the suffixes ("-hood," "-kind") which make singular terms out
of common nouns. This would give us

   (f⁵)   Lionhood is a kind
   (f⁶)   Lionkind is a kind.

Of these I shall use "-kind" although it has the disadvantage of
being used primarily to form collective nouns rather than abstract
singular terms which would stand to common nouns as "triangularity" stands to "triangular." The usage I propose has the
virtue of making "Lionkind is a kind (i.e., sort)" a true statement.
According to this usage, (h) becomes

   (h¹)   Lionkind is an abstract individual

and stands to (f) as "Triangularity is an (abstract) individual" to
"Triangularity is a quality." Furthermore, its rational reconstruction stands to

   (f⁴)   ·lion·s are common nouns

as

   (b⁹)   ·the ·triangular··s are DST's

to

   (a⁵)   ·triangular·s are (one-place) predicates.

---

[18]For convenience, I have abbreviated "distributive singular term" as DST.

Thus (h¹) becomes

     (h²)   Lionkind is an abstract individual

and is explicated by the following series

     (h³)   *The ·lion·* is an abstract individual

     (h⁴)   The ·the ·lion·· is a DST

which reduces to

     (h⁵)   ·the ·lion··s are DST's.

It will be noticed that (h⁵) can be expanded to

     (h⁶)   ·the ·lion··s are *metalinguistic* DSTs

in which respect it resembles (b⁸) and differs from

     (e³)   ·the lion·s are DSTs.

VI

We are now in a position to see more clearly why it is incorrect to say that all abstract individuals are linguistic, where "abstract individual" is given the sense of "distributive individual." For the adjective "linguistic" undergoes a subtle change in sense as one goes from explicandum to explicans (i.e., from the material to the formal mode of speech). Thus,

    —— is a *linguistic* abstract (distributive) individual

becomes

    ·——·s are *metalinguistic* distributive singular terms,

and appropriate examples of these forms would be

    The ·triangular· is a linguistic abstract (distributive) individual

    ·the ·triangular··s are metalinguistic DSTs.

Thus, since it is not true that

    ·the lion·s are *metalinguistic* DSTs

it is not true that

    The lion is a linguistic distributive individual.

If we draw the distinction between linguistic₁ (i.e., in a language) and linguistic₂ (i.e., pertaining to language), then

    —— is a linguistic distributive individual

is appropriate only where in its formal mode counterpart

    ·——·s are linguistic DSTs;

"linguistic" has not the trivial sense of "linguistic₁" (where else could a DST be but *in* a language?), but the sense of "linguistic₂" which contrasts in this context with "not pertaining to language."

It is, consequently, only if the term "abstract individual" is not given the broad scope of "distributive individual" but is restricted to qualities, relations, propositions, kinds, classes, and the like that

All abstract individuals are linguistic

expresses a truth.

VII

The above considerations also clarify the question

Are all abstract entities individuals?

If one approaches the notion of an individual in the broadest sense with Frege's notion of an object, the questions arises,

Are there any abstract entities which are *not* objects?

And the answer seems unavoidable that *of course* there are abstract entities which are not objects. That this answer is correct and (*pace* Frege) unparadoxical emerges from the following examples:

1. *The lion* is a (distributive) individual and not a kind (i.e., The ·the lion· is a DST and not a common noun.

2. Lionkind is a kind and not a (distributive) individual (i.e., The ·lion· is a common noun and not a DST).

3. *Lionkind* is a (distributive) individual and not a kind (i.e., The ·the ·lion·· is a DST and not a common noun).

4. Triangularity is a quality and not a (distributive) individual
(i.e., The ·triangular· is a predicate and not a DST).

5. *Triangularity* is a (distributive) individual and not a quality
(i.e., The ·the ·triangular·· is a DST and not a predicate).

In (1), (3), and (5), we have examples of items which are objects and not functions; in (2) and (4), examples of items which are functions and not objects. It will be noticed that the examples of items which are functions and not objects—lionkind in (2) and triangularity in (4)—are *prima facie* identical with two of the items which are objects and not functions—lionkind in (3) and triangularity in (5). That this is only superficial appearance is one of the central themes of this paper.

But if all the above are abstract entities, though some are functions and others not, it is because all of the following are true:

 6. *The lion* is an abstract entity

 7. Lionkind is an abstract entity

 8. *Lionkind* is an abstract entity

 9. Triangularity is an abstract entity

 10. *Triangularity* is an abstract entity.

What, then, we might ask, is the formal mode counterpart of "abstract entity"? Clearly it won't do to say simply "linguistic expression." For while all the following are true

 6^1. The ·the lion· is a linguistic expression

 7^1. The ·lion· is a linguistic expression

 8^1. The ·the ·lion·· is a linguistic expression

 9^1. The ·triangular· is a linguistic expression

 10^1. The ·the ·triangular·· is a linguistic expression

it is *not* true that

 11. Socrates is an abstract entity

although it is true that

 11^1. The ·Socrates· is a linguistic expression.

This points toward an interpretation of "entity" rather than "abstract entity" as the material mode for "linguistic expression," and to a distinction between "non-abstract" and "abstract" entities which reflects a basic dichotomy between kinds of linguistic expression. Just how this latter might be characterized (or, indeed, whether a simple dichotomy will do) falls outside the scope of this paper. It is worth noting, however, that there is free play in the system for a distinction between wider and narrower senses of the term "abstract entity." Thus we have already suggested that although

 The lion is a distributive individual

we need not say

 The lion is an abstract individual

but may reserve the latter category for items which satisfy the explication schema

    —— is an abstract individual

    The ·——· is a linguistic distributive individual

    The ·the ·——·· is a metalinguistic DST.

It will be useful to conclude this section with a remark on so-called "individual concepts." If the term "concept" is used in the Fregean tradition, then an individual concept would be a concept which can be satisfied by at most one individual; thus, the property of being the last person to arrive at a certain dinner party. A concept which merely in point of fact was satisfied by only one individual would not in this sense be an individual concept. Thus the abstract singular term "Socrateity" *might* be used as equivalent to "being $\varphi_1 \ldots \varphi_n$" where the latter constitute the identification criteria for the name "Socrates" and where at most one object could be " $\varphi_1 \ldots \varphi_n$." A less interesting individual concept would be the property of being identical with Socrates. Such individual concepts would share with triangularity and mankind the character of being concepts in Frege's sense, abstract entities, and (with the warnings spelled out above) abstract individuals.

In speaking of "individual concepts," however, I have in mind items which are *not* concepts in Frege's sense. In Frege's terminology they would more appropriately be called "individual senses." For just as we can say

    rouge (in French) expresses (the sense) redness

ie.,

    *rouge*s (in French) are ·red·s

so we can say

    Sokrates (in German) expresses (the sense) Socrateity

i.e.,

    *Sokrates*s (in German) are ·Socrates·s[19]

Here two things are to be noted: (1) redness is not only an ex-

---

[19]It is important not to confuse

    Sokrates (in German) expresses (the sense) Socrateity

with

    Sokrates (in German) names Socrates.

The former (but not the latter) could be true even if there were no such person as Socrates.

pressible sense, but a concept in Frege's sense, and (2) Socrateity is an expressible sense, but not a concept as Frege uses this term.

Thus construed, Socrateity, unlike Socrates and like triangularity, is an abstract individual. Here we must be careful, for it will be remembered from the opening argument of this section that both

4. Triangularity is a quality and not a (distributive) individual (i.e., The ·triangular· is a predicate and not a DST)

and

5. *Triangularity* is a (distributive) individual and not a quality (i.e., The ·the ·triangular·· is a DST and not a predicate)

are true. In the present case, by way of a parallel, we have

12. Socrateity is an individual-sense and not a (distributive) individual (i.e., The ·Socrates· is an individual constant and not a DST).

13. *Socrateity* is a (distributive) individual and not an individual-sense (i.e., The ·the ·Socrates·· is a DST and not an individual constant).

It should also be noted that although on our analysis "Socrates is an individual" and "Socrateity is an individual-sense," as we are using the latter, are strongly equivalent, actual usage restricts "Socrates" to one material mode context in addition to its non-metalinguistic use, whereas "Socrateity," which in its primary use has the sense of "Socrates" in its secondary or material mode use, also has a secondary use (cf. [13]) in which it expresses a meta-metalinguistic concept in the material mode. For this reason it would be as incorrect to say that

Socrateity is a (*non*-distributive) individual

as to say

Socrates is an (abstract) individual.

VIII

Frege's concepts are a subset of senses—predicative senses. Since the class of non-predicative senses includes many items which would traditionally have been called concepts (e.g., the senses of such expressions as "and," "not," "all," etc.[20]), the situation is fraught with the possibility of misunderstanding. Since, as I see it, Frege's distinction between concepts and objects was of decisive importance in the history of ontology, I am strongly inclined to follow his lead and limit the term "concept" to predicative senses. In accordance with this usage I shall not speak of the senses of names, logical connectives, quantifiers, or other non-predicative expressions as concepts.

IX

We must now make good a still more basic oversimplification in our rational reconstruction of such abstract singular terms as "triangularity" as the names of linguistic types which are typically embodied in our language by the designs of which they contain an illustration (i.e., as having the force, in terms of our quoting convention, of, for example, "the ·triangular·." For while these abstract singular terms *are* names of linguistic types, and, indeed, of types to which the designs they illustrate are intimately related, it is at least an oversimplification to say that the types in question are realized in these designs. The point I have in mind stands out like a sore thumb once we remember that in a perspicuous language constructed on the principles laid down in Wittgenstein's *Tractatus*, for example, the Jumblese sketched in my "Naming and Saying,"[21] basic statements are made not by concatenating predicate expressions with individual constants, but rather by writing these individual constants in various manners or styles. Thus the Jumblese counterpart of PMese

Triangular (a)

might be an *a* from one type font, thus.

a

and of

Circular (a)

an *a* from another font, and so on. Again, the Jumblese counterpart of PMese

Larger (a, b)

---

[20]That Frege thought of "p or Tom is tall" as expressing a function and hence as *predicative* is a symptom of a basic flaw in his system.

[21]*Philosophy of Science, 29:*7-26, 1962, (reprinted in *Science, Perception and Reality*).

might be an *a* and a *b* from the neutral font placed in a certain relationship, thus

     a

       b

while the counterpart of PMese

     Heavier (a, b)

might be

      a

     b

Corresponding to the PMese statement functions

     Triangular (x)
     Circular (x)
     Larger (x, y)
     Heavier (x, y)

would be variables written in the corresponding styles or manners.
Further development of Jumblese means of expression would take
us beyond our present aims. For the above is sufficient to call
attention to the fact that there are no designs in Jumblese which
play the role played by *triangular*s, *circular*s, *larger*s, etc.,
in PMese. Jumblese, in short, contains no predicate designs.

Now what this amounts to is that PMese has a greater multiplicity of *pieces* than does Jumblese for playing the same game. In
effect, the role played by *triangular*s, etc., in PMese is a *subordinate* one. Thus the role of *triangular*s is that of bringing
it about that individual constants or variables have the character
of being concatenated with a *triangular*. PMese as well as
Jumblese makes statements by tokening individual constants in
various manners, but PMese manners involve the use of designs
other than the names, whereas Jumblese manners do not. Or, to
put it somewhat differently, in Jumblese we find a smaller number
of designs, but a correspondingly greater number of ways of
forming and deploying those it has. (The subordinate move in
PMese of concatenating a *triangular* with an *a* to form *triangular (a)*—I shall use parenthesis without comment—can be
compared to the subordinate move of putting a separate crown on
a pawn to make a queen.

Now, if Jumblese has no design which plays the role played in
PMese by *triangular*s, it does have items which play the role

played in PMese by *triangular(x)*s. It does have, that is to say, items which are ·triangular(x)·s (i.e., which stand for the propositional function that x is triangular). Thus, whereas PMese has both predicates and propositional functions, Jumblese makes do with the latter.

The question now arises, shall we say that triangularity is to be construed as the type realized in our language by *triangular*s, in which case no Jumblese design would stand for or express triangularity? Or shall we say that triangularity is to be construed as the type realized in our language by certain *sentential* designs of which *triangular*s are the distinctive component? In this case, Jumblese might very well have designs which express triangularity. in spite of the fact that it has no designs which play the role played in our language by *triangular*s.[22]

To fix our ideas as to what the second approach to a reconstruction of triangularity might be, let us begin with the suggestion that

Triangularity = the ·x is triangular·

(i.e., that "triangularity" is the name in our language of the type realized in our language not by *triangular*s, but by *x is triangular*s). This suggestion has the merit of interpreting triangularity as a type which is found in Jumblese as well as PMese. Thus in Jumblese *x*s would correspond to *triangular(x)*s in PMese, and like the latter would express or stand for triangularity (i.e., would be ·x is triangular·s). This suggestion, furthermore, would fit in with the fact that the statement made by

Triangularity entails trilaterality

is often represented by the formula

"x is triangular" entails "x is trilateral."

But although the suggestion is on the right track, it won't do as it stands, for it involves a misunderstanding of what one is attempting to express by the use of the variable. That this is so stands out clearly if we compare the latter formula with its material mode of speech counterpart,

---

[22]And, consequently, could not form this name of the office in question from a design which corresponds to our *triangular* as Germans, for example, can do by using *dreickig*.

That something is triangular entails that it is trilateral. Obviously it would be a mistake to symbolize the latter as

That (*Ex*) *x* is triangular entails. . .

The "something" is playing quite a different role. To bring out what it is doing, let us consider the statements

That *a* is triangular entails that *a* is trilateral

That *b* is triangular entails that *b* is trilateral.

According to our analysis,

That *a* is triangular

has the force of

The ·*a* is triangular·

and refers to the type realized in our language by **a* is triangular**s. The expression

·*a* is triangular·

is a metalinguistic common noun which is constructed through and through on the illustrating sign design principle. If, however, we want to form a metalinguistic common noun which can be applied to the two object language statements

a is triangular

and

b is triangular,

it obviously cannot be constructed through and through on the illustrating sign design principle. If we abandoned the latter altogether, we could introduce non-illustrating common nouns, thus

(genus) INDCON; (species) INDCON$_1$ INDCON$_2$. . .

(genus) PRECON; (species) PRECON$_1$ PRECON$_2$. . .

and form the non-illustrating common nouns

PRECON$_1$INDCON$_1$, PRECON$_1$INDCON$_2$

to correspond to the illustrating common nouns

·triangular (*a*)·, ·triangular (*b*)·

and also the more generic common noun

PRECON$_1$INDCON

which would have no illustrating counterpart. Thus corresponding to

x is a PRECON$_1$INDCON$_1$

we would have

    x is a ·triangular (a)·

and to

    x is a $PRECON_1INDCON_2$

we would have

    x is a ·triangular (b)·

but there would be no illustrating counterpart to the more generic classification

    x is a $PRECON_1INDCON$

or the even more generic

    x is a PRECON INDCON.

But might there not be a way of forming metalinguistic common nouns which combine the illustrating principle with other techniques, using the latter where, as in generic representation, the former is not available (at least in a straightforward way)? Perhaps we can supplement the illustrating common nouns,

    ·a·, ·b·, ·c· . . .

    ·triangular·, ·circular· . . .

with the non-illustrating ones listed above, and contrive such mixed common nouns as

    ·triangular·INDCON

to correspond to

    $PRECON_1INDCON.$

Now it seems reasonable to reconstruct

    that something is triangular

not as the *completely* illustrating

    The ·x is triangular·

(in which case only sentential expressions with variables could realize the type referred to), but as the *mixed* expression

    The (·triangular·INDCON).[23]

If so, then the second suggestion with respect to the interpretation of "triangularity" turns into the proposal to construe it as identical in sense with "that something is triangular" as used above, and hence to be reconstructed as indicated.

---

[23] I introduce parentheses at this point to make clear that the definite article is followed by one common noun formed by juxtaposing an illustrating and a non-illustrating component.

A refinement of the above considerations points to the interpretation of the non-illustrating component of the common noun "($\cdot$triangular$\cdot$INDCON)" (i.e., "INDCON") as a *variable* with "INDCON$_1$," "INDCON$_2$," etc., as its substituends rather than as a common noun constant related to the latter as genus to species. The two interpretations are intimately related, for compare

$$x\varepsilon G \equiv x\varepsilon S_1 \text{ or } x\varepsilon S_2 \text{ or } \ldots x\varepsilon S_n$$

with

$$(ES_i)x\varepsilon S_i \equiv x\varepsilon S_1 \text{ or } x\varepsilon S_2 \text{ or } \ldots x\varepsilon S_n.$$

The reason for suggesting that the reconstruction of

that something is triangular

contains a metalinguistic variable (we have seen that it doesn't contain a metalinguistic constant which names an object language variable) is that we must account for the fact that the implication statement

That *something* is triangular implies that *it* is trilateral

connects types involving the same individual constant. This would not be represented by

The ($\cdot$triangular$\cdot$INDCON) implies the ($\cdot$trilateral$\cdot$IND-CON).

This fact suggests that the reconstructed counterpart of "that something is triangular" must be, rather,

The ($\cdot$triangular$\cdot$INDCON$_i$)

where "INDCON$_i$" is a common noun variable admitting of quantification and having "INDCON$_1$," "INDCON$_2$," etc., as substituends. And, indeed, it is a clear implication of our analysis that statements beginning

That something is triangular . . .

involve two dimensions of quantification: (1) a covert universal quantification ranging over linguistic tokens, which is also present in

That a is triangular

and is made explicit by the sequence

That a is triangular

The $\cdot$triangular $(a)\cdot$

$(t)\ t\ \varepsilon\ \cdot$triangular $(a)\cdot \rightarrow\ \ldots$

and (2) an overt existential quantification which ranges *in appearance* (as being in the material mode of speech) over objects, but actually over linguistic types belonging to the category of individual constants, and which can be represented as

(E INDCON$_i$) The ($\cdot$triangular$\cdot$INDCON$_i$) is . . .

the two combining to yield

(E INDCON$_i$) (t) t ε ($\cdot$triangular$\cdot$INDCON$_i$) → . . .

To disentangle this further involves following up the theme that to be a triangular$\cdot(a)\cdot$ is to consist of a concatenation of a $\cdot$triangular$\cdot$ with an $\cdot a \cdot$ and should cause no difficulty.

But if we so reconstruct triangularity, can we say of any expression in Jumblese that it realizes this type? A negative answer might seem to be indicated by the fact that no expression in Jumblese is the result of concatenating an individual constant with a $\cdot$triangular$\cdot$. And it does indeed follow from this that no expression in Jumblese stands for triangularity in the sense in which *triangular*s (in E) and *dreieckig*s (in G) stand for triangularity. This, however, simply reminds us that Jumblese involves no design which plays the derivative role played by *triangular*s and *dreieckig*s in PMese type languages. On the other hand, the role played by expressions consisting of an INDCON concatenated with a $\cdot$triangular$\cdot$ *is* played in Jumblese, for it is played by expressions consisting of an INDCON formed in a certain style or manner.

The question, "What Jumblese expression, if any, stands for triangularity?" as interpreted in the preceding paragraph must not be confused with the question What Jumblese expression, if any would be the translation of "triangularity"? The latter, of course, would presuppose an account of Jumblese metalanguages, a difcult but by no means impossible task which will not be attempted here. The following hints, however, might be helpful.

A. A PMese type metalanguage which specifies sentential roles which are played in a given PMese type object language by

Triangular (a), Longer (a,b)

Circular (b), etc.

and in a Jumblese type object language by

a a_b

b   etc.

would involve the definition schemata

1. $^1\mathfrak{S}_i = \varphi_i$ (INDCON)
2. $^2\mathfrak{S}_k = R_k$ (INDCON, INDCON)
3. $^1\mathfrak{S}_j = \varphi_i{}'$(INDCON), etc.

where (1) tells us that an item is an $^1\mathfrak{S}_i$ if it is a φ_i individual constant. Thus, *a*s (in Jumblese) and *triangular (a)*s (in PMese) are $^1\mathfrak{S}_i$. And (2) tells us that an item is a $^2\mathfrak{S}_k$ if it consists of an INDCON which is R_k to an INDCON.

In Jumblese, to be φ_i is to be written in a certain style, and for two expressions to be R_k is for them to be as in *a_b*. In PMese on the other hand, to be φ_i is to be concatenated with a ·triangular· and for two expressions to be R_k is for them to be concatenated to the left with a ·larger· as in *Larger (a, b)*.

B. This suggests that where a PMese metalanguage contains

φ_i (INDCON) R_k (INDCON, INDCON)

its Jumblese counterpart would contain something like

INDCON

INDCON

INDCON

(i.e., would use a style instead of concatenation with a *φ* or an *R*. And this is indeed the case. But, it is important to note, before this step can be taken, one must work out the Jumblese counterparts of such expressions as "a pawn" and "the pawn," not to mention the other expression used in clarifying the grammar of roles and offices. Some light is thrown on this by considering the following table.

TOM	Tom is a man
$(x)\ X \rightarrow X$	All men are animals
M (The)	Man is an animal

where "M" is an introduced singular term written in the appropriate manner for saying of something that it is an animal.

With these remarks in mind, it can be suggested that the Jumblese counterpart of

The ·triangular· INDCON

(which is our PMese type rational reconstruction of "triangularity" might well be) "**INDCON**" where the illustrating principle is followed by forming this metalinguistic expression in the same

style as is used in the object language to say of something that
it is triangular. Thus, assuming that Jumblese uses our quoting
convention, we would have the following counterparts

	Illustrating Jumblese ML	Illustrating PMese ML
That *a* is triangular	·a·	the ·triangular (*a*)·
{ Triangularity { That something is triangular	**INDCON**	the ·triangular· **INDCON**

To return to the primary line of thought, I conclude that
triangularity is not to be construed as *the ·triangular·*, but rather
as being the type realized in the PMese dialect of our language by
expressions formed by concatenating a *triangular* with an individual constant—and in PMese dialects of subject-predicate languages generally by bringing into an appropriate relation (e.g.,
concatenating) a ·triangular· and an individual constant.

From this point of view, the classical problem of universals
rests in large part on the fact that in such languages as English
and German expressions referring to universals are constructed on
an illustrating principle which highlights a design which actually
plays a subordinate role, and consequently tempts us to cut up
such sentences as

Triangular (*a*)

into two parts, one of which has to do with the universal rather
than the particular, the other with the particular rather than the
universal, and tempts us, therefore, to construe the statement as
asserting a dyadic relation ("exemplification") to obtain between
the particular and the universal.

The temptation in question is strengthened by reflection on
the fact that after all it *does* make sense to say

a exemplifies triangularity

which therefore strikes us as a "more explicit" way of saying what
is said by the former statement. The puzzles generated by this
line of thought are notorious. It is relevant, therefore, to ask what
light is thrown by our analysis on such statements as "*a* exemplifies
triangularity." Actually, as I have pointed out elsewhere,[24] such

---

[24]Naming and saying, *Philosophy of Science*, 29:7-26, 1962,] reprinted in *Science,
Perception and Reality*.

statements, in which "exemplifies" is technical jargon used where ordinary discourse speaks of things "having" qualities or "standing in" relations, are closely related to statements of the form

That triangular (a) is true.

And the necessary equivalence of

a exemplifies ("has") triangularity

with

Triangular (a)

is to be understood in terms of the necessary equivalence of the latter with

That triangular (a) is true

and no more than the latter is to be construed as an identity of sense.

To appreciate this, one need only see that

a exemplifies triangularity

is equivalent to

Triangularity is true of a.

For according to our analysis, the latter is to be reconstructed as

The ($\cdot$triangular$\cdot$INDCON) is true of a

which tells us that where the individual constant in question is an $\cdot a \cdot$ expressions which are ($\cdot$triangular$\cdot$ INDCON)s are true. It is therefore equivalent to

The $\cdot$triangular (a)$\cdot$ is true

which is our reconstruction of

That triangular (a) is true.

This analysis has the additional merit of making it clear that

Socrates exemplifies wisdom

does not assert a relation between Socrates and wisdom, for the *Socrates* is functioning as a metalinguistic expression in the material mode of speech. Thus the "relation" of exemplification which for Platonists binds the realm of becoming to the realm of being, and which for more moderate realists binds the "real" order to the "logical" or "conceptual" order, is an offshoot of the "relation" of truth, which analysis shows to be no relation at all, but a sign of something to be done.[25]

---

[25]Truth and "correspondence," p. 38, reprinted in *Science, Perception and Reality.* See also chapters 3 and 4 of *Science and Metaphysics,* London, 1967.

I shall conclude these investigations by asking what light, if any, is thrown on the status of relations between abstract entities by the above analysis. Consider, for example, the statement

That *a* is triangular implies that it is trilateral.

In the light of our analysis, we should expect to reconstruct this along somewhat the following lines

The ·triangular (*a*)· implies the ·trilateral (*a*)·.

But how is this to be interpreted? Since the subject is *the ·triangular·* it is clearly a universal statement. But it obviously is not telling us that wherever a ·triangular (*a*)· occurs, there also occurs a ·trilateral (*a*)·, which is clearly false. Rather it is telling us what is correct and proper with respect to the occurrence of ·triangular (*a*)·s. It is correct or proper (to introduce a theme from proof and derivation theory with respect to formalized languages) to place a ·trilateral (*a*)· in sequence after a ·triangular (*a*)·, thus

.

.

.

triangular (*a*)
trilateral (*a*)

.

.

What is to count as a placing of a ·trilateral (*a*)· in sequence with a ·triangular (*a*)· can vary as much from language to language as what is to count as a ·triangular (*a*)·. But it is worth noting that when we say

That *a* is trilateral is a consequence of the fact that it is triangular

the consequence relation between propositions to which "is a consequence of" gives expression is to be understood in terms of a placing of tokens in sequence, one variety of which is illustrated above.

The above analysis can readily be extended to throw light on statements in which one speaks of necessary connections of universals. Thus, consider

Triangularity implies trilaterality.

Unperspicuously represented, this becomes

f_1-ness R f_2-ness

and anti-platonists attempt to reduce this to

$$(x)f_1(x) \rightarrow f_2(x)$$

together with a commentary which refers to expectations or dispositions to believe. A more recent approach reconstructs it as

'$(x)f_1(x) \rightarrow f_2(x)$' is analytic

which is closer to the truth, but unless "analytic" is misused to mean "unconditionally assertable," one ground (among others) of unconditional assertability is confused with such assertability itself.[26] And when the normative character of the original statement is correctly explicated, we find

(INDCON$_i$) The ($\cdot$triangular$\cdot$INDCON$_i$) implies the ($\cdot$trilateral$\cdot$INDCON$_i$)

which is the general implication of which the illustrating instances would be, for example

The $\cdot$triangular $(a)\cdot$ implies the $\cdot$trilateral $(a)\cdot$
The $\cdot$triangular $(b)\cdot$ implies the $\cdot$trilateral $(b)\cdot$
etc.

or, in more familiar garb,

That a is triangular implies that a is trilateral
That b is triangular implies that b is trilateral
etc.

which were analysed above.[27]

---

[26]See the concluding section of Comments on Maxwell's "Meaning Postulates in Scientific Theories." In *Current Issues in the Philosophy of Science*, ed. Herbert Feigl and Grover Maxwell, New York, 1961.

[27]The considerations advanced on p. 265 suggest that the illustrating common noun "$\cdot$triangular (a)$\cdot$," which refers to $\cdot$a$\cdot$s which are concatenated with a $\cdot$triangular$\cdot$, would be more perspicuous if changed to "$\cdot$triangular$\cdot$ [$\cdot$a$\cdot$]." The latter would refer to $\cdot$a$\cdot$s which are concatenated with a $\cdot$triangular$\cdot$ as "white [dog]" might be used to refer to dogs which are white. This convention would replace the expressions on the left (below) with those on the right:

The $\cdot$triangular (a)$\cdot$ The ($\cdot$triangular$\cdot$ [$\cdot$a$\cdot$])
The ($\cdot$triangular$\cdot$ INDCON)   The ($\cdot$triangular$\cdot$ [INDCON])
The $\cdot$larger (a, b)$\cdot$ The ($\cdot$larger$\cdot$ [$\cdot$a$\cdot$, $\cdot$b$\cdot$])
The ($\cdot$larger$\cdot$ INDCON, INDCON)   The ($\cdot$larger$\cdot$ [INDCON, INDCON])

This more perspicuous convention is put to use in the following essay which is devoted to a restatement and, hopefully, resolution of the Russell paradox.

X

CLASSES AS ABSTRACT ENTITIES
AND THE RUSSELL PARADOX

I

THE implications of the theory of abstract entities which was developed in the preceding essay[1] for some classical problems pertaining to classes are interesting and, I believe, important. To show this I shall take my point of departure from the thesis, advanced in an earlier paper,[2] that the form

$x \, \varepsilon \, k$

construed as the logistical counterpart of

x is a k (e.g., x is a man)

must not be confused with the same form construed as the logistical counterpart of

x is a member of k-kind

where "k-kind" is given a technical use as a referring expression which refers to a class, and in which it is equivalent to "the class of ks." According to our analysis

x is a k

stands to

x is a member of k-kind

as

$f(x)$

to

f-ness is true of x

or, as it is often put,

x exemplifies f-ness.

I shall use "ε_1" as the logistical counterpart of "is a" and "ε_2" as the counterpart of "is a member of." The latter, then,

---

[1] I shall hereinafter refer to this essay as AE.

[2] Grammar and Existence: a Preface to Ontology, *Mind*, *69*:499-533, October, 1960, reprinted in *Science, Perception and Reality*.

is a relation word closely related in sense to "exemplifies," whereas "ε_1" is not a relation word, but is rather a syncategorematic expression which is, to use an Irish Bull, a part of the common noun which follows it. Thus, to use a familiar mode of representation,

Tom is a man

does not have the form

$(x)\ R\ (y)$

but rather

$f(x)$

and would be appropriately symbolized as

$\varepsilon_1 k(x)$ thus, is-a-man (Tom)

instead of the more familiar, but less perspicuous,

$x\ \varepsilon_1\ k.$

The first thesis I wish to advance can be summed up as follows. The form

$—\varepsilon_1—$

requires a singular term in the left hand space and a common noun in the right hand space. On the other hand, the form

$—\varepsilon_2—$

requires a singular term in each space.[3] In other words, the forms

$k\ \varepsilon_1\ k$

$k\ \varepsilon_2\ k$

$k\ \varepsilon_2\ k\text{-kind}$

are all ill-conceived, where "k" is intended to function as a common noun, and "ε_1" and "ε_2" to have the meanings specified above. There are, however, well-formed expressions in the neighborhood which can, and will, be confused with these if one overlooks the significant differences between "is a k" and "is a member of k-kind," that is to say, if one fails to distinguish between "ε_1" and "ε_2."

I shall use upper case "K_i" to form the abstract singular term which stands to lower case "k_i" as "f_i-ness" stands to "f_i." In other words, I shall drop the use of the suffix "-kind" in favor of this new device. Thus the platonistic counterpart of

$a\ \varepsilon_1\ k_1$

---

[3]This thesis will be related to a more general principle pertaining to subjects and predicates in the following section. It will also be given a nominal qualification; one which, however, does not pull its teeth.

will be

$$a \; \varepsilon_2 \; K_1 \quad (= a \; \varepsilon_2 \; k\text{-kind}).$$

If, now, we press the parallel between "ε_2" and "exemplifies," and between "K_i" and "f_i-ness," we are committed to the idea that just as, according to the argument of AE,

$$\text{redness} = \text{the} \; (\cdot\text{red}\cdot[\text{INDCON}])$$

so

$$\text{mankind}^4 = \text{the} \; (\cdot\varepsilon_1 \; \text{man}\cdot[\text{INDCON}])$$

A word in explanation of this symbolism. According to tractarian principles, one attributes a quality to a particular by writing the name of the particular in a certain style—in English PMese by giving it the property of being placed-in-parentheses-and-con-catenated-with-a-certain-predicate, thus,

$$\text{red} \; (a).$$

Correspondingly, one attributes a relation to two particulars by relating their names in a certain manner—in English PMese by putting their names in the relation of being concatenated—placed-in-parentheses—and-having-a-certain-relational-predicate-to-the-left-of-them-both, thus,

$$\text{larger} \; (a, b).$$

A perspicuous metalanguage will form the common noun which applies to tokens of the former sentence in a way which reflects the form of the metalinguistic sentence

$$\text{"red"} \; (\text{"}a_1\text{"})$$

which says of the above token of "a" (which token is here called "a_1") that it has the property of being-placed-in-parentheses-and-concatenated-with-a-token-of-"red."[5] Thus the perspicuous meta-language I have in mind gives the common noun in question the form

$$\text{"red"} \; [\text{"}a\text{"}].$$

This common noun refers to sentences which are tokens of "a" which have the property of being-placed-in-parentheses-and-con-catenated-with-a-token-of-"red." As a non-metalinguistic parallel, consider the object language sentence

$$\text{white} \; (\text{dog}_1)$$

---

[4]In our technical sense.

[5]Notice that the reference to the parentheses is made by the metalinguistic predicate "red" and not by the parentheses in the metalinguistic sentence.

which says of a certain dog that it is white. We might well use the contrived object language common noun

> white [dog]

to refer to dogs which have the property of being white.

On these same principles,

> "larger" ("a"$_2$, "b"$_1$)

would be a metalinguistic sentence which says of a certain token of "a" and a certain token of "b" that they stand in the relation of being-concatenated—placed-in-parentheses—and-having-a-token-of-"larger"to-the-left-of-them-both. The metalinguistic common noun which refers to sentences which consist of a token of "a" and a token of "b" which stand in this relation would be

> "larger" ["a", "b"].

The metalanguage we are characterizing is an *illustrating* one in that metalinguistic names of object language expressions (other than subject-predicate or relational sentences) are formed by placing quotes around the designs which—in the object language—are the expressions to be named. The preceding paragraphs are designed to explain why, although the name of a subject-predicate or relational sentence *could* be formed by placing quotes around the design which—in the object language—is the sentence, this way of forming the name would obscure the logical structure of the sentences to which it referred. If taking account of this structure were simply a matter of recognizing that such a sentence as

> red a

is a complex expression, so that its name should be formed by articulating the names of its component expressions, thus,

> "red" "a"

then one might well adopt a convention according to which the latter expression could be simplified into

> "red a."

The tractarian insight requires us, rather, to embody in our metalanguage the insight that the role of the "red" in "red a" is radically different from the role of the "a," and this is what the metalanguage we are using is designed to do.

Three additional remarks are in order. In the first place, although a metalanguage can contain illustrating names of specific object language expressions, thus

"*a*," "red," "larger," etc.,

as well as

"red" ["*a*"], "larger" ["*a*", "*b*"]

(which are illustrating names, but in a more complicated sense), it will also require non-illustrating names, thus

INDCON

which is a common noun which refers to tokens of any of the individual constants of the object language, and

¹PRECON, ²PRECON, PRECON

which apply, respectively, to tokens of any-one-place predicate, tokens of any two-place predicate and tokens of any predicate *uberhaupt* in the object language. With these resources, the list of names which apply to tokens of subject-predicate and dyadic-relational sentences in the object language would include

"red" [INDCON]
"larger" [INDCON, INDCON]
PRECON [INDCON]
PRECON [INDCON, INDCON].

The second remark is that whereas ordinary quotes are to be construed as forming an illustrating common noun for expressions in a specific language, the one which uses the quoted designs, I introduced dot quotes in *AE* to form metalinguistic expressions which are illustrating in a more sophisticated sense. Thus

·red·

is a common noun which applies to tokens of any expression in any language which has the same sense as does the illustrated design in our language.

The third remark is that metalinguistic common nouns preceded by "the" are distributive singular terms (DST). Thus

The (·red·[INDCON])]

is the DST which corresponds to the common noun

·red·[INDCON]

as

the lion

stands to

lion.

Just as statements about the lion are (with qualifications discussed in *AE*) reducible to statements about lions, so statements about the ($\cdot$red$\cdot$[INDCON]) are reducible to statements about $\cdot$red$\cdot$[INDCONS]s.

Against the background of these conventions, I introduce the following definitions:

Definition 1.

> the $PRECON_i$[INDCON] is true of the $INDCON_j$
> $=_{Df}$ the $PRECON_i$[$INDCON_j$] is true.

Definition 2.

> the $^2PRECON_k$[INDCON, INDCON] is true of the
> $<INDCON_l, INDCON_m>$
> $=_{Df}$ the $^2PRECON_k$[$INDCON_l$, $INDCON_m$] is true.

In interpreting these definitions, it should be remembered that the phrase "is true of" also occurs in the material mode of speech in which what follows it is ostensibly, in its lowest level uses, a non-metalinguistic expression, thus

> Wisdom is true of Socrates.

The significance of this point will be explored in a subsequent stage of the argument.

II

Before embarking on an explanation of the metalanguage we are using, I had offered the following rational reconstruction of "mankind," the abstract singular term referring to the class of men

> mankind $=$ the ($\cdot\varepsilon_1$ man$\cdot$[INDCON]).

According to this reconstruction, the right-hand side is the DST formed from the common noun which applies to sentential tokens which are individual constants having the property of being-concatenated-with-an-$\cdot\varepsilon_1$ man$\cdot$. Thus we have the schema

> $K = k$-kind $=$ the ($\cdot\varepsilon_1\,k\cdot$[INDCON]).

In accordance with these conventions, the ε_2-statement schema

> $a\,\varepsilon_2\,K$

is explicated by the following series

> 1. $a\,\varepsilon_2\,K$
> 2. a is a member of k-kind

3. the ($\cdot \varepsilon_1 \, k \cdot$[INDCON]) is true of the ($\cdot a \cdot$)[6]
4. the ($\cdot \varepsilon_1 \, k \cdot [\cdot a \cdot]$) is true (by definition 1, above)
5. $\varepsilon_1 \, k \, (a)$ i.e., $a \, \varepsilon_1 \, k$.[7]

Notice that the move from (2) to (3) is to be construed as a move from the material to the formal mode of speech. This move will be explored in section 5 below.

The preceding explication of "$a \, \varepsilon_2 \, K$" parallels the explication, defended in *AE*, of

a exemplifies f-ness

by the series

1. *a* exemplifies f-ness
2. f-ness is true of *a*
3. the ($\cdot f \cdot$[INDCON]) is true of $\cdot a \cdot$
4. the ($\cdot f \cdot [\cdot a \cdot]$) is true (by definition 1 above)
5. $f(a)$.

We can now turn our attention to the fact that, at least as far as the requirements mentioned, when "ε_1" and "ε_2" were distinguished are concerned, both

$$K \, \varepsilon_1 \, k$$

and

$$K \, \varepsilon_2 \, K$$

are available forms. In the former we have a singular term to the left and a common noun on the right; while in the latter we have a singular term in both places. To explore the possible significance of these forms and their relationship to each other, let us view the situation in terms of an informal Fregean distinction between objects (whether distributive or non-distributive) and functions. Thus, suppose the non-distributive objects

$$a, \, b, \, c, \ldots$$

and the functions

$$k_1, \, k_2, \, k_3, \ldots$$

(where I have, for convenience, temporarily absorbed the syncate-

---

[6]In the remainder of the paper I shall omit the "the" from the DST which follows the phrase "is true of."

[7]In the remainder of the paper I shall move directly to the form "x ε_1 k" instead of passing through the form which makes the syncategorematic character of "ε_1" and the predicative character of "ε_1 k" manifest, (i.e., "ε_1 k (x))."

gorematic "ε_1" into the function expressions). Let us construct a table of which the following is the first line:

Objects	Functions	Propositions[8]
$a, b, c \ldots$	$k_1, k_2, k_3 \ldots$	$a\ \varepsilon_1\ k_1 \ldots b\ \varepsilon_1\ k_1 \ldots$

No sooner have we set down the first line of our table, than the objects and functions of platonistic counterpart propositions demand a place in the sun. This gives us a second line, and the table becomes:

Objects	Functions	Propositions
$a, b, c \ldots$	$k_1, k_2, k_3 \ldots$	$a\ \varepsilon_1\ k_1 \ldots b\ \varepsilon_1\ k_1 \ldots$
$K_1, K_2, K_3 \ldots$	ε_2	$a\ \varepsilon_2\ K_1 \ldots b\ \varepsilon_2\ K_1 \ldots$

But our new objects also satisfy functions of the form

—— is a —— (i.e., —— $\varepsilon_1\ k$).

Thus the second line branches and the table becomes

Objects	Functions	Propositions
$a, b, c \ldots$		
$K_1, K_2, K_3 \ldots$	$\begin{cases} \varepsilon_2 \\ {}^2k_1, {}^2k_2, {}^2k_3 \ldots \end{cases}$	$\begin{cases} a\ \varepsilon_2\ K_1 \ldots b\ \varepsilon_2\ K_1 \ldots \\ K_1\ \varepsilon_1\ {}^2k_1 \ldots K_2\ \varepsilon_1\ {}^2k_1 \ldots \end{cases}$

With this step, the table begins to grow indefinitely. Let us follow one more step in its development before taking stock.

Objects	Functions	Propositions
${}^2K_1\ {}^2K_2, {}^2K_3 \ldots$	$\begin{cases} \varepsilon_2 \\ {}^3k_1, {}^3k_2, {}^3k_3 \ldots \end{cases}$	$\begin{cases} K_1\ \varepsilon_2\ {}^2K_1 \ldots K_2\ \varepsilon_2\ {}^2K_1 \ldots \\ {}^2K_1\ \varepsilon_1\ {}^3k_1 \ldots {}^2K_2\ \varepsilon_1\ {}^3k_1 \ldots \end{cases}$

Now there is much that is puzzling and problematic about this informal table. As we shall see, it makes a key assumption which is not borne out on a closer examination. Furthermore, it is not clear what significance we are to attach to the superscripts which appear before the "k"s and the "K"s of the later lines. Is a theory of types being presupposed? Or do they simply indicate the row on which the relevant "k" occurs, it being left open that "k"s with different superscripts can stand for the same function, and "K"s with different superscripts can stand for the same object? Unless

---

[8]Notice that the "ε_1" which was absorbed into the function expression in the second column to highlight its syncategorematic character has been precipitated out in the third column to permit ready comparison with the role of "ε_2."

we are forced to do otherwise in order to avoid paradox, let us make the second assumption.

Let us now note that the designation of each object occurs on the left-hand side of ε_1-statements and ε_2-statements.[9] Thus,

$$a$$

occurs in both

$$a \; \varepsilon_1 \; k_1$$

and

$$a \; \varepsilon_2 \; K_1$$

while

$$K_1$$

occurs in both

$$K_1 \; \varepsilon_1 \; {}^2k_1$$

and

$$K_1 \; \varepsilon_2 \; {}^2K_1.$$

Furthermore, the designations of all but the initial objects occur on the right-hand side of ε_2-statements.

III

Before the main argument of this paper is advanced, it should be explicitly acknowledged that it is built on the assumption, which will not be defended here, that, in Fregean terms, objects and only objects satisfy functions; that is, that

$$\emptyset(f)$$

as contrasted with

$$\emptyset(f\text{-ness})$$

makes sense only as an unperspicuous way of expressing a proposition in which "f" and "$\emptyset$" reappear, both in a predicative role; each, however, and in particular "$\emptyset$," being appropriately concatenated with a non-predicative expression. This would be the case, for example, if the use of "f" and in "$\emptyset(f)$" were introduced by the schema

$$\emptyset(f) \; =_{Df} \; (x)f(x) \rightarrow \emptyset(x).$$

If this is granted, then the expression

$$k_i \; \varepsilon_1 \; k_j$$

(where "k_i" is not being covertly used as a singular term, e.g., is

---

[9]The assumption referred to in the previous paragraph is lurking in this way of putting the matter. It will be unearthed when the argument comes to a head.

not being used in the sense of "K_i"[10]) instead of being an otherwise well-formed expression to be excluded by a stipulation recom-
mended by its paradox resolving power, would make sense only
in an unperspicuous derivative use in which, in accordance with
the above definition schema,

$$k_i \; \varepsilon_1 \; k_j$$

rewritten as

$$\varepsilon_1 \; k_j \; (k_i)$$

to bring it under the schema "$\emptyset(f)$," or, still more explicitly,
pulling the syncategorematic "ε_1" out of the "k_i," as

$$\varepsilon_1 \; k_j(\varepsilon_1 \; k_i)$$

would reduce to

$$(x)x \; \varepsilon_1 \; k_i \rightarrow x \; \varepsilon_1 \; k_j.$$

Similar considerations apply to

$$k_i \; \varepsilon_2 \; K_j$$

where, again, "k_i" is not covertly being used as a singular term,
e.g., in the sense of "K_i." As a derivative use of the expression
"$k_i \; \varepsilon_2 \; K_j$" having the form "$\emptyset(f)$" and appropriately rewritten as

$$\varepsilon_2 \; K_j(\varepsilon_1 \; k_i)$$

it would reduce to

$$(x)x \; \varepsilon_1 \; k_i \rightarrow x \; \varepsilon_2 \; K_j.$$

Whether or not—or under what conditions—the latter makes
sense, i.e., whether or not "the same object" can be a value of
an ε_1-function and an ε_2-function, thus

$$a \; \varepsilon \; k_i \text{ and } a \; \varepsilon \; K_j$$

will be explored in the argument to come.

IV

Let us now return to the task of exploring the relationships
pictured in our third table. And let us begin by recalling that
according to the analysis of abstract singular terms developed in
AE, these terms are to be construed as DSTs, i.e., as analogous to
"the pawn," save that whereas pawns are non-linguistic objects,
·red·[INDCON]s are linguistic objects, and hence,

---

[10]Another singular term in the neighborhood which "k_i" might be used, with
ambiguity, to represent is "the k_i" e.g., "the lion." So used "$k_i \; \varepsilon_1 \; k_j$" would have,
in part, the sense of "$(x) \; x \; \varepsilon_1 \; k_i \rightarrow x \; \varepsilon_1 \; k_j$."

the ($\cdot$red$\cdot$[INDCON]),

a metalinguistic DST. Thus, in accordance with this analysis and with the conventions spelled out in the opening section, the ε_1-statement, in the third line of the table,

$$K_1 \; \varepsilon_1 \; {}^2k_1$$

which has as subject the abstract singular term "K_1," has the sense of

the ($\cdot\varepsilon_1 \; k_1\cdot$[INDCON]) $\varepsilon_1 \; {}^2k_1$.

This reduces, as do all statements of which the subject is a DST, to a statement the subject of which is "($\cdot\varepsilon_1 \; k_1\cdot$[INDCON])s."
Compare

The lion is an animal

which reduces[11] to

Lions are animals.

Notice that

The lion ε_1 animal

is a derivative use of the form

$$—\varepsilon_1 \; k$$

in which it is extended from non-distributive to distributive singular terms in accordance with the schema

The $k_i \; \varepsilon_1 \; k_j \; = \; {}_{Df} \quad (x)x \; \varepsilon_1 \; k_i \rightarrow x \; \varepsilon_1 \; k_j$.[12]

If we introduce the symbol "$\subset$"—commonly called the symbol for class inclusion, but which must be as carefully distinguished from the relational predicate "is included in" as "$\varepsilon_1 \; k$" ("is a k") was distinguished from "$\varepsilon_2 \; K$" ("is a member of K")—then "lions are animals" can be represented as

lion $\subset$ animal[13]

---

[11]With qualifications explored in *AE*. See also the following note.

[12]The fact that DSTs are contextually defined in away which reminds us of the contextual definition of definite descriptions in *Principia* should keep us on our toes with respect to the logic of statements in which they occur. Thus, whereas in the case of non-distributive singular terms,

not $(a \; \varepsilon_1 \; k) \equiv a \; \varepsilon_1 \; k'$

where "k'" is the complement of "k" and can be read "non-k," the same is not true of DSTs. Thus, "it is not the case that the lion is a yearling" is not equivalent to "the lion is a non-yearling."

[13]In accordance with the text, "lion $\subset$ animal" must be carefully distinguished from "lionkind is included in animalkind." If we introduce the symbol "$<$" for

which, for present purposes, can be equated with

$(x)x\ \varepsilon_1$ lion $\rightarrow x\ \varepsilon_1$ animal.

In these terms,

the $(\cdot\varepsilon_1\ k_1\cdot[\text{INDCON}]\ )\varepsilon_1\ {}^2k_1$

reduces to

$\cdot\varepsilon_1\ k_1\cdot[\text{INDCON}]\subset{}^2k_1.$

We have just seen that

$K_1\ \varepsilon_1\ {}^2k_1$

is explicated by the series

$K_1\ \varepsilon_1\ {}^2k_1$

The $(\cdot\varepsilon_1\ k_1\cdot[\text{INDCON}])\ \varepsilon_1\ {}^2k_1$

$\cdot\varepsilon_1\ k_1\cdot[\text{INDCON}]\subset{}^2k_1.$

What, now, of the ε_2-statement

$K_1\ \varepsilon_2\ {}^2K_1$

which is also "about K_1" and is, indeed, the platonistic counterpart of the previously explicated ε_1-statement? It reduces as follows:

1. $K_1\ \varepsilon_2\ {}^2K_1$
2. The $(\cdot\varepsilon_1\ k_1\cdot[\text{INDCON}])$ is a member of ${}^2K_1$
3. The $(\cdot\varepsilon_1\ {}^2k_1\cdot[\text{INDCON}])$ is true
   of $\cdot$the $(\cdot\varepsilon_1\ k_1\cdot[\text{INDCON}])\cdot$
4. The $(\cdot\varepsilon_1\ {}^2k_1\cdot[\cdot$the $(\cdot\varepsilon_1\ k_1\cdot[\text{INDCON}]\cdot])$ is true
5. The $(\cdot\varepsilon_1\ k_1\cdot[\text{INDCON}])\ \varepsilon_1\ {}^2k_1$
6. $\cdot\varepsilon_1\ k_1\cdot[\text{INDCON}]\subset{}^2k_1.$

The character of this reduction will stand out more clearly if we compare it with the reduction of a simpler example of an ε_2-statement, thus,

1. Leo ε_2 lionkind
2. Leo is a member of lionkind
3. the $(\cdot\varepsilon_1$ lion $\cdot[\text{INDCON}])$ is true of $\cdot$Leo$\cdot$
4. the $(\cdot\varepsilon_1$ lion $\cdot[\cdot$Leo$\cdot])$ is true
5. Leo ε_1 lion.

It will be seen that to step (6) in the first of these derivations nothing corresponds in the second. This is because Leo is not a

---

"is included in," the latter has the form "$K_i < K_j$," the former the form "$k_i\subset k_j$." It is important to see that in "$k_i\subset k_j$" the expressions "k_i" and "k_j" have a *predicative* use which is founded on the fact that the statement is unpackable into "$(x)\ x\ \varepsilon_1\ k_i\rightarrow x\ \varepsilon_1\ k_j$ in which their predicative use is manifest.

distributive individual, and hence the ε_1-statement about him is a basic rather than extended use of the form "—— $\varepsilon_1 k$." From this standpoint, a more complete parallel would be the series

1. The lion ε_2 animal-kind
2. The lion is a member of animal-kind
3. The ($\cdot \varepsilon_1$ animal $\cdot$ [INDCON]) is true of $\cdot$ the lion $\cdot$
4. The ($\cdot \varepsilon_1$ animal $\cdot$ [$\cdot$ the lion $\cdot$]) is true
5. The lion ε_1 animal
6. Lion $\subset$ animal.

If, now, we compare the reduction of the ε_2-statement "$K_1 \varepsilon_2$ $^2K_1$" with that of the ε_1-statement "$K_1 \varepsilon_1$ $^2k_1$" we see that they both culminate in

$$\cdot \varepsilon_1 k_1 \cdot \text{ [INDCON]} \subset {}^2k_1.$$

This was, of course, to be expected, since the ε_2-statement is the platonistic counterpart of the ε_1-statement, i.e., stands to it as

Leo ε_2 lionkind

stands to

Leo ε_1 lion

and, more remotely, as

Tom exemplifies tallness

to

Tom is tall.

V

It is now time to recall that whereas on our analysis, neither

$k \ \varepsilon_1 \ k$

nor

$k \ \varepsilon_2 \ k$

nor

$k \ \varepsilon_2 \ K$

is, in its basic use, the schema of a well-formed formula, so that none of these provides a way of "saying of a class that it is a member of itself," the same is not true, in the first instance, of

$K \ \varepsilon_2 \ K.$

At least *some* expressions consisting of an "ε_2" with an uppercase "K" fore and aft are well-formed, and while in the example we have been considering, the two class terms were different, thus,

$$K_1 \; \varepsilon_2 \; {}^2K_1,$$

the question immediately arises: Is it possible to make statements of this form where the same class expression occurs in both places?

Let us try, to begin with,

$$K_1 \; \varepsilon_2 \; K_1.$$

This reduces as follows:

1. The $(\cdot \varepsilon_1 \, k_1 \cdot [\mathrm{INDCON}]) \; \varepsilon_2 \; K_1$
2. The $(\cdot \varepsilon_1 \, k_1 \cdot [\mathrm{INDCON}])$ is a member of K_1
3. The $(\cdot \varepsilon_1 \, k_1 \cdot [\mathrm{INDCON}])$ is true
   of $\cdot$ the $(\cdot \varepsilon_1 \, k_1 \cdot [\mathrm{INDCON}]) \cdot$
4. The $(\cdot \varepsilon_1 \, k_1 \cdot [\cdot \text{the } (\cdot \varepsilon_1 k_1 \cdot [\mathrm{INDCON}]) \cdot])$ is true
5. The $(\cdot \varepsilon_1 \, k_1 \cdot [\mathrm{INDCON}]) \; \varepsilon_1 \; k_1$
6. $\cdot \varepsilon_1 \, k_1 \cdot [\mathrm{INDCON}] \subset k_1,$

and there would seem to be no problem about such a statement being true for some values of "K_i"—for example,

Expressions which are individual constants concatenated with an $\cdot \varepsilon_1$ statement$\cdot$ are statements.

This brings us face to face with the question: Can the Russell paradox be constructed in the framework of classes as we have been explicating it? The forms

$$K \; \varepsilon_2 \; K$$

and

$$K \; \varepsilon_1 \; k$$

are *prima facie* available. The latter, however, is obviously not suited to the formation of an abstract which would serve the purpose of Russell's

$$\hat{k}(\sim (k \; \varepsilon \; k)),$$

for the latter requires that the same variable occur both before and after the "ε," whereas the expressions which occur before and after the "ε_1" of

$$K \; \varepsilon_1 \; k$$

cannot be substituends for the same variable. Roughly put, to do so would be to treat both an expression and its name as simultaneous substituends for one variable. Thus Russell's abstract cannot be generated from

$$\sim (K \; \varepsilon_1 \; k).$$

For both

$$\hat{K}(\sim(K \ \varepsilon_1 \ k))$$

and

$$\hat{k}(\sim(K \ \varepsilon_1 \ k))$$

would at best be abstract functions rather than abstracts. To get an abstract from either we would have to specify or bind the free variable.

What, then, of the form

$$K \ \varepsilon_2 \ K?$$

Here, again, the answer is no, although a bit more difficult to see. The point is essentially the same, although the appearances are different. The key question is: Is the first "K_1" in

$$K_1 \ \varepsilon_2 \ K_1$$

the same term as the second "K_1"? Indeed, is it the same term as the "K_1" of its ε_1-counterpart

$$K_1 \ \varepsilon_1 \ k_1?$$

The answer to the second question is that the subject term of the ε_2-statement stands to the subject term of the ε_1-statement as the "Socrates" of

Socrates exemplifies wisdom

stands to the "Socrates" of

Socrates is wise.

And the answer to the first question is the same.

Clearly, *if* the two "K_1"'s of

$$K_1 \ \varepsilon_2 \ K_1$$

though of similar design, and though their senses are intimately related, are not the same term, then they cannot be treated as substituends of the same variable. The expression

$$\hat{K}(\sim(K \ \varepsilon_2 \ K))$$

would be an abstract function rather than an abstract, and *which* abstract-function it would be, would depend on whether it is the variable before the "ε_2" or the variable after the "ε_2" which was intended to bear the brunt of the abstraction operator.

But *is* the "K_1" of

$$K_1 \ \varepsilon_2 \ K_1$$

thus ambiguous? That this is indeed the case can be seen by

exploring the above reduction of "K_1 ε_2 K_1." Thus, it will be noted that the phrase by which the left hand "K_1" is initially explicated turns out to be a *mentioned* item in the course of the reduction, whereas the same phrase offered in explication of the right hand "K_1" turns out to be *used but not mentioned*. The fundamental point is illustrated in the reduction of

Socrates exemplifies wisdom.

As analysed in *AE*, it includes the steps

1. Wisdom is true of *Socrates*
2. The (·wise· [INDCON]) is true of ·Socrates·
3. The (·wise· [·Socrates·]) is true
4. Wise (Socrates), i.e., Socrates is wise.

The italics in (1) highlight the fact that there the design "Socrates" is a metalinguistic expression in the material mode of speech. Thus (2) is the explicated formal mode translation of (1), and the transition from (2) to (3) is made by the use of Definition 1, above.

If this analysis is correct, and the explicitly metalinguistic character of the use of the design "Socrates" in (3) reflects a metalinguistic use in the material mode of the "Socrates" in

Socrates exemplifies wisdom,

then we have clear sailing, for the reduction of "K_1 ε_2 K_1," which is our transcription of "K_1 is a member of K_1," includes the steps, parallel to steps (2) to (4) above,

3. The (·ε_1 k_1· [INDCON]) is true
   of ·the (·ε_1 k_1· [INDCON])·
4. The (·ε_1 k_1· [·the (·ε_1 k_1· [INDCON]) ·]) is true
5. The (·ε_1 k_1· [INDCON]) ε_1 k_1.

An analysis along these lines would explain why we can ask of any given class whether or not it is a member of itself—for this is to ask

$$K_i\ \varepsilon_2 K_i?$$

a question which takes in its stride the different roles of the two "K_i"'s—but cannot meaningful ask: Is the class represented by

$$\hat{K}(\sim(K\ \varepsilon_2\ K))$$

a member of the class represented by

$$\hat{K}(\sim(K\ \varepsilon_2\ K))?^{14}$$

any more than we can meaningful ask,

x is red?

Both of the latter are question functions rather than questions.

Notice, however, that we can form the abstract

$$\hat{K}_i,\ \hat{K}_i(\sim(K_i\ \varepsilon_2\ K_i))$$

where bold italics have been used to distinguish the variable which occurs before the "ε_2" from the otherwise similar variable which occurs after it, and a subscript to make it clear that the class expressions paired have the same subscript.

VI

It may be thought that this solution of the problem is too cavalier. After all, it may be said, surely

Socrates exemplifies wisdom (*or* Wisdom is true of Socrates)

is as much about Socrates as

Socrates is wise.

Surely the "Socrates" in the former "is the same term as" the "Socrates" in the latter, and as the "Socrates" in

Socrates exists.

Now it is obvious that these "Socrates"'s are intimately related, and that they do *not* differ as do the "Plato" of

Plato is wise

and the "Aristotle" of

Aristotle is wise.

Nevertheless there are important differences between them, and the fact that "they all refer to the same man" is bound up with the fact that the different uses of the design "Socrates" involved make up a family the members of which are all related to one primary use.

Suppose it were asked, does the design "it is raining" in

It is true that it is raining

mean the same as the design "It is raining" in

It is raining

---

[14]The reason for the caution with which this question has been formulated will be found in section VII, where the logical character of abstracts will be discussed in relation to the formulation of Russell's paradox.

or the design "it is raining" in

    Jones says that it is raining?

Well, none of these has the same meaning as the English expression "It is snowing." They don't *in the ordinary sense,* "have different meanings." But they are playing different roles, of which the *primary* one is to say

    It is raining.

Thus, the sameness of meaning of the design "it is raining" in

    It is true that it is raining

and in the simple declarative sentence

    It is raining,

is bound up with the inferences

    It is true that it is raining

    Therefore, it is raining

and

    It is raining

    Therefore, it is true that it is raining;

and the validity of these inferences is compatible with, indeed clarified by, our explication of "that it is raining" as

    The ·it is raining·.

Thus in

    Jones says that it is raining

the "it is raining" is being used to form the name of a linguistic type[15] of which, if the statement is true, some Jonesean verbal behavior is a token. Otherwise put, some Jonesean verbal behavior is an ·it is raining·.

In a sense which parallels that in which "It is true that it is raining" is about the weather, "Socrates exemplifies wisdom" is about Socrates. For although the latter tells us in the first instance that sentences which are ·wise·[INDCON]s are true where the INDCONs are tokens of a certain specific INDCON, it does so by using the sign design which is that certain specific individual constant in our language, so that by knowing how to use that

---

[15]In the interlinguistic sense of this term in which it stands for a linguistic distributive object which it embodies in different languages in different sign designs. Cf. my Quotation marks, sentences and propositions, *Philosophy and Phenomenological Research, 12,* 1952.

design in our language, we know our way to
        Socrates is wise
by a route, already spelled out, where the last step is the truth
move.[16]

<h1 style="text-align:center">VII</h1>

It will be helpful to make our argument seem more relevant by
showing how the Russell paradox can be generated in the framework of classes as we have interpreted it, and in spite of all our
distinctions, if the asymmetry of the roles of the "K"'s before and
after the "ε_2" is overlooked. Before showing this, however, we
must reflect briefly on the status of abstracts. Roughly, are they
singular terms or common nouns? In Fregean words, are they
objects or functions?

In particular, do abstracts belong in the context
        —— ε_1 (abstract)
or in the context
        —— ε_2 (abstract)?

I think it clear that *primary* abstract expressions, as I shall call
them, are common nouns or predicative expressions; but that
corresponding to each primary abstract expression there will be a
secondary or "platonistic" abstract expression which stands to the
former as "lionkind" to "lion." Thus with primary abstracts the
appropriate form is illustrated by
        Leo $\varepsilon_1 \hat{x}$ (x ε_1 lion).

The corresponding statement with a secondary abstract would be
        Leo ε_2 the ($\cdot \varepsilon_1 \hat{x}$ (x ε_1 lion) $\cdot$ [INDCON]),
the equivalence of which to the former is shown by the series
        Leo ε_2 the ($\cdot \varepsilon_1 \hat{x}$ (x ε_1 lion) $\cdot$ [INDCON])
        The ($\cdot \varepsilon_1 \hat{x}$ (x ε_1 lion) $\cdot$ [INDCON]) is true of $\cdot$ Leo $\cdot$
        The ($\cdot \varepsilon_1 \hat{x}$ (x ε_1 lion) $\cdot$ [$\cdot$ Leo $\cdot$]) is true
        Leo $\varepsilon_1 \hat{x}$ (x ε_1 lion).

Let us adopt the convention of forming a secondary abstract

---

[16] I shall not pause to show how similar considerations apply to the sense in which
"Socrates exists" is about Socrates. The first step, however, would be to establish
something like the following as the analysis of "Socrates exists,"
        (E DEFDIS) Criterion (DEFDIS, $\cdot$ Socrates $\cdot$)
        and the ($\cdot E! \cdot$ DEFDIS) is true.

from a primary abstract by putting the primary abstract in braces.
Then

$\{\hat{x} \ (x \ \varepsilon_1 \ \text{lion})\}$

is the secondary abstract written above as

The $(\cdot \varepsilon_1 \ \hat{x} \ (x \ \varepsilon_1 \ \text{lion}) \cdot [\text{INDCON}])$.

We are now in a position to construct the Russell paradox on
the (false) assumption that the two "K_i"s in "$K_i \ \varepsilon_2 \ K_i$" can be
treated as substituends for the same variable.

Form the primary abstract

$\hat{K} \ (\sim(K \ \varepsilon_2 \ K))$.

This, of course, is a common noun, a predicative expression. Thus,

$(\hat{K} \sim(K \ \varepsilon_2 \ K)) \ \varepsilon_2 \ \hat{K} \ (\sim(K \ \varepsilon_2 \ K))$

is ill-formed. Furthermore, and for the same reason, this primary
abstract is not a proper substituend for the variable "K." If, however, we form the corresponding secondary abstract,

$\{\hat{K} \ (\sim(K \ \varepsilon_2 \ K))\}$, i.e.,

The $(\cdot \varepsilon_1 \ \hat{K} \ (\sim(K \ \varepsilon_2 \ K)) \cdot [\text{INDCON}])$,

both moves become permissible, as far as anything we have said is
concerned—always within the false assumption that the variable
"K" is unambiguous.[17]

Let us represent this secondary abstract by "S" and ask what
follows from each of the two assumptions,

1. $S \ \varepsilon_2 \ S$
2. $\sim(S \ \varepsilon_2 \ S)$.

From (1) we get the derivation

$S \ \varepsilon_2 \ S$
$S \ \varepsilon_2 \ \{\hat{K} \ (\sim(K \ \varepsilon_2 \ K))\}$
$S \ \varepsilon_2 \ \text{the} \ (\cdot \varepsilon_1 \ \hat{K} \ (\sim(K \ \varepsilon_2 \ K)) \cdot [\text{INDCON}])$
The $(\cdot \varepsilon_1 \ \hat{K} \ (\sim(K \ \varepsilon_2 \ K)) \cdot [\text{INDCON}])$ is true of $\cdot S \cdot$
The $(\cdot \varepsilon_1 \ \hat{K} \ (\sim(K \ \varepsilon_2 \ K)) \cdot [\cdot S \cdot])$ is true
$S \ \varepsilon_1 \ \hat{K} \ (\sim(K \ \varepsilon_2 \ K))$
$\sim(S \ \varepsilon_2 \ S)$.

---

[17]Notice that if we recognize the ambiguity of the variable, then the secondary
abstract is a DST which refers to certain sentential tokens of an irreflexive, dyadic-
relational kind, thus

The $(\cdot \varepsilon_1 < \hat{K}_i, \ \hat{K}_i > (\sim (K_i \ \varepsilon_2 \ K_i) \cdot [\text{INDCON}_j, \text{INDCON}_k](j \neq k)$
which has the form

The $^2\text{PRECON} \ [\text{INDCON}_j, \text{INDCON}_k] \ (j \neq k)$
to which Definition 2 pertaining to 'true of' applies.

From (2) we get the derivation

$$\sim(S \; \varepsilon_2 \; S)$$
$$S \; \varepsilon_2 \; \hat{K} \, (\sim(K \; \varepsilon_2 \; K))$$
The $(\cdot \varepsilon_1 \hat{K}(\sim(K \; \varepsilon_2 \; K)) \cdot [\text{INDCON}])$ is true of $\cdot S \cdot$
$$S \; \varepsilon_2 \; \text{the} \, (\cdot \varepsilon_1 \hat{K}(\sim(K \; \varepsilon_2 \; K)) \cdot [\text{INDCON}])$$
$$S \; \varepsilon_2 \; \{ \hat{K} \, (\sim[K \; \varepsilon_2 \; K]) \}$$
$$S \; \varepsilon_2 \; S.$$

Notice that although these derivatives parallel the Russell moves, they do so in a way which brings out the essential involvement of the semantical concept of truth. For that Russell's paradox is, at bottom, a semantical paradox to be handled by semantic distinctions is the fundamental theme of this paper.

XI

THE PARADOX OF ANALYSIS:
A NEO-FREGEAN APPROACH

I

Consider the argument

A. 1. The concept Male Parent is the analysis of the concept Father

   2. The concept Father = the concept Male Parent

   3. The concept Father is the analysis of the concept Father.

We shall suppose that (1) is true, without, however, committing ourselves, for the moment, to any particular explication of it. On the other hand, (3) is patently false. Yet (3) can be obtained, it would seem, from (1) by identity substitution (Subst. I) based on (2). And (2) has been thought to follow from (1). What has gone wrong?

Suppose for the moment that (2) does follow from (1). Then the trouble would lie in the substitution of identicals in the context

      . . . is the analysis of . . .

But *some* substitutions of identicals in this context are clearly appropriate, thus from (1) together with

     The concept Male Parent = the concept expressed in German by "Maennlicher Elter"

we can get

     The concept expressed in German by "Maennlicher Elter" is the analysis of the concept Father.

And it is not clear why the identity expressed by (2)—if it holds—would not permit the corresponding move which results in (3). The context in question does not flaunt an obliqueness such as that which invalidates

     The morning star = the evening star

     Jones believes that the morning star is rising

     Jones believes that the evening star is rising.

The expression "the concept Father" seems to have the same sense and the same reference in (1) as in (2), and so does "the concept Male Parent." In this respect the argument resembles

Tully was an admirer of Cicero
Tully = Cicero
Cicero was an admirer of Cicero.

To bring in an *ad hoc* principle to the effect that substitution of identicals is inappropriate to the context " . . . is the analysis of . . ." is to resolve no puzzles.

II

But even if we rule out substitution of identicals in this context, there is another mode of substitution which would seem to authorize the move from (1) to (3), for the latter need not be construed as the move from

(The concept Male Parent) is the analysis of the concept Father

to

(The concept Father) is the analysis of the concept Father
but rather as the radically different move from

The concept (Male Parent) is the analysis of the concept Father

to

The concept (Father) is the analysis of the concept Father
where the parentheses indicate the scope of the substitution. Construed in this manner, the transition from (1) to (3) would be governed by something like the following principle [Subst II:] Expressions which stand for the same concept may be substituted for each other *salva veritate*. And the relevance of this principle would require that

(4) In the context "the concept . . ." the English expressions
      "Father" and "Male Parent" stand for the same concept
and, which would seem harmless enough,

(5) In the English context "the concept Male Parent" the
      expression "Male Parent" stands for a concept.
These make possible the reasonably explicit argument

B. 1. The concept (Male Parent) is the analysis of the concept
        Father

5. In the English context "the concept Male Parent" the expression "Male Parent" stands for a concept

4. In the context "the concept..." the English expressions "Father" and "Male Parent" stand for the same concept

3. (by Subst. II) The concept (Father) is the analysis of the concept Father.

Let us disregard (5) for the moment, and turn our attention to (4). It does not sound implausible. Indeed, it has the intuitive ring of truth. It has been supported by the following line of thought, which is attractive, if not fully explicit.

C. 6. In non-oblique contexts the English expression "Father" stands for the concept Father

7. In non-oblique contexts the English expression "Male Parent" stands for the concept Male Parent

1. The concept Male Parent is the analysis of the concept Father

8. In non-oblique contexts the English expression "Father" stands for the concept Male Parent.

If the argument is good so far, who could object to

D. 7. In non-oblique contexts the English expression "Male Parent" stands for the concept Male Parent

8. In non-oblique contexts the English expression "Father" stands for the concept Male Parent

4a. In non-oblique contexts the English expressions "Father" and "Male Parent" stand for the same concept

the conclusion of which would seem to follow as the night the day. If we add the assumption that two English expressions which stand for the same concept in non-oblique contexts will also stand for the same concept—not necessarily the same concept as in non-oblique contexts—in the context "the concept...," we could move from (4a) to (4).

It would seem, then, that to avoid the paradox we must either reject the principle (Subst. II) that two expressions which stand for the same concept can be interchanged *salva veritate*, or reject one of the above steps leading to (4), or reject the idea (5) that in the context "the concept Male Parent" the expression "Male Parent" stands for a concept.

III

It should now be noticed that the principle that two expressions which stand for the same concept can be interchanged *salva veritate* is involved in two lines of thought which generate

2. The concept Father = the concept Male Parent
which is a premiss in the first form of the paradox. These two lines of thought are, first,

E. 9. The concept (Male Parent) = the concept Male Parent

4. In the context "the concept..." the English expressions "Father" and "Male Parent" stand for the same concept

5. In the English context "the concept Male Parent" the expression "Male Parent" stands for a concept

2. (by Subst. II) The concept Father = the concept Male Parent

Not to be confused with this is the argument

F. 4a. In non-oblique contexts the English expressions "Father" and "Male Parent" stand for the same concept

6. In non-oblique contexts the English expression "Father" stands for the concept Father

7. In non-oblique contexts the English expression "Male Parent" stands for the concept Male Parent

2. The concept Father = the concept Male Parent

In the light of these interconnections, what options do we have if we wish to retain both principles of substitution and also hold that the context "...is the analysis of..." is a non-oblique context? Clearly (2) must be rejected. But if we reject (2) while keeping Subst. II, we must, in the light of argument (E), reject either (4) or (5). *Prima facie* the burden would seem to lie on (4a). If it were false, *both* arguments for (2)—(F) as well as (E)—would be undercut. Yet the rejection of (4a) runs into resistance. Surely, one is inclined to say, if (1) is true, then there is a sense in which the English expressions "Father" and "Male Parent" stand for the same concept. And if they stand for the same concept in non-oblique contexts, can we stop short of (4)?

IV

Is it possible to maintain that the expressions "Father" and "Male Parent" stand for the same concept while denying that the concept Father is identical with the concept Male Parent? There would seem to be only two possibilities along this line. One involves a critique of argument (F), the other a critique of argument (E). Against argument (F) it can be suggested that the expression "stands for" is ambiguous, indeed that there are at least *three* distinguishable senses of "stands for" of which the third is the disjunction of the first two. Thus it can be claimed that instead of (6) we have

> (6′) In non-oblique contexts the English expression "Father" stands-for$_1$ the concept Father;

instead of (7) we have

> (7′) In non-oblique contexts the English expression "Male Parent" stands-for$_1$ the concept Male Parent;

whereas instead of (8) what we are entitled to is rather

> (8′) In non-oblique contexts the English expression "Father" stands-for$_2$ the concept Male Parent.

If so, (4a) would be true only in the disjunctive sense of "stand for," i.e., "stand for$_3$," thus

> (4a′) In non-oblique contexts the English expressions "Father" and "Male Parent" stand-for$_3$ the same concept.

According to this claim, argument (F) is guilty of a fallacy of ambiguity, for it becomes, when the ambiguity is made evident,

> F′. 4a′. In non-oblique contexts the English expressions "Father" and "Male Parent" stand-for$_3$ the same concept
> 6′. In non-oblique contexts the English expression "Father" stands-for$_1$ the concept Father
> 7′. In non-oblique contexts the English expression "Male Parent" stands-for$_1$ the concept Male Parent
> 2. The concept Father = the concept Male Parent.

Against argument (E) one might take a related line by suggesting that Subst. II be modified to read

> Subst. II′: Two expressions in L may be interchanged *salva veritate* if in non-oblique contexts they both stand-for$_1$ the same concept.

This modification, the force of which remains to be explored, together with the shift from (4a) to (4a′), would undercut not only argument (E) for (2), but argument (B)—the second form of the paradox of analysis—as well.

That these two lines of thought are not unrelated emerges when we press the question, What is the connection between

    1. The concept Male Parent is the analysis of the concept Father

and Subst. II? It is time we made some attempt to explicate (1). Let us try, as a first approximation,

    $1'$. An expression in L which in non-oblique contexts stands-for$_1$ the concept Father can be replaced *salva veritate* in non-oblique contexts by an expression in L which in non-oblique contexts stands-for$_1$ the concept Male Parent.

Since this proposed explication of (1) has the form of a substitution rule, we can call it "Subst. F/MP." While the proposal won't do as it stands, for it fails to account for the asymmetry of the context "... is the analysis of...," it will suffice for our present purposes.

This explication of (1) as ($1'$) or Subst. F/MP suggests an interpretation of the claim that "stands for" is ambiguous. It will be remembered that the claim involved the idea that whereas, in non-oblique contexts, the English expression "Father" stands-for$_1$ the concept Father, it does not stand-for$_1$ the concept Male Parent, but rather stands-for$_2$ this concept. The possibility occurs to us that

    $8'$. In non-oblique contexts the English expression "Father" stands-for$_2$ the concept Male Parent

can be explicated as

    $8''$. In non-oblique contexts the English expression "Father" stands-for$_1$ a concept of which the analysis is the concept Male Parent.

But while this suggests how "stands-for$_2$" might be explained in terms of "stands-for$_1$" and "is the analysis of," it fails to shed much light on "stands-for$_1$" which we have been treating as a primitive idea.

V

Now the above interpretation of (1) as Subst. F/MP brings to the fore a problem which has been lurking in the argument from the beginning. Thus, if it were granted that the context "the concept..." is non-oblique, so that in the expression "the concept Male Parent" the expression "Male Parent" stands-for$_1$ the concept Male Parent, Substition F/MP would permit the construction of the paradox as follows:

G. 1.   The concept Male Parent is the analysis of the concept Father

10.   In (1) the expression "Male Parent" occurs in a non-oblique context and stands-for$_1$ the concept Male Parent

6'.   In non-oblique contexts the expression "Father" stands-for$_1$ the concept Father

3.   (by Substition F/MP) the concept Father is the analysis of the concept Father.

If, therefore, we are to retain subst. F/MP we must deny that the context "the concept..." is non-oblique. Since Subst. F/MP has a plausible ring, the light of analysis must finally be focussed on the role of "Male Parent" in the "concept Male Parent."

What is this role? To begin with, if we are to maintain the impetus of the above argument, we must deny that in the context "the concept..." the expression "Father" stands-for$_1$ the concept Father, that the expression "Male Parent" stands-for$_1$ the concept Male Parent, and, for that matter, that the expression "Father" stands-for$_2$ the concept Male Parent. It is tempting, therefore, to suppose that in this context these expressions do not stand for concepts at all. And there is bite to this suggestion. It has even been claimed that to substitute for "Father" in the context "the concept Father" is like substituting, to use Quine's example, for the "rat" in "Socrates." This is obviously too strong a way of putting it, for whereas the "rat" in "Socrates" has no connection with the concept Rat, the "Father" in "the concept Father" has a very definite connection with the concept Father. Indeed, if "Father" (in English) did not stand-for$_1$ the concept Father in non-oblique contexts, it could not play the role it does in the expression "the concept Father"—even though in the latter expression it does not stand-for$_1$ the concept Father.

What is the role of "Father" in "the concept Father?" In its simplest terms the answer is that English expressions of the form "the concept..." are designed to *refer to* the concept which "..."

stands-for$_1$ in non-oblique English contexts. It is particularly important to see that this connection between '...' and "the concept..." is a matter of a name-forming practice and not a matter of definition. Thus we are *not* saying that (schematically)

The concept... =Df. the concept which "..." stands-for$_1$ in non-oblique English contexts.

This distinction enables us to see that

Der Begriff Vater

formed in German by a similar name-forming practice, can be in the *strictest sense* a translation of

The concept Father

for neither mentions an English or a German word, although each involves the use of a word in the same language in following the relevant name-forming practice.

The fact that the "Father" in "the concept Father" is there by virtue of a name-forming practice seems to support what otherwise would be an *ad hoc* way of avoiding the paradox (i.e., the introduction of the idea that it is inappropriate to substitute within the context "the concept..." simply to close the route from

1. The concept (Male Parent) is the analysis of the concept Father

to

3. The concept (Father) is the analysis of the concept Father.

Yet once we grant the above difference between substituting for "Father" in "the concept Father" and substituting for the "rat" in "Socrates," it is less easy to deny that the "Father" in "the concept Father" stands for a concept. Certainly the idea that it doesn't *refer to* a concept is, as Frege pointed out, an obvious paradox which is apparently on a par with denying that the "Socrates" in "the man Socrates" refers to a man. And if it *refers to* a concept, must it not stand for a concept—even though, of course, it doesn't stand for the concept to which it refers. And if it stands for a concept, it is not implausible to suppose that another expression might stand for the same concept and be interchangeable with it *salva veritate*.

A glance at the move from (4a′) to (4′) is relevant. For provided that we bear in mind the distinction between "stand-for$_1$" and "stand-for₂" it might well be the case that two expressions in English which stand-for₁ the same concept in non-oblique contexts, also stand-for₁ the same concept in the context "the concept..."—though not, of course, the same concept which they stand-for₁ in non-oblique contexts. To decide this issue we would need to know the answer to two questions: (1) What is a concept—in the sense in which "concept" has been used in this argument? (2) What is it for an expression to stand-for₁ a concept?

Thus it might be the case that the reason why it is incorrect to substitute "Father" for "Male Parent" in the "concept Male Parent" is *not* that substitution is *uberhaupt verboten* in this context, but rather that only expressions which, in non-oblique contexts, stand-for₁ the same concept are interchangeable in this context. If, for example, we suppose that a necessary condition of two expressions in English standing-for₁ the same concept is that they have what might be intuitively called "the same symbolic complexity," then it might well be the case that we could substitute "4" for the "Four" in "the concept Four" and "3+1" for the "Three Plus One" in "the concept Three Plus One," but not "4" for the "Three Plus One" in "the concept Three Plus One." This possibility will be picked up shortly.

VI

Yet the above considerations, promising though they may be, do not come to grips with a central feature of the paradox. For granted that in accordance with a name-forming practice the English expression "the concept Father" refers to the concept which "Father" stands-for₁ in English, and that the English expression "the concept Male Parent" refers to the concept which "Male Parent" stands-for₁ in English, why are we constrained to deny that these two expressions refer to the same concept? Why must we deny

2. The concept Father = the concept Male Parent?

and what exactly is wrong with the line of thought which goes from (1) to (2)? Surely one and the same concept can have two names! Thus even if "Father" and "Male Parent" are playing the name-forming role in the context "the concept...," and even if it be granted that for one reason or another it is not permissible to substitute "Father" for "Male Parent" in the context, might not the concepts named be in the strictest sense identical? Why not? and if they are, the paradox in its first form remains.

The above considerations have, indeed, undercut one line of thought which supports (2), (i.e., argument (F) which involves substitution within the context "the concept..."). But it leaves untouched the defence of (2) which derives it from (1) along the lines of argument (F). We have, indeed, given a friendly nod to the idea that, properly formulated as (F'), the argument reveals itself to involve a fallacy of ambiguity. But at the moment the distinction between "stand-for$_1$" and "stand-for$_2$" remains *ad hoc* and intuitive. Besides, there is strong temptation to think that (2) is true.

Yet (2) is, indeed, taken at its face value as a statement of identity, false. There is, however, a true statement in its neighbourhood which is easily confused with it, namely

11. Father = Df. Male Parent

In its primary sense (but see below) this statement does, indeed, admit expansion to

11'. The concept Father = Df. the concept Male Parent

but only if " = Df." is read "equals by definition" and the statement is taken to assert an equality or equivalence (in a sense to be analyzed) of the two concepts in question, rather than their identity.

We can, indeed, say

12. Fathers are by definition male parents

which amounts to

12'. (x) x is a father $\equiv x$ is a male parent

together with a commentary to the effect that (12') is not an empirical assertion, but rests on the explicitly analytic truth

13'. (x) x is a male parent $\equiv x$ is a male parent

together with something like our Substitution F/MP and premises (6) and (7).

Furthermore, since (13) is equivalent to a statement of class identity

13'. Male Parent = Male Parent

there is an identity statement

12″. Father = Male Parent

which, when the identity sign is enriched with the commentary "Df." can easily be confused with (11), or, at least, lead us to assume that because the *class* Father can be shown to be *identical* with the *class* Male Parent by an appeal to Subst. F/MP, the same must be true of the *concept* Father and the *concept* Male Parent. The resulting interpretation of (11′) as a variant of (2) is a disaster, for, as we shall see, (11′), correctly understood, is strictly equivalent to (1), and, as we shall also see, the truth of (1) is *inconsistent with* the truth of (2). A concept cannot be identical with the concept of which it is the analysis.

VII

In spite, however, of the coherence of the distinctions we have been drawing, the claim that the concept Father is not identical with the concept Male Parent is likely to strike one as an unnecessary multiplication of entities. This is certainly the case if one construes concepts as not only public, intersubjective entities, which is obviously true, but as enjoying *chorismos* not only with respect to Becoming, but also with respect to discourse and thought. Is there, one might ask, an archetypal Father as well as an archetypal Male Parent? Could the Divine Craftsman, perhaps, exemplify the one without exemplifying the other? And what grounds could there possibly be for choosing the one rather than the other?

The answer lies in recognizing that although concepts are public, intersubjective entities, so also are institutions. And just as the existence of an institution is logically tied to the existence of persons—though not of this or that particular person—so the existence of concepts is logically tied to the existence of persons and their ability to participate in intersubjective discourse. The existence of a game lies, in its primary sense, in the fact that there are people who know how to play it. Now concepts, as I see it, are linguistic objects in the sense in which the various pieces involved in the game of chess (e.g., the pawn) are chess objects. Thus, just as the pawn can be realized in material objects of different shapes, sizes and composition, so the concept Father can be realized in different linguistic materials or sign designs. From this point of view, the German sign design *Vater*, the

French sign design *Pere*, and the English sign design *Father* are all realizations of the concept Father in different materials. In their respective languages, they all stand-for₁ the concept Father. A similar situation obtains with respect to the sign designs *Maennlicher Elter*, *Parent Mâle*, and *Male Parent*, which are all realizations or embodiments, in their respective languages, of the concept Male Parent.

But whereas the concept Father is a non-composite linguistic object, and is realized or embodied in sign designs which are not structures of sign designs, the concept Male Parent is a composite linguistic object in the sense that any realization or embodiment of it must consist of a realization of the concept Male concatenated, in a manner characteristic of the language in which it is realized, with a realization of the concept Parent. If, therefore, we interpret concepts as linguistic objects along the above lines, we can see how the concept Father and the concept Male Parent might be *equal* or equivalent in a very strong (and special) sense, without being identical. For we see why the expressions "the concept Male Parent" and "the concept Father" are not to be construed as two differently formed names of the same concept.

Thus, as we saw in an earlier section, the expression which follows the rubric "...the concept..." must be an expression which, in non-oblique contexts, stands-for₁ the concept to which the whole expression refers. That is to say, on the present interpretation, it must be a design which, in English, embodies the linguistic object which is the concept in question. But just as to embody a certain chess object is to be, for example, a pawn; so to embody the linguistic object which is the concept Father is to be a ·father·. The convention for dot quotes differs from that for ordinary quotes in that whereas "father" is a common noun which is used to refer to instances of the design *father* as playing in English a role which could be played by instances of other designs, "·father·" is a common noun which is applicable to items which play this role *whatever their design may be and to whatever language they may belong*. Of course, the formation of this common noun involves the use of the design which plays this role in English, but, as pointed out in Chapter 9, this design is involved in the name-forming capacity only, and not as a criterion for being a

·father·. To be a ·father·, then, is to be an item which in some language plays the role played, in non-oblique contexts, by instances of the design *Father* in the language (in this case English) to which the common noun "·father·" belongs. *To stand-for$_1$ the concept Father is to be a ·father·.*

On the other hand, to be a ·Male Parent· is to be a concatenation of two designs in the same language, one of which is a ·male·, the other a ·parent·. It follows that no ·father· can be a ·male parent· (i.e., that no expression which stands-for$_1$ the concept Father can also stand-for$_1$ the concept Male Parent).

The above considerations explain why (2) is false, and thus cut off one path, argument (A), to the paradox of analysis. They also serve to clarify, as we shall see, the grounds on which the second form of the paradox, argument (B), has been criticized in earlier sections.

VIII

We have seen that to be a ·male parent· is to be a complex expression, whereas to be a ·father· is to be a simple expression. Thus the interchangeability of ·male parent·s and ·father·s which is their equality, is a matter of the interchangeability of a complex and a simple expression which has always been recognized to be an essential feature of classical (or "analytic") definition. Thus (1), and with it Subst. F/MP, becomes

Subst. ·f·/·mp·: ·father·s (which are simple expressions) can be interchanged in any language with ·male parents· (which are complex expressions)

where the asymmetry of complexity shown by the principles is formulated in the parenthetical remarks. Notice that reference to "non-oblique contexts" has been dropped. The reason should be clear. In what are called "oblique contexts," a design which would otherwise be, for example, a ·father· is not a ·father· but, rather, something else.

Notice, furthermore, that I have dropped the pharse "*salva veritate.*" It might be thought that the reason for doing this is that "*salva veritate*" is too weak, and should be strengthened to "with saving of sense." If, however, the latter phrase is interpreted to mean "with identity of sense" it would be a mistake to put it in.

For, as we have seen, while more than an extensional equivalence between the concept Father and the concept Male Parent is involved, this something more is not an *identity* of these concepts. If, however, the phrase is interpreted to mean "with equal sense," it is indeed an appropriate addition, for the holding of Subst. ·f·/·mp· *is* the equality of the two concepts, and may suitably be noted in a parenthetical remark.

To pick up where the last paragraph but one left off, notice that in the expression "the concept Father," the design *Father* is not a ·father·, but rather, to make the point in first approximation, a · ·father· ·. This brings with it a number of clarifications. In the first place, it explains why Subst. ·f·/·mp· does not authorize the move from

> 1. The concept Male Parent is the analysis of the concept Father

to

> 3. The concept Father is the analysis of the concept Father.

thus blocking the second mode of constructing the paradox of analysis, argument (B). For (1) has the form

> 1″. ·male parent· is the analysis of ·father·

and in (1″) the design *male parent* is not a ·male parent·— nor, indeed, an expression of any other kind, but rather something which contributes to the forming of an expression, a · ·male parent· ·, in accordance with an expression-forming practice.

In the second place, it also explains why certain substitutions in the context "the concept . . ." are *in principle* permissible. Thus, suppose that two simple English expressions *red* and *ded* play the same role, have the same use, in short, are synonyms in the strictest sense. Each can be used to form an expression which refers to the linguistic "piece" which plays this role, thus

> The concept Red (i.e., [the "piece"] ·red·)
> The Ded (i.e., [the "piece"] ·ded·)

In the expression "the concept Red," the *Red* is a · ·red· ·, while in the expression "the concept Ded" the *Ded* is a · ·ded· ·. Here, however, in contrast to the case of the concepts Father and Male Parent, we *can* say

> The concept Red = the concept Ded

(that is, in first approximation,

(the "piece") ·red· = (the "piece") ·ded·);

the senses of the two sides of this identity are different, the difference being rooted in the difference of the resources mobilized by the practice in accordance with which the two expressions referring to the same role were formed.

Again, it enables us to see that the expression "the concept Father" is, after all, analogous to "the man Socrates" in that what follows the phrase "the concept" is an expression which refers to a man. For, whereas in "Tom is a father" the *father* is a ·father· and, therefore, a predicative expression, in "the concept Father" the *Father* is not a ·father·. Here we must be careful, for if we go on to say, as in a sense we must, that instead of being a ·father· it is a ··father··, we will not have explained how it can be a *referring* expression, for a ··father·· is as much a common noun as a ·father·.

It will be remembered that I wrote above that in the expression "the concept Father" the *Father* is not a ·father·, but *to make the point in first approximation, a* ··father··. Why a "first approximation"? The answer will illuminate not only the puzzle raised by the last paragraph, but also the relationship between

Subst. ·f·/·mp·: ·father·s may be interchanged in any language with ·male parent·s

(to which we were led by modifying Subst. F/MP in accordance with later developments) and

1″. ·male parent· is the analysis of ·father·.

The point is a simple one which concerns the difference between a common noun and the corresponding singular term formed from it as "the pawn" is formed from "pawn" or "the lion" from "lion."

Statements of the form

The K is f

imply the corresponding statement of the form

Ks are f

and they can be "introduced" from the latter, provided that certain *conditions* are met.[1] In this sense, statements about the K are reducible to statements about Ks.

---

[1]These points are discussed in some detail in Chapter IX above.

Consider now the statement

　　14. "run" is a verb

This obviously entails, and is, in the above sense, reducible to

　　15. "run"s are verbs

where "run"s are what Peirce would call tokens of the type "run." Thus (14) has the form

　　14'. the "run" is a verb

(i.e., in [14] the expression "run" is functioning as what I have elsewhere[2] called a distributive singular term (DST), one that is formed from the common noun "run" which is the root of the plural found in [15]). Exactly the same is true of (1''). It has the form

　　1'''. The ·male parent· is the analysis of ·father·s

and is, in the above sense, reducible to

　　1.'''' ·male parent·s are analyses of ·father·s

which is identical in sense with Subst. ·f·/·mp·, although to develop this point to bring out its full significance would take another paper of almost equal length.

Finally, we see that the expression "the concept Father" has a form which can be represented by

　　the concept ·father·

only if we agree to use dot quotes expressions both as common nouns and as DSTs, letting the context decide which is appropriate. If we did so, we would be extending to dot quotes a convention characteristic of ordinary quotes. We say not only

　　"but" is a conjunction

where "but" is a DST, but also

　　the first word on the page is a "but"

where it is a common noun. If, therefore, we wish to avoid misunderstanding, we can write

　　The concept, the ·father·.

It will doubtless have occurred to the reader that the use of a capital letter, as in

　　The concept Father

or the use of italics, as in

　　The concept *father*

---

[2]*Loc. cit,*

are more familiar, but less clarifying, ways of expressing the peculiar role played by expressions in the context "the concept..." For an additional discussion of expressions of the form represented by "the concept Father," with particular reference to Frege's puzzles about whether or not the concept Father is a concept, the reader is referred to Chapter IX. It is, however, important to call attention to the fact that concepts in Frege's sense are a subset of the concepts with which we have been concerned. Our use of the word "concept" corresponds rather closely to Frege's notion of sense. His concepts are what we would distinguish as the predicative variety of concepts.

XII

NOTES ON INTENTIONALITY

My aim in this paper is to develop, in fairly short compass, some central themes pertaining to intentionality. Since I do not have the space for a useful discussion of even a few of the major approaches to this complex topic, I shall limit myself to sketching the kind of position I am inclined to hold, and contrasting it with a carefully worked out alternative which belongs in the same philosophical neighborhood.

I shall assume that there are inner conceptual episodes proper ("thoughts") which are expressed by candid overt speech. These episodes can be referred to as "mental acts" provided that one is careful not to confuse "act" with "action" in the sense of piece of conduct." Thoughts are acts in the sense of *actualities* (as contrasted with dispositions or propensities).[1]

I shall not attempt to botanize the varieties of mental act. Their diversity corresponds to the diversity of the linguistic utterances which, in candid or uncontrived speech, they find their natural culmination. I shall focus my attention on such thoughts as are expressed by subject predicate empirical statements, and make use where possible of the tidy forms of PMese.

I said above that candid meaningful linguistic utterances express thoughts. Here it is essential to note that the term "express," indeed the phrase "express a thought," is radically ambiguous. In one sense, to say of an utterance that it expresses a thought is to say, roughly, that a thought episode *causes* the utterance.[2] But there is another and radically different sense in which an utterance can be said to express a thought. This is the sense in which the utterance expresses a proposition (i.e., a thought in Frege's sense (*Gedanke*)—an "abstract entity" rather than a mental

---

[1]This is not to say that there are no such things as mental actions in the conduct sense, but they have a more complex structure.

[2]I say "roughly," because the word "cause" is a dangerous one unless used with proper care. Here it means that the occurrence of the thought explains (on certain assumptions about the context) the occurrence of the utterance.

episode). Let me distinguish between these two senses of "express" as the "causal" and the "logical," and between the two senses of "thought" by referring to *thinkings* and *propositions*. These distinctions are represented by the following diagram:

$$* \text{ proposition that-}p$$

Thinking that-p $* \rightarrow *$ speaking that-p

This diagram obviously raises the question, What is the relation between the thinking that-p and the proposition that-p? One possible move is to treat the relation between the speaking and the proposition as the logical product of the causal relation between the speaking and the thinking and a relation between the thinking and the proposition, thus

$$* \text{ proposition that-}p$$

Thinking that-p $* \rightarrow *$ speaking that-p

(Roughly, for a speaking to mean that-p is for it to be caused by a thinking that-p.)

Another possible move is to treat the relation between the thinking and the proposition as the logical product of the causal relation between the speaking and the thinking and a relation between the speaking and the proposition, a situation which the first diagram can also be used to represent. (Roughly, to be a thinking that-p is to be an episode of a sort which causes speakings which express the proposition that-p.)

I propose, instead, to work with the following more complex framework in which the idea that thinkings belong to "inner speech" is taken seriously, and combined with the idea that expressions in different languages can stand for (express in the logical sense) the same proposition. It can be represented, at least initially, by the following diagram:

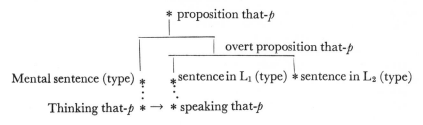

According to this account, neither the relation of the speaking to the proposition nor the relation of the thinking to the proposition is to be analyzed as a logical product along the lines of previous paragraphs. This claim is intended to be compatible with the idea that there is an internal relation between the idea of a speaking expressing a certain proposition and the speaking being caused, *ceteris paribus*, by a thinking which expresses the same proposition.[3]

The structure of the above diagram can perhaps be clarified by pointing out that according to the position I am defending, the framework of thinkings is an analogical one the *fundamentum* of which is meaningful overt speech, (i.e., speech which is understood in terms of the uniformities and propensities which connect utterances with (1) other utterances (at the same or different level of language), (2) with the perceptible environment, and (3) with courses of action (including linguistic behavior). I say uniformities, but the uniformities are not *mere* uniformities, for they are grounded in rules in a way most difficult to analyze, but which involves the causal efficacy of rule expressions.[4]

Thus the concept of a proposition as something which can be expressed by sentences in both Mentalese and, say, English is an analogical extension of the concept of a proposition as something that can be expressed by sentences in both English and German. My next move, therefore, will be to explore what it is for a token of a sentence in, for example, German to express a proposition.

Instead, however, of dealing with this topic directly, I shall ask the closely related question, What is it for a German noun, say "Himmel," to express a concept: the concept sky?[5]

I have written on a number of occasions[6] that "meaning is not

---

[3]It is important to distinguish between two senses of "meaningless utterance": (1) An utterance is meaningless if it does not token a properly formed expression in a language. (2) An utterance is meaningless if it is uttered parrotingly by one who does not know the language. It is worth reflecting on the idea of a meaningless mental utterance. We might not call it a thinking, but it would stand to thinkings as meaningless utterances stand to "saying something."

[4]See Wittgenstein: *Philosophical Investigations;* also my essay Some reflections on language games, *Philosophy of Science, 21,* 1954 (reprinted in a revised version as Chapter 11 of *Science Perception and Reality*).

[5]In Fregean terminology, both concepts and propositions, as I am using these terms, are *senses,* and I am exploring what it is for a sentence to express a sense by asking the parallel question about less complex expressions.

[6]Cf Empiricism and abstract entities, in *The Philosophy of Rudolf Carnap*, Open

a relation," although statements about what expressions mean "convey" information which would be directly expressed by statements among which would be the relational ones. I want now to make additional payments on these promissory notes.

The hypothesis I wish to propose is that

'Himmel' (in German) means sky

has the sense of

'Himmel's (in German) are ·sky·s

or, in PMese

'Himmel' (in German) $\subset$ ·sky·

where ' ·sky· ' is a common noun which applies to items in any language which play the role played in our language by the sign design which occurs between the dot quotes, and the specific word "means" serves to indicate that the context is linguistic, and to remind us that in order for the statement to do its job directly, the unique common-noun forming convention must be understood, and the sign design *sky* must be present in the active vocabulary of the person to whom the statement is made, playing there the role played by "Himmel" in German.

To characterize a statement of the form

A $\subset$ B

as "relational" is a mistake of the same nature as characterizing

p or q

as a relational form, or

$\sim$ p

as predicating negation of a state of affairs. The first of these statements is equivalent by definition to

x (xεA) $\rightarrow$ x (xεB)

and, ultimately, to

(x) xεA $\rightarrow$ xεB.

The expressions "A" and "B" which appear in "A $\subset$ B" are no more to be construed as proper names then these same expressions as they appear in its unpacked equivalents. As a first approximation we can say that "A $\subset$ B" preserves the predicative character

---

Court, 1964, pp. 431-468, especially pp. 464 ff.; also Empiricism and the philosophy of mind, in *Minnesota Studies in the Philosophy of Science*, Vol. I, Minneapolis, 1956, pp. 253-329. Reprinted as Chapter 5 in *Science, Perception and Reality*, especially p. 31.

of these expressions which is explicit in the latter statement.[7]
"A ⊂ B" must not be confused with its higher order counterpart,

> The class of A's (or A-Kind) is included in the class of
> B's (or B-kind)

which is, in its way, a relational statement. The distinction is
closely parallel to that between the non-relational statement form
"fa" and its higher order counterpart "A exemplifies f-ness,"
which is discussed in the next paragraph.

It will probably be objected that the above account simply
disguises the relational character of meaning. For surely, it will
be said, the role played by the design *sky* in our language is that
of expressing the concept sky and that consequently I have no
more shown that meaning is non-relational than I would have
shown that largeness is non-relational by pointing out that

> New York is large

has the non-relational form

> $f(x)$.

To come to grips with this challenge I must draw on the resources
developed in Chapters IX and XI. I explored there the equivalence
of statements of the forms

> The K is f
> Ks are f.

In the first of these forms, the DST occurs in the subject position.
We now take into account the fact that it can occur in the predicate,
thus

> Tom loves the brimming glass.

If this can be construed as equivalent to

> Tom loves brimming glasses,

we are confronted with the equivalence schema

> . . . (verb) the K
> . . . (verb) Ks.

The suggestion naturally arises that

---

[7]Strictly speaking, of course, the predicates in the latter are "εA" and "εB" in
which the "A" and "B" are the differentiating components and the "ε" serves (like
"is a" in English) as a syncategorematic component which expresses the classificatory
rather than adjectival character of the predicates. See opening paragraphs of chapter
10 above, also Counterfactuals, dispositions and the causal modalities, in *Minnesota in
Studies the Philosophy of Science*, Vol. II, pp. 225-308, especially pp. 252-266.

'Himmel's (in German) express the concept sky

has the sense of

'Himmel's (in German) express (the concept) the ·sky·

which reduces, in accordance with the above schema, to

'Himmel's (in German) express ·sky·s

If we interpret 'express' to be a specialized form of the copula, then the statement we are analysing stands to

'Himmel' (in German) means sky

as

 ... are the K

to

 ... are Ks.

If so, to claim that 'Himmel' (in German) means sky *because* 'Himmel' (in German) expresses the concept sky is analogous to claiming that Tom loves brimming glasses because Tom loves the brimming glass.[8]

If we extend these considerations to the case of sentential expressions, we see that

"Es regnet" (in German) means *it is raining*

is, at bottom, the non-relational PMese statement

"Es regnet" (in German" $\subset$ ·it is raining·

and that although it has an unperspicuous counterpart, namely,

"Es regnet" (in German) expresses the proposition that it is raining.

The existence of the latter does not point to a relational analysis of meaning statement.

I have argued elsewhere[9] that the truth of statements in a language is to be defined in terms of the truth of propositions. In the framework sketched above, the definition can be represented by the following shema

S (in L) is true $=_{df}$ (Ep) S (in L) means p, and that-p is true

If this seems to involve a conflation of two radically different variables, namely, "that-p" and "p" the appearance is an illusion,

---

[8]For a discussion of the expression "The Concept Father" which throws additional light on the above, the reader should consult the concluding sections of Chapter XI.

[9]Truth and "correspondence," *Journal of Philosophy*, *59*, 1962. (Reprinted as Chapter 6 of *SPR*.)

for the propositional expression "that-p" is related to "p," as it occurs in the context "S (in L) means p," as "the bishop" in

The bishop is a diagonal mover

to "bishop" in

Bishop $\subset$ diagonal movers

They are at the same level of language,[10] and hence no fallacy of treating expressions at different levels as values of the same variable is involved in the above definition. Explicated it now becomes

$$S \text{ (in L) is true} =_{df} (E \cdot p \cdot) S \text{ (in L)} \subset \cdot p \cdot \text{ and } \cdot p \cdot \subset \text{true}$$

Once one makes the move of accounting for the truth of statements in language in terms of the propositions they express, the philosophical problem of truth becomes that of explaining how statements like

That it is raining is true

are related to their lower level counterparts, thus

It is raining.

Gustav Bergmann, in an important essay on intentionality,[11] makes an interesting use of the structure of Carnap's definition of "true sentence in L" in which he applies it to the truth of the propositions, thus

$$\text{That-p is true} =_{df} (Eq) \text{ that-p means q and q}$$

Bergmann argues that statements of the form

—— means . . .

are either "analytic" or "self-contradictory" according to extended applications of these terms which he finds to be justified by the fact that these applications bring together things which belong together. (Just what the *intension* is which is supposed to be common to the original and extended applications is left obscure— a matter of being decidable on purely quasi-linguistic grounds).

The initial effect of this approach is to make it appear that Bergmann is assimilating the way in which "it is raining" occurs on the right hand side of

That it is raining means it is raining

---

[10]This point is elaborated and defended in Abstract entities, *Review of Metaphysics*, *16*:627-671, 1963.

[11]Intentionality, in *Semantics*, Rome, 1955, reprinted in *Meaning and Existence*, Madison, 1960, pp. 3-38.

to the way in which it occurs in analytic extensional contacts, thus on the right hand side of

Not (it is raining) or it is raining

To switch the metaphor, his logically atomistic left hand works on the principle that the only way in which "p" can occur in sentential contexts is if the latter are truth functional, so that in order for "it is raining" to occur in "that it is raining means it is raining" the latter statement must be analyzable in terms of truth functional connectives in such a way that the apparently *predicative* character of "means" disappears.[12]

His equally agile right hand, however, works on the principle that "means" functions as a predicate. Is it a predicate? It cannot, he assures us, be analyzed into the familiar connectives. Yet its character as predicate is *somehow* bogus. At this juncture, Bergmann simply tells us that "means" is a *unique* connective. His purpose is clear. If "means" is a *connective*, then "it is raining" genuinely occurs on the right-hand side of ". . .means it is raining" while if it is *not reducible* to the familiar connectives, it must be *added* to PMese to capture the unique character of mentalistic discourse. Bergmann is on to something important, but his formulations strike me, to use a Russellian metaphor, as light-fingered.

What is the alternative? As I see it, the correct move is not to introduce a new "connective," but to explore in greater detail the unique way in which "it is raining" occurs in "it is true that it is raining." But before doing so, let me note that on the view sketched earlier in the paper, as well as on Bergmann's view,

That it is raining means it is raining

is analytic. On my view, however, it is analytic in a straightforward sense, for it amounts to nothing more than

·It is raining· ⊂ ·it is raining·.

The crucial difference between our two accounts concerns the concept of a proposition. On my view, it is essential to distinguish

---

[12]In his *Introduction to Semantics*, Carnap so introduces "designates (in L)" that "it is raining" does genuinely occur on the right-hand side of

S designates (in L) it is raining

by defining it in terms of disjunction, conjunction, and identity construed as a PMese connective. This generates *at best* the "telephone directory" account of meaning and truth correctly satirized by Max Black in his well-known paper on the Semantical definition of truth, *Analysis*, 1947.

between a proposition and the mental sentence directly tokened by mental acts or thinkings. Bergmann runs these two together with, as I see it, disasterous consequences to his whole philosophy of mind. For this running together, when combined with the insight that it is just as appropriate to speak of what mental sentences mean, leads him to the mistaken conclusion that statements about *the meanings of propositions* are basic to the theory of mind, meaning, and truth.

Thus, if we use " <Es regnet> " to stand for the kind of "mental act which occurs in the mind of German-speaking people and finds its overt expression in candid utterances of 'Es regnet'," then it makes as good sense to say

<Es regnet> (in the minds of German speakers) means it is raining[13]

as it does to say

"Es regnet" (in German) means it is raining

That there is a close connection between these statements is clear, but it is not such as to make (using a corresponding convention)

<It is raining> (in the minds of English speakers) means it is raining

as trifling as

That it is raining means it is raining.

Inner sentence episodes can differ in their descriptive character and yet express the same proposition, just as can overt sentence episodes.[14]

And just as the generically specified character of the shapes and motions and relative locations demanded of chess pieces *must* have determinate embodiment in actual games, so the generically specified character of pieces, positions, and moves, which is common to determinate ways of playing the same conceptual game, must

---

[13]I pointed out above that the concept of a proposition as expressed by mental and overt sentences is an analogical extension of the concept of a proposition as something expressed by overt sentences. Roughly, to be a that-p item in the more inclusive sense is to be an item of a kind which plays a role in *either* thinkings *or* overt speakings which is similar in relevant respects to that played in our overt speech by the design represented by "p."

[14]There is, indeed, every reason to suppose that Japanese inner speech differs systematically from English inner speech in a way which reflects the differences between these two languages.

be determinately embodied in the natural order. In other words, while a mental act which expresses the proposition that it is raining is *ipso facto* an ·it is raining,· it must also belong to a specific variety of ·it is raining,· just as a token of the corresponding English sentence is not only an ·it is raining· but has the specific empirical character by virtue of which it sounds (or reads) like *that*.

The fact that conceptual "pieces" or "role-players" *must* have determinate *factual* character, even though we don't know what that character is save in the most generic way, is the hidden strength of the view which identifies mental acts with neurophysiological episodes.[15]

If the foregoing remarks are correct, then whereas the truth of mental statements must, like that of overt statements, be defined in terms of the truth of propositions, according to the schema

$$S \text{ (in } L) \text{ is true} =_{df} (E \cdot p \cdot) \ S \text{ (in } L) \text{ means } \cdot p \cdot$$
$$\text{and } \cdot p \cdot \subset \text{ true}$$

the truth of propositions is *not* to be so defined, but requires a radically different treatment.

I shall limit my positive account to the truth of empirical propositions and to the bare bones of that. The central theme is that the "inference" represented by the statement

.
.
.

It is true that Tom is tall
Tom is tall

.
.
.

Differs radically from the inference represented by the sequence

.
.
.

Tom is tall and wise

---

[15]This point is elaborated in Philosophy and the scientific image of man, in *Frontiers of Science and Philosophy*, Robert Colodny, ed., Pittsburgh, 1962. (Reprinted as Chapter 1 in *Science, Perception and Reality*; see especially Section VI.

Tom is tall

.

.

.

or

.

.

.

There is lightning
It will thunder

.

.

.

In the latter two examples, the sequences are authorized by principles which do not themselves belong in the sequences. In the first example, however, the inscribing of ·Tom is tall· is a performance which has as its authority a statement which is inscribed above it.

It might be thought that I am offering something like the "warranted assertability" theory of truth, according to which the first sequence has the form

.

.

.

The tokening of ·Tom is tall· is warranted
Tom is tall

.

.

.

But to make this move is to confuse truth with probability, for, presumably, to be warranted is to be warranted by evidence. There is, indeed, a close connection between truth and probability, but it is not as simple as that.

What is the basic job of empirical statements? The answer is, in essence, that of the *Tractatus* (i.e., to compete for places in a picture of how things are, in accordance with a complex manner of projection). Just how such a manner of projection is to be described is a difficult topic in its own right.[16] The important thing for our purposes is that the relation between conceptual picture and objects pictured is a factual one. Thus, whereas an item in the picture is, say, an ·fa·, and the concept of an ·fa· ultimately involves (as does the concept of a pawn) the concept of what it is to satisfy a norm or a standard, the point of the norms or standards pertaining to conceptual ·"pieces" is to bring it about that *as items in the natural order* they picture the way things are.

To say of a basic empirical preposition, e.g., that-fa, that it is true is to say that an ·fa· belongs in a telling of the world story which it is the business of empirical inquiry to construct. And the statement,

> An ·fa· belongs in the story

makes sense even where one neither knows nor has good reason to think that an ·fa· belongs in the story. If, however, one constructs two columns, a right hand one purporting to be a fragment of the story, and to the left a fragmentary list of statements about what belongs in the story, then it is clear that to inscribe ·An ·fa· belongs in the story· in the latter left-hand column is to be committed to the inscribing of an ·fa· in the right-hand column and vice versa. If we represent this committment by

> That-fa is true: fa

then we can say that the implication statements

> That-fa is true implies that-fa
>
> That-fa implies that that-fa is true

are derivative from the former in that the latter are vindicated by pointing out that the pair of inscriptions referred to above can be regarded as a special case of both of the kinds of sequence represented by

> .
>
> .
>
> .
>
> That-fa is true
> fa
>
> .
>
> .

---

[16]I have explored this topic in the paper on Truth and **"correspondence,"** referred to in footnote 9 above.

.

.

.

.

fa

That-fa is true

.

.

.

which it would be the point of the implication statements to authorize.

Notice, in conclusion, that the *practical* connection between inscribing ·That-fa is true· and inscribing ·fa· is a special case of a family of practical connections. Another example is that which relates ·that-fa implies that-ga· to world-story telling. Commitment to ·that-fa is true· picks for further consideration out of all constructable world stories those which include an ·fa·. Commitment to ·that-fa implies that-ga· picks out those which do not include an ·fa· unless they include a ·ga·, nor a competitor of ·ga· unless they include a competitor of ·fa·.

XIII

THEORETICAL EXPLANATION

I

MY PURPOSE in this paper is to discuss some of the features of theoretical explanation which have been at the center of the philosophical stage in recent years. Since the term "theory" covers importantly different types of explanatory systems, each of which is capable of generating philosophical perplexities, let me make it clear from the outset that I shall limit myself to theories of the type which, to speak informally, explain the behavior of objects of a certain domain by "identifying" these objects with systems of objects of another domain, and deriving the laws governing the objects of the first domain from the fundamental laws governing the objects of the second domain. This schema, which has been deliberately designed to highlight the topics which I wish to discuss, covers two importantly different but, as I hope to show, importantly similar, types of theoretical explanation:

1. The explanation of the behavior of "observable" things in terms of "unobservable" things, as in the kinetic theory of gases.

2. The explanation of the behavior of the "unobservable" things of one theoretical framework in terms of the "unobservable" things of another theoretical framework, as in the explanation of the behavior of chemical substances in terms of atomic physics.

I have put the expressions "observable" and "unobservable" in quotation marks because they are technical terms which differ in important respects from their counterparts in ordinary usage. Thus it is not absurd to speak of observing viruses and protein molecules through an appropriately constructed electron microscope. But, as is evident, this extended use of the term is built on the physical theory of the instrument and how it relates to the physical systems which can be observed by its use. Again, to identify the objects observed by its use as "protein molecules" or "viruses" presupposes biochemical theory and pathology. Furthermore, it is particularly clear that the observations made by the use of an instrument cannot be the grounds on which we accept the theory of the instrument. For until we have the theory of the instrument, we *logically* can't make observations with it, though, of course, we can observe it and its behavior as a perceptible physical object.

Thus, although observation in the extended sense provides data for the elaboration of theories pertaining to objects which are not observable in the absence of theory-laden instrumentation, the concept of such observation presupposes the concept of unaided perception, and it is the latter, as submitted to scientific discipline, which the philosopher of science refers to as observation in his technical sense. There are many problems pertaining to unaided sense perception which are still matters of dispute among philosophers. I shall avoid these problems and simply assume what practicing scientists take for granted, that in sense perception we have direct access to public physical objects and processes, and can distinguish between favorable and unfavorable circumstances for telling *by looking, listening,* etc. what perceptible characteristics can reliably be ascribed to these objects and processes. It is customary to call these perceptible characteristics "observable properties" and their linguistic expression "observation predicates." The concept of what one can tell about an object or process by looking, listening, etc. does not cover the same ground in all contexts. Thus a clinical psychologist can tell by looking that a patient is depressed, and many people can tell by looking that a certain object is ten feet high. Reliability and intersubjectivity with respect to a given science at a given stage of its development determine what, for that science, can be told by looking. Implicit in the above discussion are distinctions which can be tabulated as follows:

1. Observable things and processes.
2. The observable properties of observable things and processes.
3. Unobservable things and processes.
4. The unobservable properties of unobservable things and processes.

This classification makes no pretense of being exhaustive. Indeed, a glance at it cannot help but raise the questions:

1. Can observable things and processes have unobservable properties?

2. Can unobservable things and processes have observable properties?

The second question is by no means unambiguous, but a possible example would be

Can a system of sub-atomic particles be liquid?

I shall say something about questions like this at the end of the paper. Of more immediate interest is the first question. The answer is clearly affirmative. There are, however, two types of unobservable property which an observable object might have

1. Specific gravity.

2. The property of consisting of subatomic particles.

The second type is problematic. In effect, to say that observable objects can have such a property implies an affirmative answer to the question, "Can a system of subatomic particles have an observable property?" We shall accordingly postpone considering this type of unobservable property of observable objects until we take up the latter question. It is worth pointing out, however, that if our initial characterization of one of the varieties of theory with which we shall be concerned (i.e., theories which explain the behavior of a domain of observable objects by *identifying* them with systems of certain unobservable objects) is taken at its face value, it must be true that

1. Observable objects have unobservable properties of the second type listed above.

2. Systems of unobservable objects have observable properties.

What this does is bring out the full force of the word "identity" and, as a result, generates some measure of perplexity with the idea that to accept chemical theory is to accept the idea that the water in a glass of water is identical with a quantity of H_2O.

II

But before we can make any headway in this and other issues pertaining to theories, additional distinctions must be drawn. The best place to begin is with the first category of unobservable

characteristics which observable objects can have. The ones I
have in mind have in common the fact that they are explicitly
definable in terms of observable properties. Here the important
thing to note is the revolution which modern logic has brought
to the concept of explicit definition. The days when the paradigm
of a definition was

x is a man $=$ $_{df}$. x is a living organism *and* x is rational

have gone forever. Notice that the right-hand side of this definition
includes the logical expression "and." The revolution in the theory
of definition brought with it, among other things, a recognition
of the importance of definitions in which other logical expressions
play the role played above by "and." Modern philosophy of
science lays particular stress on definitions in which the right-hand
side is conditional in form, thus:

x is water soluble $=$ $_{df}$. if x is put in water, then x dissolves.

So-called *operational definitions* have this form. It is sometimes
thought that the use of operationally-defined terms introduces an
anthropomorphic element into the content of science by introducing a reference to the activities of scientists into the very
concepts in terms of which the world is to be scientifically described. This is a simple misunderstanding. Compare the two
definitions

(i) x is water soluble $=$ $_{df}$. if x is put in water, then x
       dissolves

(ii) x is water soluble $=$ $_{df}$. if x comes to be in water, then
       x dissolves

The first does contain an anthropomorphic element, for *putting
things in water* is something people *do*. On the other hand, the
second definition, though conditional in form, has in place of
"is put," "comes to be," and has no anthropomorphic content.
To every operational definition there corresponds a conditional
definition which makes no reference to operations. Thus, operational definitions are that subspecies of conditional definitions
where the antecedent is a state of affairs which can be realized
by a doing on the part of the scientist. It is, therefore, convenient
to formulate them in terms of this doing. This *methodologically*
important formulation, however, can always be discounted and

the operation word replaced by an expression making no reference to human activity.

It is sometimes thought that even observation predicates should be said to be "operationally defined" because their importance lies in the fact that one can tell that they apply to something by "performing the operation of looking (in controlled circumstances)." The reason given is a true proposition, but it does not support the proposal, which blurs the distinction between predicates which, whether or not they are defined in terms of operations, can be determined to apply to an object by performing an operation. These two notions do not coincide. The latter is more inclusive than the former. And if one takes "pencil and paper operations" into account, the class of predicates the applicability of which to an object can be determined by performing an operation becomes unilluminatingly large.

Let us introduce the expression "empirical predicate" to cover not only observation predicates but predicates which are directly or indirectly defined in terms of observation predicates and, of course, the vocabulary of logic. An empirical property is one the linguistic expression for which is an empirical predicate. Defined empirical predicates are a subset of empirical predicates, and operationally defined empirical predicates a subset of defined empirical predicates.

Fruitful empirical predicates are those which occur in inductively confirmed generalizations. As Professor Bergmann has emphasized, any predicate which is defined in terms of well-formed expressions consisting of observation predicates and logical words is meaningful in the sense that it stands for a property. On the other hand, it may be meaningless in the sense of pointless or lacking scientific significance.

The theory of measurement is a large topic about which it is better to say nothing rather than little. I must, however, call attention to the fact that what might be called ground floor metrical predicates are operationally defined. Yet, as Hempel and others have pointed out, these operationally defined metrical predicates are tied in ways which have not yet been fully analyzed, to metrical predicates which involve the real number system. If one compares, as seems reasonable, the relation of these "idealized" metrical predicates to operationally defined metrical predicates to that of theoretical to empirical predicates generally, then already in the theory of measurement one runs into the problem of the reality of theoretical constructs. It will be clear from the general tenor of this paper that in this context also I would be strongly inclined to give an affirmative answer. But there are sticky issues in this neighborhood, and I am happy that I can sweep this issue under the rug.

III

There are many interesting questions relating to operationally defined predicates. Some of these are logical; thus it is pointed out that to say that something is soluble is to say that if it *were* put in water it *would* dissolve, which confronts one with the problem of subjunctive conditionals and causal modalities. Then there is the problem of how one establishes that a particular object has a conditional property such as is defined by an operational definition. If one has an inductive generalization to the effect that all objects of kind K are soluble, and knows that this object is of kind K, then one is indeed entitled to say that this object is soluble. But this pushes the problem one stage back, for, it would seem, the evidence for the generalization that all K's are soluble must include statements of the form "this K is soluble" which are known to be true independently of the generalization. It must, it would seem, be possible to know about a particular object that it has a certain conditional (or, as it usually called, dispositional) property without reference to any kind to which it may or may not belong. Thus, if we perform the relevant operation repeatedly on the object and as often get the appropriate result, we can argue inductively,

> At t_1 this was O'd and R ensued
> At t_2 it was O'd and R ensued
>
> . . . .
>
> At t_n it was O'd and R ensued
> *Therefore* (supposing this to be all the evidence) it is probable that if it were *now* O'd, then R would ensue

This induction, if repeated successfully with other objects which were all of a certain kind to which the original object belongs, would authorize the generalization

If things of kind K are O'd, then R ensues

i.e.,

Things of kind K have the property D

where D is operationally defined in terms of O and R.

This line of thought works reasonably well with conditional properties like elasticity, but runs into trouble with "inflammable." Here the induction must rather be of the form

This piece of paper was heated and burned
That piece of paper was heated and burned

.   .   .   .

The other piece of paper was heated and burned
Therefore, probably pieces of paper are inflammable.

Here the kind, the operation, and the result are all involved in the basic induction. Needless to say, the structure of such an argument, to be plausible, would be far more complicated, but these hints should help relieve any perplexities of principle.

IV

Let us now focus our attention on the idea of a set of inductively confirmed generalizations pertaining to a certain domain of objects. These generalizations may be either "universal" or "statistical," but since the topics I shall discuss, at least in the scale in which I shall treat them, do not hinge on this distinction, I shall assume that they are universal in form, and represent them as follows:

G_1. if A then B
G_2. if C then D

.   .   .   .   .

G_n. if X then Y

where the upper case letters in the if-then statements represent empirical predicates, and "if A then B" is to be read: If any object or group of objects of the domain has the property A, then the object or group of objects has the property B. "A" and "B" may, of course, stand for empirical properties of any degree of complexity. Spatial and temporal relations are tacitly included.

Now according to the standard account of theories of the kind we are considering, a theoretical framework which is to explain generalizations G_1 to G_n will consist of two sets of propositions:

1. A deductive system consisting of postulates and the theorems they logically imply. The vocabulary of the system consists of two parts: (a) the vocabulary of logic and mathematics, which has its ordinary sense, and (b) the distinctive vocabulary of the theory, which, in its turn consists of two parts: (b_1) primitive terms, (b_2) defined terms. Taken simply as belonging to the deductive system, both primitive and defined terms are *uninterpreted*. This does not mean—*pace* Nagel—that they are *variables*.

2. A set of correspondence rules which correlate some expressions belonging to (b_2), above, with empirical predicates which occur in $G_1 \ldots G_n$. These rules do not suffice to correlate the primitive vocabulary of the theory with empirical predicates. If they did, the "theory," if successful, would simply be a representation of empirical generalizations in the form of a deductive system.

The correspondence rules are so chosen that ideally they correlate the inductively established generalizations $G_1 \ldots G_n$ with theorems in the deductive system, and correlate no theorem in the deductive system with an inductively disconfirmed empirical generalization. If it succeeds in doing this, the theory is insofar confirmed. If, moreover, the correspondence rules correlate a theorem in the deductive system with a lawlike statement in the empirical framework which has not yet been put to the test, and it is then put to the test and is inductively confirmed, this is taken to be a particularly striking confirmation of the theory.

Now the deductive system of a theory is often formulated with reference to a model. A domain of objects is pointed to, which either behaves in ways which satisfy the postulates of the deductive system, or can be imagined to do so without an absurdity which would deprive the reference to them of any value or point. The model serves a number of purposes. The most obvious is to make the theory intuitive and aid the imagination in working with it. But more than this it fills, an important need in that whereas the basic magnitudes of the empirical framework are operationally defined and are therefore rooted in a background of qualitative content, the basic magnitudes of the theoretical framework, in the absence of a model, would in no way point to a foundation in nonmetrical, qualitative distinctions which might stand to them as the qualitative dimensions of observable things stand to the metrical properties which are operationally defined with respect to them. The theory would leave them "abstract" in a sense which reminds us of Whitehead's charge of "vacuous actuality" against scientific materialism. The basic magnitudes of the theory would simply point forward to the more complex theoretical properties which can be defined in terms of them, and would find their *be all and end all* in the theorems which save the appearances (empirical generalizations). Now by virtue of their visualizable character, models provide a surrogate for the "qualitative" predicates which must, in the last analysis, be the underpinning of theoretical magnitudes if they are to be the sort of thing that could "really exist," if this phrase can be given a stronger interpretation than that of the irenic instrumentalist. Needless to say, the qualitative dimensions which provide the content for the metrical form of theoretical entities need not be the perceptual qualities of the model. It would be odd if the only qualitative dimensions of the world were those which are, in the last analysis, tied to the sensory centers of the human brain.

Thus, however important the heuristic function of the model, and however important the layer of analogical meaning which the theoretical predicates acquire by being explained in terms of the model, the theory is not about the objects of the model, nor do theoretical predicates stand for properties of the objects in the model. The reference of the theory, if it can be said to have reference, and the meanings of the predicates of the theory, insofar as these are more than an adumbration of things to come, are to be understood in terms of the deductive system and the coordination of the theory with the empirical generalizations it is designed to explain. This brings me to the topic of correspondence rules.

V

The first thing to note is that our previous characterization of correspondence rules was too narrow. We need a more inclusive concept of which the type of rule referred to above is a special case. Correspondence rules in this broader sense are rules correlating theoretical predicates with empirical predicates. Within this broader classification we can distinguish:

1. Rules which correlate predicates in the theory with empirical

predicates pertaining to the objects of the domain for which the theory is a theory, where the important thing about these empirical predicates is that they occur in empirical laws pertaining to these objects. It is not important that these predicates be *observation* predicates or related to observation predicates by particularly short definitional chains, nor that these definitions be operational. I shall call these rules *substantive correspondence rules*.

2. Rules which correlate predicates in the theory with predicates which, though empirical, need not pertain to the domain of objects for which the theory is a theory. (They may pertain, for example, to an instrument, e.g., a spectroscope.) In the case of rules of this type, it is essential that the empirical predicates be observation predicates or related to them by operational definitions. I shall call these rules *methodological correspondence rules*.

The distinction stands out more clearly in terms of illustrations. Thus a correspondence rule of the substantive type would be

Temperature of gas   <———>   Mean kinetic energy of
in region R is   molecules in region
such and such   R is such and such

where, although it is true that since the temperature of a particular gas can be calculated from experimental data, the correspondence rule provides a path which can take us from an empirical description to a theoretical description, the primary point of the rule is not of this methodological character, but rather to permit a correlation of a theorem in the deductive system with an empirical law, thus the Boyle-Charles law.

Compare, on the other hand,

Spectroscope appropriately <———> Atoms in region R
related to gas shows   are in such and such
such and such lines   a state of excitation

Correspondence rules of this kind differ from the above in that whereas in the former case it would not be absurd to say that the rule in some sense *identifies* temperature with the mean kinetic energy of its molecular constituents, it would be absurd to say of the latter that it *identifies* spectral lines with the state of excitation of the atoms. Again, since spectroscopes are not gases, they do not belong to the domain of which the theory is a theory. On the other hand, the spectroscope must be related to a gas in an appropriate manner, and we can certainly say that the property of causing certain spectral lines, which *is* a property, albeit relational, of an object belonging to the domain of the theory, is correlated by the correspondence rule with the state of excitation of the atoms. But all this does is make manifest that the theory of the instrument enables a detection of the theoretical state by virtue of a connection of that state with processes (electromagnetic vibrations) which can be registered by the instrument.

It is important to note that whereas in the example used, the connection between the observable spectrum and the theoretical state of the gas involves a well-developed and articulated theory, this need not be the case. Correspondence rules of the methodological type can be built on a very schematic and promissory-noteish conception of *how* the observable phenomena are connected with the theoretical states.

It is correspondence rules of the first or substantive kind which have fascinated philosophers of science. As I pointed out above, it is not implausible to formulate them as statements of identity. Yet here we must be careful, for while it is *very* plausible to say that gases *are* populations of molecules, it is by no means as plausible to make the same move with respect to empirical and theoretical *properties*. However tempting the idea might appear to start with, it is difficult to see just what could be meant by saying that a property defined in terms of observable characteristics is identical with a property defined in terms of theoretical primitives. Could one, perhaps, take seriously the idea that gases are identical with populations of molecules, while denying that the empirical properties of gases are identical with the theoretical properties of populations of molecules? This move is sometimes made. But if, as I suspect, the two identifications are inseparable, the *prima facie* implausibility of the identification of empirical and theoretical properties must militate against the *prima facie* plausibility of the identification of empirical and theoretical objects.

VI

I think that some light can be thrown on this puzzle by considering the case where it is not a question of "identifying" empirical properties with the corresponding theoretical properties, but rather properties defined in one theoretical framework with properties defined in a second theoretical framework to which the first theory is said to be "reducible." The stock example is the reducibility of the objects of current chemical theory to complexes of the objects of current atomic physics. To speak of this reduction as accomplished fact is probably to idealize the actual situation, but since philosophers are always concerned with what might in principle be the case, to understand what the structure of such a reduction would be if it were to exist will serve our purpose.

In speaking of reduction, one must be very careful not to think of the reduction of the content of one scientific theory to that of another as amounting to the reduction of one *science* to another. For even if the former reduction has been successfully achieved, the two sciences will normally remain distinct at the empirical level. Thus the science whose theory has been reduced will concern itself as before with a narrower domain of empirical objects (chemical substances and processes), will use different experimental techniques, and will gain access to concepts in the unified theory by different operational routes and at a different level of the theory.

But before spelling out these differences in more detail, let us see how the theme of *identification*, which is present in the concept of *reduction*, is to be understood. If we suppose that the two theories prior to the reduction have been formulated as deductive systems, then the distinctive vocabulary of each theory had no definitional connection with that of the other. The only connection between them was "round about," in that the domain of empirical objects with which the one theory (chemistry) was concerned is a subset of the domain with which the other (atomic physics) is (in principle) concerned.

But if, as the concept of reduction implies, theoretical propositions in chemistry are to be derived from theoretical propositions in atomic physics, this unconnectedness of the two vocabularies must be overcome. Chemical expressions must be correlated with physical expressions. Thus, if a certain chemical process is to be explained in terms of atomic physics, the statement formulating the law governing this process must be correlated with a sentence derivable in atomic theory which is to be the explanation of this process. This correlation will consist of rules which are like the substantive correspondence rules we have been considering, with the difference that they do not correlate theoretical with empirical predicates, but expressions in one theory with expressions in another. Again, like the correspondence rules we have been considering, they are not logically true; they are not true by virtue of the meaning of the expressions they correlate. And also like them they are adopted on scientific and, therefore, broadly speaking, empirical grounds. This latter fact is ultimately Nagel's ground for calling them "bridge laws," which I find a most misleading expression. I propose, instead, to introduce a still broader sense of "correspondence rule" in accordance with which what I have been calling substantive correspondence rules can connect either a theoretical predicate with an empirical predicate (which is the case we have already considered) or a predicate in one theory with a predicate in another (which is the case we are now considering).

Now although the correspondence rules which connect theory with theory are not true by virtue of the *antecedent* meanings of the two sets of theoretical expressions, the situation involves a dimension of linguistic free play which is not present, at least at first sight, in the case of rules connecting theoretical with empirical expressions. For as far as the deductive cores of the two theories is concerned, there is no reason why the two theoretical vocabularies built from two sets of theoretical primitives could not be *replaced* by one vocabulary built from one set of primitives—those of atomic physics. The primitive vocabulary of unreduced chemical theory would reappear; this time, however, not as primitives but as defined terms in the reducing theory. The inter-theory correspondence rules would have been replaced by definitions. Notice that before this step was taken, we would be in a frame of mind similar to that in which we found ourselves with respect to kinetic theory. On the one hand, we would be strongly inclined to say that the *objects* of chemical theory are identical with systems of objects of the atomic physical theory. (Thus compare "a minimum quantity of hydrogen is an atomic system consisting of such and such a nucleus and one electron" with "a gas is a population of molecules.") On the other hand, we would clearly *not* be entitled to say that the predicates of chemical theory have the *same sense* or stand for the *same properties* as any predicates of atomic physics.

But in the case of the reduction of one theory to another we can *bring it about* that the identity statements are unproblematic, both with respect to objects and with respect to properties, by making one unified vocabulary do the work of two. We give the distinctive vocabulary of chemistry a new use in which the physical and the chemical expressions which occurred in substantive correspondence rules now have the same sense.

Yet in explicating this identity of sense we must not forget what was said above about the difference between reducing a theory and reducing a science. It was pointed out that to reduce chemical theory to physical theory is by no means to reduce chemistry to physics. The replacement of the substantive correspondence rules which related the original theories by explicit definitions leaves relatively untouched the correspondence rules, both substantive and methodological which tied the two theories to their empirical domains. To use a picture, a situation in which two balloons (theories), one above the other, each tied to the ground at a different set of places (theoretical-empirical correspondence rules), and each vertically tied to the other by various ropes (theoretical-theoretical correspondence rules), has been replaced by a situation in which there is one taller balloon which, however, is tied to the ground by two sets of ropes, one of which connects the lower part of the balloon to the places where the lower balloon was tied, while the other connects the higher part of the balloon to the places where the upper balloon was tied.

VII

If we put this by saying that the language of identity is appropriate to an informal formulation of substantive correspondence rules of the theory-theory type because they are candidates for ultimate replacement by definitional identities, the question arises, "Are the substantive correspondence rules which relate empirical predicates pertaining to gases to theoretical predicates pertaining to populations of molecules capable of similar treatment?" This, as I see it, is the heart of the problem of the reality of theoretical entities. It is, in effect, the problem "Can observable things be reduced (in principle) to the objects of physical theory?" Notice that if the substantive correspondence rules of a physical theory adequate to such a reduction were to be replaced by definitions, it would be a matter of defining the empirical vocabulary in terms of the theoretical vocabulary, and not vice versa. The impossibility of defining theoretical concepts in observational terms has been a cornerstone of the argument.

Does it make sense to speak of turning empirical predicates—and in particular observation predicates—into definitional abbreviations of complex theoretical locutions? Could observation predicates be so treated while continuing to play their perceptual role as conditioned responses to the environment? I see no reason in principle why this should not be the case.

From the standpoint of the methodology of developing science, it might seem foolish to build physical theory into the language of observation and experiment. A tentative correlation of theoretical and empirical terms would seem more appropriate than redefinition. But this is a truism which simply explains what we mean by developing science. But the perspective of the philosopher cannot be limited to that which is methodologically wise for developing science. He must also attempt to envisage the world as pictured from that point of view—one hesitates to call it Completed Science—which is the regulative ideal of the scientific enterprise. As I see it, then, substantive correspondence rules are anticipations of definitions which it would be inappropriate to implement in developing science, but the implementation of which in an ideal state of scientific knowledge would be the achieving of a unified vision of the world in which the methodologically important dualism of observation and theoretical frameworks would be transcended, and the world of theory and the world of observation would be one.

In my opinion, also, the only alternative to this conception is the instrumentalist conception of theories as deductive systems, the distinctive vocabulary of which consists of what, in the context of pure geometry, are called uninterpreted expressions, doomed as a matter of principle to remain so. As functioning in the theory they would have a *use*, but this use would be simply that of serving as essential cogs in a syntactical machine which provides an external systematization of empirical statements. The instrumentalist conception of theories correctly stresses that theories have this use and are *meaningful* in the sense that they have this use. But surely our willingness to use the language of identity in connection with empirical and theoretical objects involves a commitment which goes beyond anything which would be implied by correspondence rules if these were formulated ascetically, in accordance with instrumentalist convictions, as syntactical bridges between a *language* and a *calculus*. I do not think that this willingness rests on a mistake.[1]

---

[1]For an application of this approach to the mind-body problem, see Chapter XV. For a discussion of explanation in terms of thing kinds and causal properties, see also Counterfactuals, dispositions and the causal modalities, in *Concepts, Theories and the Mind-Body Problem*, ed., Herbert Feigl, Grover Maxwell, and Michael Scriven, Minneapolis, 1958, especially Part II, sections 46-54.

XIV

SCIENTIFIC REALISM OR IRENIC INSTRUMENTALISM
A Critique of Nagel and Feyerabend on Theoretical Explanation

I

PROFESSOR J. J. C. Smart[1] correctly locates my views on the topics he discusses, taken as a whole, somewhere in the middle between those of Ernest Nagel and Paul Feyerabend. Any such one dimensional ordering of course does violence to the complexity of the issues and the many combinations of agreement and disagreement this complexity permits. But with respect to the large scale contrast he is drawing, I think that Smart is right in the following sense: I tend to agree with Nagel or Feyerbend on each of the major points, but to agree with neither on all of them. Roughly, I tend to agree with Nagel on methodological topics, with Feyerabend on ontology, and with each of them in turn on key epistemological issues.

Since, of the two, Nagel has given the far more comprehensive and systematic account of theoretical explanation,[2] one which not only continues the classical tradition on this subject, but is itself already a classic, it is clearly good strategy to begin by concentrating on those features of Nagel's account which bear on the questions raised by Smart, and then proceed to examine the somewhat more impetuous, but challenging and illuminating views which Feyerabend has expressed on these issues.

The theories which raise in paradigm form the philosophical puzzles with which Smart is concerned are of the type which postulate "unobservable" micro-entities to explain the behavior of the "middle size" objects of perceptual experience. Not all theories, even as scientists use the term, are of this type, and many subtle philosophical problems are raised by theories of other types.

---

[1] In "Conflicting views about explanation," *Boston Studies in the Philosophy of Science, Volume II*, edited by Robert S. Cohen and Marx W. Wartophy, New York, 1965.

[2] In his *The Structure of Science*, New York, 1961.

Some of these additional problems are also raised by micro-theories—e.g., the problem of the relation of mathematically idealized concepts to coarser grained concepts admitting of perceptual discrimination. The following discussion, however, will focus attention, by and large, on problems *peculiar* to micro-theories.

Before I turn to Nagel's views on micro-theoretical explanation, it will be useful to make a preliminary comment on Feyerabend's notion[3] that "common sense" is a "theory" which, like all theories, should be abandoned by scientists, except for practical purposes, when a better theory comes along. The term "theory" is one of those accordion words which, by their expansion and contraction, generate so much philosophical music. And while I agree with Feyerabend that the conceptual framework of "common sense" is, in the last analysis, false, I find it confusing rather than clarifying, for reasons which will emerge in the course of the argument, to speak of this framework as a false *theory*.

Now if one uses the phrase "the framework of common sense" in such a way that it includes common sense *beliefs* in its reference, then this framework would, indeed, include not only empirical generalizations, but theoretical fall-out from earlier science and even proto-theories of its own. But not all subject-matter dependent universal propositions to which common sense is committed are properly characterized as *beliefs*. There are many principles about physical objects and the perception of them ("categorial principles" they might be called) which are constitutive of the very concepts in terms of which we experience the world. And while I agree with Feyerabend that this does not exempt them from criticism and possible replacement, it is, as I see it, incorrect to compare this possible replacement to the replacement of a corpuscular by a wave theory of light, or dephlogistication by oxidation.

What would the conceptual framework of common sense be a theory *of*? Granted that common sense beliefs *within* this framework include proto-theories about specific subject matters capable, in principle, of being characterized without the use of the vocabulary of these proto-theories, what is the framework itself a theory of? A *trivial* answer is, of course, available, namely, "Common sense objects and events." But this would be like answering the question

---

[3]Cf. Smart, pp. 159, 162.

"What is atomic theory a theory of?" by saying "Atoms." A *false* answer is also available, namely, "Sense impressions."

If we distinguish, in the spirit of the classical account, between the "internal" and "external" subject matters of micro-theories, so that in the case of the kinetic theory of gases, for example, molecules and their behavior would be the "internal" subject-matter of the theory, and gases as empirical constructs defined without reference to molecules its "external" subject-matter, then, as I see it, the conceptual framework of common sense has no *external* subject-matter and is not, therefore, in the relevant sense a theory *of* anything.

Feyerabend, of course, emphatically rejects phenomenalistic accounts of experience according to which the primary objects of knowledge are sense impressions. Thus he rejects the move according to which physical object statements stand to sense impression statements as, according to the classical account of theories, statements about populations of molecules stands to observation framework statements about gases. Thus he rejects, and rightly so, the idea that the framework of physical objects is *in the classical sense* a theory of which the external subject matter is sense impressions. Nevertheless, there is a sense in which for Feyerabend the framework of physical objects is a theory *with respect to* sense impressions, for he emphasizes that it is in terms of the framework of physical objects that, in perception, we conceptually respond to the impressions of sense.[4] Since, as he sees it, the language in which we *respond to* sense impressions is different from (indeed, incommensurable with) the language in which these sense impressions themselves are described,[5] there is no reason, he feels, why the scientist should not train himself to respond to his sense impressions by still another incommensurable language—the language of micro-physical theory. In *this* sense, one theory *with respect to* sense impressions would be replaced by another.

---

[4] Explanation, reduction and empiricism, *Minnesota Studies in the Philosophy of Science*, Vol. III, p. 35.

[5] In developing his "pragmatic theory of observation," which will be examined below, he emphasizes that the meaning of an observation predicate is not determined by the sensory state to which it is a response. This point is spelled out in great detail on pages 38-42 and 94 of the essay referred to in the previous footnote. He goes so far as to say on page 39 that "the fact that a statement belongs to the observational domain has no bearing on its meaning."

From this point of view, the correspondence rules which, according to the classical analysis, correlate micro-theoretical constructs with observation framework counterparts are excess baggage, as is the very contrast between internal and external subject matters. The important thing is to get the language of the theory connected *not* with another language, but with the sense impressions of the scientist. And because the concept of language-language correspondence rules and the related distinction between internal and external subject matters play an unimportant role in Feyerabend's account of micro-theoretical explanation, the only *important* sense in which, for him, a theory is a theory *with respect to* something is a matter of its being a behavior orienting perceptual response to that something. In *this* sense, though not in the ordinary sense, the framework of physical objects *is* a theory with respect to sense impressions. It is this conception, as I see it, which underlies Feyerabend's willingness to speak of common sense as a theory.

But before these remarks can be put to use in a general assessment of Feyerabend's views, we must return to our general strategy and to Nagel.

II

According to Nagel's reconstruction,[6] the following elements must be distinguished. They are more or less explicitly present in the actual practice of micro-physical explanation and would be explicitly present in a micro-theoretical counterpart of Plato's Ideal State:

1. The deductive system T_D
2. The *partial* interpretation of T_D by correspondenece rules which correlate expressions in T_D with empirical predicates in the observation framework. By doing so, these rules correlate theorems in the theory with general propositions formulated in terms of these empirical predicates. Some of these propositions are inductively confirmed (empirical laws); none of them are disconfirmed; some are hypotheses whose possible confirmation is placed by the theory on the scientific agenda.
3. The model: a *complete* interpretation of T_D.

---

[6] *The Structure of Science*, pp. 90ff.

Of these items, (1) and (2) are substantive parts of the theory. Whether, and if so in what sense, this is also true of (3) will be explored subsequently.

Let me go into these features in somewhat greater detail. In the first place, Nagel thinks of the non-logical vocabulary of the deductive system, T_D as consisting of predicate variables.[7] This, I believe, is a serious mistake which is rooted in an inadequate conception of what makes a non-logical predicate meaningful. It stands, as we shall see, in the way of a genuinely realistic interpretation of micro-theoretical entities.

Certainly the form of words

> If two Ps are on an L, then there is another P which stands
> to them in R

could be a statement function containing predicate variables "P" "L" and "R." It *would* be so if it was intended to substitute for them or submit them to quantification. But this *need* not be the intent and, in the case of pure geometry and micro-theories, it is *not* the intent. Clearly, it is only if, and to the extent that, we have predicate constants with the ideal syntactical articulation of mathematical geometry that we can formulate true statements which satisfy mathematical statement functions in the sense that they have constants where the statement functions have variables. But the whole point of the empiricist explanation of ideal geometrical predicates as elements in a deductive system is to account for the existence of such ideally articulated conceptual structures. If, however, the predicate expressions of a deductive system are *essentially* variables, the statement functions of the system *could* have no statement counterparts with predicate *constants* for which they were true—surely an incoherent notion.[8]

The moral is that the logical space of pure geometry must contain predicate constants as well as predicate variables, and this means that strictly speaking implicit definition pertains to predicate constants.

It must, indeed, be granted that a non-logical predicate constant which isn't connected with extra-linguistic objects is not,

---

[7]*Ibid.*, p. 91. See also p. 141 ff.

[8]To make the same point in a simpler context, the individual variable "x" in "Fx" would be a sham if, although the predicate "F" were conceptually consistent, there *could* be no individual constant for which "Fx" was true.

in the full sense, meaningful. But not being extra-linguistically meaningful must not be identified with being a variable.

Thus, an adequate philosophical treatment of the predicate expressions of a pure geometry must specify a primary use in which they constitute a special class of predicate constants. How is this special class to be characterized? The answer lies in remembering that a pure geometry becomes a physical geometry by virtue of being connected by correspondence rules with empirical predicates pertaining to perceptually discriminable features of physical things.[9] Since the implicit definition of predicates by the postulates of a deductive system is not sufficient to give these predicates extra-linguistic meaningfulness, we can say that *qua* implicitly defined they are *candidate* constants. Their role is not that of being substituted for or quantified over, but that of being available for connection with extra-linguistic fact.

As I see it, then, just as the predicate expressions of a pure geometry, construed as a system of implicit definitions, are not variables but candidate predicate constants, so the predicate expressions in a micro-theory *qua* deductive system are not to be construed as variables, but as *candidate predicate constants* which, *to put the matter in first approximation*, get their extra-linguistic meaningfulness from the correspondence rules which connect them with constructs in what Bergmann has called the "empirical hierarchy."

Now Nagel sees that the idea that micro-theoretical predicates are variables generates the question "How can theoretical sentences be true or false?" Would they not actually be sentence functions, and no more true or false than 'x is a man'? His answer, of course, taken from Ramsey, is that the conjunction of theoretical postulates

---

[9]These remarks apply to the idealized geometrical space of macro-physical objects. The point they enable me to make about the status of the predicates of micro-theories remains valid even though, as a final step in our philosophy of physical geometry, we bypass Space as a postulated quasi-physical *Unding* consisting of a continuum of geometrical objects (points) which satisfy non-logical predicate constants, and use the correspondence rules to connect operational geometrical measures and locations directly with appropriate structures in the domain of real numbers. The possibility of this latter move clarifies the sense in which Space, as contrasted with actual and possible physical relationships (overlappings and coincidences) among its 'contents,' is an *Unding*. Additional problems are raised by the physical geometry of micro-physical entities.

is to be construed as preceded by an existential quantification of the predicate variables. This desperate expedient runs up against the objection based on the above analysis that it is logically odd given that "f" is a *descriptive* predicate variable, to suppose that the theoretical statement

(Ef) (x) fx

might be true even though no substitution instance of the function "fx" *could* be true. But, on Nagel's view, the only descriptive predicate constants which are available belong to the empirical hierarchy, and no empirical attributes satisfy the conditions laid down by micro-theoretical postulates.[10] Only a neo-pythagorean— such as Carnap, on occasion, tends to be—would be happy with substitution instances involving purely arithmetical expressions.

Furthermore, it should be noted that the Ramsey sentence approach to theoretical sentences is inconsistent with the idea that theoretical statements can be factually true in the full sense in which statements in the observation framework are now conceived to be true. For the full sense of "factually true" requires that there be a level of factual truth in which objects are directly "mapped" or "pictured" by atomic statements as linguistic events *in rerum natura*. Truth functional combinations of atomic statements and quantified statements are to be construed as recipes for constructing such maps or pictures, which latter do not themselves contain logical connectives or operators.[11] On Nagel's approach, it is *in principle* impossible for theoretical language to contain linguistic events to perform this role—for it can contain no sentences free of quantification. Such mapping or picturing as could be done by theoretical sentences must, on his view, be *indirect*, essentially mediated by correspondence rules correlating theoretical statements with statements involving predicates in the empirical hierarachy.

---

[10]Cf. Grover Maxwell, The ontological status of theoretical entities, *Minnesota Studies*, Vol. III, pp. 16-17; also my The Language of Theories, in *Current Issues in the Philosophy of Science*, ed. by Herbert Feigl and Grover Maxwell, New York, 1961, p. 68. The latter essay is reprinted, with minor revisions as Chapter 4 in my *Science, Perception and Reality*. The corresponding reference is to p. 117.

[11]For an elaboration of this thesis concerning factual truth, which stems from Wittgenstein's *Tractatus*, see my Truth and "correspondence," *The Journal of Philosophy*, 59, 1962. (Reprinted with minor revisions as Chapter 6 in *Science, Perception and Reality*.) Also see paragraph below.

III

But before I explore the topic of the factual truth of theoretical sentences, I want to call attention to another and more
subtle way in which the idea that only predicate constants in an
antecedent observation framework actually stand for properties or
attributes can lead to a mistaken account of the meaning of theoretical predicates. It is more subtle, because it claims to be free
from the myth of the given. I have in mind Miss Hesse's conception
of the role of models and analogies in theory construction.[12]

It will be remembered that while Nagel gives models and
analogies an important heuristic role in theory construction, and
stresses their role as imaginative aids to theoretical thought,
he emphasizes that the scientific *content* of the theory derives
not from models or analogies but from the implicit definition of
theoretical predicates by the postulates in which they occur,
together with the correspondence rules which connect theoretical
terms with expressions in the empirical heirarachy.[13] This is at
best a half-truth.

It is a half-truth because theoretical postulates are often specified
in a way which *logically* involves the use of the model. And even
when a set of postulates is explicitly given in the form prescribed
by contemporary logical theory, it turns out, in actual practice,
(although *ideally* it *need* not) that the conceptual texture of theoretical terms in scientific use is far richer and more finely grained than
the texture generated by the explicitly listed postulates. This is
particularly true with respect to the categorial structure of what
are lumped together from an abstractly logical point of view as
"predicates" and "functors." The thingish or quasi-thingish character of theoretical objects, their conditions of identity, and the
dispositional or non-dispositional character of attributes are some
of the more familiar categorial features conveyed by the use of
model and analogies.[14]

Notice that I am *not* saying that these features *could not* be
fully captured by the explicit working of a logistically contrived
deductive system. To suppose otherwise is to return to some form

---

[12]Mary B. Hesse: *Models and Analogies in Science*, London, 1963.

[13]Nagel, *op. cit.*, p. 95ff.

[14]See also my remarks on the role of models in theory construction, pp. 327-9 ff. above.

of abstractionism or giveness. I simply call attention to the fact that the ability to capture these features in this logistical manner presupposes a degree of success in analyzing the categorial framework of scientific concepts which has to date been at best approximated in some limited areas. The familiar controversy over the logic of field concepts is a case in point. And who would be so rash as to say that the categorial structure of spatial and temporal concepts has been conclusively settled?

The notion of a micro-theory, the conceptual texture of which is completely captured by an explicit set of postulates, is, perhaps, a realizable ideal, but it is not realized in fact. The principal model of a theory does not play the *external* role of being an alternative realization of a *conceptually independent* set of postulates construed as propositional functions.

But how is the conceptual dependence of the theory on the model to be construed? Miss Hesse, if I understand her correctly, construes theoretical concepts pertaining to micro-theoretical entities as *identical with* concepts pertaining to the entities of the model, once these entities have been purged of those features which constitute the known negative analogy. This I regard as a serious mistake which rests on a tacit extension to all analogies of a logical feature of the simple case with which her analysis begins. She asks us[15] to consider the case of the earth and the moon. Here the known positive analogy consists of attributes known to be shared by those two objects; the known negative analogy consists of attributes known to be possessed by one but not the other; while the neutral analogy consists of attributes known to be possessed by one but whose possession by the other is problematical. The key feature of this account is the fact that it is in terms of the identity and difference of attributes of particulars.[16] And while one may sympathize with Miss Hesse's attempt[17] to analyze similarity in terms of identity and difference of attributes, it must be pointed out that not all similarity is similarity of *particulars*. And once one takes into account the fact that attributes themselves as well as particulars may be similar, the way is open for distinc-

---

[15]Hesse, *op. cit.*, p. 64ff.
[16]P. 65.
[17]P. 78.

tion between what might be called "first order" and "second order" similarity between particulars. In a simple case of first order similarity, two particulars would share an *identical* attribute. In a simple case of second order similarity, two particulars would have *similar* attributes.

Put in these terms, the question with which I am concerned becomes: Is the analogy between molecules and billiard balls a matter of particular molecules and billiard balls sharing *identical* attributes, or is it, at least in part, a matter of their having *similar* attributes. As I see it, it is the concept of similar or analogous attributes which is the key to the understanding of theoretical explanation.

But in what, it will be asked, does the similarity of attributes consist? Without attempting a complete analysis of the ways in which attributes can be similar, enough can be said, I believe, to bring out the importance of the idea for the philosophical analysis of theoretical explanation. A simple example is the similarity of moments in a temporal series with points in a line. For, to nail down a logical point, the analogy between moments and points is not a matter of moments and points having certain attributes in common, but for moments on one hand and points on the other to have properties which, though they have no *first order* properties as common constituents, do have certain *second order* properties in common, e.g., transitivity.

The fact that what is *said* by characterizing *to the left of* and *before* as transitive can be *shown* without the use of the predicates standing for a second order property by exhibiting the postulates which hold of these relations, should not lead one to underestimate the role of reference to second level properties in science. For in the above example, the ability to *exhibit* second order similarities presupposes the separate existence of the two conceptual frameworks of space and time. But the distinctive feature of the use of models and analogies in theory construction is that the conceptual framework of the theory is *generated* by specifying the analogies which are to obtain. Thus, as a first approximation, it can be said that models are used in theory construction to specify new attributes as *the attributes which* share certain higher order attributes with attributes belonging to the model, fail to share certain others (the negative analogy)—and which satisfy, in addition, the conditions laid down by the relevant correspondence rules.

But, it may be said, if the higher order attributes you have in mind are such "formal" properties as transitivity and asymmetry, your answer can explain at most some very skeletal features of theoretical attributes. Furthermore, the move would be unnecessary, since it is exactly these formal properties of attributes and relations which can readily be exhibited by explicit postulates. This objection overlooks, in the first place, the indefinitely large number of such formal attributes of attributes and the complexity of which they are capable. Once again, what is possible *in principle* is mistakenly used in an explication of scientific practice. Thus we may not in fact be able to pick out from a model and formulate in tidy fashion the propositional functions which would serve as the positive and neutral analogies in a completely explicit theory. And while, by the same token, we would not have tidy expressions in actual use corresponding to these propositional functions, as "transitive" and "transitivity" correspond to

$$(x)(y) \ xRy \cdot yRz \rightarrow xRz$$

our language *does* contain adequate resources for referring to second order attributes by more complex locutions.

To see this, we must note that to refer to a specific second order property is, in first approximation, to refer to the corresponding propositional function. Thus

Before is asymmetrical

has, again in first approximation, the sense of

"$(x)(y) \ xRy \cdot \sim yRx$" is true of *before*

(i.e., becomes true on the substitution of "before" for "R").

Not only can we refer to specific second order properties (i.e., mention specific propositional functions of second order), we can make *general* reference to such properties. Thus, in a simple case, we can say of two dyadic relations that they share *some* functions involving a dyadic predicate variable together with appropriate quantification over particulars. Furthermore, we can, by imposing additional conditions, specify to which subsets of second order properties those which are shared by the relations belong. Thus the logical space of second order attributes admits of all the techniques of indefinite reference and definite description. And when we take into account the open texture and vagueness with which reference can be made, we begin to see how models can be the *fundamenta* of open-textured reference to second order attributes.

It was pointed out above that there is no limit in principle to the number or complexity of formal second order attributes. It should now be pointed out that it is not necessary that all of the predicate expressions of the propositional functions to which reference is made be predicate *variables*. Thus, an explication of the analogy between color and sound involves picking out propositional functions which have predicate *constants* in common (e.g., "perceptible") in addition to the variables corresponding to the color and sound predicates being compared.

As I see it, then, models provide a basis for a more or less vague and open-textured reference to a framework of propositional functions which the predicates of a theory are to satisfy. They are specified as *the functions which* hold, with certain qualifications, of the predicates which apply to the entities of the model. I say "with certain qualifications" because the reference to a model is accompanied by what I have called[18] a "commentary" which eliminates specific functions from the analogy and modifies others. The important point is that these relatively precise qualifications operate within the context provided by an intuitive grasp of the framework of the model which it would be difficult if not impossible to articulate in terms of an explicit list of postulates.

But whereas in the above "rational reconstruction" of the use of models in theory construction it is implied that different sign designs would be used for the introduced theoretical predicates and the predicates of the model on the basis of which they are introduced, it should be noted that in actual fact the same designs may be used. That the predicates involved in theoretical explanation may be subtly ambiguous, having different meanings in different contexts, could easily be overlooked and lead to a failure to distinguish the conceptual framework of a theory from the conceptual framework of the model on which it depends.

---

[18]In Empiricism and the philosophy of mind, *Minnesota Studies in the Philosophy of Science, I:*313.

Notice also that the above explication involves a three-fold distinction between

1. the objects of the unqualified model
2. the objects of a revised model which preserves the perceptual and imaginative role of the predicates of the unqualified model, but modifies the internal structure of the model in accordance with the commentary. The revised model involves, therefore, a controlled incoherence, an example of which is the visualizability of the imperceptible particles of micro-physics.
3. the objects of theory.

The importance of distinguishing between (2) and (3) is that it puts the finishing touch on the idea that the positive analogy between theoretical entities and empirical constructs is not a simple matter of the identity of some of their first level attributes with those of perceptible things. Only if we recognize that the analogy between micro-physical entities and the entities of the model[19] is not to be construed in terms of the identity or difference of first order attributes, can we appreciate how the use of models in theoretical explanation can generate *genuinely new* conceptual frameworks and justify the claim to have escaped from the myth of the given.

Having made this point, it must now be emphasized that it is only from the standpoint of a rational reconstruction that we can draw a tidy distinction between three sets of entities, as in the preceding paragraph.

This tidy threefold distinction is, I believe, philosophically clarifying as a framework on which to project the various ways in which theories are used. But it can be philosophically misleading, if taken as a report of explicitly drawn distinctions in the practice of science. Thus, instead of putting the point substantively in

---

[19] I say *the* model because the concept of model here is not simply that of a model in the set theoretical sense (in which any theory would have an indefinite number of models). The relevant concept is a methodological one pertaining to theoretical concept formation. That even in this methodological sense two (or more) models can be jointly used as a basis for introducing theoretical concepts is granted—compare the role of wave and particle models in quantum mechanics. This joint use as a *fundamentum* does not require that they be jointly used in application, and, indeed, in the latter use the models are incompatible. This incompatability is, I believe, given its proper location by the above account.

terms of a distinction between the entities of the model, the entities of the revised model and the corresponding theoretical entities, one can speak of a model and the various roles it performs in theoretical explanation. And while Miss Hesse's account fails, as I see it, to do justice to the complexity of these roles, it does have the virtue of stressing the essential and intrinsic involvement of the conceptual framework of the model in the conceptual framework of the theory.

The temptation to identify the theory with the qualified or revised model (to which, I believe, Miss Hesse succumbs) would indeed be overpowering if, inclined to take a realistic view of theories, one thought that only by such identification could the theory be provided with predicate *constants*. But this motive has, I believe, been undercut by the above critique of Nagel's interpretation of the predicate expression of a micro-theory. We have seen that predicate variables *do* come into the picture, but they come in not as theoretical language predicate variables, but as implicit in the specification of the second order attributes which are conceived to be shared by first order attributes in the theoretical domain with first order attributes in the domain of the model.

IV

I find lurking in Nagel's account the presupposition that for an expression to become a meaningful descriptive predicate constant it must be given a place—for example, by explicit definition—within the antecedent observation framework. This presupposition would simply rule out the idea that theory construction could be a technique for enriching or revising this framework—though not, of course, the idea that theoretical considerations enable one to pick out constructs and hypotheses *within* the observation framework which are likely to prove fruitful.

It is this presupposition which, as I see it, insures the ultimate shipwreck of Nagel's higher synthesis of instrumentalism and realism. It ultimately rests, as I diagnose the situation, on an interpretation of a predicate's

standing directly[20] for a property of things

---

[20]As contrasted with standing for a property *via* a definition chain.

with its

being associated with a property of things.

This interpretation makes the meaningfulness of fundamental descriptive predicates a matter of a psychological connection between predicates and properties *construed as extra-linguistic entities.* It is the supposedly extra-linguistic character of these properties or attributes which is thought to guarantee them a status independent of the vicissitudes of human concept formation.

This realistic[21] interpretation of the perceptible attributes of things is, as I see it, aided and abetted by a confusion between the "of-ness" of sense impressions and the "of-ness" of thought. Thus

Jones has a sense impression of a red triangle

tells us about a non-conceptual state of Jones. On the other hand,

Jones is under the perceptual impression that there is a red triangle (in front of him)

i.e.,

There appears to Jones to be a red triangle in front of him

tells us about a conceptual state of Jones. There is, of course, a close connection between these two kinds of state. Roughly, we explain the latter in terms of the former. To confuse them, however, is to identify the *conceptual* awareness of an item *as* red and triangular with a non-conceptual state of affairs. There arises the bastard notion of a *pre-conceptual* awareness of items as being red and triangular which is supposed to be the language independent foundation on which the meaningfulness of language rests.

V

Of the dogmas of classical empiricism, two have been generally abandoned. These are the twin ideas that empirical knowledge rests on an absolute foundation of knowledge pertaining to sense-data, and that the content of genuine descriptive concepts is derived from sense data. These "dogmas" have increasingly been replaced by an anthropologically-oriented interpretation of the conceptual framework in terms of which we perceive the world as

---

[21]The term "realism" is here used in the sense in which it contrasts with "conceptualism" and "nominalism," rather than that in which it contrasts with phenomenalism.

a form of group life which has evolved from rudimentary beginnings by a process of adaptation which can be compared—in ways which are not well understood—to natural selection. This conceptual framework, though *brought into play by* sense impressions is not, at least primarily, *about* sense impressions.

It is in the spirit of this approach that Feyerabend correctly argues that although the meaningfulness of observation predicates requires that they be *responses to* sense impressions, it does not require that they stand for properties which either common sense or theoretical psychology or even ideal neuro-physiology would attribute to these impressions.

From the pragmatic picture of language as a technique of behavioral orientation, the conclusion might be drawn that we are free to replace, segment by segment, the framework in terms of which we perceive the world, by scientifically contrived structures which enable a more subtle orientation and fewer surprises. Thus, one who is at home in the micro-physics of his day would be free to train himself to respond to his environment in terms which, though they externally resemble the vocabulary of his fellow man, have as their descriptive conceptual content highly derived constructs in this theoretical framework. We are free, so to speak, to pour new conceptual content into old bottles.

And, indeed, as Feyerabend develops his "pragmatic theory of observation," this seems to be what he is telling us. According to him, the perceptual predicates which lie at the base of the empirical hierarachy are simply those which are in *de facto* possession of this behavior guiding role, and are subject to dispossession by any system of predicates which does the job better. As he sees it, it is simply untrue that an expression can become a descriptively meaningful predicate constant only if given a place in the *antecedent* observation framework. There is, indeed, no such thing as *the* observation framework. Observation frameworks come and go. For a descriptive predicate to be factually meaningful, it is sufficient that it belong to the current empirical hierarchy—i.e., to a framework in terms of which the relevant language using organisms—in this case scientists—currently orient themselves to, and cope with, their internal and external environment.

But though I am in general sympathy with Feyerabend's pragmatic theory of observation, I do not think that it will do as it stands. There is a core of truth in the concept of "*the* observation framework" and, indeed, of the abstractionist approach to basic empirical concepts which survives the exorcising of givenness. And, in my opinion, although Feyerabend arrives at the ontological truth that the world is in principle what scientific theory says it is, he does so by chopping the structure of science with a cleaver rather than carving it at its conceptual and methodological joints. As I see it, only someone who is unaware of the subtle interdependence of the various dimensions of the framework of empirical knowledge would speak cavalierly of the piecemeal replacement of part by scientifically better part.

We have come to issues in which the philosophy of science shows its organic connection with less exotic branches of the philosophical enterprise. And the first point to be made is that to reject the myth of the given is not to commit oneself to the idea that empirical knowledge as it is now constituted has no rock bottom level of observation predicates proper. It is to commit oneself rather to the idea where even if it does have a rock bottom level, it is *still* in principle replaceable by another conceptual framework in which these predicates do not, *strictly speaking*, occur. It is in this sense, and in this sense *only*, that I have rejected the dogma of given-ness with respect to observation predicates.

The second point to be made is that it is, in my opinion, a serious mistake to move, as Feyerabend seems to do,[22] from the propositions:

1. It is *possible* to train micro-theorists and their experimental colleagues to respond directly to visual stimulation by the use of sentences in the framework of micro-theory.

2. Every physical process can *reasonably* be described in micro-physical terms.

3. It is *possible and reasonable* to train physicists and chemists to tell by looking that certain specific micro-physical processes are going on in certain specific contexts (i.e., to respond directly, knowing that one is in such a context, to visual stimulation with sentences in the language of micro-theory, in a way which is reliable and known to be reliable). (For example, it is possible and reasonable

---

[22]Cf. Smart, p. 11; also pp. 3, 7.

to train a physicist to tell what a particle is doing in a cloud chamber [i.e., to know what it is doing without inferring this from non-theoretical sentences *via* correspondence rules].)

to even the first—let alone the second—of the following propositions:

4. It is reasonable to train scientists to respond in all kinds of circumstances to visual stimulation with sentences in the framework of micro-physics (e.g., when chopping wood or drawing water).

5. It is reasonable to train scientists to respond to visual stimulation in all circumstances with sentences in the framework of micro-physical theory *only* (i.e., to *abandon* the perceptual use of the framework of common sense).

Let me emphasize that I am as firmly convinced as Feyerabend of the truth of the following proposition:

(α) Micro-physical entities do not have the second class existence of mere "conceptual devices."

(β) The framework of common sense is radically false (i.e., there *really* are no such things as the physical objects and processes of the common sense framework).[23]

(γ) Propositions (α) (β) are to be clarified in terms of the concept of its being reasonable *at some stage* to abandon the framework of common sense and use only the framework of theoretical science, suitably enriched by the dimension of practical discourse.[24]

But, as I see it, the ontological theses formulated by (α) and (β) involve no commitment to the idea that the time for scientists to abandon the framework of common sense is *now*.

Indeed, all the methodological gain which the *exclusive* use of theoretical constructs would bring can be achieved by the use

---

[23]This does not, of course, mean that there are no tables or elephants, but rather that tables and elephants as conceived by common sense do not really exist (i.e., that these concepts are in *principle* to be replaced by a counterpart built on a theoretical foundation). For an explication of what is meant by "really exist" in this context, see "Empiricism and the Philosophy of Mind," 39ff.

[24]This aspect of the situation, which is not stressed by Feyerabend, is illustrated by the practical dimension of such common sense concepts as that of what it is to be a hammer.

of correspondence rules as in the classical account, together with the direct use in experimental situations referred to in (3) above. On the other hand, taken seriously, as we shall see, the *abandonment* of the common sense framework would result in serious methodological and conceptual loss.

To develop this point, I must return to the topic of what is meant in this connection by "the framework of common sense." Previously I distinguished between common sense *beliefs* and common sense *principles*. The former are in no way binding on the scientist. Nor are the conceptual *constructs* of common sense binding on the scientist. It is the rock bottom concepts and principles of common sense which are binding until a total structure which can do the job better is actually at hand—rather than a "regulative ideal."

That this bindingness is *methodological* and is incompatible with neither the *ontological* thesis that the world as conceived by common sense is, in the Kantian sense, phenomenal, nor with the *epistemological* thesis that it is the task of theoretical science to give us an accurate picture of things, is the fundamental contention of this essay. To which it is anti-climax to add that no one who stresses the methodological primacy of the framework of common sense is committed, as Feyerabend seems to think he is, to preserving either outmoded common sense beliefs (which is obvious) or common sense constructs (e.g., our everyday concepts of *up* and *down*) in the corpus of science.

But, it will be asked, is not this talk of the "methodological primacy" of the common sense framework, this talk of "foundation" and "super-structure," "basic concepts" and "constructs," "principles," and "beliefs" simply an attenuated form of the myth of the given, a ghostly survival of abstractionism and self-evidence? I cannot hope to do justice to this challenge on the present occasion.[25]

I shall limit myself to present one central line of thought which illustrates the broad strategy by which I would meet it.

The idea that the framework of common sense has a rock

---

[25]It is met, I believe, by the argument of Chapters I, II, and V of *Science, Perception and Reality*, London, 1963, and applied specifically to the mind-body problem in Chapter XV below.

bottom does not require that this rock bottom consist of sense impressions. The framework of common sense is a framework of (among other things) colored physical objects extended in space and enduring through time. And while objects which are red on the facing surface have the power to cause normal observers in the standard conditions to have sense impressions of red, this is incorrectly taken to mean that the physical property of being red on the facing side is to be analyzed in terms of this causal power.

As Berkley, Kant, and Whitehead, among others, have pointed out, physical objects cannot have primary qualities only—for structural and mathematical properties presuppose what might be called "content qualities." And unless one falls into the trap of thinking of the framework of physical objects as a common sense theory evolved with unconscious wisdom to explain the manner in which sense data occur, it will scarcely do to say that the content qualities of physical objects are conceived, by a common sense use of analogy, to be the physical counterparts of the qualities of data (i.e., to play in the realm of physical things the content-role played in sense data by sense qualities). For if the conceptual space of common sense physical objects is *underived*, their content qualities must be *directly* rather than *analogically* conceived, for it is only in terms of perceived, and therefore conceptualized, qualitative difference that form and structure can be distinguished.

Thus the rejection of a phenomenalistic analysis of the framework of common sense requires that the physical objects of this framework have perceptible qualitative content. And once one realizes this, one sees that there is no alternative to construing these physical objects as colored in the literal occurent sense. One might wish to say that this framework—which has as its central constituents items which are in *this* sense colored through and through[26]—is, from the standpoint of theoretically-oriented science, *false*, although enabling a behavioral adjustment of sufficient accuracy for the practical purposes of life. But false or not, such is the framework of common sense.

Again, the rejection of given-ness is compatible with a distinction between the attributes which physical objects and processes

---

[26]As a paradigm case, think of a pink ice cube.

can *strictu sensu* be perceived to have, and those which they can be perceived to have in less stringent senses. Thus, I can perceive that this is a pad of writing paper—indeed perceive it *as* a pad of writing paper—but *strictu sensu* I perceive that it is, for example, a physical object which, on the facing side, is rectangular, yellow, and lined with parallel blue lines. It should not be necessary to point out that the distinction in question does not require that a perception of the pad *as a pad* consists in perceiving it as an object which is rectangular and yellow with blue lines on the facing side, and inferring that it is a writing pad.

If the framework of common sense physical objects is analyzed along the preceding lines it is easy to see that while the fundamental concepts of the framework are not concepts of sense impressions, they are concepts which, so to speak, project or transpose the attributes of sense impressions into the categorial framework of physical things and processes. But although the conceptual framework of physical color is in this sense ontologically grounded in visual impressions, the conceptual framework in terms of which common sense conceives these impressions is itself an analogical offshoot from the conceptual framework of physical color and shape.[27] To put the matter in Aristotelian terminology, visual impressions are prior *in the order of being* to concepts pertaining to physical color, whereas the latter are prior *in the order of knowing* to concepts pertaining to visual impressions.[28] This is what I referred to above as the kernel of truth in the classical empiricist doctrine that concepts of the qualities of sense are formed by "abstraction" from sense impressions.

We saw above that the logical status of color as qualitative content is an essential part of the common sense framework of physical objects. We have also seen that this logical space is a

---

[27]For an elaboration of this point see the concluding paragraphs of "Empiricism and the Philosophy of Mind;" also *Science, Perception and Reality*, pp. 47-49; 91-95; also The identity approach to the mind-body problem, *Synthese*, 1964.

[28]That common sense concepts of sense impressions are *in principle* as subject to replacement by concepts belonging to an adequate neurophysiology as the common sense framework of physical objects by an adequate micro-physics, is the key to the solution of the mind-body problem. But any solution along these lines which fails to preserve the conceptual space of color, sound, taste, etc., suitably transposed, has lost touch with rather than solved the problem.

conceptual projection of certain attributes of visual sense impressions. We are therefore in a position to make two key points:

1. The abandonment by scientists of the conceptual framework of common sense physical objects would involve either the abandonment of the conceptual space of color *tout court*, or the retention of this conceptual space as it reappears in its analogical offshoot, the conceptual space of sense impressions. The latter would be cut off from its foundation and left to wither on the vine. In either case, the conceptual space of the qualities of sense ("secondary qualities" in one use of this phrase) would disappear from the public observation base of science. It would enter science only in linguistics, in the study of the structure of the language of non-scientists—and of scientists only to the extent that their sense impression talk continued to reflect the pre-revolutionary framework of common sense physical objects.

2. Only when the conceptual space of sense impressions has acquired a status which is not parasitical on the framework of common sense physical objects—in other words, only with the development of an adequate scientific theory of the sensory capacities of the central nervous system—could the framework of common sense be abandoned without losing conceptual contact with a key dimension of the world.

VI

I have said that to a first approximation I agree with Nagel that the framework of common sense is methodologically indispensable, but with Feyerabend that it is in principle false. I have sketched an argument for the first half of this thesis. Let me now attempt to bring the entire thesis to a second degree of approximation by taking a closer look at the second half.

The key to the ontological issue is the concept of a correspondence rule and its place in the classical account of theoretical explanation. Since I have already made clear my sympathy with Nagel's qualified endorsement of the classical dualism of observation and theoretical frameworks, the problem will be to show how this dualism can be reconciled with the assertion that in principle it is the framework of theory *rather than* the observation framework which is real.

The crux of the matter concerns the correspondence rules which connect theoretical concepts with observation framework counterparts, and, in particular, those which can informally be said, in a comfortable but problematic sense, to "identify" macro-objects and -processes with systems of micro-objects and -processes.[29]

These correspondence rules, by correlating concepts in the two frameworks, also correlate theorems in the deductive system of the theory with general propositions in the observation framework. Let us refer to these general propositions as the observation framework counterparts of the theorems. Here it is vital to note that there are two importantly different types of candidates which satisfy the general criterion for being an observation framework counterpart (i.e., which can be characterized as lawlike statements in the observation framework), correlated with theorems in the theory by correspondence rules. These are

1. lawlike observation framework counterparts which are *compatible* with the observational evidence;
2. lawlike observation framework counterparts which not only satisfy condition (1), but which were accepted, and would still be accepted, on purely inductive grounds (i.e., in the absence of theoretical considerations).

The distinction is crucial, for it is clear that a counterpart which satisfies condition (1) need not satisfy condition (2) (i.e., need not be the lawlike statement which it would be reasonable to accept on purely inductive grounds, nor even contain the empirical concepts which it would be reasonable to construct and use in the absence of theoretical considerations). It is characteristic of good theories to show observational counterparts in sense (2) to be false. On this point I am in substantial agreement with Feyerabend.

It should therefore be clear that the role of substantive correspondence rules is not to tie theoretical propositions to antecedently established observational counterparts in sense (2), but to tie them to observational counterparts in the weaker sense specified

---

[29]In other words, with what I have elsewhere (above, pp. 329 ff.) called "substantive," as contrasted with "methodological," correspondence rules.

in (1). By so doing, the theory, taken in conjunction with other knowledge, typically provides an explanation *not* of the antecedent generalizations which were based on purely inductive grounds, but rather of why the inductive use of observational evidence came as close as it did to yielding the observational counterpart in sense (1). [30]

Nor is the role of substantive correspondence rules in the reduction of one theory to another that of correlating theorems in the reducing theory with the postulates of the theory to be reduced *as it existed before the possibilities of reduction were considered in detail.*[31] The theory to be reduced is typically modified in subtle ways, a fact which may well lead to a revision of the correspondence rules which connect the theory to be reduced with observation framework counterparts, thus generating revised lawlike statements which are inductively indiscriminable both from those to which unaided induction would point and those which were accepted in the light of the unmodified theory.

VII

There are no puzzles in principle about the status of substantive correspondence rules which connect theory with theory. One can envisage with equanimity the replacement of two correlated theoretical structures by one structure of constructs and theorem in which the correspondence rules have (*pace* Nagel) been replaced by straight-forward definitions. This unified structure would, of course, be methodologically tied to the observation framework by two different systems of methodological correspondence rules—although the systems would tend to overlap—because the reduction of the theoretical framework of one science to that of another must

---

[30]As I put it in The language of theories in *Current Issues of the Philosophy of Science*, ed. by Herbert Feigl and Grover Maxwell, New York, 1961, "...[micro-] theories about observable things do not explain empirical laws, they explain why observable things obey, to the extent that they do, these empirical laws; that is, they explain why individual objects of various kinds and in various circumstances in the observation framework behave in those whys in which it has been inductively established that they do behave." (p. 71).

[31]This point is not clearly distinguished by Feyerabend from the foregoing since he tends to run together problems pertaining to the relation of one theory to another theory with problems pertaining to the relation of theory to empirical generalizations. (Nor does Nagel always keep these two types of problems sufficiently apart.)

not be thought to be the reduction of one *science* to another. The latter truth is, as I see it, misinterpreted by Nagel to demand that the substantive correspondence rules cannot, in principle, be replaced by definitions.

It is rather the case of those substantive correspondence rules which connect micro-theoretical with empirical constructs, and which, if one were to take seriously their analogy with the rules which connect one theory with another, would tempt one to speak of "reducing" the observation framework to the framework of the micro-theory, which generates philosophical perplexity. One can understand how primitives in chemical theory might come to be defined as predicates in a deductive structure shared by physics with chemistry. After all, as *theoretical* concepts they were in jeopardy to begin with; they were the fruit of postulational concept formation, and could be modified or abandoned at the drop of a good reason. But basic observation framework attributes *seem*, as we have noted, to have an absolute status independent of thought and language. The corresponding predicates seem, therefore, to lack the vulnerability of theoretical primitives and to be immune to replacement by micro-theoretical concepts.

This, however, as I have already pointed out on p. 351 above is an illusion which has its source in the fact that the perception of an object as red and triangular involves not only the *concept of a red triangle*, but also the *sense impression of a red triangle*. The latter is, as we have noted, a non-conceptual state of the perceiver. Thus, to put it bluntly, the phrase

      sense impression of a red triangle

refers to items which would exist even if there were no conceptual frameworks, whereas the phrase

      concept of a red triangle

obviously does not. If, therefore, one confuses the role of the phrase

      of a red triangle

in the former[32] with its role in the latter, the object language character of the former role may be attributed to the latter, and the "of-ness" of perceptual thoughts will be interpreted as a relation *in re* between thoughts and extra-conceptual items—in this case the property of being a red triangle.

---

[32]Cf. Section V.

The truth of the matter, however, is that in the phrase
>concept of a red triangle

the sign designs "red" and "triangle" are being used in "second
intention," as the scholastics put it, to form expressions which
classify conceptual items. And while it is true that the thought of
a red triangle is related to redness and triangularity and, indeed,
the property of being a red triangle, these latter items do not
have the absolute status "independent of thought and language,"
which is supposed to render the observation framework predicates
which express them immune to the fate of theoretical primitives.[33]
To see that theoretical *particulars* are not doomed to a second
class status, it is necessary to see that theoretical *attributes* are not,
as a matter of principle, second-class cousins of the perceptible
attributes of perceptible things.

Once we recognize that to say of a predicate that it stands
for a certain attribute, e.g., triangularity, is not to characterize
it as related to an item in the extra-conceptual order, but to
tell us that the predicate functions linguistically as does the predicate built into the attribute expression, thus, "triangular," our
attention is focussed on *how* this predicate functions. And this
takes us from "stands for attribute" talk to talk about specific
matter-of-fact relations between the predicate and the linguistic
and non-linguistic situation in which it is used.

And here the key point is that whereas in
>1. "φ" (in L) stands for triangularity

the term "triangularity" refers to a conceptual item, in
>2. "This is φ" (in L) is a perceptual response to triangular
>things

the phrase "triangular things" does not. The latter formulates
a necessary condition of "φ" being an observation predicate of L.
And whereas in (1) "φ" must be the *translation* in L of "triangular,"
so that both expressions must belong to the same conceptual

---

[33]For a general defense of the thesis that the *esse* of attributes, not only theoretical
attributes but even perceptual attributes is *concipi*, and a more detailed application
of this thesis to the problem of the status of theoretical entities, see the essay on "The
Language of Theories" referred to in footnote 27 above. A technically more adequate
statement and defense of the thesis is given in Abstract entities, *Review of Metaphysics*,
16:627-671.

framework, the same is not true in (2). It *could* be correct to say both

2′. "This is red" (in E) is a perceptual response to systems of particles emitting such and such electromagnetic radiation

and

2″. "This is a system of particles, etc." (in scientese E) is a perceptual response to red objects.

These distinctions put us in a position to explain the feeling philosophers have had that theoretical predicates have a "second class" meaningfulness. For to commit oneself to the idea that the connection of theoretical statements with the extra-linguistic order is in principle either *always* or *primarily* mediated by observation framework statements to which transition is made by correspondence rules, is to deny to theoretical expressions the direct language-entry transitions which make the observation framework more more than a syntactical game.[34]

Clearly, a theoretical framework can achieve first-class status only if a proper subset of its expressions acquire a direct role in observation. This Feyerabend sees, and it is the central truth in his account. It is indeed important to note that theoretical expressions can acquire a reporting role—that we can "tell by looking" that certain theoretical states of affairs obtain.

But Feyerabend seems to me to confuse the sound philosophical point that realism with respect to theoretical entities involves the idea that *in principle* theoretical expressions could take over and monopolize the direct response role which they now share, to a limited and subordinate extent, with expressions belonging to the framework of common sense, with the unsound idea that this "take over" is a live option *hic et nunc*. He thus turns a sound ontological insight into methodological error.

Nagel, on the other hand, reifies methodological insight into ontological error. His concessions to realism are superficial and leave untouched the hard core of instrumentalism in his position.

---

[34] I have used the phrase "language-entry transition"—which contrasts with both "intra-linguistic move" and "language-departure transition"—in Some reflections on language games, *Philosophy of Science*, *21*, 1954, reprinted in a revised version as Chapter 11 in *Science, Perception and Reality*.

VIII

Unimpressed by the fact that it can be methodologically useful to train oneself to respond directly to experimental (or clinical) situations in the language of a theory, and recognizing that the ability to so respond exists in an ambience of common sense, the extirpation of which would be folly, Nagel commits himself to the idea that the framework of common sense is *in principle* indispensable. By so doing he dooms theoretical frameworks to an in *principle* second class status as contrasted with the *de facto* (and methodologically reasonable) second class status they currently possess.

Nagel avoids the appearance of doing this by mislocating the issue. He compares the instrumental character of theories to the instrumental character of empirical laws in their capacity as "material rules of inference," and argues that "there is, on the whole, only a verbal difference between asking whether a theory is satisfactory (as a technique of inference) and asking whether it is true (as a premise)."[35]

Let us examine this parallel. Nagel begins by pointing out that instead of going from the premises

    All A is B

and

    Wellington is A

to the conclusion

    Wellington is B

in accordance with a formal principle of inference, we can go directly from

    Wellington is A

to

    Wellington is B

in accordance with a material principle of inference which can be represented for our purposes as

    from "x is A" infer "x is B."

He argues that the question as to the soundness of this principle is equivalent to the question as to the truth of "All *A* is *B*."

Nagel's concept of a material principle of inference is, as we

[35] *The Structure of Science*, p. 139.

shall see, the concept of what I shall call a "dependent" principle of inference. To bring this out, let us consider another argument which can be constructed from the above materials. One can go directly from

All A is B

to

Wellington is B

in accordance with the principle

from "All A is B" infer "Wellington is B."

Here the question as to the soundness of the principle is equivalent to the question as to the truth of "Wellington is A."

Let me represent the two "material" (i.e., dependent) principles as follows:

1.   ⌈(all A is B)

 "x is A" └————> "x is B"

2.   ⌈(Wellington is A)

 "All A is B" └————> "Wellington is B"

and let me call the parenthetical adjuncts to the arrows the "presuppositions" of the principles. Finally, let me represent a dependent principle of inference which leaves its presupposition unspecified, but indicates that there is one, by the form

  "..." └————> "..."

Corresponding to (1) and (2) we would then have

 1. "x is A" └————> "x is B"

 2'. "All A is B" └————> "Wellington is B"

With these distinctions in mind,[36] let us explore Nagel's use of his concept of a material rule of inference to clarify his "irenic instrumentalism," his higher synthesis of the claims of instru-

---

[36]Material rules of inference in Nagel's sense (which is concerned, in more traditional terminology, with enthymemes) must be distinguished from material rules in the full-blooded sense which illuminates traditional puzzles concerning lawlike statements, inductive argument, and counterfactual conditionals. According to the latter conception, a lawlike statement is *as such* a principle of inference and is "material" in that the validity of the argument it covers depends on the descriptive predicates involved, and not on its governing enthymemes in which the major premise—the supposed lawlike statement—is suppressed. Induction is correspondingly analyzed not as the establishing of descriptive statements to the effect, for example, that all

mentalism and realism. His general idea is that realism stresses the use of theoretical sentences as *premises* in theoretical explanation and insists that theoretical sentences are either true or false; instrumentalism, on the other hand, stresses the use of theoretical sentences as *principles of inference* and insists that the relevant question is not "true or false" but "satisfactory or not satisfactory?" All this (argues Nagel) is much ado about nothing, the two ways of putting the matter being equivalent. Is he right?

Let us first consider the case where a theory functions as a premise in a formally valid argument. It will be convenient to use expressions of the form "θ_i" and "O_j" to represent theoretical and observation framework predicates respectively, and the variable "x" to range over whatever it is that pragmatists means by "situations." In these terms the formally valid argument in question would presumably look something like

$$(x) \; \theta_1 x \rightarrow \theta_2 x$$
$$(x) \; O_1 x \rightarrow \theta_1 x$$
$$(x) \; \theta_2 x \rightarrow O_2 x$$

Therefore,

$$(x) \; O_1 \rightarrow O_2 x$$

The first premise would be a theorem in the theory; the second premise the counterpart of a correspondence rule correlating "O_1" with "θ_1"; the third the counterpart of a correspondence rule correlating "O_2" with "θ_2"; and the conclusion a lawlike statement in the observation framework.

Let us now ask about the form of the material principle of inference which would be used when the theory is functioning as a "technique of inference" rather than a premise. Clearly it must be the dependent principle

$$\text{"}O_1 x\text{"} \; \underset{\xrightarrow{\hspace{2cm}}}{\overline{\left|(T_1 \cdot T_2 \cdot T_3)\right.}} \; \text{"}O_2 x\text{"}$$

---

objects of a certain kind A are also B, but as a reasoned *decision* to adopt a material principle of inference which authorizes reasonings which can be illustrated by: "Although this is not known by observation or testimony to be B, it is A and so, in all probability, is B." For a defense of this approach to lawlike statements and induction, see my Counterfactual conditionals, dispositions, and the causal modalities, in *Minnesota Studies in the Philosophy of Science*, Vol. II, ed. by Herbert Feigl, Michael Scriven, and Grover Maxwell; and Induction as vindication, *Philosophy of Science*, *31*, 1964.

Where the premises of the formally valid argument are represented by the expressions "T_i"[37] If the presupposition of this dependent principle is left to be supplied by the context, it becomes

$$\text{MP}_T: \text{``}O_1x\text{''} \quad \longrightarrow \quad \text{``}O_2x\text{''}$$

It would then seem open to Nagel to say that the question whether the material principle of inference MP_T is *satisfactory* is equivalent to the question whether the theory or more specifically "$T_1 \cdot T_2 \cdot T_3$" is *true*.

But what is meant by "satisfactory" in connection with material principles of inference? One possible meaning is "truth preserving." And, indeed, in the original example one shows that

$$\text{``}x \text{ is } A\text{''} \quad \longrightarrow \quad \text{``}x \text{ is } B\text{''}$$

is truth preserving by showing that the statement which it presupposes (i.e., " All A is B") is true.

But that MP_T is truth preserving is shown *not* by showing that its theoretical presupposition ("$T_1 \cdot T_2 \cdot T_3$") is true, but rather by showing that the corresponding observation framework material rule of inference

$$\text{MP}_O: \quad \text{``}O_1x\text{''} \quad \longrightarrow \quad \text{``}O_2x\text{''}$$

which is the indeterminate form of

$$\begin{array}{c} (x)\ O_1x \to O_2x \\ \text{``}O_1x\text{''} \quad \longrightarrow \quad \text{``}O_2x\text{''} \end{array}$$

is truth preserving. And this, on Nagel's analysis is equivalent to showing that

$$(x)\ O_1x \to O_2x$$

is a true lawlike statement.

Notice, therefore, that the expression

$$\text{``}O_1x\text{''} \quad \longrightarrow \quad \text{``}O_2x\text{''}$$

is ambiguous: if the context is theoretical explanation, it is the indeterminate form of

$$\begin{array}{c} (T_1 \cdot T_2 \cdot T_3) \\ \text{``}O_1x\text{''} \quad \longrightarrow \quad \text{``}O_2x\text{''} \end{array}$$

---

[37]The situation can alternatively (but equivalently) be represented by analyzing the use of the theory as a "technique of inference" as a matter of *deriving* the material rule of inference

$$\text{``}O_1x\text{''} \quad \longrightarrow \quad \text{``}O_2x\text{''}$$

from the material rules of inference corresponding to "T_1," "T_2" and "T_3."

and its indeterminate or context dependent form should be represented as

$$\text{MP}'_\text{T}: \quad \text{``}O_1x\text{''} \overset{\text{(theory)}}{\underset{\longrightarrow}{\rule{0pt}{12pt}\phantom{xxxx}}} \text{``}O_2x\text{''}$$

If, on the other hand, the context is induction and the explanation and prediction of particular empirical matters of fact, it is the indeterminate form of

$$\text{``}O_1x\text{''} \overset{(x)\ O_1x \rightarrow O_2x}{\underset{\longrightarrow}{\rule{0pt}{12pt}\phantom{xxxx}}} \text{``}O_2x\text{''}$$

and its indeterminate and context dependent form should be represented as

$$\text{MP}'_\text{O}: \quad \text{``}O_1x\text{''} \overset{\text{(observation)}}{\underset{\longrightarrow}{\rule{0pt}{12pt}\phantom{xxxx}}} \text{``}O_2x\text{''}$$

There is, however, another possible meaning for "satisfactory" in connection with theories as "techniques of inference." It could mean "leading to observation counterparts which are experimentally confirmed." It would be only too easy to run these two senses of satisfactory together if one thinks of truth as warranted assertibility. All one would have to do is argue that the warranted assertibility of theoretical sentences is a matter of leading to experimentally confirmed lawlike sentences in the observation framework.

But to make *this* move is to drape an instrumentalist account of theories in the language of factual truth. Theoretical principles construed as the instrumentalist construes them could legitimately be said to have warranted assertibility and even to be "factually true" in a weak sense which simply contrasts them with mathematical and logical truths, as depending for their warranted assertibility on experimental considerations. But in the full sense of "factually true" in which we think of statements in the observation framework as factually true, no statement in a framework which is, *as a matter of principle*, limited to an indirect encounter with the world mediated by a correspondence rule can be said to be factually true. In the observation framework we must distinguish between the truth of lawlike statements which, as material principles of inference, are indeed instruments, and the truth of singular descriptive statements. Unless a corresponding distinction can be drawn, in principle, between the truth of theoretical principles and the truth of singular theoretical statements, theoretical frameworks are limited to an instrumental role. The scientific realist must take singular theoretical statements seriously.

And factual truth in the full sense involves, as Nagel seems to realize[38] without drawing its full consequences, a picturing or mapping of events in nature by linguistic or, more generally, conceptual episodes in their own capacity as natural events. "Picturing," in this sense, which involves "semantic uniformities" of the "thing→language," "language→language" and "language→action" types, is often confused (as in the classical correspondence theory of truth) with the "equivalence" expressed by the schema

   that-p is true = p

which is as relevant to mathematical, logical, and ethical propositions as to statements of empirical fact.[39]

Thus, to say that theoretical statements are capable of factual truth in the full sense is to say that a stage in the development of scientific theory (including the theory of sentient organisms) is conceivable in which it would be reasonable to abandon mediation by substantive correspondence rules in favor of a direct commerce of the conceptual framework of theory with the world. Such direct commerce exists already in limited contexts, and, to the extent that it does exist, theoretical frameworks enjoy in anticipation the first class status which would be theirs in that "long run" in terms of which, according to Peirce, we conceive the scientific enterprise and the "truth" about "what really exists," which is its formal, final, and efficient cause.

---

[38] *The Structure of Science*, p. 139.

[39] For an elaboration of this point and a discussion of the picturing relation see Truth and correspondence, *Journal of Philosophy*, 59:29-56, 1962. Reprinted with minor alterations as Chapter 6 of *Science, Perception and Reality*.

XV

THE IDENTITY APPROACH TO THE
MIND-BODY PROBLEM[1]

I

M Y PRIMARY aim in this paper is to set the stage for a discussion of some of the central themes in the so-called "identity" approach to the mind-body problem. I particularly have in mind Herbert Feigl's elaborate statement and defense of this approach in Volume II of the *Minnesota Studies*. A secondary but more constructive purpose is to bring out some of the reasons which cause me to think that the theory is either very exciting but false, or true but relatively uninteresting.

I shall begin with a preliminary formulation of the identity theory which will highlight the topics I propose to discuss. Roughly put, the theory claims that what it calls "raw feels"—a technical expression which is intended to cover impressions and images pertaining to the external senses, as well as bodily sensations and feelings in a more usual sense—are identical with "brain states." It hastens to add that in speaking of "raw feels" as identical with "brain states" it does not simply mean that the very same logical subjects which have "raw feel" characteristics also have "brain state" characteristics, or that "raw feel" characteristics do not occur apart from "brain state" characteristics, but rather that the very characteristics themselves are identical. As Feigl puts it, "raw feel" universals are identical with certain "brain state" universals.

This rough and ready formulation of what is actually a highly sophisticated philosophical thesis blocks out three topics with which any attempt to assess the identity theory must come to grips. Each of these topics turns out on the most cursory inspection to involve highly controversial issues which are at the very center of the philosophical stage. I shall not attempt to resolve all or, indeed, any of these issues. My aim will rather be to thread my

---

[1]This paper was prepared for and presented at the Boston University Colloquium for the Philosophy of Science, April 10, 1963.

way through them in such a way as to bring out the common ground I share with the identity theory and thus make possible a meaningful joining of issues.

It will not have passed unnoticed in this particular climate of opinion that the identity theory as formulated above is committed to the idea that it makes sense to speak of the identity of attributes or universals. This is the first of the thorny topics on which *something* must be said. This may be the place, but it is not the time to develop a theory of abstract entities. I shall simply mobilize some of the pre-analytic strands which any theory must take into account, and develop them in a way which gives the claim that "raw feel" universals are identical with certain "brain state" universals or at least have the appearance of being in keeping with the spirit of a scientifically-oriented philosophy.

Universals, then, are a subset of abstract entities. Their distinctive feature is that they are expressed in language by predicates (e.g., "red") or by predicative expressions (e.g., "three feet long," "between red and yellow in color"). I shall say that predicates (under which term I shall usually include predicative expressions) "stand for" or "express" universals. Universals may be referred to as well as stood for or expressed. But predicates do not *refer to* universals; indeed, they are not referring expressions at all. Among the expressions which refer to universals, a particularly important role is played by those which are formed from predicates or predicative expressions which stand for or express the universals to which reference is made; thus,

> Triangularity
>
> Being three feet long
>
> Being between red and yellow in color.

Universals are public objects. They are identities not only with respect to their many instances, but also with respect to the many minds which think in terms of them, and the many languages which give expression to them. This inter-subjective and inter-linguistic character must be accounted for by any adequate theory of abstract entities. Equally important, and even more "platonistic" in tone, is the distinction which must be drawn between those universals which have been "discovered" or have come to be "known" and those which have not, and, within the sphere of the former, between those which are effectively taken account of by our language, and those which are not. To unpack this a bit, I shall assume that a universal is "discovered" or comes to be "known" in the course of coming to know what *use* a predicate would have to have in order to stand for or express it. The universal is effectively taken account of by our language if our language contains a predicative expression which actually has this use.

Notice, therefore, that while we can refer to unknown or undiscovered universals (I drop the quotation marks from these metaphorically-used terms) and to universals which are not effectively taken account of by our language, only universals which are effectively taken account of by our language can be referred to by referring expressions formed from predicates which stand for or express them. Thus, although we can refer to the unknown property of persons which would explain their telekinetic powers, our language contains no predicate which stands for or expresses this property.

> Two universals are identical if, were a language to contain predicative expressions which stand for or express them, these predicative expressions would either independently have the same use, or one would be a definitional abbreviation of the other.

Clearly, much of the burden of the above distinctions is borne by the word "use" and the phrase "the same use." My general strategy is clear. It is to connect "realistic" talk about universals with "nominalistic" talk about linguistic expressions. My further strategy would be to connect talk about the use of expressions with talk about uniformities in the occurrence of linguistic inscriptions, and, therefore, to build a bridge to "behavioral criteria of synonymy." But that is strategy for a war and not a battle. Here I shall limit myself to pointing out that the patterns of use I have primarily in mind are (1) the reporting or observation pattern, and (2) the consequence pattern. The latter is, roughly, the pattern which would find its explicit formulation in what Carnap calls "transformation rules," L-transformation rules, P-transformation rules, and others. I add "and others" to Carnap's list because it is not clear that it is an exhaustive classification. Other possible candidates are "bridge laws" and "correspondence rules."

I pointed out above that we can refer to universals for which we have no corresponding predicates. There are two types of case, one of which is, for our purposes, uninteresting. Thus there is a sense in which it can be said that there are color universals for which we have no predicates. We can imagine that we had no predicate for the color between red and yellow. It should be noticed, however, that while we might not have had the predicate "orange," we might well have had the predicate expression "between red and yellow in color." And, indeed, to be in the logical space of color is to have predicate expressions adequate to the job of introducing predicates in the narrower sense, thus "orange."

The interpretation of statements asserting the identity of universals, where the logical space of the universals is in this sense familiar, is relatively straightforward. Consider, for example:

> The universal which. . . . = the universal which. . . .

We can distinguish two forms the descriptions might take: (1) Each locates a universal with respect to a point outside the logical space of the universal located. Thus,

> The color of Plato's beard = the color of your father's moustache.

Here, if we have the relevant information, we can go from one of the descriptions either directly to an illustrating name of the universal (i.e., a name formed appropriately from the predicative expression which stands for it), thus

> The color of Plato's beard = orange (i.e., being orange)

or to a description which locates the universal with respect to the logical space to which it belongs, thus

> The color of Plato's beard = the color between red and yellow.

(2) In the second type of case, at which we have just arrived, at least one of the descriptions locates the universal with respect to the logical space to which it belongs. Where we have a predicate which expresses the color between red and yellow, we can move from the above (supposing that predicate to be "orange") to

> The color of Plato's beard = orange (i.e., being orange).

If we do not have such a predicate, we at least have the predicate expression "between red and yellow in color," and can say

The color of Plato's beard = being between red and **yellow** in color,

and could introduce a predicate having the use of "orange."

The important case of referring to universals for which we have no corresponding predicates is that of referring to what I have called unknown or undiscovered universals. Consider, thus,

>   1. The property which an adequate theory of telekinesis—if we but had it—would ascribe to persons having this power.

Contrast this with

>   2. The property which the theory (current) of chemical interactions assigns to catalysts.

In (2) it is implied that we have a predicate in our language which stands for or expresses the property in question. Not so in case (1). There the property in question is referred to by relating it to the properties expressed by the predicates of the science of telekinesis at its operational and instantially inductive level. The logical space of these empirical constructs is not that of the properties to which access would be gained by constructing a sound theory of telekinetic phenomena.

In general, then, the universals which it is the task of theoretical science to "discover" are referred to *via* a reference to the unborn or undeveloped theory, the predicates of which would stand for or express them, and, therefore, *via* a reference to the logical space of the empirical properties of the phenomena to be explained by the theory.

Yet the predicates of even sketchily developed theories express or stand for universals. Here it is essential to note that as a theory develops, its predicates cannot, in general, be said to continue to stand for or express the same universals.[2] This brings me to a fundamental point which adds an element of symmetry to our previous classification of universals. To the classification (which highlights the temporal dimension);

---

[2] It should not be assumed that the evolution of the use of a predicate is to be construed as a matter of its successively standing for a series of universals to which the concept of evolution does not apply. If, as I have argued in Chapter IX above, universals are linguistic roles, they share in their own way the evolutionary and revolutionary vicissitudes of games and institutions.

1. Not yet discovered.

2. Discovered or known:

> a. Not yet effectively taken account of by our language
>
> b. Effectively taken account of by our language

we must now add a third heading under (2)

> c. No longer effectively taken account of by our language

and a new major category:

3. Lost, or, so to speak, undiscovered universals.

These considerations strongly suggest that the objective or "platonistic" status I am ascribing to universals might be construed in a Peircean way as relative to the continuing scientific community. Thus, if on hearing the above proliferation of universals, one is tempted to expostulate, "which of these universals *really* exist?" I would reply by recalling Peirce's characterization of a true proposition as one that the continuing scientific community would ultimately accept—and then I would change the subject.

II

Now if the claims of the identity theory are placed in the frame-word of the above distinctions, it is clear that the theory does not assert the identity of "raw feel" universals with certain "brain state" universals which are effectively taken account of by existing language. For on the above analysis, this would involve that some "brain state" predicates have the same use as "raw feel" predicates. And this is obviously not the case. The claim is, rather, that among the universals which would find expression in the predicates of a to be developed "brain state" theory, some are identical with "raw feel" universals.

At first sight, this is hardly much better. For, it might be urged, how could any predicates in a "brain state" theory have the same use as "raw feel" predicates? After all, the latter doesn't even presuppose the knowledge that there are such things as brains! But before we take up this and other objections, we must explore the notion of a "raw feel" universal.

III

The "rawness" of "raw feels" is their non-conceptual character. The sense in which "raw feels" are "of something" is not to be assimilated to the intentionality of thoughts. To say that they are non-conceptual is, of course, not to deny that they can be referred to and characterized by the use of concepts, or even directly responded to by concepts in direct self-knowledge.

The word "feel" in the expression "raw feel" is an extension to all sense modalities of a use of the word "feel" which has its ultimate source in such contexts as,

    1. He felt the hair on the back of his neck bristle.

In this primary context, "to feel" is clearly a cousin of "to see," and feeling in this sense can properly be classified as a mode of perception. Notice that feeling in this sense is conceptual; a propositional attitude. One would, perhaps, be more comfortable about this remark if the example had been,

    2. He felt that the hair on the back of his neck was bristling.

The relation between (1) and (2) is an interesting and important topic in the philosophy of perception. I shall simply assume on the present occasion that (1) is a stronger form of (2) which emphasizes the noninferential character of the experience.

Notice that to ascribe a perceptual propositional attitude to a person in the form,

    3. He perceived that-p

is to endorse the proposition involved in the attitude. We can, however, ascribe the same propositional attitude in a non-endorsing way by using such locutions as

    4. He thought he perceived that-p

    5. It seemed to him that he perceived that-p

    6. It appeared to him that-p

    7. He was under the (perceptual) impression that-p

None of these is completely neutral with respect to endorsement. They all tend to imply the falsity of the proposition involved in the attitude, and have other overtones which are irrelevant to my purpose. I shall make a technical use of (7) in which it will imply neither the truth nor the falsity of the proposition involved in the perceptual propositional attitude. Thus the statements,

8. He was under the tactual impression that the hair at the back of his neck was bristling

9. He was under the visual impression that there was a red and triangular physical object in front of him

ascribe perceptual propositional attitudes while making no commitment concerning the truth or falsity of the proposition involved in the attitude.

Now a classical theme in the philosophy of perception is that the truth of statements such as (9) implies the occurrence of something which is variously called a "(visual) sensation" (a sensation of a red triangle) or a "(visual) impression" (an impression of a red triangle), where this occurrence is understood to be a non-conceptual episode which *somehow* has the perceptible qualities which the propositional attitude takes to be exemplified in the world of perceptible things. Thus, the fact that a person is under the visual impression that a certain stick in water is bent is taken to imply that he is having a visual impression of a bent object. I shall assume that this is true. This does not mean that I accept the "sense datum inference," for it should not be assumed that to have a visual impression is to sense a sense datum as these terms are used in classical sense-datum theories.

Notice that visual impressions are classified by the use of the word "of" followed by the phrase which would appear in the statement of the propositional attitudes which imply their occurrence, thus

Impression of a red and triangular object

corresponds to

Impression that there is a red and triangular object in front of one.

The idea that there are such non-conceptual episodes was put to use in explaining, for example, how a straight stick (in water) can look bent, and a red object (in green light) look black. It was postulated that the propositional attitude ascribed by

He is under the visual impression that there is a black object in a certain place

involves, among other things, (1) the occurrence of an impression of a black object, (2) the occurrence of the thought that there is a black object in a certain place, the thought (or perceptual judg-ment, as it was called) being evoked by the impression. Roughly speaking, *impressions that* were construed as conceptual responses to *impressions of.* To this was added the idea that while in standard conditions viewing red objects results in an impression of a red object, and viewing bent objects results in an impression of a bent object, in non-standard conditions (e.g., viewing a straight stick in water) the viewing of an object that is not bent may result in an impression of a bent object, and the viewing of an object that is not red may result in an impression of a red object.

Although the examples I have been using come from vision, exactly the same distinctions were drawn in the case of feeling. Here "feeling *of . . .*" is the counterpart of "visual impression of . . . ." We can therefore understand the philosophical use of the expression "raw feel" as an extension to all modes of perception of an expression which stands for the non-conceptual kind of episode, which explains why a person can be under the impression that he is being pricked by something sharp when this is not the case.

I pointed out that sense impressions or raw feels are classified according to the perceptible qualities which are ascribed to some part of the world by the perceptual propositional attitudes which they evoke, and which characterize their standard causes. As I see it, the "of" phrases in

> Sense impression of a red triangle
> Raw feel of being pricked by a sharp object

are adjectives which, in addition to classifying raw feels *extrinsically* by their causes and effects, also classify them with reference to their intrinsic character.

How are we to understand the intrinsic character of raw feels? Obviously the sense impression of a red triangle is not, in the literal sense, either red or triangular; nor is the raw feel of being pricked by a sharp object a being pricked by a sharp object. The most that can be said is that the families of qualities and relations which intrinsically characterize raw feels or sense im-pressions correspond in a certain way to the families of qualities and relations which characterize perceptible objects and processes. (The scholastics took the different, and ultimately unsatisfactory, tack of holding that the characteristics were the same, but the mode of exemplification different.) I shall return to this point later. For the moment I shall simply say that the logical space of the qualities and relations which characterize raw feels is, in certain respects, isomorphic with the logical space of the perceptible qualities and relations of physical objects and processes. It would be useful, therefore, to introduce predicates for raw feels which are formed from predicates which stand for perceptible qualities and relations by adding the subscript "s." Thus a triangular$_s$ impression or raw feel would be one which in standard conditions is brought about by viewing a triangular object and which, *ceteris paribus*, results in being under the impression that a triangular object is before one.

It will have been noticed that even my characterization of the intrinsic properties of raw feels has been, so to speak, extrinsic. For I characterized them in terms of their correspondence with the perceptible qualities and relations of physical objects and processes. It might be inferred from this that I think of our access to the logical space of impressions as indirect, as based upon a prior access to the logical space of perceptible qualities and relations. I shall postpone taking a stand of my own on this matter, and limit myself for the moment to pointing out that the type of identity theory I am examining rejects this suggestion and insists that our access to the logical space of sense impressions or raw feels is direct and, indeed, is the presupposition of our access to the logical space of physical objects and processes. It insists, indeed, that the qualities and relations of "raw feels" are "directly given" and that physical objects and their properties are "existential hypotheses" whose reality is guaranteed by the fine job they do of saving the appearances.

Finally, a categorial point about raw feels which is implicit in the preceding remarks. They are construed as "pure episodes" and are contrasted with dispositions and mongrel categorical-hypothetical states. It should be noticed that the fact that one has in some sense "privileged access" to a state of oneself doesn't by itself imply that this state is a pure episode. Children can be trained to respond linguistically to Skinnerian states of their organism. Nor, as this point in turn suggests, need "privileged access" be construed in terms of classical theories of the given.

The identity theory we are examining, however, is committed to the idea that raw feels are pure episodes and that raw feel facts are "given" in something like the classical sense.

IV

Before taking the bull by the horns, a word or two about the other terms of the identities envisaged by the identity theory. It will be remembered that according to the theory, raw-feel universals are identical with certain brain-state universals. Which brain-state universals? Indeed, which brains?

For there is, in the first place, the brain as an empirical object to which empirical properties definable in observation terms can be ascribed. Can raw-feel universals be identical with universals which characterize the empirical brain? They cannot, of course, be identical with any universals expressed by empirical predicates defined in terms of the publicly observable features of the brain, for raw feels are pure episodes which are public only in the sense that others can infer that which is given to oneself. (What authorizes the inference is, of course, a classic question.) Nevertheless, it is important to see that there is a sense in which it is perfectly legitimate to suppose that raw feels *are identical with* certain states of the empirical brain. This, for the simple reason that it makes sense to suppose that they *are* states of the empirical brain. Imagine a person who has been defleshed and deboned, but whose nervous system is alive, intact, and in functioning order. Imagine its sensory nerves hooked up with input devices and its motor nerves hooked up with an electronic system which enables it to communicate. Without expanding on this familiar science fiction, let me simply suggest that we think of what we ordinarily call a person as a nervous system clothed in flesh and bones. In view of what we know, it makes perfectly good sense to introduce the term "core person" for the empirical nervous system, and to introduce a way of talking according to which raw feels and, for that matter, thoughts are in the first instance states of "core persons" and only derivatively of the clothed person.

I submit that in this sense most scientifically-oriented philosophers think of raw feels and thoughts as brain states. But while the thesis that raw feel universals *are*, in this sense, brain states and therefore trivally[3] identical with certain brain-state universals is almost undoubtedly *true*, it is relatively non-controversial and unexciting. Only a Cartesian dualist would demur.

For the claim that raw feels and thoughts are in this sense identical with brain states simply transfers the episodes and dispositions initially attributed to persons to the central nervous system, now conceived of as a core person. All of the important philosophical problems pertaining to the relation of mental states to physical states remain.

These considerations give proper perspective to the fact that the brain state universals which, according to the identity theory, are identical with raw-feel universals, are universals which would be expressed by certain predicates of an as yet to be elaborated *theory* of brain activity. Thus, instead of the relatively unexciting claim that raw-feel universals are identical with certain brain-state universals, where this reduces to the claim that raw feel universals *are* brain-state universals (i.e., ascribable to brains as core persons) the identity theory claims that raw-feel universals are not only brain-state universals in this unexciting sense, but are identical with certain universals to be "discovered" in the course of developing a scientific theory of brains.

Thus the question arises, "Is it reasonable to suppose that the scientific study of brains will lead to the discovery of brain-state universals which are identical with raw-feel universals?" And to this question we are strongly tempted to answer "No!!" For interpreted along the lines sketched at the beginning of this paper it becomes, "Would an adequate theory of brains contain predicates which had the same use as raw-feel predicates?" And the idea that this might be so has a most implausible ring. It will be useful to formulate some of the objections which this idea tends to arouse.

The first is that since predicates which would stand for the relevent brain-state universals are *ex hypothesi* theoretical predicates, they would not have the avowal or reporting use which is characteristic of some, if not all, raw-feel predicates. To this objection the identity theorist replies that once the theory was developed,

---

[3]Compare the trivial move from "shapes are properties of physical objects" to "shapes are identical with certain properties of physical objects."

people could be trained to respond to the brain states in question with the predicates of the theory—which would thus gain an avowal use.

The second objection is that raw-feel predicates do not have a theoretical use, or, to put it in the material mode, raw feels are not theoretical entities. Here the identity theorist might reply that the *other*-ascriptive use of raw feel predicates is, in effect, a theoretical use. The force of this reply will be explored subsequently.

The third objection is the challenge "How can a predicate which applies to a single logical subject (a person) have the same use as a predicate which applies to a multiplicity of scientific objects?" The effect of this challenge is to make the point that the identity theory involves not only the identity of raw-feel universals with certain brain-state universals, but of persons with systems of scientific objects. The identity theorist can be expected to reply that it is enough for his purposes if raw-feel universals which differ only in this categorial respect from the raw-feel universals expressed by predicates which apply to persons as single logical subjects are identical with certain brain-state universals. We shall leave this reply untouched, although we shall return to something like it at the end of our argument.

The fourth objection, however, is the most familiar and goes to the heart of the matter. "How," it asks, "can a property which is in the logical space of neurophysiological states be identical with a property which is not?" Otherwise put, "How could a predicate defined in terms of neurophysiological primitives have the same use as (be synonymous with) a predicate which is not?" To this question the inevitable answer is "It could not."

V

It might seem, as it has to many, that this is the end of the matter. The identity theory is absurd, and that is all there is to it. And, indeed, the identity theory as we have so far described it has no obvious defense against this standard objection. Yet it is not difficult to discern the fundamental strategy of the identity theorist in the face of this objection. It consists in an appeal to a supposed analogy between the speculatively entertained identity of raw-feel universals with brain-state universals, and the once speculative but now established identity of chemical universals with certain micro-physical universals. The story is a familiar one, and I shall not bore you with the details. The relevant points are quickly made. Suppose U_C is a certain universal which the predicate "P_C" in the chemical theory current at time T stands for. And suppose that this chemical theory has a degree of sophistication essentially that of chemical theory today, but that microphysics current at T is rudimentary. An "identity theorist" puts forward at T the thesis that chemical universals will turn out to be identical with certain to-be-discovered micro-physical universals (i.e., universals which would be expressed by the predicates of a more sophisticated micro-physics). An opponent raises the following objections:

1. How can micro-physical predicates which are not tied to Chemical Laboratory observables have the same use as chemical predicates which are?

The "identity theorist" replies that once the theory is developed, these defined micro-physical predicates are given this new use, and therefore acquire a chemical-theoretical role.

2. How can the predicates of current chemical theory, which have no definitional tie to micro-physical primitives, have the same use as any predicates of future microphysical theory which will have such a tie?

This objection corresponds to the fourth and most telling objection to the mind-body identity theorist. And once again the objection is, in a certain sense, decisive. But here the "identity theorist" has available to him a move which is, at first sight, not available in the raw-feel, brain-state case. He can argue that *both* of the universals involved in the identification are *to be discovered* universals, the chemical ones as well as the micro-physical ones. Roughly, the identity claim takes the form,

The universals which will be expressed at T' by the predicates of a more adequate theory of chemical processes are identical with the universals which would be expressed at T' by the predicates of a more adequate micro-physical theory,

and while the universals which the predicates of chemical theory current at T express would not be identical with micro-physical universals, the universals which would be expressed by its more powerful successor might be.

For just as universals can be "discovered" and "given effective expression in our language" by our coming to use predicates in various ways, so universals can be "abandoned," and even lost, by no longer finding expression in our language. A chemical predicate which at T did not stand for a micro-physical universal may come to do so at T'. And the chemical universal for which it stood at T may be left in the lurch for a more sophisticated face.

The situation can be represented as one in which chemical theoretic predicates cease to stand for universals which are merely constantly co-exemplified with micro-physical universals ("bridge laws") and come to stand for micro-physical universals. The identification is *made* rather than *discovered*—though the possibility of identification is discovered.

VI

Is anything like this move possible in the raw-feel, brain-state case? Can the identity of raw-feel universals with brain-state universals be assimilated to the identity of chemical and micro-physical universals? Can raw-feel predicates and brain-state predicates be regarded as on the move towards a possible synonymity as was correctly predicted for the predicates of chemical and micro-physical theory? Summarily put, can raw feels be *reduced* to neurophysiological states?

This suggestion runs up against the obvious objection that according to typical identity theories, raw feel predicates, at least in their first-person use, are as *untheoretical* as predicates can be. Unlike the predicates of chemical theory, they are not on the move towards a more adequate logical space which they might come to express. Like the Bostonian, they are *there*. This is often put by saying that they "label" directly given qualities and relations.

And even if the identity theorist were to hold that the *other*-ascriptive use of raw-feel predicates is to be reconstructed as involving two stages:

1. The postulation of inner episodes to account for the perceptual behavior (including verbal behavior) of *others*

2. The identification of these theoretical inner episodes with the raw feels given to self awareness (i.e., the identification of theoretical *kind* with the given *kind*),[4]

the *further* move of reducing the *other*-oriented theoretical episodes to neurophysiological states would simply conflict with the identification formulated in (2).

Suppose that at this point the identity theorist switches his tactics to conform to his reductionist strategy and abandons the thesis of given-ness. In other words, he now argues that instead of the use of raw-feel predicates being a confluence of two autonomous uses, a *self*-ascriptive use in which they "label given universals" and an *other*-ascriptive use in which they can be compared to theoretical predicates, the theoretical use in the explanation of perceptual behavior is primary and is an *anybody*-ascriptive use, and that such avowal or reporting use as raw-feel predicates have is a dimension of use which is built on this anybody-ascriptive theoretical use. Would not this complete the parallel with the chemistry-physics model? For if both raw-feel and brain-state predicates are theoretical predicates, can we not conceive of a reduction of raw-feel theory to brain-state theory?

If the concept of reduction is construed on the model of the physics-chemistry case, then, as I see it, the answer is "No." For reduction in this sense is a special case of the identification of universals located with respect to two theoretical structures which are expected to merge. Roughly, instead of the primitive predicates of one theory ending up as *defined* predicates in the unified theory—which is the chemistry-physics case—these primitive predicates may end up as *primitive* predicates in the unified theory. In effect, the to-be-discovered sense-impression universals would be no more complex than the sense-impression universals expressed by current sense-impression predicates; they would have a different categorial framework, and be logically related to (but *not* complexes of) universals expressed by other primitive predicates in the to-be-achieved unified sense-impression, brain-state theory. The logical space of sense-impressions would, so to speak, have been transposed into a new key and located in a new context. It would not, how-

---

[4]Notice that this approach has the merit, at least, of meeting some of the objections to the instantially inductive form of the argument from analogy.

ever, have become internally more complex in the way in which the logical space of chemical properties becomes internally more complex by virtue of their identification with micro-physical properties. That is to say, there would be no increase in complexity with respect to what might be called the factual content of sense-impression universals; such increased complexity as occurred would be of a logical character. Roughly, the new sense-impression universals would be exemplified not by single logical subjects (persons), but rather by a manifold of logical subjects which might be called—borrowing a term without its philosophical commitments—sensa.

But if sense-impression or raw-feel theory is to merge with brain-state theory, the latter phrase must be used in its proper sense of "theory adequate to explain the properties of empirical brains as core persons" and freed from any commitment to the idea that brain theory is of necessity a theory the scientific objects of which, nerves, are reducible, along with their properties, to systems of micro-physical particles in a sense which implies that all the predicates of an ideal brain theory would be definable in terms of micro-physical primitives none of which apply *exclusively* to micro-physical systems which are the theoretical counterparts of brains.

Thus, if the objects of brain-state theory are conceived to be reducible to micro-physical objects (however un-thingish) by an adequate micro-physical theory, the latter phrase must connote *not* "micro-theory adequate to the explanation of inanimate physical objects" (as it often tends to do), but rather "micro-theory adequate to the explanation of any physical object, animate or inanimate."

Thus it is my conviction that a theory which is to explain the properties of core persons will involve a family of families of predicates which would be a categorial transformation, but not substantive reduction, of raw-feel predicates, and which would apply only to systems of scientific objects which are the theoretical counterparts of empirical brains. Thus I accept the identity theory only in its weak form according to which raw feels or sense impressions are states of core persons, and according to which, therefore, the logical space of raw feels will reappear transposed but unreduced in a theoretical framework adequate to the job of explaining what core persons can do. In my opinion, such a theory is not yet even on the horizon.

The fundamental point I wish to make in defense of this thesis is that if one thinks of "sense impressions" or "raw feels" as theoretical constructs introduced for the purpose of explaining "discriminative behavior" such as is found in white rats, then there is no reason to suppose that the postulated states might not be identified with neural states and conceived of as reducible along the lines described previously. It is therefore crucial to my thesis to emphasize that sense impressions or raw feels are common sense theoretical constructs introduced to explain the occurrence *not* of white rat type discriminative behavior, but rather of perceptual propositional attitudes, and are therefore bound up with the explanation of why human language contains families of predicates having the logical properties of words for perceptible qualities and relations.

Finally, it must be remembered that although the framework of raw feels is a theory, the logical space of the attributes of raw feels is modeled on that of the perceptible qualities and relations of physical objects and processes; and this logical space is, in an important sense, *closed*. Perceptible qualities and relations are, as the identity theory indirectly acknowledges, pure occurrent qualities and relations. They are neither dispositional nor mongrel states. To say of a physical object that it is red and triangular is not to ascribe a power or disposition to it, though it is, in a very strong sense, to imply that it has certain powers and dispositions. Now it is not the logical spaces of occurrent perceptible qualities and relations which generate the demand for scientific explanation, but rather the logical space of the powers and dispositions of physical objects and processes. Here one must be careful, for there is clearly a sense in which the latter space is an off-shoot of the former. Roughly, it is not such facts, expounded in a "phenomenology" of sensible qualities and relations, as that to be orange is to be between red and yellow in color, which demand scientific explanation, as it is such nomological facts as that black objects sink further into snow that white objects when the sun is shining. And when physical theory explains these causal powers by "identifying" perceptible things and processes with systems of micro-physical objects, the "identification" is not to be construed as involving a *reduction* of perceptible qualities and relations to the qualities and relations of scientific objects, but rather as a *correlation* of these two sets of qualities and relations by means of "bridge laws." *How* this correlation is to be construed, and whether, unlike perceptible qualities and relations, the physical objects and processes which exemplify them can be reduced (i.e., *identified* [rather than merely correlated with] systems of scientific objects), are questions which transcend the scope of this essay, although they must be given an acceptable answer by a realistic interpretation of scientific objects such has been presupposed throughout the entire argument.[5]

---

[5]For an exploration of this problem, see Chapters XIII and XIV above; also the early chapters in my *Science, Perception, and Reality*, Routledge and Kegan Paul, 1963.

XVI

SCIENCE AND ETHICS[1]

THE fundamental data of ethics are the concrete moral judgments and evaluations which we and other peoples make on particular occasions. They include the general maxims and principles which are formulated in reflective moments and which play a central role in passing our way of life on to the next generation.[2]

These same data are also data for the anthropologist. This generates the question, "What is the difference between the approach of the anthropologist and the approach of the philosopher?" One possible answer is that the anthropologist is concerned with a question of *fact*. He is concerned to discover what moral principles are in fact *espoused* by various cultures (including his own), whereas the philosopher is concerned to determine which set of moral principles is *true*. This answer is not without merit, but it is a radical oversimplification.

Let us begin by exploring the situation as it appears to the anthropologist. He attempts to structure the moral consciousness of the culture in terms of some such distinction as

1. The spontaneous evaluations of particular acts and situations made by members of the culture. These are his fundamental data.
2. What I shall call intermediate principles or maxims.
3. The "first principles" which express the most basic and general evaluations in terms of which the former would be justified.

Let me explain these distinctions by means of a simple analogy.

1. Particular evaluations: The Smiths are coming tonight. We ought to buy playing cards.

---

[1]A revised version of a paper read to the Phoebe Griffin Noyes Library Association, Old Lyme, Connecticut, on January 26, 1960.

[2]It is always dangerous to take copybook maxims at their face value, for to be a realistic expression of our fundamental moral convictions, they would have to be accompanied by a complicated set of qualifications which specify exceptions, make clear what kind of context is presupposed, and stipulate an order of priority for those situations in which different maxims would call for opposite plans of conduct.

2. Maxim: When the Smiths come, we play bridge.

3. First principle: When one has guests, one ought to do what the guests like.

The maxim is derivable from the principle together with the fact that the Smiths like to play bridge. The same "first" principle together with the fact that the Joneses like to dance generates the maxim, "When the Joneses come we dance."

Another example: A nomadic tribe amid hostile tribes.

1. Particular evaluation: It's time to put Mom and Dad away. (They can't keep up with the tribe.)

2. Maxim: When people can't keep up with the tribe, they should be put away.

3. First principle: People who endanger the safety of the tribe should be put away.

Sophisticated cultures abound in abstract formulations of maxims and "first" principles, though, as was pointed out above,[3] what people formulate as general moral propositions are not necessarily adequate expressions of the way they actually think on moral matters. The formulated maxims and principles are almost always oversimplified to a high degree.

The best way of finding out what people's attitudes really are is to watch what they do and say in concrete situations and, by using the "hypthetico-deductive method" determine what small number of abstract principles would lead to the concrete evaluations actually made and acted on in the culture in question, if these principles were espoused by the culture and applied in terms of what it believes about the world and about the consequences of actions. If these hypothesized principles coincide with what is actually said, so much the better; but what is said should never be taken at its face value. The fundamental moral attitudes of the culture need never have received explicit formulation.

Suppose, then, that an anthropologist studies a number of cultures and looks for the "first principles" of their moral frameworks. It is obvious that the intermediate principles or maxims he finds will differ, often drastically, from culture to culture. The maxims of an agricultural community are notoriously different from those

---

[3]Footnote 2.

of hunting communities. But this difference at the intermediate level is compatible with agreement at the level of first principles. Would the anthropologist find such agreement? This question enables us to explore one sense of the phrase "cultural relativism." This sense concerns a matter of fact.

Thus, suppose he found agreement; that all disagreement at the level of maxims and concrete judgments could be accounted for in terms of the different circumstances of the cultures and their different beliefs about nature and about the consequences of their action. Would this agreement show that the principles in question were true or correct or valid? How does one show a first principle to be not only *held* but *rightly held*? Can one?

Suppose, on the other hand, that he found different cultures to have different first principles. Would it make sense to ask which is correct or true? Could the different cultures not only in point of fact have different first principles, but rightly or justifiably have them?

> The claim that they have different principles would be cultural relativism as a *scientific* or *factual* thesis.
>
> The claim that each *rightly* has its own first principles would be cultural relativism as an *ethical* or *evaluative* thesis.

Is it, perhaps, the task of the anthropologist not only to discover what principles are espoused by a culture, but whether the principles are rightly espoused? If the latter, on what grounds would he argue? Consider a culture in which a high degree of aggressive behavior is sanctioned among young men. Dueling is encouraged, and suppose that this aggressive behavior is sanctioned, so to speak, as an end in itself and not a means of training men for the rigors of war. The anthropologist might see that if the culture persists in this policy, its stock will deteriorate and the culture will be in danger of perishing. Can he argue as anthropologist that the policy is bad or incorrect? Or take the case of a culture which adopts a policy of celibacy and continence as a way of life. In both cases, the anthropologist can say

> If these principles are maintained, the culture will be in danger of disappearing.

And obviously he can conclude that the policy is wrong or incorrect if he assumes that the disappearance of the culture is a bad thing.

Another example: A culture has a system of practices which result in an ant-like way of life, monotonous, conforming, but warm and comfortable. He can argue that if its members changed their way of life, they would have more ups and downs and perhaps less comfort and more anxiety, but would, on the other hand, have a richer esthetic and intellectual life. Can he argue as anthropologist that the culture ought to change its way of life? Or ought not?

Obviously, at this point, the anthropologist must take into account his own principles; the fundamental attitudes in terms of which he and his fellows approach problems of living. Anthropologist, know thyself! And if he does a bit of auto-anthropology and discovers what his first principles are, can he say that his principles are the *correct* ones and mean anything more by this than they are *his*?

We can now distinguish between three dimensions of ethical theory:

1. Descriptive or anthropological ethics (including auto-anthropology).

2. Normative ethics. Its aim is to discover the true first principles of conduct and evaluation; if there are such things as true moral principles and a method of discovering them.

3. Criteriological ethics. Its concern is with how one can settle a dispute about which (if any) moral principles are true—by rational means (as opposed to brute force or propaganda). Criteriological ethics is concerned with the very possibility of normative ethics as a rational discipline.

These three branches of ethics are paralleled in the field of scientific knowledge by the distinction between

1. The history and anthropology of science. What beliefs do such and such people *have* about the workings of the world and how did they come to have them?

2. Science. What beliefs about nature are *true*?

3. Scientific methodology (or criteriology). What are the

criteria of a good scientific theory; what constitutes a
good reason for accepting a scientific hypothesis?

The philosopher is particularly concerned with criteriological
questions. Thus he wishes to know whether it makes sense to say
of a set of moral first principles that they are not only accepted,
but correct or true, and how one would go about defending by
rational means the assertion that they are true. In short, he wants
to know *whether* moral principles can be rationally justified and,
if so, how.

With the above distinctions under our belt, let us try to get an
overall picture of what philosophers have had to say on the subject.
We have seen that particular moral judgments are justified by
subsuming them under intermediate principles or maxims, and
that intermediate principles are justified by subsuming them under
more general principles and, ultimately, first principles. This kind
of justification is purely logical. Its forms are illustrated by

> I ought to help Jones because Jones is hungry and penniless, and
> one ought to help people who are hungry and penniless.
> One ought to assist people who are hungry and penniless because
> people who are hungry and penniless are in distress, and one
> ought to help people who are in distress.

This mode of justification appeals to logical consistency. There
would be a logical inconsistency in holding the general principle
and yet, granting that Jones is hungry and penniless or that people
who are hungry and penniless are in distress, rejecting the specific
application.

But mere logic cannot commit us to the principles themselves.
The denial of a moral principle is never absurd in the way in
which a contradiction is absurd. Logic by itself can discover
relations of consistency and inconsistency between our principles.
It can classify them according to their degrees of generality. It
can show that one principle follows from another. But when it
comes to the most abstract and general principles—first principles—
of a moral code, logic by itself is powerless to decide whether they
are *worthy* of acceptance.

(It is worth pausing to note that the language by which we
classify actions often reflects a commitment to principles: e.g.,
"murderer" means, roughly, unjustified homicide. Thus, there is

indeed a sense in which it is "flying in the face of reason" to deny that murder is wrong. It is equally, and for similar reasons, flying in the face of reason to deny that a *Euclidian* straight line is the shortest distance between two points. It is only when these commitments are peeled away from the formulation of the principles that the powerlessness of logic to certify them becomes apparent.)

Is there any way in which a rational choice can be made between competing first principles? To this question philosophers have traditionally given three answers: rationalism, empiricism, and skepticism. In order to explain these three positions, let me introduce the notion of a "rational discipline." By this phrase, I shall mean a field of inquiry in which good reasons can be offered for answers to questions belonging to the field. The empirical sciences are clearly rational disciplines in this sense. The physicist knows when he has good reasons for answering a question in one way rather than another. So does the biologist and the historian. The mathematical sciences are also rational disciplines in the sense that mathematicians, by and large, agree on when there are good reasons for accepting a certain mathematical proposition as true.

If we leave aside the historical sciences which are concerned with particular matters of fact, and concentrate our attention on those disciplines which seek to establish laws and principles, we see that they fall into two groups, according to whether or not they make use of empirical or observational evidence. Thus, a physical theory, however abstract its principles, must ultimately stand or fall on the evidence provided by observation and experiment. The "first principles" of the theory are justified by the ability of the theory as a whole to do its job, which is to enable us to understand the general course of experience.

Again, pure mathematics is a rational discipline. It is not, however, an empirical science. Mathematicians use pencil and paper not, of course, to make experiments, but simply because thinking on paper is more reliable (and capable of being checked and rechecked) than thinking in one's head. Pure mathematics is, so to speak, an armchair science. In philosophical terminology, it is *a priori*.

Pure mathematics is not only an *a priori* discipline in the sense that it doesn't appeal to observation and experiment (a negative point). It is also, speaking positively, *a formal* discipline. Within a mathematical system more specific principles can be justified by deriving them logically from more general principles. The same is true of an empirical science. But when we ask how the more general principles—the first principles—are justified, the answer is quite different from that appropriate to the empirical sciences. It is simply that to deny these principles leads to contradiction. Not only the *coherence* of a mathematical system, but its very *truth* is a matter of consistency.

Pure mathematics tells us nothing about the specific properties of things. Its truths hold of any consistently thinkable world, however strange and uncouth. The proposition that two plus two equals four tells us that it would be inconsistent to say

> There are two plus two apples on this table, but three altogether (or five or more)

—inconsistent, however, in a more complicated way than is
> This table top is both round and square.

The mathematically formulated hypotheses of physics tell us something specific about the world, not by virtue of being mathematical, but by virtue of being mathematically formulated empirical hypotheses. In this respect, they resemble

> This table is eight feet long.

which is not a mathematical statement, although it uses the mathematical concept of *eight*. If mathematics is a formal discipline, the same is clearly not true of physics, chemistry, and biology. Worlds are consistently thinkable which obey laws quite different from those of the actual world. Let us say that a rational discipline makes a *commitment* about the world if it makes claims which go beyond the demands of mere consistency—if it makes statements about the world in which we live which would not be true of all consistently thinkable worlds. Mathematics makes no commitment in this sense; physics and the empirical sciences do.

Notice that we have drawn two contrasts:

1. between rational disciplines, *based on observation* and those which are *not*,
2. between rational disciplines which *make a commitment* and those which do *not*.

How do these two contrasts correlate? Are they, perhaps, two ways of drawing the same distinction? This question is the crux of classical philosophy.

The issue can be put as follows:

> Are there any rational disciplines—bodies of knowledge with objective criteria for evaluating answers to questions falling within their purview—which are *a priori* like mathematics but which, unlike mathematics, make a *commitment* about the world.

Philosophers who answer in the affirmative are called rationalists; for they hold that important truths about the world and man can be established by mere reflection, by a method other than the experimental method characteristic of the empirical sciences. Among the candidates proposed for such bodies of truth are (1) philosophy itself; (2) rational theology, and (3) normative ethics.

Empiricists, traditionally, are philosophers who argue that all rational disciplines which commit us beyond the limits of mere consistency belong to the empirical sciences. It follows from their position that if a commitment is not a testable empirical hypotheses, it falls outside the realm of rational discussion.

This opposition between rationalism and empiricism is expressed in ethics as the opposition between the claim that the first principles of morals are known *a priori* and the claim that they are empirical hypotheses which it is the responsibility of science (in particular, biology, psychology, and sociology) to test and confirm or refine.

It has become clear that neither of these positions is satisfactory. Not rationalism, for once it is granted that no contradiction or inconsistency is involved in denying a moral principle, what reasons could mere armchair thinking have for preferring it to its alternatives? *Ex hypothesi* it is a *first* principle and cannot be derived from a higher one. If it could, the same question would arise concerning the latter. The rationalist falls back on *intuition*. Pure thought simply *sees* certain moral principles to be true, but has no way of supporting its intuition with reason. This view plays into the hands of skepticism, for it is notorious that in different cultures and in different persons in the same culture, "pure reason" makes contradictory deliverances. And according to in-

tuitionism there is no way of arbitrating between contrary in-
tuitions. There would seem to be no significant difference between
an intuition which cannot be supported by reasons, and a basic
commitment which we *make* without being able to *justify*.

Nor does empiricism fare much better. For while observation
and experiment and scientific method do provide good reasons
for general commitments about the world, these commitments
concern what *is* the case rather than what *ought to be* the case.
Thus even the anthropological study of what things people value,
what they approve and disapprove, and of the circumstances in
which people tend to value one thing rather than another, gives
us knowledge about what is *valued* or *prized*, but not about what
is *valuable* in the sense of *worthy* of being valued. Certainly a scientific knowledge of the needs and abilities of men would play a
determining role in shaping the actions and policies of one who
already has a moral perspective. But mere knowledge of things
as valued or prized does not present them to the knower as *values*
(i.e., as things which, other things being equal, *ought* to be brought
about or realized).

The failure of both rationalism and empiricism seems at first
sight to leave us no alternative but skepticism, the view that moral
principles are commitments which we find ourselves having, indeed,
which we have been brought up to have, but which are incapable
of rational justification. Curiously enough, in order to escape from
this dilemma, we must first plumb the depths of the skeptical point
of view. And to set the stage for this we must look at a different
dimension of what we have called "criteriological" ethics. We
have been stressing the question "Can ethical first principles be
given a rational justification? And if so, how?" Or, to put it somewhat differently, "Can a good reason be given for committing
oneself to a set of ethical first principles without contradicting
their status *as* first principles?" But recent criteriological ethics
has stressed rather the questions "What exactly are we saying of
a state of affairs when we say that it is intrinsically *good*, worth
having for its own sake?" and "What exactly are we saying of an
action when we say that it ought to be done?" Recent philosophy
has rightly paid a great deal of attention to problems pertaining
to meaning and the clarification of meaning. In ethics, this em-

phasis led for a time to an almost exclusive concern with "the meaning of ethical terms."

It would seem evident that there is an intimate connection between concepts pertaining to the intrinsic value of states of affairs and concepts pertaining to what people ought to do. Reflection on this fact has often generated the idea that one of these two groups of concepts can be explicated or defined in terms of the other. Thus, according to one group of philosophers, the concepts of duty, right, and wrong, which pertain to action, are to be explicated in terms of the concept of the intrinsic value of the consequences of action. Roughly,

$$\text{x ought to do A} =_{df} \begin{array}{l} \text{the consequences of A could} \\ \text{be intrinsically better than} \\ \text{the consequences of any al-} \\ \text{ternative action open to x.} \end{array}$$

Other philosophers have found it more plausible to orient the explication in the opposite direction and have proposed definitions of the following types:

$$\begin{array}{l} \text{States of affairs} \\ \text{of kind S are in-} \\ \text{trinsically good} \end{array} =_{df} \begin{array}{l} \text{in so far as an action open} \\ \text{to one would bring about a} \\ \text{state of affairs of kind S} \\ \text{one ought to do it} \end{array}$$

or

$$\begin{array}{l} \text{States of affairs of} \\ \text{kind } S_1 \text{ are intrin-} \\ \text{sically better than} \\ \text{states of affairs} \\ \text{of kind } S_2 \end{array} =_{df} \begin{array}{l} \text{if of two actions open to x} \\ \text{one would bring about } S_1 \text{ while} \\ \text{the other would bring about} \\ S_2, \text{ then, in so far forth, x} \\ \text{ought to do the former} \end{array}$$

The issues we are concerned with now, however, are sufficiently general not to depend on a decision between these two points of view. For whether the first principles of ethics are principles concerning what actions one ought to do or principles concerning what states of affairs are intrinsically good, the problem remains: "What new meanings, if any, are involved when we move from simply describing how things are or might be—with no use of distinctively ethical terms—to saying of a state of affairs that it is or it would be *good*, or of an action that it *ought to be done?*

As a matter of historical fact, the basic distinctions were thrashed out in connection with the meaning of the term "good," since it was, on the whole, taken for granted by British and American philosophers in the early years of this century that "good" was a more basic notion than "ought."

The argument developed as follows: (1) we must obviously distinguish between a good thing or state of affairs (in short a good) and its goodness (i.e., the property by virtue of which it is good). More accurately, since, as we shall see, there are two senses in which a property might be that "by virtue of which" something was good, we must distinguish between the good thing and that property the having of which *constitutes* its being good. (2) Even when people agree as to what items are good, they may disagree in the accounts they give of the property the having of which constitutes their being good. Not only philosophers, but people generally can agree in the *application* of a term (roughly its denotation) but disagree in their account of what the term *means* (i.e., its "sense" or "intension"). A notorious example is the term "cause." People agree, by and large, about *what* causes *what*. But if asked to explain what it means to say that something, *x*, *causes* something else, *y*, the accounts are almost as many as the people who give them. (3) It is important to see that the fact that different philosophers have offered different accounts of causation does not imply that these philosophers used the word "cause" in different senses in their non-philosophical discourse. The meanings of words (including their ambiguities) are public, intersubjective facts, and while a person may use a word in a *stipulated* sense, stipulated senses presuppose a vocabulary with non-stipulated senses which has the public status of a custom or practice or institution. Words do not mean what the user thinks they mean. It is possible to use a word meaningfully and correctly but give, when asked, a mistaken account of its meaning. If merely by virtue of being able to use a word correctly a person had the ability to give a clear and distinct explanation of its meaning, one of the most difficult tasks of philosophy—explaining the meaning of these abstract terms which crystalize the symbolic forms of human discourse—would be a task for children.

Now as Moore[4] saw it, there were three possibilities:

1. The adjective "good" stands for a property which is also signified by an expression belonging to a vocabulary other than that of ethical discourse, that is to the vocabulary of one of the disciplines which is concerned with what *is* or *is not* the case, as contrasted with what *ought* to be the case. Representative views of this kind are those in which "good" stands for a biological property (e.g., "conducive to survival") or a psychological property (e.g., "pleasant," "approved of by the speaker,") or a sociological property (e.g., "approved of by one's social peers"). These alternatives barely scratch the surface of this type of approach to the concept of intrinsic value.

2. The adjective "good" stands for a property which is uniquely ethical and can neither be equated with nor defined in terms of any property with which sciences of what is the case are directly concerned.[5]

3. The word "good" does not stand for a property at all. Moore himself, in his early writings, seems to have assumed that since "good" is an adjective, it either stands for a property as "circular" stands for circularity or else is a *flatus vocis*.

Regarding the latter alternative as absurd, he dismissed (3) and focussed his attention on the problem of choosing between (1) and (2). As is well-known, he decided in favor of (2) and defended his decision by interesting and important arguments about which it may be worth while to say a few words.

The first line of thought can be summed up as follows: Suppose it is claimed that two predicative expressions, each of which may be either simple or complex, have the same sense. Represent these two predicate expressions by "P_1" and "P_2" respectively, and let "x" refer to a subject to which these predicates are appropriately

---

[4]G. E. Moore: *Principia Ethica*, Chapter I.

[5]The psychologist and the sociologist are, of course, concerned with the predicate "believed to be good" and with such facts as that John believes x to be good. But it would obviously be absurd to define the predicate "good" in terms of the predicate "believed to be good."

(thought not necessarily truly) applied. Now form the question

Is x, granted that it is P_2, P_1?

For example

Is x, granted that it is bounded by three straight lines, triangular? Is x, granted that it is a featherless biped, human? Is x, granted that it is approved of by me, good?

Moore points out that if such a question, in spite of the concessive clauses, is *open*, then it cannot be true that the two predicate expressions have the same sense. He proceeds to test representative views of type (1) each of which claims that "good" has the same sense as a predicate expression in a vocabulary which is used when one's concern is simply to state what is or is not the case in a certain domain of fact, without any commitment as to what ought or ought not to be the case. He claims that if one constructs for each such claimed identity of the form

"P_1" has the same sense as "P_2"

a corresponding question of the above form, the latter is readily seen to be an open question. He contends that every such claimed identity is false, and that the only identities which are not clearly ruled out by this test are those in which both predicate expressions are patently ethical, e.g.,

"good" has the same sense as "ought to be desired"
"good" has the same sense as "worthy or worth having for its own sake."

Moore also argued[6] that any adequate account of the property *good* must preserve the *prima facie* contradictoriness illustrated by the dialogue

Mr. A: x is good
Mr. B: x is not good

whether A and B are different members of the same cultural group or members of different cultural groups. He argues (and this is a recurring pattern of argument in his philosophy) that it is more probable that a philosophical view which rejects this *prima facie* (but by no means superficial) contradictoriness is based on a mistake, than that the contradictoriness is an illusion. This argument

---

[6]*Ethics*, Chapter III.

provides an additional ground for rejecting views of the type illustrated by

x is good = I like x

x is good = my culture approves of x

These and other considerations led Moore to the following theses:

1. Goodness is a simple property.

2. Goodness is a uniquely ethical property. It does not fall within the province of the empirical sciences.[7]

3. Goodness is a "resultant quality." If anything has the property of being good it must have it by virtue of being of a certain sort or kind. An example might be

    x is good *because* (and in so far as) it is a feeling of pleasure

    which corresponds to the principle

    if anything is a feeling of pleasure, then it is (in so far forth) good.

    The properties which, though they are not identical with goodness, are the grounds of goodness might be called, with C. D. Broad,[8] "good-making properties." According to Moore, there are a number of "good-making properties," thus, among others, the properties of being a consciousness of pleasure, of being a state of knowledge, and of being an affectionate and loving frame of mind.

4. True principles of the form

    P_1 is a good-making property

    are "synthetic necessary truths" and our knowledge of them is neither deductive nor inductive. They are first principles whose evidence must be self-evidence. Moore's position is, therefore, a clear cut and straight forward example of the *rationalistic* type of criteriological ethics.

---

[7]The property of being *believed to be good*, of course, does belong in the province of the empirical sciences. But, of course, a parallel distinction can be drawn in the case of *divisible by two* and *believed to be divisible by two*. The sense in which *P* is a constituent of *believed to be P* calls for careful analysis.

[8]Some of the main problems of ethics, *Philosophy*, *21*, 1946. (Reprinted in Feigl and Sellars: *Readings in Philosophical Analysis*, New York, 1949).

There are many interesting features of Moore's position which would have to be taken into account if our purpose was to present it as a reasonably lifelike representation of moral experience. To put some flesh on the above bare bones, we would have to discuss his views on such topics as the commensurability of values, the relation of intermediate principles to first principles, and, which for Moore is a special case of this, the relation of principles of obligation to principles of value, etc. For our purposes, however, the bare bones of Moore's argument suffice, for in terms of them we can explain the distinctive trait of ethical skepticism in the early post-Moore period.

In his later writings, Moore supplemented his earlier and essentially negative characterization of the property for which the predicate "good" stands as a "non-natural" property with a no less negative, but potentially far more illuminating characterization of it as a "non-descriptive" property. By thus distinguishing "descriptive" properties (e.g., circularity), the ascription of which to an object describes it (as circular), and "non-descriptive" properties (e.g., goodness), the ascription of which to an object does not describe it, he raised the question, "What is one doing with respect to an item when one ascribes goodness to it, if one is not *de*scribing it?" It was not long before the general lines of an answer were forthcoming. But the initial formulations were so inadequate, so burdened with positivistic commitments, that the insight they contained had a difficult time surviving.

I shall take a brief look at these initial formulations in a moment. But it will be instructive to develop Moore's distinction between "descriptive" and "non-descriptive" properties in a way which joins more directly with the best contemporary thinking on the subject. To come to the point directly, suppose we were to say that goodness is a normative property,[9] what would this (intuitively) imply? Surely that goodness is a resultant property by virtue of which that which possesses it has a claim on our conduct and on the attitudes and choices which manifest themselves in our conduct. The term "claim" is not, of itself, particularly illuminating. It does, however, serve to convey the essential truth that

[9]There is no intention here to imply that "descriptive" and "normative" exhaust the varieties of property.

a norm or standard in the desired sense is something which, when the individual recognizes it as such, has a unique resonance in his affective life. It is somehow an essential fact about that which we believe to be good that we *care* about it, are *concerned* about it. Roughly speaking, goodness is a property which is such that *in the absence of contrary aims and desires*, to believe that a certain state of affairs would be good is to be disposed to act in such a way as to bring it about.

Now if one is not content to postulate the existence of such a property, and attempts to explain its possibility, the fact that the properties which modern empirically and scientifically-minded philosophers have taken as "paradigm cases" of properties are without exception such that

1. If anybody believes that x is ϕ, he tends to approve of x

is always synthetic. This is obviously true in the case of such a property as circularity. But even when "ϕ" stands for the property of being approved of by the person in question, the statement is still logically synthetic. In the absence of a reassessment of the structure and scope of the "space" of *properties* which succeeds in demonstrating that in the case of goodness the statement corresponding to (1) is logically analytic, a phenomenologically adequate account of goodness must claim that (1) is true *ex vi terminorum*, and, if it sees no grounds for expecting that such a demonstration might someday be forthcoming, that it is a synthetic necessary truth. As is well-known, those who, under the influence of Moore, took goodness to be a unique, resultant, and normative property took the latter course. We thus see that the sophisticated, ethical rationalist invokes the concept of synthetic necessary truth at two crucial junctures in his theory:

1. The first principles of value or obligation are synthetic necessary truths

2. The connection between goodness or obligation and approval is a synthetic necessary truth.

Let me end this part of my argument by pointing out that according to a position which accepts (2) there would be no *contradiction* in the idea of a community which intellectually knows what sorts of things are intrinsically good (or what kinds of actions ought to be done in various kinds of circumstances) and yet has no concern or (in the broad sense) feeling about these items *qua* being good or *qua* what ought to be done. If the idea of such a community is nevertheless held by these philosophers to be absurd, they must trace the absurdity to *a priori* insight, to intuitive *evidence*, in short, to synthetic *a priori* knowledge.

Now recent ethical skepticism, under the name "emotivism" or "non-cognitivism," developed within the framework of Moore's analysis, but adopted the alternative, which Moore was unable to take seriously, that "good" does not stand for a property at all—unique or non-unique, natural or non-natural, descriptive or non-descriptive. Thus, to choose one of the earlier and less sophisticated formulations of emotivism, Ayer, in his *Language, Truth, and Logic*, after agreeing that the views Moore criticizes will not do, and acknowledging that if one of these was the only alternative, Moore's position with its unique, non-natural, non-empirical, non-descriptive resultant property of goodness, and its synthetic necessary first principles of value, would carry the day—a result which would conflict painfully with the epistemology developed in earlier chapters of the book—announces to us that the dilemma is to be overcome by escaping between the horns. In spite of the fact that "good" functions grammatically as an adjective, its job is quite other than that of standing for a property, even though standing for a property is what adjectives usually do. He calls attention to the difference between "expressing" or "evincing" an emotion and describing oneself as having the emotion. "I am angry" is the first person present tense counterpart of "he was angry", and is either true or false. A person, however, can *express* his current anger (but no one else's anger, or his own past or future anger) by using an expletive, or speaking in an angry tone of voice. Sentences of the form "x is good," although they grammatically resemble sentences which are used to ascribe properties, have as their primary function to give expression to the speaker's attitude. They ape sentences which are used to ascribe properties and by doing so give objective and rational protective coloring to the business of expressing one's attitudes. But in their primary use, they do not ascribe properties or assert propositions and are neither true nor false. The *prima facia* contrariety between x is good

and

x is bad

which Moore had emphasized, is interpreted by Ayer and his disciples as the expression of a "disagreement in attitude," where a clash between attitudes is to be understood in terms of the incompatability of the states of affairs which would result from implementing them.

Now emotivism was on to *something*. The best way to see this is to notice that it makes analytic the connection between *believing something to be good* and *being positively concerned about x*, which for the ethical rationalism sketched above is synthetic *a priori*. It does so, however, by trivializing the connection into a tautology, for it turns believing *x* to be good into "believing" *x* to be good and simply *equates* the latter with approving of *x*.

Indeed, early emotivism assimilated ethical judgments "so-called" to the non-rational, non-conceptual order by a liberal use of non-rational, non-conceptual models. Thus, an examination of Ayer's discussion shows that he compares ethical statements (1) to symptoms of feeling in the narrow sense illustrated by pain, thus "bad" to "ouch," and (2) to *stimuli* which arouse or provoke other people into action in a manner reminiscent of the con-ditioned responses exhibited by a trained soldier being put through the manual of arms by a barking sergeant. But even though words of command can *become* response-evokers, commands, and, more obviously, requests, belong to the conceptual order and so do the forms of words which we use to express our appraisals and evalu-ations.

It is by now a familiar story that *crude* emotivism failed to distinguish between emotions and attitudes. Attitudes are settled ways of viewing the world. They are commitments which manifest themselves in a variety of ways. In different circumstances, radi-cally different ways of behaving, thinking, and feeling can be expressions of the *same* attitudes. Thus, an attitude of superiority to a certain group can find its expression in one situation in an outburst of anger, and in another by a cool withdrawal. Attitudes can be compared to long-range policies. Emotions, on the other hand, are short-run outbursts highly colored by visceral sensations and incipient activity. It is possible to regard ethical statements as expressions of *attitudes*, but not to compare them in their capacity as ethical statements to shrieks of joy or cries of anger.

Crude emotivism failed equally to distinguish between emotions and feelings in the narrower sense in which pain is a feeling. When a person feels pain and says "ouch," the "ouch" is a symptom of pain. It belongs to the sub-rational level of human behavior. One must not confuse between "is an expression of" and "is a symptom of." It is as rational beings that we feel emotions, and while expressions of emotion are neither true nor false, nevertheless the devices by which emotions are expressed are as much a part and parcel of the inter-subjective symbolic forms of human discourse as the vocabulary of description and explanaton which philosophers, with few exceptions, have placed at the center of their interest.

As a result of these two confusions, emotivism overlooked the fact that attitudes and the expression of attitudes belong to the *rational* order—which is not, of course, to say that there are no *ir*rational attitudes, but rather no *non*-rational ones. It is as a rational being that a man has attitudes. All commitments, scientific as well as ethical, are attitudes, and in no case is an attitude a sensation or feeling which accompanies a "pure thought."

Before I attempt to characterize the distinctive traits of the attitudes we call moral or ethical, I want to return to the topic, central to the controversy between Moore and the emotivists, as to when a word stands for a *concept*. For central to the emotivist's contention that

> "good" is "cognitively meaningless" and *merely* expresses an emotion, etc.

is a theory as to when words belong to the conceptual order. Crude emotivism was developed by philosophers (e.g., Ayer) who held that if a word is not (1) a logico-mathematical word expressing a *formal* concept or (2) definable in terms of perceptable (or introspectable) states of affairs with the aid of logico-mathematical words, and expressing an *empirical* concept, it does not belong to the conceptual order at all and merely apes words which do. It belongs rather, with "ouch" and "hup." Concept empiricists were dominated by the ostensive training aspect of learning how to use words: the formation of habits of responding to *things* with *words*. But it is obvious that we learn the use of many words where such a correlation does not even make sense. This is surely the case with *logical* words and reflection shows it to be equally true of such words as "was," "will be," "this," and, to move closer to practical discourse, such words as "shall," as in "I shall do A."

I shall not press this point, but rather proceed directly to formulate a different criterion as to when a word stands for a concept or, more accurately, belongs to the conceptual order. The criterion I wish to recommend has two virtues as over and against concept empiricism:

1. It explains why both formal and empirical words belong to the conceptual order

2. It permits—indeed requires—the recognition that other words belong to the conceptual order.

The criterion I propose is that a word stands for a concept when there are good arguments in which it is essentially involved. Consider the following three arguments:

1. This is *red*
   therefore, it is *extended* and *not green*

2. Tomorrow *will be* Tuesday
   therefore, yesterday *was* Sunday

3. I *shall* get to Hartford by 8 *PM*
   therefore, I *shall* leave New Haven before 6 *PM*.

Once such a humble word as "shall" is seen to belong to the conceptual order, the way is clear to recognizing that "good" and "ought" belong there too. Indeed, I would argue that the meaning of "ought" is related to that of "shall" and is indicated, roughly, by the context

We shall all always (other things being equal) do A in C (i.e., "ought" statements express [presumptively] shared *intentions*, where "intention" is used in an extended sense to cover moral attitudes, and where the scope of "we" includes everybody that we recognize as one of *us*).

But before I carry this further, I must pick up a theme from an earlier stage of the argument. It concerns the possible parallel between the empirical sciences as rational disciplines and a putative rational discipline of normative ethics. If we turn our attention to the former, we find that we must distinguish between three ways in which statements belonging to an empirical science of an advanced type (e.g., chemistry or physics) are capable of rational justification. The first of these, which raises serious problems which transcend the scope of this essay, concerns the move from statements reporting the results of experiment or controlled observation to the acceptance of a generalization applying to all cases in which the same conditions are realized. The problem of the rational warrant for moves of this kind is the classical problem of induction, and will not concern us here.

More germane to our purpose is the structure of reasoning at the level of theoretical explanation. The distinction I had in mind is that between the logical derivation of statement from statement *within* the framework of the theory, and the reasoning by which we justify the decision to adopt the framework. Reflection on the former type of move readily generates a distinction between the more general principles of the theory, and the implications they have for a wide variety of specific conditions and circumstances which can be formulated in terms of the theory. And if, by a certain idealization, we construe the theory as a deductive system, we are led to a distinction between the first principles or fundamental postulates of the theory and the derivative principles or theorems which follow from them in accordance with logical procedures.

Our rational warrant for accepting the first principles of the theory clearly cannot consist in the fact that they have been logically derived from other statements of the theory. If this were the case, it would simply mean that they were misdescribed as the *first* principles of the theory. On the other hand, the decision to accept the theory of which these principles are the first principles can be given a rational defense. Let us follow a terminological suggestion by Herbert Feigl and say that a set of theoretical first principles is *vindicated* by giving a successful rational defense of the decision to espouse it.

The rational defense of a decision is a piece of practical reasoning, and, in the type of case with which we are now concerned, involves the relationship of means to end. Thus we are concerned with reasoning of the form

I shall do that which is conducive to E.

Doing A is conducive to E. So I shall do A.

Notice that the major premise of this reasoning is a statement of intention. The reasoning relates a specific course of action to this intention.

If this distinction between the logical derivation of statement from statement within a theory and the vindication of the first principles of the theory is to be of assistance in understanding the rational status of normative ethics, we must presumably be able to put our finger on sound arguments of the form

I shall do that which is conducive to E.

Doing Action$_1$ in Circumstance$_1$, Action$_2$ in Circumstance$_2$, etc., is conducive to E

Therefore: (1) I shall do Action$_1$ in Circumstance$_1$, etc.

(2) I shall espouse the principles: "Anybody shall do Action$_1$ in Circumstance$_1$," etc.

(3) I shall support the general practice of doing Action$_1$ in Circumstance$_1$, etc.

But what could be the end, E, in terms of which the espousal of moral first principles is to be rationally defended? In the case of scientific theory, the end is presumably the goal of providing scientific understanding, the ability to explain and predict phenomena falling under the scope of the theory.

To answer this question, or at least indicate the lines along which an answer might be found, let me return to the basic line of argument. It will be remembered that we have emphasized the distinction between statements which, as expressing attitudes, belong to the conceptual order, and mere symptoms of feeling ("ouch," etc.) which, though socially conditioned, do not belong to the conceptual order. What, we must now ask, is the distinctive character of those attitudes which we call moral? One essential trait, emphasized by the German philosopher Kant, but illustrated also by the Golden Rule, is that they are attitudes in which we view ourselves *impersonally* ,and approve or disapprove of *our* doing something in certain circumstances because we would approve or disapprove of *anyone* behaving in that way under similar circumstances. Moral attitudes are in this sense impartial. They are also, I have suggested, inter-personal or shared attitudes in the sense that their proper expression involves not simply "I intend, approve, etc.," but rather "we intend, approve, etc." They are subjectively universal (inter-personal) as well as objectively universal (impartial).

Let us suppose then that ethical principles express *impersonal* attitudes towards life and conduct in the sense just defined. What becomes of the problem of justifying ethical principles? It becomes the following:

> Granted that I and my fellow man have been brought up to have such and such impersonal commitments concerning what is to be done in various kinds of circumstances, is there any reason why I should not let these commitments wither away and encourage self-regarding attitudes, attitudes which, in the vernacular, look out for Number One?

It is reasonable to suppose that it is to each of our advantages to have other people have moral attitudes. A society in which everyone was guided by intelligent self-interest might work if people were intelligent and knowledgable enough. But a moment's reflection makes clear how very intelligent and knowledgable and cool-headed they would have to be. Thus, as things stand, it is clearly to each of our advantages that *other* people have the moral point of view.

But is there any reason why we should nourish our own commitment to a system of moral principles? Self-interest, certainly as ordinarily construed, cannot do it, for while it can lead us to do for the most part the actions which morality enjoins, it does so only as a means of gaining rewards and avoiding penalties, and has no tendency to take us to, or support, the impersonal point of view.

The only frame of mind which can provide *direct* support for moral commitment is what Josiah Royce called Loyalty, and what Christians call Love (Charity). *This is a commitment deeper than any commitment to abstract principle.* It is this commitment to the well-being of our fellow man which stands to the justification of moral principles as the purpose of acquiring the ability to explain and predict stands to the justification of scientific theories. This concern for others is a precious thing, the foundation for which is laid in early childhood, though it *can* come about, in adult years, through the little understood phenomena of conversion and psychotherapy.

I said above that a society based on intelligent self-love might survive if its citizens were intelligent and knowledgable enough. I will close this essay by adding that recent psychological studies make clear what has in a sense been known all along, that the ability to love others for their own sake is as essential to a full life as the need to feel ourselves loved and appreciated for our own sakes—unconditionally, and not as something turned on or off depending on what we do. This fact provides, for those who acknowledge it, a means-end relationship around which can be built practical reasoning which justifies a course of action designed to strengthen our ability to respond to the needs of others. Thus *really* intelligent and informed self-love supports the love of one's neighbor, which alone directly supports the moral point of view when, as the eighteenth century British divine, Bishop Butler, put it, we sit down in a cool hour and ask why we should do our duty.

INDEX

413